The Passionate Beechers

The Passionate Beechers

A Family Saga of Sanctity and Scandal That Changed America

Samuel A. Schreiner, Jr.

WILEY

John Wiley & Sons, Inc.

Published by John Wiley & Sons, Inc., Hoboken, New Jersey
Published simultaneously in Canada

Photo credits: pp. 26, 27, 43, 110, 111, 177, 275, 308, 309 (top), 330, and 331, the Harriet Beecher Stowe Center, Hartford, Conn.; p. 42, the Schlesinger Library, Radcliffe Institute, Harvard University; p. 309 (bottom), the Mark Twain House, Hartford, Conn.

Excerpts included in this book are from *Saints, Sinners and Beechers* by Lyman Beecher Stowe. Copyright © 1934 by Bobbs-Merrill Company; copyright renewed 1962 by Lyman Beecher Stowe. Reprinted with the permission of Simon & Schuster, Inc.

For general information about our other products and services, please contact our Customer Care Department within the United States at (800) 762-2974, outside the United States at (317) 572-3993 or fax (317) 572-4002.

Wiley also publishes its books in a variety of electronic formats. Some content that appears in print may not be available in electronic books. For more information about Wiley products, visit our web site at www.wiley.com.

Library of Congress Cataloging-in-Publication Data:

Schreiner, Samuel Agnew.
   The passionate Beechers : a family saga of sanctity and scandal that
changed America / Samuel A. Schreiner, Jr.
      p. cm.
   Includes bibliographical references and index.
   ISBN 0-471-41484-0
   1. Beecher, Lyman, 1775-1863. 2. Beecher family. 3. Congregational
churches—United States—Biography. I. Title.
BX7260.B33.S33 2003
285.8′092′273—dc21

                                                         2002154454

Printed in the United States of America
10 9 8 7 6 5 4 3 2 1

For Dorrie, the one and only "love of my life"

Contents

Acknowledgments

Few writers of nonfiction can claim to work alone. Certainly I am not one of them. In the beginning, I have always needed a touchstone for the ideas that almost mysteriously surface in my head. Over a period of thirty years and for more than a dozen books, the touchstone for me has been my agent, Phyllis Westberg, of Harold Ober Associates. Then I have needed an appreciative and understanding editor to provide critical encouragement of the work in progress. For this project, that person has been Hana Umlauf Lane of John Wiley & Sons. Digging for the facts to enrich the account is a little like mining for gems; help is required to map out and light the way. As in many of my earlier ventures, I have leaned heavily on Blanche Parker and her associates in the research department of the Darien Library to find materials I needed. I am also greatly indebted to the staff of the institutions where the letters and other memorabilia of the Beecher family are stored: the Harriet Beecher Stowe Center in Hartford, Connecticut; the Yale University Library in New Haven, Connecticut; and the Schlesinger Library of Radcliffe Institute for Advanced Study at Harvard University in Cambridge, Massachusetts. And I must acknowledge that this work could never have been done without the willingness of my wife and family to do without my presence and services when I was off exploring Beecherland.

Prelude

"Thanks to God, we's free"

NEVER IN THE LONG HISTORY of Charleston, South Carolina, had there been anything like the gathering in Zion Church on Calhoun Street on that March Sunday morning. In the eyes of the few members of Charleston's prominent families left to witness this happening, it was a humiliation, an abomination. More than any other event in four truly dreadful years, this Sunday service marked an end to the prideful, gracious way of life that had made Charleston the glory of the South.

Although Zion was one of the city's largest churches, the building could hardly hold the worshipers who jammed its pews and stood along its aisles. Since almost all of them were in uniform, the view from the pulpit was like looking at a restless dark blue sea with hundreds of human heads bobbing above the surface. What made this view so exceptional in Charleston was the color of those heads—every shade of black. For the people in this congregation it was a morning of miracles, and they were here to thank God for passing them.

The uniformed men formed a regiment called the Thirty-fifth United States Colored Troops. It was one of the all-black units in the Federal forces that were romping through a bleeding Southland during that spring of 1865. The soldiers of the Thirty-fifth enjoyed the special distinction of being one of the first volunteer units recruited from among escaping slaves. For each man in that regiment the primary miracle was just being there in church and alive instead of lying among the dead they had left in the fields during fierce fights around the perimeter of a besieged Charleston. A close second to that miracle was the feeling of being free, of being a man who owned his own body. And it was another kind of miracle that a church in which to give thanks had remained standing while a third of the city's buildings had been turned into rubble or ash by four years of shelling and uncontrolled fires.

1

When the regiment's colonel came through the church door at the appointed time, the men in the pews scrambled to their feet. Somebody sounded a note, and the congregation turned into a full-throated chorus, singing:

My country 'tis of thee
Sweet land of liberty.

It was a hymn that Colonel James C. Beecher had taught his men shortly after he had brought them together for the first time at New Bern, North Carolina, in the summer of 1863. A minister in civilian life, Beecher acted as both chaplain and commanding officer. Here in Charleston, the singing soldiers watched admiringly as this man who had led them through victorious combat strode down the aisle. Still in his thirties, he was tall and handsome and vigorous. In splendid full-dress uniform with sword clanking at his side, he had the bearing of a true military man, and the beard flowing down to his chest suggested a mind with the gravity of a prophet. Arrived at the pulpit, Beecher unbuckled his sword and laid it on the lectern. As at that first service in New Bern, the theme of his sermon was the blessing of living in a land of liberty. Years later, the regiment's surgeon, Dr. Marcy, would recall that "he took for his text, 'The liberty wherewith Christ hath made us free.' His impassioned oratory at times swayed the vast audience as a mighty wind the tree tops, again, recounting God's care for his children, it fell as the soft dews from heaven, and there was not a dry eye in the house, and when at the close all bent in prayer, broken sobs and utterances of 'Thanks to God, we's free,' attested to his power."

Shortly after that service, Colonel Beecher received a copy of General Order No. 50, dated March 27, 1865, from the War Department in Washington:

Ordered—

First. That at the hour of noon, on the 14th day of April, 1865, Brevet Major-General Anderson will raise and plant upon the ruins of Fort Sumter, in Charleston Harbor, the same United States flag which floated over the battlements of that fort during the rebel assault, and which was lowered and saluted by him and the small force of his command when the works were evacuated on the 14th day of April, 1861.

Second. That the flag, when raised, be saluted by one hundred guns from Fort Sumter.

Third. That suitable ceremonies be had upon the occasion, under the direction of Major-General William T. Sherman, whose military operations compelled the rebels to evacuate Charleston or, in his absence, under the charge of Major-General Q. A. Gillmore, commanding the Department. Among the ceremonies will be the delivery of a public address by the Reverend Henry Ward Beecher.

Fourth. That the naval forces at Charleston, and their commander on that station be invited to participate in the ceremonies of the occasion.

By the order of the President of the United States.

Edwin M. Stanton
Secretary of War

Although fighting went on to the north of Charleston, where Sherman was squeezing Confederate general Robert E. Lee's army from the south as General Ulysses S. Grant was squeezing it from the north, General Order No. 50 reflected the jubilant mood in Washington. All hands there believed that a ceremony just weeks away at Fort Sumter in the very spot where the war had begun would serve as a most appropriate celebration of the certain coming of peace. It was Secretary Stanton who made the suggestion at a cabinet meeting of using Henry Ward Beecher as the orator. President Abraham Lincoln agreed enthusiastically. Not only could they count on a ringing patriotic speech from the nation's most famous preacher, but also the appointment would reward Beecher for what he had done to tilt public opinion to the Union side during a speaking tour of the British Isles in 1863. In fact, Lincoln regarded the Beecher family as having had a great deal to do with the recent course of the nation's history. When Henry Ward's sister Harriet Beecher Stowe visited him in the White House, he had acknowledged the influence of her world-renowned novel *Uncle Tom's Cabin* by his greeting: "So this is the little lady who started this big war." Whether the president was aware of it or not, Stanton thought that sending Henry Ward Beecher to Charleston would be a kind of reward to the whole family as well. Only months before, he had personally issued a pass authorizing Frankie Johnson to go through the battle lines to marry Colonel James Beecher, the youngest of the clan, and he knew that orders had already been cut to put the colonel in command of the northern part of Charleston with a promotion to the rank of brevet brigadier general.

By the first of April, Colonel—now General—Beecher's black troops were quartered in the Citadel, and he and Frankie took over one of the few fine houses still standing on the corner of Charlotte and Meeting Streets. Because of its imposing facade, a popular song from *The Bohemian Girl*—"I Dreamt That I Dwelt in Marble Halls"—came to Frankie's mind when she first saw it. Unfortunately, that feeling did not last when they inspected the inside and discovered that only two of the many rooms contained furniture. Not for the first time James expressed regret about all the fine furniture that he had seen go up in flames when his raiding parties torched plantation houses throughout the countryside around Charleston. After the first shock wore off, Frankie, a resourceful and gutsy woman, shrugged and said, "Well, we'll borrow mattresses from Dr. Marcy's hospital stores, and treat our guests to a taste of our army picnic life."

This would be Frankie's first opportunity as a new member of the Beecher family to entertain her husband's celebrated older brother, and she would not skimp on providing at least one touch of elegance to her empty home. Even though the only thing left standing on many Charleston properties were chimneys—known to the locals as "Sherman's sentinels"—roses bloomed above the weeds in once carefully cultivated gardens. As a Connecticut Yankee, Frankie was purely fascinated by such flowering so early in the year. Knowing of Henry Ward's passion for flowers from family lore, she brought so many roses into the house that James playfully complained that he could not find an empty tumbler to get a drink or a basin to wash his hands. But her efforts were appreciated by her guests from the still-chilled north, who also were cheered when they learned of Lee's surrender at Appomattox on April 9 from another ship when their steamer *Arago* arrived off Charleston Harbor. That news made for a joyous family reunion. As Frankie wrote later, "Everyone was so jubilant over the fact that 'the cruel war was over' that we would not have murmured at any kind of hardship. Fortunately, we had secured the services of one of the best of the famous South Carolina cooks, and our first breakfast of deviled crabs and corned bread, cooked over the open fire in the usual far away kitchen, was worthy of the occasion."

Without knowledge of the family, no observer would have concluded that the general and the minister were brothers when the Beacher party arrived in good time for the high noon ceremonies at Fort Sumter. At fifty-two, Henry Ward was beginning to show signs of aging and soft living. He was shorter than his brother and thickening at the waist, while James was lean and hard from his time in the saddle. Carelessly dressed as always in rumpled clothes, Henry Ward was clean-shaven, with a mane of unfashionably long hair. He was every inch the civilian in contrast to his soldierly brother. They differed in features almost as much as in dress. Henry Ward had a nose too prominent and lips too full to be called handsome, but his expression reflected his friendly and generally sunny personality. James had more finely chiseled features, and there was an intriguingly guarded aspect to his appearance, as if he were holding his real feelings back.

Once a formidable high-walled fortress that covered the whole of an island off the mouth of Charleston Harbor, Fort Sumter was a scene of devastation as great as that in the city it was built to guard when Charleston's citizens feared only enemies from across the seas. Henry Ward Beecher was an emotional man whose strong feelings surfaced easily. Aboard the *Arago,* he had wept for joy at the news of Appomattox, though while going through the streets of Charleston, the sight of the ruined, abandoned homes had brought tears of sorrow to his eyes. Here at the very heart of a social system that he hated to the point of being willing to sacrifice his own life and those of his loved ones to bring it down, he was suddenly confronted with the price that people who had once been his countrymen had been forced to pay to satisfy his hatred. Ever a quick study who regularly improvised his sermons and speeches, Beecher rearranged his thoughts to incorporate the emotion of the moment, even as he watched General Robert Anderson raise the flag and heard the triumphal booming of a hundred of the cannons surrounding the harbor that the Union forces had used to wreak this terrible destruction.

When the time came for his speaking, Beecher chose a pile of rubble a little higher than most as a platform so the crowd could better see and hear him. With his long hair lifting in the breeze and a smile on his face, he saluted General Anderson and spoke directly to him:

Today you are returned again. We devoutly join with you in thanksgiving to Almighty God that he has spared your honored life and vouchsafed you the honors of this day. The heavens over you are the same, the same shores, morning comes, and evening as they did. All else, how changed! These shattered heaps of shapeless stone are all that is left of Fort Sumter. Desolation broods in yonder sad city—solemn retribution hath avenged our dishonored banner! You have come back with honor, who departed hence four years ago, leaving the air sultry with fanaticism. The surging crowds that rolled up their frenzied shouts as the flag came down are dead, or scattered, or silent, and their habitations are desolate. Ruin sits in the cradle of treason. Rebellion has perished. But there flies the same flag that was insulted. With starry eyes it looks all over this bay for the banner that supplanted it, and sees it not. You that then, for the day, were humbled are here again, to triumph once and forever. In the storm of that assault this glorious ensign was often struck; but, memorable fact, not one of its stars was torn out by shot or shell! It was a prophecy! It said: "Not one state shall be struck from this nation by treason!"

Rejoicing in the restoration of the Union, Beecher went on to remind his listeners of how the people of the North and the South had stood shoulder to shoulder during the Revolution and throughout the establishment of a new nation. He was transposing from a theme of triumph to one of mercy, which he sounded when he said, "I charge the whole guilt of this war upon the ambitious, educated, plotting political leaders of the South. They have shed this ocean of blood." After dwelling on the misery and havoc these leaders had caused for which they deserved no mercy, Beecher continued in a softer tone: "But for the people misled, for the multitudes drafted and driven into this civil war, let not a trace of animosity remain. The moment the willing hand drops the musket, and they return their allegiance, then stretch out your own honest right hands to greet them. Recall to them the old days of kindness. Our hearts wait for their redemption. All the resources of a renovated nation shall be applied to rebuild their prosperity and smooth down the furrows of war."

Beecher could not ignore the sight of black soldiers in blue standing before him, nor the stories he had heard of their valor from brother James across the breakfast table. They were living refutation of all the mistaken myths about their race and especially the widely expressed claim that "niggers won't fight." Throwing a salute in their direction, he said:

No other event of the war can fill an intelligent Southern man of candid nature with more surprise than the revelation of the capacity, moral and military, of the black race. It is a revelation, indeed. No people were ever less understood by those most familiar with them. They were said to be lazy, lying, impudent, and cowardly wretches, driven by the whip alone to the tasks needful for their own support, and the functions of civilization. They were said to be dangerous, blood-thirsty, liable to insurrection, but four years of tumultuous distress and war have rolled across the area inhabited by them, and I have yet to hear of an authentic instance of the misconduct of a colored man. They have been patient and gentle and docile in the land, while the men of the South were away in the army, they have been full of faith and hope and piety, when summoned to freedom they have emerged with all the signs and tokens that freedom will be to them what it was to be—the swaddling band that shall bring them to manhood. And after the government, honoring them as men, summoned them to the field, when once they were disciplined and had learned the art of war, they proved themselves to be not second to their white brethren in arms. And when the roll of men that have shed their blood is called in the other land, many and many a dusky face will rise, dark no more, when the light of eternal glory shall shine upon it from the throne of God.

Beecher's speech deliberately echoed Lincoln's second inaugural address a little more than a month before. A man whom Henry Ward had come to regard as a personal friend and a great moral leader, Lincoln had said: "With malice toward none, with charity for all, with firmness in the right as God gives us to see the right, let us strive on to finish the work we are in, to bind up the nation's wounds, to care for him who shall have borne the battle and for his widow and orphan, to do all which may achieve and cherish a just and lasting peace among ourselves and all nations." That the leader who spoke these words was assassinated on the night when the victory he had won was celebrated at Fort Sumter remains one of history's grimmest ironies.

For the Beecher brothers, as for a whole nation, what had seemed to be an end to a challenge that had taxed all the resources they possessed in the way of energy and determination had suddenly become the beginning of a new and equally important challenge. With the fires of hatred rekindled in the North by the assassination and in the South by emancipation, the establishment of a more perfect union as heralded in Henry Ward's speech was a matter of deep doubt. From his pulpit and publications, Henry Ward would have to plead with his fellow countrymen to be understanding and compassionate; as a commander responsible for order and purposeful activity to a large segment of a society turned upside down, James would have to deal with an infinite number of practical problems. Fortunately, the Beecher brothers knew that they would at least have the strong support of active and influential siblings. Four living brothers also were ministers, and three of their four sisters had established national and international leadership positions through their writings, speeches, and organizational activities. If, as Lincoln suggested, Beechers had made the war, they would now feel charged to make the peace. They had learned that it would not be easy from half a century of trying to sell their gospel of love to their fellow men; hatred found a readier market. Nevertheless, the Beechers would go on trying, since the mission that they had been trained for from the cradle was simply to save the world.

1

"The Chariot of Christ"

"I WISH, DEAR ESTHER, you would write me all the news. We get no paper, and know no more of the affairs of the world than if we were not in it," Mary Foote Hubbard reported from East Hampton, Long Island, New York, to her sister in Connecticut on an undated day in January 1806. "Here we are so still, so quiet, so dull, so inactive, that we have forgotten but that the world goes on the same way. We have forgotten that there are wars, murders, and violence abroad in the earth, that there are society, and friendship, and intercourse, and social affection, and science and pleasure, and life, and spirit, and gayety, and good-humor, alive still among the sons of earth. All here is the unvaried calm of a—frog pond, without the music of it. We neither laugh nor cry, sing nor dance, nor moan, nor lament."

Although few could have predicted it on that cold January evening, the beginning year would be the last year for a century in which anyone connected with the Beecher family could honestly pen such a letter. It is a wonder that even then Mary Hubbard, writing in a cramped corner of an overcrowded household, would complain of calm and quiet. She was turning into a permanent guest in the home of her brother-in-law, the Reverend Mr. Lyman Beecher, pastor of East Hampton's Presbyterian Church. In addition to the minister himself and Mary's older sister, Roxana, there were four Beecher children under six years of age, two black indentured servant girls who were not much older, a black housekeeper, and five female borders living under the same roof with her. The boarders were students in a school that Roxana conducted in the house during daylight hours in an effort to stretch her husband's four-hundred-dollar-a-year salary into a living for them all, and Mary's function was to assist her sister in this work.

9

Undoubtedly Mary Hubbard's wistful words were prompted more by thoughts of the life that she might have led than the one that she was living. She and her siblings in the Foote family had been reared with great expectations. Their home was Nutplains, their Grandfather Ward's two-hundred-acre place in North Guilford on the Connecticut coast just east of New Haven. A general in Washington's army during the Revolutionary War, Andrew Ward was the leading light of Guilford society and the town's representative in the state legislature. Although the general was a Congregationalist and patriot, his only child, Roxana, had married Eli Foote, a New Haven lawyer, and, as a dutiful wife, had adopted her husband's Tory allegiance to the crown and his Episcopalian religious preference. When Roxana was widowed by Foote's untimely death from yellow fever, her father welcomed her and her ten children back to the sheltering comfort of Nutplains and created a not unusual Connecticut household of divided loyalties. The general was open-minded enough to switch to his daughter's church so that they could attend services together, and he viewed her continuing loyalty to George III as a harmless eccentricity. Wanting his grandchildren to share his understanding and tolerance, he saw to it that they were supplied with the means to do so by loading his saddlebags with the latest books and periodicals every time he rode back from a legislative session in Hartford. In the matter of prompting enlightenment and discussion of important issues of the day, he did not discriminate between the girls and boys in the large brood he had taken under his wing. He was equally supportive when Samuel, the most adventurous of the brothers, elected to go to sea, and when Mary, the prettiest of the sisters, went off to Jamaica at age eighteen as the bride of a young man from a good Connecticut family who boasted of the prosperous plantation he owned on the island.

Within the Foote family it was tacitly agreed that Mary had made a better catch with her beauty in the person of John Hubbard than Roxana had with her virtue in the person of Lyman Beecher. Her mother's namesake, Roxana was in many respects the most accomplished of all the Footes. Tall and handsome rather than pretty, Roxana not only acquired all the feminine skills—sewing, spinning, painting, accompanying her own singing on the guitar—with ease, but she also exhibited an almost masculine grasp of mathematics and science. She eagerly devoured all the literature her grandfather brought into the house, often propping a book up where she could read while carrying out some mindless physical activity such as spinning. Despite her intellect and talents, Roxana was shy. Except with intimates and children, trying to share her thoughts with other people would cause her to blush embarrassingly, and she was not comfortable with physical contact. Roxana was also good. As the second child of a widowed mother, she learned early to subordinate her own interests to the demands of caring for younger siblings. Having been introduced to her parents' Episcopalian version of Christianity at age five, Roxana was to say in midlife that she could never recall a day going by without resorting to prayer. It was her goodness, freely acknowledged and heavily relied on by all who knew her, that attracted a young theological student at Yale named Beecher when he came calling at Nutplains.

Lyman Beecher was no stranger to the Foote family. He had grown up in Guilford, a community small enough that everything was known about everybody. Like the first Andrew Ward to come to the New World, the first Beecher—a widow named Hannah with a son named John—had settled in Connecticut in the 1630s. But their descendants had followed very different paths. Early on, Andrew Ward became a member of the state's High Court, or legislature, and succeeding generations of Andrew Wards were military officers and political leaders. John Beecher's descendants were sturdy blacksmiths, admired in New Haven for their sagacity as well as their strength. It was said that the first person whom Roger Sherman, Connecticut's great statesman of the Revolutionary era, consulted to get the temper of the people when coming home from some important national gathering such as the Constitutional Convention was his blacksmith, David Beecher, Lyman's father. Lyman's birth in 1775 was a traumatic event for all concerned. His mother delivered at seven months a creature so scrawny that the women attending her laid him aside as lifeless. When the baby stirred on his own and caught their attention, the woman who washed and dressed him said, "It's a pity he didn't die with his mother like this." After his mother died of consumption two days later, his bereaved and overburdened father arranged for Lyman to be reared on the North Guilford farm of the boy's uncle, Lot Benton. The hard labor of helping on the farm turned an unpromising infant into a young man as hard-muscled as his father, but in the process his active mind developed a distaste for farming. Sensitive to what appeared to be their charge's unusual mental capacity, his Uncle Lot and Aunt Benton made an arrangement with his father for Lyman to enter Yale and become the first Beecher to acquire a college education. Even so, in the eyes of the long-established Footes, Lyman was a problematic suitor for what he himself would call "the Queen of all those girls."

In eighteenth-century Connecticut, Congregational ministers reigned supreme. Theirs was the tax-supported religion of the state, and in many, if not most, communities the Congregational ministers decided who should occupy the seats of temporal power as well as who should go to heaven. Becoming one of these highly respected, even revered, power brokers was the ambition of most young men fortunate enough to attend the state's institution of higher learning at New Haven. But the challenges and rewards involved in the new and democratic nation arising from the Revolution were attracting more young men to the study of law by the time Lyman entered Yale. In fact, sixteen of Lyman's thirty classmates were headed for the bar instead of the pulpit, and he was midway through his undergraduate years before he fell under the spell of the charismatic divine who headed Yale, Dr. Timothy Dwight. During a revival conducted by Dr. Dwight, Lyman experienced what was called a "conversion" in the Calvinist theology prevailing in Congregational and Presbyterian denominations. It was an experience so charged with powerful and confusing emotions that few could find words to describe it. Beecher gave up on attempting to subject conversion to "the test of close metaphysical analysis," but more than half a century later he was eloquent in asserting what it did for him: "I soon found myself harnessed to the Chariot of Christ, whose wheels of fire have rolled onward, high and dreadful to his foes, and glorious to his friends. I could not stop." To do his part in hauling that chariot, Lyman decided to become a minister and enrolled for an extra year in theological school after his graduation in 1797.

It was during that year that he came courting Roxana. Instead of being overawed by the erudite and comparatively sophisticated Footes and their impressive surroundings, the farm boy who had once admired them from afar was concerned as to whether they could meet the standards of his converted self. They were, after all, Episcopalians and therefore outside the pale of the Calvinist elect. According to the stern doctrine that the Puritans brought with them to the New World, all human beings were subject to damnation as sinners because of Adam's fall. Although Jesus had atoned for man's sin on the cross, the salvation that he promised would come only to the elect who were privileged to go through that rather mysterious process of conversion. As implied by the word *elect*, people could not reason or will themselves into a conversion experience or earn it by good works. It had to be a gift from God, who predestined the course of all human lives. The role of the church and its ministry was to awaken those fortunate elect to the gift they could have by admitting and repenting of their sinful natures and surrendering themselves completely to the will of God. Only when this happened could they count themselves among the saved and entertain the hope of going to heaven. The necessary view of oneself as a hopeless sinner could be depressing and painful, and Lyman endured a year of anguish before he hooked onto that fiery chariot. Ironically, Lyman's new conviction led him to worry that the personality traits that made Roxana lovable in human terms constituted a heresy in the form of a "natural goodness" that would blind her to the need for a supernatural conversion.

The doubts about the state of her soul that Lyman raised in his letters to her would have brought an end to the affair for almost any other woman than Roxana Foote. Her own deep religious beliefs, however inspired, allowed her to appreciate Lyman's sincerity and view his concern for her salvation as an expression of love. When he was present in person, she was aware that she had an instinctive need for a man whose nature was a complement to her own. He was as voluble as she was silent, as nervous as she was calm, as ardent as she was cool. Although he could not be called handsome because his nose was too long and his ears too large, his face was alive with expressions of his ever-changing emotions. He had the saving grace of humor and fun to lighten his piety. Still, there was a brief time when the questions he raised made her think so hard about the nature of her own faith in God that she was upset and depressed to the point of causing her family to worry about her sanity. All this came to an end during one of Lyman's visits when he gave her the final test of Calvinism: Would she rejoice if God were to damn her for his own glory? Her reply was instinctive. "Wouldn't being damned mean being horribly wicked? To believe that my being horribly wicked would contribute to the glory of my Heavenly Father is unthinkable," she said. Startled by her honesty and logic, Lyman said, "Oh, Roxana, what a fool I've been!" Even though Roxana never surrendered her belief in a compassionate and reasonable God, Lyman accepted her wrestling with his questions to the point of acknowledging a sinful nature as a conversion experience, and they were married in harmony in the same year that Lyman was called to a Presbyterian pastorate at East Hampton, Long Island.

In 1800 the Beechers welcomed a new year and a new century by bringing into the world a new life in the form of a girl whom they christened Catharine. Roxana's mother and young sister Mary sailed over from Connecticut to help her through the first months with the baby. Being in that household gave Mary, who had grown up in a fatherless family, an idea of what marriage might be like when, and if, she accepted a serious suitor. Roxana seemed to be content, and she was the same serene and somewhat distant sister she had been at Nutplains. She kept peace in the house by agreeing with everything Lyman said and by trying to anticipate his every whim. Through his sermons and the several prayer sessions that he held at home every day, Lyman stayed in close touch with God and tried to discern and pass on the Almighty's will for everyone in every aspect of life. As a convicted agent of the Lord, he cut a commanding figure in the eyes of his congregation and his family. He was so earnest about being good and doing good for others that it was hard to argue with him. But Mary rather hoped that the man to whom she gave her hand would not be as bossy as Lyman could be and—to be honest— would be better looking and have better prospects. She did not want to scrimp and slave and save and talk about taking in boarders just to make ends meet, as Roxana was doing. When Roxana complained mildly to Lyman about their finances, he would just shrug and say, "The Lord will provide."

Mary thought that she had found a man more to her liking when she had boarded at New Haven a ship bound for Jamaica as the wife of John Hubbard. Family and friends agreed that she had made a good catch and could look forward to a life of luxury and plenty in what Hubbard insisted was a heaven on earth. On the voyage, Hubbard turned out to be pleasantly tender and attentive, and the island was as beautiful as her husband had pictured it to be—and as hot. Within days, the beauty would cruelly taunt her like a dream of imagined bliss. Only the heat remained real, for she found herself in a hell instead of a heaven on earth. Trying to get to know the kitchen help so that she could better manage the manor house on the plantation, she was informed, as if she should already have known it, that the lovely, milk-chocolate children who seemed to enjoy free run of the house had been sired by the master. Grinning and laughing, one of the cooks proudly claimed motherhood. When confronted with this news, Hubbard grinned, too, and said, "Think nothing of it. It's the custom here, but now that you are with me, my love, there will be no more need for that sort of thing." Worse than the fact of it was her husband's casual acknowledgment of what was a dreadful sin in the light of all that she had ever been taught. Because he was aware of her grandfather's high standing back in Connecticut, Hubbard felt obliged to assent to his bride's desire to go home as soon as possible. Awaiting passage, she had to linger on in a place she loathed long enough to learn that, bad as it was, her husband's sin was as nothing compared to the general mistreatment of the slaves who labored in the island or were traded in the markets in transit to America.

Although she was still only nineteen when she finally returned to Nutplains, Mary Foote Hubbard was aged beyond her years by her disillusioning experience. She would bear a lifelong load of bitterness over betrayal by a person she had trusted and thought she loved and of hatred for slavery and everybody associated with it. Staying long at Nutplains was out of the question. Leaving a husband under almost any circumstances would be viewed as a disgrace and failure by their solid, churchgoing friends and neighbors. She would be too embarrassed, too ashamed, to explain her actions in detail. So she had welcomed Roxana's invitation to come over to East Hampton and help her with the school. Except for moments of homesickness like those that prompted her letter to Esther on that cold January evening, she was grateful for the opportunity to be of service among people who loved and respected and understood her.

Busy though she was bearing children and teaching, Roxana had worked wonders in making her household an example of civilized living in a rustic wilderness. She had made and laid the first rugs on floors and hung the first curtains in windows that were ever seen in the district, painted colorful designs on crudely wrought furniture, and even put her scientific bent to practical use by designing and having built a Russian stove that she had read about. As for Lyman, children were mellowing him. He turned half child himself when he took a break from work to tease and frolic with them, but then he turned half God again when he disciplined them for their transgressions. The children seemed to absorb energy from his warmth like flowers opening to the sun as they seemed to seek rest in the cool, calm, moonlike radiance from their mother. Mary was especially appreciative of the fact that the young black girls, Zillah and Rachel, were treated like members of the family who would be free to make lives of their own when their indenture ran out. The contrast between their treatment and fate and that of even children begotten by the master in Jamaica gave her hope that the evil of slavery could one day be eradicated. On the whole, as the oldest Beecher sibling, Catharine, would remember about the times in East Hampton, "there was a free and easy way of living, more congenial to liberty and society than to conventional rules."

Certainly, Lyman's relationship with Catharine was anything but conventional. He displayed no disappointment that his first offspring was not a son. From the first he called her "Thou little immortal" (a gift from God), and he cherished her as such. His reward was to discover very early that she had a quick, bright mind and a physical structure like his own. She took after him in looks and in a nervous craving for the outlet of physical activity. He began taking her with him at a very early age on his pastoral rounds to the Montauk Indian villages in the area or on more pleasurable fishing and hunting outings. The most exciting events for the whole community were whale sightings. When the cry went up, nearly everybody, including Pastor Beecher with daughter Catharine in tow, would rush to the beaches and boats. Lyman would leave Catharine on the beach with the other children and women to watch the fun while he would take an oar in one of the boats. Like her father, Catharine was neither squeamish nor fearful. When a whale was beached, she liked to watch men carve it up. As to her fearlessness, she passed the unexpected, playful tests her father gave her with high marks. She would recall with pride all of her life that she had not screamed in panic or begged for mercy when he dangled her out of the highest window of the house on one occasion or when he ducked her head under in a washtub full of water on another. Her marks in her mother's schoolroom were nothing to boast about or remember. It was too tempting to stare out the window across half a mile of sand and scrub growth to the sea and dream of far-off places.

There was never a question of Lyman's turning Catharine into a surrogate son. Her mother and Aunt Mary made sure of that. Roxana drilled her in the practical, housekeeping aspects of becoming a woman. What with managing the household and delivering William in 1802 and Edward in 1803 and baby Mary in 1805, Roxana had little time or inclination for the kind of play that Catharine enjoyed with her father or for the kind of bonding that Catharine had with Aunt Mary. Mary fed the girl's imagination by reading Scott and Burns and Byron with her. Mary also schooled Catharine in the feminine graces. When a practical Roxana wanted to crop Catharine's hair, for instance, Mary insisted that it be left long. Then she dressed Catharine's hair in different ways to demonstrate to Catharine herself and to her parents how attractive the girl could be. If her father could discard his ministerial duty to play like a child, Aunt Mary could go even further. She could be a child in her understanding and sympathy "with all the little half-fledged wants and ambitions of childhood," as Catharine put it later in describing her relationship with her aunt. She was fond of referring to her Aunt Mary as "the poetry" of her childhood and candidly admitted that she felt closer to her than to Roxana. She would grudgingly learn the skills and perform the tasks that her mother demanded, but she would willingly perform any service for Aunt Mary.

For Lyman, spurts of play with his children were like hissing jets from the safety valves on the steam engines that were being used on a tramway in Boston and from what he had heard on a boat in Scotland. The steam driving Lyman was heated by the fire of his faith. He was a serious man engaged in the most serious business of all—the saving of souls. Unlike his sister-in-law, Lyman never had the feeling of being out of touch with the world, perhaps because he regarded it as his duty to attend meetings of the Presbytery, the Synod, and even the General Assembly, the higher bodies of the Presbyterian Church. They would take him all over Long Island, down to New York, and on into New Jersey and Pennsylvania. There he would meet fellow clergymen and get a feeling for what was happening all over the country, and he didn't like most of what he was hearing.

As a staunch Federalist, a member of the party that was once headed by a conservative and reverential man like George Washington, he feared that the country was literally falling apart under a chief magistrate like this godless Democratic-Republican Jefferson. Thomas Jefferson had come back from his time as minister to France with an undue admiration for the bloodthirsty French revolutionists, who showed as little respect for the church as for the crown. Lyman had become an admirer of Emperor Napoleon, who was not only restoring law and order to France but also had demonstrated his belief in a higher than human power by having the pope come all the way from Rome to crown him in Paris. The latest news, that the emperor's armies had defeated the Austrians at Austerlitz, was welcome to Lyman, who felt that all the old courts of Europe were in need of cleansing.

Ironically, Jefferson might never have become president in 1801 if General Alexander Hamilton, who had inherited leadership of the Federalists, had not worked so hard in the House of Representatives to be sure that it would break the tie between Jefferson and Aaron Burr, another Democratic-Republican, in Jefferson's favor after thirty-five ballots. Again, in 1804, Jefferson might not have been reelected if there had not been dissension within the Federalist Party, and again both Burr and Hamilton were deeply involved. When it became obvious that Jefferson wanted to replace him on the ticket with Governor George Clinton of New York, a more moderate Republican, Burr decided to run for Clinton's office. Fearing that Jefferson's purchase of the Louisiana Territory from France would mean a permanent shift in power to the slaveholding South and West, a group of New England Federalists proposed that the northeastern states, including New York, secede and form a new nation. They met secretly with Burr and offered him their immediate support in the New York election and held out the possibility of making him president of that new nation if their plans worked out. Alexander Hamilton, appointed general and then secretary of the treasury by Washington, believed firmly in the union of all the states they had led to victory in the Revolution. He feared and mistrusted Burr, also a war hero and charismatic politician who had established a strong power base among the working classes through an organization in New York called Tammany Hall. If the New England secessionists supported Burr, the Federalist vote would be split, and Burr would certainly be elected to a position from which he could seriously threaten the union. In the process of trying to head off this movement, Hamilton wrote a private letter to a fellow Federalist in which he said that "Burr is a dangerous man and one who ought not to be trusted with the reins of government." When these words became public in the summer of 1804, Burr challenged Hamilton to a duel and killed him.

In the eyes of Lyman Beecher, this was a tragedy with dreadful consequences. The story, at least in Federalist circles, was that Burr had practiced with a pistol assiduously to improve his marksmanship before the duel, while Hamilton, whose son had been killed in a political duel three years before, told his seconds that he would deliberately fire over the head of his opponent. In the event, Hamilton did miss, and Burr's aim was deadly. Quite apart from the personal sorrow that Hamilton's death had brought to his family, the wound to the nation was still festering. Although there were no laws against dueling per se and it had been an accepted practice among gentlemen sensitive about their honor since the first settlers arrived in America, Burr thought it wise to leave his New York mansion under cover of darkness on the night of Hamilton's death. But he brazenly turned up in Washington to complete his term as vice president by presiding over the Senate during the impeachment trial of U.S. Supreme Court associate justice Samuel Chase in early 1805. Lyman did not know whether to believe the talk that Jefferson entertained Burr at dinner in the White House and thanked him for getting rid of his political enemy. But there was a great deal of substance to the talk that Jefferson, who wanted to see Chase impeached, turned against Burr for running a trial that let Chase off the hook. By 1806 a footloose Burr was said to be leading an expedition into the Southwest to detach those territories from the union, annex Mexico by force, and make himself emperor of a new nation.

That Burr would be involved in such a traitorous scheme was nearly incredible to Lyman in view of the man's background. His father was Aaron Burr, Sr., the second president of the College of New Jersey, which became Princeton University; his maternal grandfather was Jonathan Edwards, a great Calvinist theologian whose work and words were an example and inspiration for Lyman. When his son-in-law died, Edwards took over the presidency of Princeton for a few months before his own death. An orphaned Burr attended Princeton, where he made a record as one of its most brilliant students and where he had a friend and collegemate named James Madison, who was now Jefferson's secretary of state. Burr's sister Sally married a Princeton graduate, Tapping Reeve, who founded one of the nation's first and best law schools at Litchfield, Connecticut, and Burr studied there until he joined Washington's army. Rising through the ranks to become a lieutenant colonel, Burr distinguished himself in a number of campaigns, including the march on Québec and the Battle of Monmouth. He was credited with saving a whole brigade from capture during the retreat from Long Island. How could a man like this stray so far from living by the faith of his fathers? This was one of the most troublesome aspects of the duel for Lyman, who simply could not let it go without doing something about it.

There was no way of erasing that particular blot from history, but Lyman believed there should be a way of preventing such a tragedy in the future. Lyman decided that it should be the task of Calvinist Christians to see that dueling, which was obviously a sin in God's eyes since it led to murder, was made a crime in the eyes of men. But what could he do about it? He was only thirty-one and pastor of a church so small in a community so far off any beaten path that he had to ride fourteen miles round-trip on horseback to get his mail. For him, it would be a very far reach to any of the levers of power that could eliminate a social evil that for centuries had not only been tolerated but also too frequently used by the very men who controlled those levers. Nevertheless, Beecher decided that he would use the only means at hand and denounce dueling from his own pulpit to a handful of fishermen and farmers and Indian basket weavers. Like Martin Luther before him, he could do no other. When asked many years later by his biographers for whom the Hamilton-Burr duel was ancient history why he had made what seemed a futile gesture, he said, "[T]here never was such a sensation as that produced through the whole country. When I read about it in the paper, a feeling of indignation was roused within me. I kept thinking and thinking, and my indignation did not go to sleep. It kept working and working, and finally I began to write. No human being knew what I was thinking and feeling, nor had any agency in setting me at work. It was the duel, and myself, and God, that produced that sermon."

Beecher thought that the sermon was received well enough by his own congregation that he preached it again when the Presbytery met at

Aquebogue on April 16, 1806. Although astonished by the subject matter, some of his ministerial colleagues thought that he should try to have
it published. Thus encouraged, Beecher went to work on polishing it. He
read draft after draft to a captive audience at home—Roxana, Mary Hubbard, and his own sister Esther, who was then visiting. Although he
accepted some of their suggestions for minor changes, he was well aware
that they did not represent an unbiased public and that they were
unlikely to challenge his good sense in publishing at all. When he and
the rest of the family were satisfied with the script, he sent it over to
Gardiner's Island for a critique by the island's hereditary owner, John
Lyon Gardiner, the only person in the neighborhood who had the education and sophistication to be of such help in Lyman's opinion. After two
weeks of awaiting Gardiner's reaction, he went to the island himself.
Gardiner was not there, but his wife knew about the sermon. "Have you
found it yet?" she asked. Found it? Beecher did not know that it was lost,
and the story she told him nearly took the heart out of him. Gardiner
had given the handwritten manuscript, the only copy in existence, to
another man returning to the mainland for delivery to Beecher. The man
put it in the pocket of his jacket. While rowing he got so warm that he
threw off his jacket. When he picked up the jacket to get out of the boat,
he found the sermon missing. He did recall hearing something like a
splash and assumed that the manuscript had fallen into the water.

For Beecher this bad news came as if God had decreed that he desist.
He still had his notes and early drafts, but he dreaded the task of putting
it all together again. Then came more news that called for some action
by somebody. Down in a place called Nashville, Tennessee, an admired
former judge named Andrew Jackson shot and killed a lawyer. Beecher
could not help noting that these were two more men trained in the law
as those members of the New York bar, Hamilton and Burr, had been. Yet
they also felt free to stage a duel. Obviously there was pressing need for
laws that would make this form of murder a crime. Although still reluctant to reconstruct his manuscript, Beecher thought that the least he
could do would be to make certain that the messenger had not dropped
it before boarding his boat. Gardiner had some forty laborers on his five-
hundred-acre island farm, and Beecher went over to contact as many of
these men as possible and offer a five-dollar reward for finding the lost
manuscript.

When a month went by with no word, Beecher nearly gave up hope.
Then one day, as he was cutting wood for the home fires, he saw a man
running toward him waving something in the air. It was his manuscript,

and it was in good condition. Gardiner had wrapped it in paper and wound it tightly around with yarn. This created enough protection to keep the manuscript dry during the short time it spent at sea. There had been a storm on the evening of the day that the package was lost overboard. High winds and a higher-than-usual tide deposited it above the normal tide line not far from the island's boat landing "as Providence had ordered it," in Beecher's words.

This divine encouragement caused Beecher to have it put in print by a local publisher, who could not afford to distribute it beyond the villages on that far tip of Long Island. There was very little reaction from a population that was largely Democratic-Republican and did not wish to dwell on a subject that might put their leadership in a bad light. Once more Beecher thought that his work was destined for oblivion, but once more Providence decreed otherwise. A copy found its way into the hands of a prominent New York City minister, John M. Mason, who reviewed it favorably in his periodical *The Christian's Magazine*. After that the subject was brought up at a meeting of the Presbyterian Synod in Newark, New Jersey, where Beecher himself was on hand to explain his proposal for the formation of societies against dueling. The young man from a rural pastorate was surprised to meet strong opposition to his point of view from a doctor of divinity whose metropolitan pastorate contained wealthy and prominent men who considered dueling a proper, if not precisely Christian, way of settling affairs of honor. Beecher offered an eloquent defense of his position and lit a fire that would not be extinguished. As a supportive doctor of divinity at the meeting said, "The light in the golden candlestick of East Hampton began to be seen afar."

These happenings ordered by Providence made of Beecher a name to reckon with throughout the Congregational and Presbyterian communities of the Northeast. Mary Foote Hubbard, who would spend the rest of her life helping with a growing Beecher family, would never again have to complain of being mired in a soundless frog pond.

2

"Up for the war"

One rat slipped on Miss Katy's toes
And danced about the room.
While with the tongs and candlestick
Two others kept the tune.

One rat jumped onto Harriet's bed
And began to gnaw her nose.
The other chose another extreme
And nibbled Mary's toes.

So BEGAN A LENGTHY POEM by which Catharine Beecher tried to calm the
fears and overcome the disgust of the younger sisters who shared a bedroom with her in the big, old house on North Street in Litchfield, Connecticut. She was the oldest and considered to be the wittiest of the
Beecher brood. Her favorite game was playing with words, and often she
would use them to express the wry humor with which the family viewed
life's vicissitudes. This particular scourge was hardly exaggerated by the
vivid imaginations of the children. Their very sober father, the Reverend
Mr. Lyman Beecher, admitted in a letter to a friend that "rats, abundant
as usual, rattle over our head o'night in troops." Until this year of sorrows, it had been possible for Catharine to treat a tribulation like rats in
the walls lightheartedly simply because their lives had otherwise been so
idyllic since father Lyman had been called to the pulpit of Litchfield's
Congregational Church. Now the future seemed clouded and uncertain,
and only the past looked bright.

Back in 1810 there had been general rejoicing in the house at East
Hampton when Lyman broke the news that they would be moving to

Connecticut. The family had continued to grow. Although baby Harriet had lived only a month, infant George was thriving at a year. Lyman's reputation as a fiery preacher of Calvinist doctrine also had been growing. But his $400 annual stipend from the East Hampton Presbyterian congregation had stayed at $400. Despite Roxana's effort with her school and boarders, the family had never made ends meet, and they were $500 in debt. The pastor gave his flock fair warning that he would have to leave them for the sake of supporting his family unless they could give him at least $500 a year. Only after the Litchfield church offered Beecher $800 and he announced a departure date was any effort made to detain him. How Beecher felt about this show of indifference by people he had labored to save for ten years was evident in his last sermon, a classic exposition of Calvinism. He began by giving himself credit for leading some of them through the conversion process to the point where he was sure that he would one day meet them again in "the world of glory." But then he let the rest of them have it:

> And what shall I say to you, my dear hearers, of decent lives and impenitent hearts, to whom, through the whole period of my ministry, God by me has called in vain? God is my witness that I have gravely desired and earnestly sought the salvation of your souls, and I had hoped before the close of my ministry to be able to present you as dear children of God. But I shall not. My ministry is ended, and you are not saved. But I take you to record this day that I am pure from your blood, for I have not shunned to declare, to you especially, the counsel of God. I have proclaimed abundantly, and proved by Scripture argument, your entire depravity, the necessity of being born again, the obligation of repentance and faith, and the terrors—the eternal terrors of law and Gospel both, if you do not repent and plead with you, from Sabbath to Sabbath, to be reconciled to God, and now I leave you still in arms against God—still in the gall of bitterness—still in the kingdom of darkness, and with the melancholy apprehension that all my labors for your good will prove only a savor of death. Once more, then, I proclaim to you all your guilt and ruin. Once more I call upon you to repent, and spread before you the unsearchable riches of Christ, testifying to all of you that there is no other name given under heaven whereby we must be saved, and that he that believeth shall be saved. And now I have finished the work which God has given me to do. I am no longer your pastor, nor you the people of my care, to the God who committed

your souls to my care I give you up, and with a love which will
not cease to glow till the lamp of life expires, I bid you farewell.

How the congregation felt after hearing themselves so roundly damned
was never recorded. But many years later Mrs. Gardiner, the lady of Gardiner's Island and wife of the man whose careless handling of Beecher's
sermon on dueling very nearly ended a spectacular preaching career before
it began, told a Beecher biographer, "[I]t was his leaving that was the cause
of my conversion. I thought when he went that the harvest was past, the
summer ended, and my soul not saved." And it was Beecher's uncompro-
mising position on the requirements for salvation that brought a call
from Litchfield where Congregationalists were concerned about inroads
being made upon the true faith by theists and Unitarians and Roman
Catholics and all manner of lesser and looser Protestant denominations.

For Beecher, there was much more than financial relief involved in
choosing Litchfield over East Hampton as a soul-searching ground. Located
in the hills of northwestern Connecticut, it was then the fourth-largest
town in the state and a crossroads of the stage routes between Boston and
New York and Albany and the coast. With the nation's first law school
and first academy for young women, it was a seat of learning second only
to New Haven, the site of Yale University. The Congregational Church
was still the tax-supported established religious institution of the state,
and its minister was automatically a personage second to none in any
community. Beecher felt that a word spoken in Litchfield would be a
word likely to be carried anywhere and everywhere.

Occupying such a high public position as well as that of paterfamilias in
need of housing a dozen family members, relatives, and servants, Beecher
had to acquire a suitable residence. He was fortunate to find an empty
white frame house set just off the main street on an acre and a half of
land. A square house with a hipped roof, it contained a dining room and
three other rooms on the first floor and four bedrooms on the second. It
had a large kitchen, well room and woodshed in an attached L, and there
were two barns to house the vehicles and animals. There was yard enough
for a garden in summer and the necessary woodpile in winter, and the
views of the higher hills and ponds surrounding Litchfield were spectacular. Lyman acquired all this for $1,350, slightly less than he had realized
on the sale of his East Hampton house. The rats were a questionable
bonus of which the eager buyer was presumably unaware.

Roxana set about using all of her housekeeping skills to make the
house livable and attractive. The feature most appreciated by all the other
members of the family was a duplicate of the Russian stove that she had

designed in East Hampton. Set in the dining room on the first floor, it provided heat for three rooms on that floor and three more above. Writing home on a winter day, a newcomer to the Beecher household reported, "I am now sitting in my chamber (and it is cold weather), but I should think it agreeable summer." Roxana also continued giving birth to new Beechers in what had become a two-year cycle. Another Harriet, named for the infant who had died in East Hampton and for one of the Foote sisters, was born in 1811; Henry Ward, named by his Grandmother Foote, who was on hand for the birth, in memory of two sons whom she had lost in infancy, arrived in 1813.

With more mouths to feed and a presence to maintain as family to the pastor of the established church in a center of wealth and sophistication, the Beechers soon discovered that $800 in Litchfield did not go any farther than $400 in East Hampton. Debts mounted. As a result of her experience in East Hampton, Roxana knew just what to do about it. Both Judge Reeve's Law School and Miss Pierce's Female Academy drew students from all over the country, and there was no place for these young people to live but as boarders in private homes. Through family connections, Roxana was able to borrow enough money to build an addition to the house with a large meeting room on the first floor and four bedrooms above that she could rent out, and a study in the attic for Lyman. It is not surprising that the Beecher children would recall throughout their lives the almost continuous excitement of growing up in such a household in such a town.

Because so much was happening in their own lives in those early years in Litchfield and because of the community's inland isolation in the hills of Connecticut, the Beechers paid very little attention to the troubles being visited upon their young nation by war with England. In Litchfield, a Federalist stronghold, the conflict, remembered as the War of 1812, was called "Mr. Madison's war," blaming it by inference on the president and his Democratic-Republican colleagues. Only 316 Connecticut citizens served in Mr. Madison's war, compared to some 3,600 in the Revolution. The war was so unpopular throughout New England that it exposed the same fault in the supposedly perfect union that the Louisiana Purchase had done before it. The commercial interests of the North, with a need for freedom of the seas and foreign markets, were often at variance with the rural interests of the South, with a lust for more land and slaves to work it. Discussion of states' rights and the validity of secession must have been lively in the Litchfield law school, and a seed may have been planted there in the mind of one of its most noted graduates, John C. Calhoun, that would later burst into full flower in the warmth of his native South Carolina.

For more than half of the century that the Beecher family was prominent in American life, photography did not exist at all, and it was not easily available during the rest of their years. It is not surprising that, except for the most celebrated among them, few likenesses were made, and this is especially true for the older of Lyman Beecher's children.

Firstborn Catharine Beecher, who never married, was a leading educator and writer. As shown in this photograph, she maintained a wide correspondence with society's movers and shakers on behalf of women's education until weeks before her death.

The oldest son, William Beecher, who became a minister like his father and brothers, was the least well known of them all. The troubles he had in obtaining and keeping pastorates led the rest of the family to call him unlucky.

As rigid in mind as he appears to be in body, Edward Beecher earned an enviable reputation as an educator, minister, and theologian, but he never achieved the popular acclaim of his younger brother Henry Ward Beecher.

The only member of the family to lead a completely private life, Mary Beecher Perkins nearly achieved her one ambition—to live to be a hundred. Pictured here shortly before she died at ninety-five, she also retained her distinguishing beauty.

It may have been more than irony that Judge Reeve was brother-in-law to Aaron Burr, also a student of his and a potential tool of Federalist secessionists in 1804. Burr's mysterious movements in the Southwest during the next few years had caused him to be tried for treason on the orders of President Jefferson. Burr had been acquitted in 1807 after a much-publicized trial in Richmond presided over by Supreme Court chief justice John Marshall. Burr then spent four years hiding out in Europe and, by 1812, was back in New York practicing law and grieving over the death of his only child, Theodosia, in a disaster at sea. Some Litchfield citizens or students were certainly participants in the gathering of disgruntled Federalists known as the Hartford Convention that would go down in history as a nearly seditious movement. Although there were some serious British raids on towns along the Connecticut coast as close as forty miles from Litchfield, the only suffering that its residents shared with most people in the Northeast was economic. Ever practical of necessity, Roxana Beecher probably spoke for most of her friends and neighbors when she wrote to a friend, "We feel the war somewhat more than we should one between the Turks and Crim Tartars, inasmuchas, for the most part every article is double and treble the former price, and some things even more than that."

As in East Hampton, the one member of the family who was concerned about national and world affairs was Lyman. He came down from the hills frequently to deliver guest sermons in other pulpits and attend church meetings, and he kept up a lively correspondence with fellow churchmen. To him, a war in which Washington was invaded by British forces and the president driven from the White House and the union threatened with secession was a grave matter. He would later recall the troubled times in oratorical style: "Our dangers in the war of 1812 were very great, so great that human skill and power were felt to be in vain. Thick clouds begirt the horizon, the storm roared louder and louder, it was dark as midnight, every pilot trembled, and from most all hope that we should be saved was taken away; and when the peace came, we said, 'Our soul is escaped as a bird from the snare of the fowler. The snare is broken and we are escaped.'" But in keeping with his feeling that human power was in vain with respect to the war, Pastor Beecher devoted much of his personal power in those years to what he saw as a social evil that, like dueling, had a more widespread, enduring, and damaging effect on the body politic.

Not long after his arrival in Litchfield, Lyman was one member of what they called a consociation—a gathering of pastors from a group of churches—to attend the ordination of a young man named Heart. Here is Lyman's description of what happened there to light a new fire under him:

> The preparation for our creature comforts in the sitting room of Mr. Heart's house, besides food, was a broad sideboard with decanters and bottles, and sugar, and pitchers of water. There we found all the various kind of liquors in vogue. The drinking was apparently universal. This preparation was made by the society as a matter of course. When the Consocation arrived, they always took something to drink round, also before public services, and always on their return. As they could not all drink at once, they were obliged to stand and wait as people do when they go to mill. There was a decanter of spirits also on the dinner-table, to help digestion, and gentlemen partook of it through the afternoon and evening as they felt the need, some more and some less, and the sideboard with the spillings of water, and sugar and liquor, looked and smelled like the bar of a very active grog shop. None of the Consocation were drunk; but that there was not, at times, a considerable amount of exhilaration, I can not affirm. When they had all done drinking, and had taken pipes and tobacco, in less than fifteen minutes there was such a smoke you couldn't see. And the noise I cannot describe; it was the maximum of hilarity. They told their stories, and were at the height of jocose talk. They were not old fashioned Puritans. They had been run down. Great deal of spirituality on Sabbath, and not much when they got where there was something good to drink.

Although Lyman had sold wine to his fellow students while working his way through Yale, conversion there had changed his view of "ardent spirits." When he encountered the same sort of behavior at a second ordination in Connecticut, he reported that "it woke me up for the war"—his kind of war. At a meeting of the General Association of Congregationalists in Sharon, Connecticut, in June 1811, he heard his fellow ministers wringing their hands at what they perceived as an alarming increase in intemperance all around them. The general consensus of the meeting was that nothing could be done about it, but in Lyman's case "the blood started through my heart when I heard this, and I rose instanter, and moved that a committee of three be appointed immediately, to report at this meeting the ways and means of arresting the tide of intemperance." The association agreed to Lyman's proposal and appointed him chairman of the committee. By the next day, Lyman delivered a seven-step program of practical measures such as "That members of Churches abstain from the unlawful vending, or purchase and use of ardent spirits as a part of hospitable entertainment in social visits" and "That parents cease from the ordinary use of ardent spirits in the family, and warn their children of the evils and dangers of intemperance." Lyman Beecher had lit another fire with his report that would not burn out but would grow into a conflagration by the end of the century. Many historians, in fact, credit him with being a founder of the temperance movement that peaked in the establishment of national Prohibition.

People who drew the conclusion from public activity of this kind that the Reverend Mr. Beecher was a dour killjoy did not really know the man or had never been inside that big, old house on North Street. Making music was one of his joys, and the arrival at the Litchfield house of a piano that he had somehow managed to beg, borrow, or steal in New Haven was a major event in the family life. Catharine learned to play it, and her father would play along with his violin while they all sang. Spirited renditions of hymns were the order of most days. But sometimes on a Sunday night, after he had been through the rigors of conducting three or four solemn services—and especially if Roxana had gone to bed early—Lyman would gather the children together, kick off his shoes, take up his violin, and dance to Scottish jigs. Roxana would put a stop to this behavior when she heard it in progress, but not because she objected to secular music. She resented the fact that Lyman's dancing would add to her chore-filled days by wearing out the socks she knitted and darned for him.

Despite his warnings of damnation and hellfire from the pulpit, Lyman Beecher at home and in the streets was a kindly, somewhat eccentric figure who wore knee britches long after they had gone out of fashion and salted his conversation with the dry wit characteristic of the New England farmer. Some of his sayings were cherished and passed down through generations of the family. Lyman's theological positions often attracted sharp criticism. Asked why he did not respond in one such instance, he said, "Once I threw a book at a skunk and he had the best of it. I made up my mind never to try it again." On another occasion, he explained his attitude about the fuss he could sometimes stir up in the religious press by quipping that "I don't mind because when I see the feathers fly, I know I've hit my bird!" He was not above complaining about his audiences. Of those who did not get his message, he said, "Wish the Creator had made fewer people and given them more brains." Of those who seemed to hang on his every word, he said that they made him "think of a dead partridge on a dead limb, watching me when I'm trying to get a shot at him." But he also possessed the self-deprecatory grace of a wise comedian. When a member of his congregation commented after one service that he had been speaking very loudly, he responded, "Oh, yes, the less I have to say the louder I holler." With his head so often in the theological clouds, Lyman could have an absentmindedness about mundane affairs that sometimes proved trying to his levelheaded wife. An avid fisherman, he kept a rod at the ready hidden under a bridge across a fish-lively stream. Crossing this bridge on the way to preach one Sunday morning, he calculated that he had a few minutes to spare when he saw activity in the stream, and he ran down, threw out his line, and caught a fish worth keeping. With time running out he tucked the fish in a pocket of his frock coat and barely mounted the pulpit on time. A week later, when Roxana went to the closet to brush off her husband's Sunday-go-to-meeting coat in time for services, the aroma of a forgotten fish nearly turned her stomach.

Although Lyman would praise Roxana for the perfect submissiveness demanded of a wife to a husband demanded by his creed, her very presence within his household along with that of her sister Mary kept the door open to the rest of Roxana's unsubmissive family. One member of that family whose visits were especially prized by the Beecher children was their bachelor uncle Samuel Foote, the mariner. He was a handsome charmer whose wide-ranging travels as captain of a square-rigged clipper ship armed him with enthralling tales of exotic lands and peoples and customs. He not only presented them with a sea chest of intriguing presents from the Orient and South America but also gave them the more priceless gift of glimpsing an open mind. Samuel Foote was not in awe of Lyman Beecher. Samuel had an intelligence to match the pastor's and could be as articulate, perhaps even more so, in that he could express his thoughts in fluid French or Spanish if need be. Fortunately for the children's development, there was little that Lyman Beecher relished more than a good argument. So sure was he of his own beliefs that defending them against other points of view would only sharpen them, like drawing a knife across a whetstone. Thus Uncle Samuel was free to provoke Lyman into rebuttal and startle the children by insisting that Muslims, Catholics, Jews, and other infidels he met in his travels were as religious in their own way as any Congregationalist or Episcopalian and often more Christian in their behavior. Samuel and his sister Mary shared the same literary tastes, and he would bring her new works by Scott and Byron and America's rising literary light, Washington Irving. Mary would read these works aloud to whatever family members or outside visitors cared to listen. Still a young and attractive woman, Mary's presence and her interests often drew students of the law school to the Beecher house.

In that sense Mary Foote Hubbard's death in the early morning hours of September 1, 1813, from the wasting lung disease then called consumption, was a sad loss to the community as well as the family. At thirteen Catharine was old enough to know that she personally had lost the "poetry" of her childhood, but she would help to keep memories of things that her Aunt Mary said and did so much alive that two-year-old Harriet would reminisce about Mary as if she, too, had consciously partaken of that poetry. Lyman's behavior at the time of that death was an indication of why all the Beecher children continued to have a warm relationship with their father despite episodes of stern discipline in which the rod was not spared and constant demands for an unattainably high standard of thought and conduct. In some senses Mary Hubbard was the worm in the Calvinist apple that Lyman held out to his children. Lyman's own account of Mary's death has to be seen in that light to be fully appreciated:

> She died in my arms. A few hours before her death I sat behind her on the bed, holding her up, and she asked me to sing,
>
>> Jesus make a dying bed
>> Feel as soft as downy pillows are,
>> While on his breast I lean my head
>> And breathe my life out sweetly there.
>
> After singing I took her up and held her in my arms sitting in the rocking chair. "Oh," she said, "How distressed I am!" I comforted her by telling her that it would be over in a few minutes. And it was.

In a household bustling with so much young and new life—Henry Ward was only three months old—even this death could not cast a long-lived pall. Their faith assured them that there was a heaven where Aunt Mary, however Episcopalian she might have been, would be a happy soul. Although she was of a very different and less engaging personality, Aunt Esther, Lyman's unmarried stepsister, was living just down the street with her mother and would gradually ease into the family to take Mary's place. Most of the children were too young to be affected by the death except for Catharine and Edward, a serious, sensitive, and precocious boy. Feeling that Mary, who knew her so well, would smile down upon her, Catharine continued to live a life that Harriet would recall as "a constant stream of mirthfulness." She was admittedly as indifferent a student at Miss Pierce's as she had been at her mother's school in East Hampton, but her quick mind allowed her to guess her way through examinations. Still dreamy, she read all the novels and poetry she could find. In view of the fact that she remained closer to her father than any of the other children, her account of how she reacted in those years to the religion that Lyman made a daily staple of all of their lives is revealing and prophetic:

My strict religious training made little impression, for I rarely heard anything of that which seemed so dull and unintelligible. Up to the age of sixteen my conceptions on this subject were about these: that God made me and all things, and was very great and wise and good; that he knew all I thought and did, that because Adam and Eve disobeyed him once only, he drove them out of Eden, and then so arranged it that all their descendents would be born with wicked hearts, and that, though this did not seem either just or good, it was so; that I had such a wicked heart that I could not feel or act right in anything until I had a new one; that God only could give me a new heart; that, if I died without it, I should go to a lake of fire and brimstone, and be burned alive in it forever; that Jesus Christ was very good, and very sorry for us, and came to earth to save us from this dreadful doom; that revivals were times when God, the Holy Spirit, gave people new hearts; that, when revivals came, it was best to read the Bible, and pray, and go to meetings, but that at other times it was of little use. This last was not taught, but was my own inference.

My mind turned from all this as very disagreeable. When led by my parents and Christian friends to it, I tried to do as they told me, because I saw they were anxious and troubled, and I wished to relieve them. Two or three times when I saw my father so troubled, I took "Doddridge's Rise and Progress of Religion" and tried to go through the process there laid down, but with utter failure. Meantime, I rarely heard any prayers or sermons, and at fifteen I doubt if the whole of my really serious thoughts and efforts would, except the above, have occupied a whole hour.

It is no wonder that Lyman was troubled by the failure of revivals to give his daughter a new heart. He had gone through conversion during a revival, and they were an important part of his ministry in East Hampton and Litchfield. Driven by his own conviction, Lyman would put heart and soul into those meetings, where for a week or more he would preach a sermon every day and more on Sunday and counsel those people who were moved by the spirit between times. After one of these revivals, Lyman experienced a physical and nervous breakdown of a kind that he would pass on to a number of his equally high-strung children. Unable to carry on with his work, he tried a long vacation of hunting and fishing on trips to places as far away as Niagara Falls and Maine. When that activity did not help him, he consulted a Boston doctor, who diagnosed his problem as dyspepsia and overwork and prescribed a return to the farm labor of his childhood as a possible cure. Lyman bought eight acres adjacent to his home, hired a helper, and acquired the necessary equipment such as a yoke of oxen and a plow. For a whole season he stayed away from his books, worked the land all week, and delivered a sermon extempore on Sundays. Once recovered, he turned the experience into "clinical theology." Instead of asking inquirers at revivals about their souls, he often startled them by asking about whether they exercised or their bowels moved regularly in order to help distinguish between "dyspepsia and piety."

In keeping with her cycle, Roxana Foote Beecher gave birth in 1815 to yet another son, whom they christened Charles. It was not long after that birth that she began feeling symptoms of the same disease that had claimed her sister Mary's life. She managed to hide them from her busy husband until an August day in 1816, when he took her with him in the buggy on a visit to a parishioner. On the way back home, the brisk northwest wind turned unseasonably cold, and the chill of it caused Roxana to tell Lyman that she would not be with him long. Looking hard at his wife, Lyman saw "that she was ripe for heaven." From that point on, what Lyman called "galloping consumption" took over, and in six weeks Roxana was dead. She faced her coming death with the same calm reserve that she had faced life's other trials. She gathered her children around her and expressed her desire that all of her sons, including baby Charles, would serve the Lord as ministers. She smiled as her husband told her, "Roxana, you are now come unto Mount Zion, unto the city of the living God, the heavenly Jerusalem, and to an innumerable company of angels." An outside witness to her death, Mrs. Tapping Reeve, reported, "It is a most moving scene to see eight little children weeping around the bed of a dying mother, but, still, it was very cheering to see how God could take away the sting of death, and give such a victory over the grave." Thought too young to be taken to the burial, three-year-old Henry Ward revealed a surprising and sensitive understanding of what had happened. Found digging in the yard by Catharine a few days later, he told her, "I'm going to heaven to find Ma."

For Catharine this was the death that took more than the "poetry" of childhood out of her life. It took her whole childhood. As the oldest of the children and a girl as well, she felt obliged to help her father as much as she could in the management of the family. Although her stepgrand-mother and Aunt Esther gave up their own home to move into the house on North Street, it was Catharine who tried to keep some poetry in the lives of her siblings in the face of Aunt Esther's stern New England cleanliness and godliness. Mottoes she quoted such as "A place for every-thing and everything in its place" and "Waste not, want not" suggest the kind of order that Aunt Esther tried to establish in that teeming house-hold. One child, Edward, was away at school in South Farms and another, Harriet, had been sent to Nutplains to live with the Foote fam-ily temporarily. But there were still enough young ones left to keep their caretakers busy. As Catharine wrote to her Aunt Harriet at Nutplains:

> William is in Mr. Collins's store but boards at home. Mary goes to school to Miss Pierce, and George to Miss Collins. Henry is a very good boy, and we think him a remarkably interesting child, and he grows dearer to us every day. He is very affectionate, and seems to love his father with all his heart. His constant prattle is a great amusement to us all. He often speaks of his sister Harriet, and wishes spring would come, so that she might come home and go to school with him. Charles is as fat as ever, though he is much less trouble, and can take more care of himself. He can speak a few words to express his wants, but does not begin to talk.

The year of 1817 began as a year of sorrows for all of the Beechers, a year of emptiness at the core for a family that almost unknowingly had revolved around Roxana's solid presence. Catharine was especially aware of her father's lost feelings, but her own feelings were very mixed when Lyman went on a preaching mission to Boston that was treated with smirks and whispers throughout the community. An upset Mary came home from Miss Pierce's school to tell Catharine that the other girls were saying that the pastor had gone wife-shopping. Whether the preaching mission was a success or not, the wife-shopping certainly was. After her father told her that he had found a new companion, Catharine engaged in some carefully crafted correspondence with her. But Lyman's arrival home one night after another trip with a new Mrs. Beecher came as a surprise to the younger children. Although possibly gilded by time, the written recollection of Harriet, who had come home from Nutplains, is probably a true reflection of the family's change in mood after an uncertain year of bereavement and separation:

> I was about six years old and slept in the nursery with my two younger brothers, Henry and Charles. We heard father's voice in the entry, and started up in our little beds, crying out as he entered our room, "Why, here's pa!" A cheerful voice called out from behind him, "And here's ma."
>
> A beautiful lady, very fair, with bright blue eyes and soft auburn hair bound round with a black velvet bandeau, came into the room smiling, eager and happy looking, and, coming up to our beds, kissed us and told us that she loved little children and that she would be our mother. Never did stepmother make a prettier or sweeter impression. The next morning I remember we looked at her with awe. She seemed to us so fair, so delicate, so elegant that we were almost afraid to go near her. She was peculiarly neat and dainty in all her ways and arrangements; and I remember I used to feel breezy and rough and rude in her presence. We felt a little in awe of her, as if she were a strange princess rather than our own mamma; but her voice was very sweet, her ways of moving and speaking very graceful, and she took us up in her lap and let us play with her beautiful hands, which seemed wonderful things made of pearl and ornamented with strange rings.

It is to be regretted that there is no record as to how this dainty princess reacted to the dance of rats overhead. But her presence lifted the weight of sadness and responsibility from Catharine's shoulders enough to let her again take a light view of domestic disasters and have fun with words. A neat and graceful woman such as Harriet described must have been upset enough when a clumsy serving girl broke the best piece of crockery in the house to inspire this lament by Catharine:

> Come all, and list a dismal tale!
> Ye kitchen muses, do not fail,
> But join our sad loss to bewail.
> High mounted on the dresser's side,
> Our brown-edged platter stood with pride;
> A neighboring door flew open wide,
> Knock'd out its brains, and straight it died.

Come, kindred platters, with me mourn;
Hither, ye plates and dishes, turn;
Knives, forks and carvers all give ear,
And each drop a dish-water tear.
No more with smoking roast beef crown'd
Shall guests this noble dish surround.
No more the buttered cutlet here,
Nor tender chicken shall appear;
Roast pig no more here show his visard,
Nor goose, nor even goose's gizzard.
But broken-hearted it must go
Down to the dismal shades below;
While kitchen muses, platters, plates,
Knives, forks and spoons upbraid the Fates;
With streaming tears cry out, "I never!
Our brown-edged platter's gone forever!"

3

"No child prepared to die"

IN THE YEAR 1825, the Reverend Mr. Lyman Beecher had to face up to a long-delayed and much-dreaded decision. Should he—could he—leave Litchfield? With a salary that had not been increased by a dollar in fifteen years, he had never been able to make ends meet and was now burdened and embarrassed by debts he might never be able to pay. His marriage to Harriet Porter had so far resulted in three more children, the youngest not yet a year old, and there might well be more to come. Thank God for a woman with the kind of spunk and drive that was making Catharine independent and a help to so many of her siblings. But William was still floundering around, and Edward's education at Yale had been a drain on the family finances, though worth every penny of it in view of the young man's outstanding academic achievements. There were three more boys to be put through college if their mother's dying wish that they become ministers were to be granted. It was, of course, his living wish as well, and no doubt he would want to see the baby Tom follow along the same path. With Lyman himself, it might be a matter of now or never, since he would turn fifty this year, an age that already made him a poor candidate for congregations seeking a new pastor. However many reasons there were to leave Litchfield, there seemed to be more to stay in a place where the family had been happy despite some sad losses and where he had saved so many souls not only among his own people but also through revivals round about. Not least among the reasons to stay was the fact that he had nowhere else to go.

In the end, Lyman dodged a decision by presenting his dilemma to the congregation. He reminded them that they had not offered to raise his salary in all the years he had served them, and he described in detail the nearly heroic efforts his devout wives and supportive children had made to get along on eight hundred dollars a year. "My investigation of my struggles to make ends meet had convinced me that there is an annual deficiency in my salary of two hundred dollars wholly irremediable by any possible efforts of my own or by any authorized reliance upon Providence," he told his flock. Then, in keeping with the rules of the church, he asked the congregation to dismiss him, climbed down from the pulpit, and walked home. It was a gamble, but the odds were very much in favor of their coming up with those two hundred dollars instead of sending a man who had served them well for fifteen years packing. He would not have dared to take such a gamble in the lean years of Mr. Madison's war or after the financial panic of 1819 brought on a national depression. But money was flowing again into the pockets of the substantial members of his congregation, with a promise of more to be made now that the Erie Canal was opening the way west, and a tariff to protect the products of New England manufacturers was in place, and a sound New Englander, John Quincy Adams, was in the White House, never mind the talk that he was there instead of General Jackson only because of a suspicious deal to make Henry Clay his secretary of state for Clay's support. However it came about, Clay was a go-ahead man who would look out for American commerce and not let the old money of Europe call the shots.

In the house on North Street, feelings were mixed as the family awaited the outcome of Lyman's sermon. For the younger children, Litchfield had been a place of wonder and learning, the only place they had ever known, and the older children had been brought over from Long Island at too early an age to think of any other place as home. Unlike the children or Roxana, who had a family complex at Nutplains an easy ride away, Harriet Porter Beecher had no roots and no relatives in Litchfield or all of Connecticut. More aware than Lyman of their financial situation, she could hope that the prospects would be better almost anywhere else. Although she believed in doing the Lord's work, she was not used to the genteel poverty so often imposed on ministers.

Harriet Porter grew up in Portland, Maine, where her father was a respected and prosperous physician. Among her uncles were the nationally famous King trio—William, the first governor of Maine; Rufus, the senator from New York and twice the U.S. minister to Great Britain; and Congressman Cyrus. Visiting in Boston, Harriet met Lyman and heard him preach at the Park Street Church when he was on his wife-shopping trip in 1817. As his daughter Harriet had been, Lyman was smitten by Miss Porter's delicate beauty—"fine China," as someone described her.

But he was even more attracted by the nature and extent of her religious faith. She had obviously undergone a Calvinist conversion so successfully that she feared for the souls of her parents, who believed that a benevolent God would welcome them into heaven without a supernatural experience—her father because of his good works as a doctor; her mother because she had already suffered so many earthly ailments and disappointments. When Lyman followed Harriet home in the process of an ardent courtship, her worldly parents tried to convince her that he was literally a poor prospect with his rustic ways and all those children to raise on a minister's income. But Harriet was already twenty-seven and in danger of becoming a spinster. Like Roxana, she found Lyman, still in full vigor at forty-two, as persuasive on his knees as in the pulpit above her. How could she resist him when—as she wrote to Catharine Beecher in a polite exchange of letters to prepare for her arrival in Litchfield—she considered him to be a "messenger from the court of Heaven"?

There must have been butterflies in Harriet's stomach on that night when her carriage first drew up in front of the white house on North Street. What would she find inside? What were all those children like, and how could she manage them with so little experience? Beginning with the scene romanticized by young Harriet, glimpses of life in Litchfield from the new bride's early letters to family and friends would indicate that she was pleasantly surprised. The society of this remote place was far more impressive than she had imagined. Judge Reeve and his wife, for instance, and the governor of Connecticut, Oliver Wolcott, who had his home in Litchfield, were among the first to call at North Street to welcome her. As to family life, she wrote:

> It seems the highest happiness of the children (the larger ones especially) to have a reading circle. They have all, I think, fine capacities, and good taste for learning. Edward, probably, will be a great scholar. He and William are soon to be absent, and never very much more be under parental instruction, but I trust they will carry principles with them which shall remain always, and the fruit of them bear testimony to the benefit of early education. Catharine is a fine-looking girl, and in her mind I find all that I expected. She is not handsome, yet there is hardly anyone who appears better. Mary will make a fine woman, I think, will be rather handsome than otherwise. She is twelve now, large of her age, and is almost the most useful member of the family. The four youngest are very pretty. George comes next to Mary. He is quite a large boy, takes care of the cow, etc.; goes to school, though his father expects to educate him. He learns well.

Harriet and Henry come next, and they are always hand-in-hand. They are as lovely children as I ever saw, amiable, affectionate, and very bright. Charles, the youngest, we can hardly tell what he will be, but he promises well. Catharine and Mary take all the care of the children morning and night, etc. They go to school except Charles, and stay all day, so that we have not much noise. The boys are up before it is quite day, and make fires, and we are all down and have prayers before sunrise.

The garden yields plenty of vegetables for the year, plenty of cherries, and the orchard furnishes cider and apples enough. A barrel of apple-sauce is made in the fall, which the children use instead of butter, Mr. Beecher's and my nine o'clock supper is always sweet apples and milk.

Mr. Beecher's labors are greater than any minister's I know. . . . His people are so scattered that his parochial duties are fatiguing and difficult. If any thing would induce him to change his residence, it would be a more compact society. The attachment of his people to him is very gratifying. I witness it myself with great delight. I like Mr. Beecher's preaching as well as ever. His sermons are chiefly extemporaneous. They are animated, and have much effect.

Along with a second marriage, Lyman Beecher found himself dealing with what was beginning to look like a new nation in his eyes. The Federalist Party in which he had put his trust since the days of Washington was rapidly vanishing, with only 42 Federalists as against 141 Democratic-Republicans in the House and 14 Federalists against 34 Democratic-Republicans in the Senate of the Fifteenth Congress that convened in late 1817. With James Monroe, the last of the Virginia dynasty, as chief magistrate for two terms, it would be called the era of "good feelings," possibly because Monroe's party faced so little opposition. In reality, as conservative Federalists lost their grip on power, a creeping grassroots democracy was greening the land south and west and was killing off a unity of belief in this still-new nation. States entering the union wanted to have their own way in settling what was already the most divisive issue of all: slavery. The once-Federalist North wanted to stop its spread, while the Democratic-Republican South wanted to extend it to the Pacific. This annual struggle within Congress would end in a compromise in 1820 that granted statehood to free Maine and to slave Missouri to maintain an equal balance in the Senate. It would satisfy neither side and sorely disappoint Lyman, who had always had black people within his household and regarded the slavery issue as a moral rather than a political matter.

The younger the Beechers, the brighter they burned.

Always a dreamer and a listener, Harriet Beecher Stowe absorbed the events and culture around her like a sponge. She would turn her observations and thoughts into some of the best-selling novels of her time, most notably *Uncle Tom's Cabin*.

Henry Ward Beecher is pictured here at the height of his fame—and infamy—in the 1870s. His defiant posture and casual attire attracted as many men as women to his crowded services at Plymouth Church in Brooklyn. On annual lecture tours he carried his popular gospel of love to unchurched millions across America.

Poet, musician, preacher, gifted with the family's most unusual imagination, Charles Beecher endured numerous personal tragedies, heresy trials, and professional failures without losing his loving temperament and the belief he preached of a glorious heavenly life to come.

More disturbing and personally damaging to Lyman than the divisiveness with regard to slavery was the disestablishment of religion in his native Connecticut. In 1818, with his Litchfield neighbor and friend Oliver Wolcott in the governor's chair, Connecticut adopted a new constitution under which the Congregational Church would no longer be acknowledged as the state's official denomination and receive tax support. Although he may not have been aware of it at the time, this development undoubtedly would be a factor in Lyman's willingness to gamble on losing his Connecticut pulpit. The happy hunting ground for Congregational ministers that he had known all of his life would be changed in unpredictable ways. In a sermon he delivered at the time, he lamented the change. Calling his denomination the "rock" upon which Connecticut institutions had been built, he said in part:

> But at length the multiplication of other denominations demanded such a modification of the law as should permit every man to worship God according to the dictates of his conscience, and compel him to pay only for the support of the Gospel in his own denomination. The practical effect has been to liberate all conscientious dissenters from supporting worship which they did not approve—which the law intended, and to liberate a much greater number, without conscience, from paying for the support of the Gospel anywhere—which the law did not intend.
>
> While it accommodates the conscientious feelings of ten, it accommodates the angry, revengeful, avaricious, and irreligious feelings of fifty, and threatens, by a silent, constant operation, to undermine the deep-laid foundations of our civil and religious order. . . . Let the wastes multiply till one third of the freemen shall care for no religion, one third attach themselves to various seceding denominations, and a remnant only walk in the old way, and the unity of our counsels and the vigor of our government would be gone.

If the state's slipping from its Calvinist foundation distressed Lyman, an apparently similar development within his own family caused him anguish and despair. "But while I am as successful as most ministers in bringing the sons and daughters of others to Christ, my heart sinks within me at the thought that every one of my own dear children are without God in the world, and without Christ, and without hope," he wrote to his oldest son, William, who was away at school in 1819. "I have no child prepared to die, and however cheering their prospects for time may be, how can I but weep in secret places when I realize that their whole eternal existence is every moment liable to become an existence of unchangeable sinfulness and woe."

Sickness and death were frequent visitors in every household, and the Beechers' was no exception. Despite his labors for the Lord, Lyman did not expect that his family would be exempt from such common occurrences, but he sincerely believed that the kind of faith he preached could comfort them in illness and take the sting out of death for the converted, as it had for Roxana. So he worried and wept over what he believed to be the lost state of his unconverted children, and the events in the North Street house in June of the year after his letter to William had given him cause for his woes. In a letter to Edward, away at Yale, on June 20, 1820, Catharine set the scene:

> We are all anxious and troubled at home. Frederick [her two-year-old stepbrother, the firstborn of Harriet Porter Beecher] has had the canker, or scarlet fever, very badly. For two or three days we have despaired of his life. Last night he nearly suffocated with the phlegm, but this morning he is much better, and we hope his greatest danger is over. Last night Harriet was seized violently with the same disease, and we know not how it will terminate. Dr. Sheldon is a most excellent physician, and we hope his care and the mercy of God will save our dear Harriet and Frederick, and we use all the precautions we can to prevent the other children from taking infection.

Lyman seized on the crisis in his new son's life to push conversion on Edward in a letter of June 22:

> I hope your health may be preserved, and your life, for usefulness in the Church of God. Most earnestly I pray that I may never have the trial of weeping over you, on a dying bed, without hope. What shall it profit you though you should gain all knowledge and lose your own soul? Awake, my dear son, to righteousness! I must entreat you no longer to presume on the continuance of a vapor to reject the mercy of the Gospel.
>
> It has seemed for a while here as if God was about to sweep us away with a stroke. Causes of alarm came clustering around me: Frederick hopeless, Harriet violently seized, William more unwell, Charles stuck a pitch fork into his foot; the other children exposed to a terrible and contagious disorder; your eyes

threatened; your mother feeble and greatly afflicted. My cup seemed to admit no more of feeling and fear. But God has pitied and reprieved.

But God did not reprieve, and Catharine brought the drama to a close on June 23 with a letter to the Foote relatives at Nutplains. Her father's adjective "hopeless" would not apply to little Frederick in her account of the sad event, and it would be apparent in the very near future that Catharine was perhaps unconsciously arriving at a very different understanding of the nature of God than the one being thrust on her. She also revealed a talent for more than comic verse that would lead to a more personal tragedy in which she would have great need of such an understanding:

Disease and death have visited our house. The scarlet fever has prevailed here and little Freddy was seized, and this morning, without much struggling, breathed his last. Were it not for the support of religion, I think mamma would sink, but she is a most eminent Christian, and feels resignation and comfort from above.

I wish you could see how beautiful he looks even in death. I think I never beheld any thing earthly so perfect and lovely as his little corpse. His hair curls in beautiful ringlets all over his head, and he looks so natural and unaltered, one would think him in a peaceful slumber. I can not bear to think he must be laid in the grave.

Yesterday Harriet was seized violently with the same disease, and last night we were almost distracted for fear we should lose them both.

Our friends here are very kind, and do every thing for our assistance and comfort. It recalls every moment the heavy day when my dearest mother died. Oh, may the repeated admonitions not be lost on her children!

Sad dawned the morning of the day
That saw our sweetest flower laid low;
The weeping heavens were hung with clouds
And Nature seemed to feel our woe.

We laid him in his infant grave,
The fairest form of earthly mould,
Death ne'er could choose a sweeter flower
To deck his bosom cold.

Yet oft kind mem'ry's gentle hand
Shall lead him smiling to our view,
Recall his pretty prattling ways,
To wring our hearts, yet soothe them too.

Dear cherished child, though few the days
To cheer our hearts thou here was given,
When earth is past, thy cherub smiles
Shall sweetly welcome us to heaven.

Lyman's greatest concern was for the older children, of course, the readers so admired by his new wife who should be able to understand from his sermons and family worship and the kind of religious reading that Catharine did that they were in peril unless they could get themselves to undergo conversion. For most of the Litchfield years, the younger children were not expected to do more than memorize the catechism and behave well during family prayers and church services. In Harriet's remembrance, "most of father's sermons were as unintelligible to me as if he had spoken in Choctaw." With a family on their mother's side of different persuasion, there was a certain amount of confusion for a child to handle. On one of Harriet's long visits to Nutplains, Harriet's Aunt Harriet Foote, "the highest of High Church women," persuaded her to memorize the High Church catechism, which began with a question easy enough to enlist the child's interest: "What is your name?" But then Aunt Harriet thought that she might be creating a problem for her niece back in Litchfield, since her father was a Presbyterian minister and tried to get young Harriet to memorize the Assembly's catechism as well. It began with a question so far above the child's head—"What is the chief end of man?"—that Harriet balked, and in her recollection of the incident she was "overjoyed" to hear her aunt tell her grandmother that it "would be time enough for Harriet to learn the Presbyterian catechism when she went home."

Harriet's shadow, Henry Ward, was equally impervious to received religion in his early years. He had a built-in resistance to anything handed down from on high at home, school, or church. A weak memory and a speech impairment made both retention and recitation, the twin tools of learning, difficult and embarrassing for him. But he had a vast interest in all outdoors and in the living things he saw there—insects, birds, animals, flowers, trees. He was also full of energy and willingness to learn and perform useful tasks. He once listed the jobs he could handle before he was ten: sew, knit, scour knives, wash dishes, set and clear table, cut and split wood, make fires, feed cattle, curry horses. The last listed chore was to "go to school—and not to study." This admission was made long after the fact, as was his confession about confessing in his reminiscences:

> When I was a child, if I had done wrong, I never told it to my schoolmaster. I am afraid I told him a great many other things! Why? Because he had a magisterial air, and my faults struck against a stone wall, as it were, when I went to him. But there were members in my father's family—one of my sisters, a maiden aunt of whom I have spoken before and several others—to whom I dared to go and speak about my faults. When I ran away from school I dared to tell them that I was sorry for what I had done, for from them I neither got a cuff, nor a scolding, nor exposure. I knew that instead of bringing me into trouble they would hide my faults and shield me. And I recollect distinctly that with such persons it was easy for me to be frank. To them I could so confess my sins that penitence followed.

Fortunately for a boy prone to mischief, Henry Ward had a sunny, winning personality, and he charmed his Aunt Esther and an older black woman who helped around the house. As for his sister Harriet, they were simply "hand-to-hand" in the words of his stepmother, Harriet Porter Beecher. For Henry Ward, this second mother was no China doll but more of a stone wall, like his teacher. Her polish and piety put him off; he considered her so cold that he could "not recollect ever to have had from her one breath of summer." Deserted, as he felt, by his real mother at age three, Henry Ward was always in search of love—an "outgushing" person who "wanted to be running on somebody all the time." His step-mother could never be that somebody, and his father was not often there for him. When Lyman was available, he was capable of showing the kind of tenderness that caused his children to question the stern and rigid doctrine he preached. Recalling a time when he had a toothache, Henry Ward said, "I went to my father's room, and he put his hand upon my head, and with tones of great kindness and love said, 'You have got a toothache, my dear boy! Come get in with me and cuddle down by my side,'—how that filled me with affection, and such gladness that I forgot the toothache! It was quite lost and gone. I slept."

Lyman was never really distant from the children. When he involved them in work around the place, he often joined them and turned it into a form of fun. While they all sat around peeling apples for the sauce, for instance, he and George, the best reader of the group, would take turns reciting passages from the latest Scott novel or a poem by Byron. Like his admiration for Napoleon, Lyman's appreciation of Byron was surprising in view of the poet's wild reputation. But he knew that Byron had a Calvinist background and was sure that he could be saved if only he could hear a few of Lyman's sermons. The talk of Byron would have strange consequences for little Harriet, sitting quietly in the family circle and taking it all in. Sometimes Lyman would deliberately provoke argument about some theological question so that his children would learn to defend their beliefs. At other times there might be discussion of some current event. With consequences far greater to her life than the matter of Byron, Harriet was first made aware of slavery as an evil at the tender age of seven when she heard her father preach and talk about the Missouri Compromise. As Lyman exposed the anguish of his soul over the plight of slaves, he could bring tears to the eyes of members of his family and crusty old farmers in his congregation. But the fun in the Beecher work parties was more often physical than intellectual. They would go on fishing and hunting and nut-gathering expeditions, and they would all pitch in to cut, split, and stack the winter's wood that parishioners dumped in their yard as part of the pastor's compensation. Harriet was always a little jealous of the boys, and one of her great memories was a time when she was allowed to help with the wood stacking and got a pat and a cherished word from her father that she was his "best man." Harriet would later draw a vivid picture of the lighter side of Litchfield life in an essay on country pleasures:

> My father was fond of excursions with his boys into the forests about for fishing and hunting. At first I remember these only as something pertaining to father and the older boys, they being the rewards given for good conduct. I remember the regretful interest with which I watched their joyful preparations for departure. They were going to the Great Pond—to Pine Island—to that wonderful blue pine forest which I could just see on the horizon, and who knew what adventures they might meet? Then the house all day was so still; no tramping of laughing, wrestling boys, no singing and shouting; and perhaps only a long seam on a sheet to be oversewed as the sole means of beguiling the hours of absence. And then dark night would come down, and stars look out from the curtains, and innuendos would be thrown out of children being sent to bed, and my heart would be rent with anguish at the idea of being sent off before the eventful expedition had

reported itself. And then what joy to hear at a distance the tramp of feet, the shouts and laughs of older brothers; and what glad triumph when the successful party burst into the kitchen with long strings of perch, roach, pickerel, and bullheads, with waving blades of sweet-flag, and high heads of cat-tail, and pockets full of young wintergreen, of which a generous portion was bestowed always upon me. These were the trophies, to my eyes, brought from the land of enchantment. And then what cheerful hurrying and scurrying to and fro, and waving of lights, and what cleaning of fish in the back shed, and what calling for frying pan and gridiron, over which father solemnly presided; for to the last day he held the opinion that no feminine hand could broil or fry fish with that perfection of skill which belonged to himself alone, as king of woodcraft and woodland cookery. I was always safe against being sent to bed for a happy hour or two, and patronized with many a morsel of the supper which followed, as father and brothers were generally too flushed with victory to regard very strictly dull household rules.

The music that began with the arrival of the piano would continue to be a primary source of family entertainment. The volume and frequency of performances, if not the quality, increased as Mary, like Catharine, learned to play the piano, William and Edward took up the flute, Lyman joined in with his violin and a boarder, Louisa Wait, "sang so beautifully." These family concerts, according to Harriet, "filled the house with gladness." Into this scene one day walked a young Yale professor, Alexander Metcalf Fisher. Fisher's first acquaintance with Litchfield was a Sunday layover there during a leisurely chaise trip through the Connecticut back country. To while away a few hours of that empty day, Fisher went to hear two sermons by Lyman Beecher, a figure well known in New Haven for his continuing friendship with faculty members and moral and financial support of his alma mater where his son, Edward, was then enrolled. As an intellectual who enjoyed writing and reading verse, Fisher was attracted to poems appearing in *The Christian Spectator* and attributed to one C. D. D. Fisher knew that Lyman Beecher was a founder of the magazine who signed his contributions D. D. A little investigation revealed that the mysterious C. D. D. was Beecher's daughter Catharine, who may have thought that she would get more readership if she were mistaken for a man. In any event, Fisher took advantage of the fact that a classmate was going to preach for Beecher one Sunday and went along to Litchfield with him. It was simply a ruse to gain an introduction to the poetess he admired, and it worked. Fisher walked Catharine home from church and was invited to stay for dinner and accompany her to the afternoon services. Being also a piano player and composer of some skill, Fisher spent the intervals between eating and worshiping in playing and singing duets with Catharine. For a shy, scholarly young man like Fisher, this musical blending with an obviously intelligent young woman like Catharine was an irresistible invitation to further acquaintance.

When Fisher asked Lyman for permission to call on his daughter, the minister was only too willing. From his Yale contacts, he was well aware of Fisher's high standing in that intellectual community. Fisher was as close to a genius as any of his faculty colleagues had ever known. Son of a Franklin, Massachusetts, farmer, he had first revealed his remarkable mind when, at age ten, he wrote a textbook titled A Practical Arithmetic because he did not like the one assigned in class. At fourteen he entered Yale, graduating as "the first scholar in his class" at eighteen in 1813. Raised in as stern a Calvinistic tradition as the Beechers, he spent a year studying for the ministry at Andover Theological Seminary but returned to Yale as a tutor and in 1818, at age twenty-three, was named adjunct professor of mathematics and natural philosophy, as physics was then called. But he also dabbled in philosophy, astronomy, Hebrew, Latin, Greek, architecture, and music. Among his publications was a Hebrew grammar, a book on astronomy titled Journey to the Moon and Some of the Planets, and an article "Musical Temperament" in The Journal of Science. From Lyman's point of view, the only thing missing in the young man's curriculum vitae was any mention of a conversion, but then his Catharine could not lay claim to one either, much to Lyman's sorrow.

Considering the facts that Catharine had been described as "not handsome" and that marriage was the most acceptable future for a young woman—in fact, nearly the only one to be contemplated in her circles—and that she and Fisher seemed to have so much in common, Catharine's attitude when the professor's intentions became clearer must have puzzled her enthusiastic father. During the time of Fisher's courtship, Catharine spent part of the year in New London, where she had taken a teaching position. As a result, much of the courtship itself and of her thinking about it ended up in letters. Although Fisher wrote "pretty" letters, Catharine was concerned about his deep involvement with the sciences that were as yet of little interest to her. "It always seemed to me that devoted and exclusive attention to the abstract sciences almost infallibly will deaden the sensibilities of the heart and destroy social habits," she wrote to her father. Although an admirer of intellect, Catharine said that she would prefer a husband "with a social disposition and an affectionate heart" to "the greatest mathematician and philosopher in the country." At one point near the end of 1821, Catharine even threatened to break off the correspondence, but Fisher evidently had the perseverance to match his intellect. Early the next year, Catharine wrote of a change of heart to Louisa Wait, the songstress boarder who had remained a close friend even after she left school to go home to Philadelphia:

> Now I suppose I must tell you all about it. I wish you were lying beside me warm in bed, and I could tell you a mighty interesting tale but now I can barely give you the outline which you must fill up. Soon after you left here I received a queer letter from the Professor and I returned a queer answer, and our correspondence continued with an abundance of spunk on both sides, until I refused to correspond any longer—this brought matters to a crisis as the doctors say—he proposed a personal interview to which I finally consented and last Tuesday evening he arrived—and you cannot think what a long string of misunderstandings there was all around, but we finally found that we both loved each other too well to quarrel any longer and we soon met on such terms as all lovers should meet. He staid two or three days and I soon felt no doubt that I had gained the whole heart of one whose equal I never saw both as it represents intellect and all that is amiable and desirable in private character. I could not ask for more delicacy and tenderness—all that I regret is that we must be so soon and so long separated.

Catharine went on to explain that Fisher would be leaving that spring for a long-planned year in Great Britain and Continental Europe to press the flesh with professional contacts in the universities there and to brush up on spoken French. In the brief time before sailing, Fisher spent as many hours as possible in Litchfield, where the now open romance became the talk of the town's young people as well as Catharine's siblings. Horace Mann, one of Judge Reeve's law students and later one of the nation's great educational pioneers, wrote home that "Professor Fisher of New Haven has been making love" to one of the brightest girls in town. Lyman informed the Nutplains contingent through his brother-in-law George Foote that "we have lately had a visit from Prof Fisher, which has terminated in a settled connection, much to my satisfaction, as well as of the parties. He goes to Europe in the spring, and returns in a year and then will expect to be married."

As with so many human expectations, this one was never to be fulfilled. The ship on which Fisher sailed went down in a storm off the Irish coast, and he was one of the twenty-one cabin passengers to go to the bottom with her. Catharine was devastated, almost as much by a letter she got from her father as from the news itself. The minute he heard the news on May 29, 1822, Lyman took pen in hand and got off to a fairly good start: "My dear Child—on entering the city [New Haven] last evening, the first intelligence I met filled my heart with pain. It is all but certain that Professor Fisher is no more. Thus have perished our earthly hopes, plans, and prospects. Thus the hopes of Yale College, and of our country, and, I may say, of Europe, which had begun to know his promise, are dashed. The waves of the Atlantic, commissioned by Heaven, have buried them all." With that Lyman then launched into a murky passage of verbiage that could only be read as an expression of doubt as to where Fisher would now be spending eternity, since he had not undergone a conversion. Instead of offering comfort, he was using the tragedy to urge conversion on Catharine. "And now, dear child, what will you do?" he concluded. "Will you turn at length to God, and set your affections on things above, or cling to the shipwrecked hopes of earthly good? Will you send your thoughts to heaven and find peace, or to the cliffs and winds, and waves of Ireland, to be afflicted, tossed with tempest, and not comforted?"

Catharine's distress over her father's letter was evident in her response in early June to a more sympathetic letter from her brother Edward, who had himself just gone through conversion and was planning on becoming a minister. "Your letter came at a time when no sympathy could soothe a grief 'that knows not conscious name,'" she wrote. "Yet it was not so much the ruined hopes of future life, it was dismay and apprehension for his immortal spirit. Oh, Edward, where is he now? Are the noble faculties of such a mind doomed to everlasting woe, or is he now with our dear mother in the mansions of the blessed? . . . Could I but be assured that he was now forever safe, I would not repine. I ought not to repine now, for the Judge of the whole earth can not but do right." Thus began a deep, no-holds-barred, three-way exchange of letters and notes in which a tortured Catharine would dispute the nature of God and his government of the universe with her dogmatic father and only slightly less convicted brother. In a follow-up to her first letter a month later, Catharine told Edward that "the difficulty in my mind originates in my views of the doctrine of original sin"—the belief that all human beings were born in such a sinful state because of Adam's sin that they were destined for eternal damnation unless they were converted. Catharine simply could not make herself feel that she was "totally and utterly without excuse" for being born with a sinful nature, as the doctrine seemed to demand. She admitted that she had "implanted within a principle of selfishness . . . in the existence of which I am altogether involuntary." But she added, "When I have confessed my sins to God, there has always been a lurking feeling that, as God had formed me with this perverted inclination, he was, as a merciful being, obligated to grant some counteracting aid." In other words, she was contending that she already had within herself the capacity to overcome her besetting sin—selfishness—without the miraculous intervention demanded by the process of conversion. Trying to make herself believe in original sin depressed Catharine to the point that "when I look at little Isabella [her stepsister born that year], it seems a pity that she ever was born, and that it would be a mercy if she was taken away." Caught in a desperate struggle between what her mind told her was reasonable and what she had been taught, she reported that "my hours are passing away as the smoke, and my days as a tale that is told. I lie down in sorrow and awake in heaviness, and go mourning all the day long. There is no help beneath the sun, and whether God will ever grant His aid He only knows."

Apparently Edward shared this letter with his father, who wrote to him in August that "Catharine's letter will disclose the awfully interesting state of her mind. There is more movement than there ever existed before, more feeling, more interest, more anxiety, and she is now, you perceive, handling edge-tools with powerful grasp. . . . I am not without hope that the crisis approaches in which submission will end the strife. She is hard pressed, and, if not subdued, I should fear the consequences." Lyman's concern for Catharine's soul was particularly acute since she, as his firstborn and so many ways like himself, remained a favorite child and a powerful example to all the others. Already shocked by Fisher's death and the tragic end to a beguiling romance, the younger children were aware of the tension between Lyman and Catharine but baffled by the cause of it. Through the open door to his father's study, ten-year-old Henry Ward once heard his big sister weeping as she tried to reason with Lyman. This scene may well have taken place after an exchange of notes between them. Even though they lived in the same house, they sometimes found it easier to communicate some feelings in writing.

On a paper she left on Lyman's desk, Catharine wrote,

> I am like a helpless being placed in a frail bark, with only a slender reed to guide its way on the surface of a swift current that no mortal power could ever stem, which is ever bearing to a tremendous precipice, where is inevitable destruction and despair.

If I attempt to turn the swift course of my skiff, it is only to feel how powerful is the stream that bears it along. If I dip my frail oar in the wave, it is only to see it bend to its resistless force.

There is One standing upon the shore who can relieve my distress, who is all powerful to save, but He regards me not. I struggle only to learn my own weakness, and supplicate only to perceive how unavailing are my cries, and to complain that He is unmindful of my distress.

Lyman turned Catharine's note over and wrote a message on the other side. It is unclear whether he meant it to be read as the voice of God or his own, but there wasn't then a great difference between the two for the Beecher children:

I saw that frail boat with feeble oar, and that rapid current bearing onward to destruction an immortal mind, and hastened from above to save. Traveling in the greatness of my strength, I have pressed on through tears and blood to her rescue.

It is many days, many years, I have stood on the bank unnoticed. I have called, and she refused, I stretched out my hand, and she would not regard. At length I sunk the bark in which all her earthly treasure was contained, and, having removed the attraction that made her heedless, again called, and still I call unheard. My rod has been stretched out and my staff offered in vain. While the stream prevails and her oar bends, within her reach is My hand, mighty to save, and she refuses its aid.

What shall I do? Yet a little longer will I wait, and if she accept my proferred aid, then shall her feet be planted on a rock, and a new song be put into her mouth. If she refuse, the stream will roll on, and the bark, the oar, and the voyager be seen no more.

Catharine's answer to that, if any, was unrecorded, but events gave her an opportunity to get away from daily confrontation with Lyman and develop her own thinking. Before he sailed, Fisher had left instructions that two thousand dollars of his estate should go to Catharine if he did not survive the trip. To collect this inheritance and to get acquainted with the family that would never be hers, Catharine went up to Franklin in the fall of 1822 for a prolonged stay with the Fishers. The theological discussions by letter with her father and brother continued through the rest of that year and into the next. She was horrified to discover that the

Fisher family's minister was even more certain than Lyman that her lost love was lost indeed. But she was elated to discover by going through his diaries and papers and talking to his friends and family that the professor's personal character was without blemish. The tone of the exchange with Lyman lightened a little when Catharine reported getting comfort from a book that pictured Christ as "merciful, lovely and compassionate," and Lyman allowed that she might be taking a small step in the right direction. But Catharine obstinately took an even stronger stand in opposition to her father's view when she wrote,

> When I think of Mr. Fisher, and remember his blameless and useful life, his unexampled and persevering efforts to do his duty both to God and man, I believe that a merciful Savior has not left him to perish at last; that if he had delayed an answer to his supplications till the last sad hour, it was then bestowed; and that in the Day of Judgment we shall find that God is influenced in bestowing his grace by the efforts of men, that he does make the needful distinction between virtue and vice, and that there was more reason to hope for one whose whole life had been an example of excellence, than for one who had spent all his days in guilt and sin.

While arguing in favor of his father's theology, Edward tried to be a bit kinder to his distressed sister with advice such as "Trust in him [Jesus] and he will give you that peace which passeth all knowledge." Unlike his father, Edward could descend in the same letter from the high plain of spiritual advice to the lowly field of domestic matters with such instructions as "I wish the striped pantaloons I send to be lengthened as the other pair was" and "I wish you would be very particular and very certain to have my shirts, vest, cravats and stockings washed and sent down Monday." Catharine's head was not always in the theological clouds, either. In a letter to her father in the spring of 1823, she pointed out that she had used Fisher's library to bone up on such subjects as chemistry, logic, arithmetic, and algebra to tutor his siblings still at home. She had heard that there was need for a good girls' school in Hartford, where Edward was then teaching at a boys' school, and she suggested that she might be qualified to start one. Unable to save his daughter's soul, Lyman was nevertheless willing to help her improve the conditions of her earthly existence. He went to Hartford, satisfied himself that there was such a need by inquiring around, and started raising funds. By May 1823 Catharine was in Hartford starting her school.

The school was turning out to be an idea whose time had come and a literal godsend to the Beecher family by 1825, when Lyman was awaiting the outcome of his gamble with the Litchfield congregation. Catharine had recruited Mary as a member of the faculty; Edward as a consultant; and George, Harriet, and Henry Ward as pupils. After services on the Sunday of Pastor Beecher's request for dismissal, there was no congregational response. Nor was there word on Monday. Whether or not they decided to raise his salary, their hesitation in doing so was galling to Beecher, and he was nursing bitter thoughts on his way to the post office that day. There he discovered that his plight had not been overlooked by the Providence that had served him so often and so well in the past. Inside an envelope from the Hanover Street Church in Boston was a letter asking him to take over their pulpit at the handsome salary of two thousand dollars a year.

The timing of that call seemed evidence enough to assign its origin to Providence. But Lyman Beecher knew that he deserved it. Throughout his Litchfield years, he had assiduously cultivated the Congregationalists in Boston, the mother city of the Puritan faith. He had preached there whenever he could, and his mission was sometimes accomplished under heroic circumstances. Asked to help out at a Boston revival in the winter of 1822, for instance, he "went on horseback, started just after the great snow storm, before the stage had broken the paths. I rode in cattle paths, sometimes my saddle bags touching the snow on either side. At the time Dr. Jackson had prescribed mutton chops, and I had to carry a supply along in my saddle bags, and have them cooked at the country taverns where I stopped." From his experiences there, Beecher did not have to wonder why he had been called to Boston. Unitarianism was growing so fast that it had taken over many churches and was capturing the minds of many influential intellectuals. In that very year of 1825, an organization called the American Unitarian Association was formed to spread its gospel across the nation. A rock of Calvinism like Lyman Beecher was needed to stem that heretical tide. He would not be going for the money but to meet a challenge that the Lord was thrusting on him.

4

"Beloved and affectionate children"

"HERE WE ARE AT LAST at our journey's end, alive and well," Catharine Beecher wrote to her sister Harriet. To be able to describe herself and her fifty-six-year-old traveling companion, their father, Lyman, as "alive and well" in that year of 1831 after a trip of many hundreds of miles from New England to the "Queen City of the West"—Cincinnati, Ohio— could be considered news. Much of the journey was by stage over roads so rough as to jar the bones or so soft with mud as to cause the horses to slip and slide and the carriage to sink to its hubs. Some of it was aboard riverboats where the rock and roll was soothing but the rough part was the company—men who ate with their knives, spewed tobacco juice in all directions, filled the cabin with smoke from their cigars and pipes, and swore a blue streak. But, given the fact that they arrived in good health, the tribulations of the trip itself were not worthy of mention, as Catharine continued:

> We are staying with Uncle Samuel [Foote, the once bachelor and mariner whose wife had made settling somewhere on dry land a condition of accepting his proposal] whose establishment . . . is on a height in the upper part of the city, and commands a fine view of the whole of the lower town. The city does not impress one as being so very new. It is true everything looks neat and clean, but it is compact, and many of the houses are of brick and very handsomely built. The streets run at right angles to each other, and are wide and well paved. We reached here in three days from Wheeling, and soon felt ourselves at home.

The next day father and I, with three gentlemen, walked out to Walnut Hills. The country around the city consists of a constant succession and variety of hills of all shapes and sizes, forming an extensive amphitheatre. The site of the seminary [Lane, a new and struggling institution whose trustees were beseeching Lyman Beecher to leave a thriving Boston church to become its president] is very beautiful and picturesque though I was disappointed to find that both river and city are hidden by intervening hills. I never saw a place so capable of being rendered a paradise by the improvements of taste as the environs of this city. Walnut Hills are so elevated and cool that people have to leave there to be sick, it is said. The seminary is located on a farm of one hundred and twenty five acres of fine land, with groves of superb trees around it, about two miles from the city. We have finally decided on the spot where our house shall stand in case we decide to come, and you cannot (where running water on the seashore is wanting) find another more delightful spot for a residence. It is on an eminence, with a grove running up from the back to the very doors, another grove across the street in front, and fine openings through which the distant hills and the richest landscape appear.

I have become somewhat acquainted with those ladies we shall have the most to do with, and find them intelligent, New England sort of folks. Indeed, this is a New England city in all its habits, and its inhabitants are more than half from New England. The Second Church, which is the best in the city, will give father a unanimous call to be their minister, with the understanding that he will give them what time he can spare from the seminary.

I know of no place in the world where there is so fair a prospect of finding everything that makes social and domestic life pleasant. Uncle John [Foote] and Uncle Samuel are just the intelligent, sociable, free, and hospitable sort of folk that everybody likes and everybody feels at home with.

The folks are very anxious to have a school on our plan set on foot here. We can have fine rooms in the city college building which is now unoccupied, and everybody is ready to lend a helping hand. As to father, I never saw such a field of usefulness and influence as is offered to him here.

Catharine was supremely confident that she could meet the needs of the Cincinnati elite for their daughters' schooling. Starting back in 1823 with a rented room above a harness shop and her next younger sister Mary as assistant, she had built the Hartford Female Seminary into an institution with its own building, a faculty of eight, and a student body of more than a hundred in eight short years, the only rival in the nation to a similar school run by Emma Willard in Troy, New York. It had not been easy. Just twenty-three herself when she started the school, Catharine had very little experience in teaching and none in administration, and she was burdened with a troubled heart and mind as a result of her lover's death and her religious disagreements with her father. But she nevertheless had strong family support, an asset that would be of incalculable value to all of the Beechers through all of their years.

In the very beginning, there had been three siblings boarding with Catharine in the same Hartford home—Mary; brother Edward, who was still teaching in the Hartford Grammar School; and their younger brother George, who was a pupil in that school. In their respective periods of free time, Edward tutored Catharine in Latin, then a universal discipline in any higher education. The school brought in so little money in the first year that she had to write to Litchfield to ask her father to pay for Mary's winter clothes—"a new great coat, a frock and a bonnet which will amount to 20 dollars." By the next year, when Edward had moved on to Andover Seminary, Catharine was able to rent a house of her own, which became the Hartford annex to the Beecher homestead in Litchfield. In addition to Mary and George, she would be housing two new pupils, Harriet and Henry Ward; a number of paying boarders; and Aunt Esther Beecher to manage the housekeeping.

Still shy and retiring, Harriet had demonstrated considerable writing ability by winning the class essay contest in her last year at Miss Pierce's school and evidently was a promising candidate for more education. As for the runaway scholar Henry Ward, the hope in sending him to Hartford was that his older sisters could do a better job of stuffing some learning into his ten-year-old head than several previous schoolmasters. A recorded scene from school days in Hartford shows what they were up against. As the only boy in a class of more than thirty girls, Henry Ward learned to cover his embarrassments at making mistakes by clowning. Although the laughter he provoked was rewarding to him, it was disruptive to the class. To promote the dull study of grammar, the teacher would divide the class into competing groups and stage a contest, with rewards going to the side with more right answers. At such times neither side wanted Henry Ward, whose mistakes or clowning could turn them into losers. Sensing her brother's pain at being rejected, sister Mary took him aside before one contest to drill him in the rules of grammar.

"Now, Henry, A is the indefinite article, you see, and must be used only with a singular noun," she said. "You can say *a man*, but you can't say *a men*, can you?"

"Yes, I can say *amen*, too. Father always says it at the end of his prayers."

"Come, Henry, don't always be joking. Now decline *he*. Nominative, *he*; possessive, *his*; objective, *him*. Now, you can say *his* book, but you can't say *him* book."

"Yes, I do say hymn book, too."

At that, Mary had to laugh; Henry had scored again. But she persisted. "But now, Henry, seriously, do attend to the active and passive voice. Now, *I strike* is active, you see, because if you strike you do something. But *I am struck* is passive, because if you are struck, you don't do anything, do you?"

"Yes, I do; I strike back again."

A scene like that may account for the fact that, while there was much exasperation over Henry Ward's academic performance, there never seemed to be serious worry about the working of his mind. Beneath the boy's genial, often clowning facade, there was a troubled spirit. The sensitivity that made him aware of the theological conflict between his oldest sister and their father drove him to worries about the state of his own soul. No matter how his eyes glazed over or his mind wandered during sermons and prayers, he had caught the drift of his father's harsh doctrine: Everybody was born bad and headed for hell until God somehow reached down and saved a few people. This applied especially to children, and his father's inability to offer hope to friends and relatives of dying children was chilling. When a friend of his own age died, Henry Ward was terrified that it could happen to him, too. "At intervals for days and weeks, I cried and prayed," he said. "There was scarcely a retired place in the garden, in the wood-house, in the carriage house, or in the barn that was not a scene of my crying and praying. It was piteous that I should be in such a state of mind, and that there should be nobody to help me and lead me out to the light. I do not recollect that to that day one word had been said to me, or one syllable had been uttered in the pulpit, that led me to think there was any mercy in the heart of God for a sinner like me." That a young boy could suffer so from Calvinist tongue-lashings is confirmed by Henry Ward's tag-along younger brother

Charles, who recalled "sitting under the old fashioned Litchfield pulpit, before I was nine years of age, with face concealed and tears rolling down upon my coat, as I alternately listened to his [Lyman's] words, and trembled lest my agitation be detected."

Fortunately for his sanity then and his future career, Henry Ward was getting a subliminal view of a very different religion from an unusual source. In the rather crowded house on Litchfield's North Street, he was assigned a bunk in a room with Charles Smith, a black man who did chores around the place. When the boy went to bed, he would usually find the man reading his Bible by the dim light of a single candle. Smith never let the boy interrupt him. A truly pious man, he would read aloud and pray and sing and actually laugh with joy at the biblical passages depicting a loving Lord who had come to save the poor and humble while Henry Ward cuddled down into his covers and drifted off to sleep. "I bear record," a mature Henry Ward would say of Charles Smith, "that his praying made a profound impression on my mind. I never thought whether it was right or wrong. I only thought, 'How that man does enjoy it! What enjoyment there must be in prayer such as his!' I gained more from that man of the idea of the desirableness of prayer than I ever did from my father and mother." When Charles Smith did talk directly to Henry Ward about the soul, he described it as something to be saved rather than damned.

Henry Ward always felt that, whether by coincidence or intent, his banishment to the Hartford annex had something to do with his troubled mood. If so, it was a wise move, because the boy would be under the sympathetic eye of a sister who could understand his feelings. Catharine was still far from reconciled with her father's doctrine even though brother William had managed to have a conversion experience, and young Harriet laid claim to one just before coming to Hartford. Older and more mature than Henry Ward, as girls tend to be, Harriet was alert when her father launched into one of his extempore sermons in which

> he spoke in direct, simple and tender language of the great love of Christ and his care for the soul. He pictured Him as patient with our errors, compassionate with our weaknesses and sympathetic to our sorrows. . . . I sat intent and absorbed. Oh! how much I needed just such a friend. I thought to myself. . . . My whole soul was illumined with joy and as I left the church to walk home it seemed to me as if Nature herself were hushing her breath to hear the music of Heaven.
>
> As soon as father came home and was seated in his study, I went up to him and fell in his arms saying, "Father, I have given

myself to Jesus and he has taken me." I shall never forget the expression of his face as he looked down into my earnest childish eyes; it was so sweet, so gentle and like sunlight breaking upon a landscape. "Is it so?" he said, holding me silently to his heart, as I felt the hot tears fall on my head. "Then has a new flower blossomed in the kingdom this day."

Catharine was skeptical when she heard this sweet story. There was nothing in it of the agony of coming to terms with one's own sinful nature, a step in the Calvinist conversion that Catharine herself was not willing to take. When a supposedly converted Harriet tried to join Hartford's First Congregational Church, the Reverend Joel Hawes, a friend of Lyman's, came to the same conclusion as Catharine and asked Harriet one of those questions that Calvinists used to test true belief: "Harriet, do you feel that if the universe should be destroyed, you would be happy with God alone?" Harriet's response was a hesitant yes, but Dr. Hawes pressed on: "You realize, I trust, in some measure at least, the deceitfulness of your heart and that in punishment for your sins God might justly leave you to make yourself as miserable as you have made yourself sinful." That's just what God did through the agency of Dr. Hawes to the fourteen-year-old who had come to him so eagerly. As she wrote to brother Edward at Andover, "My whole life is one continued struggle: I do nothing right. I yield to temptation as soon as it assails me. My deepest thoughts are very evanescent. I am beset behind and before, and my sins take away all my happiness." Her internal distress showed in her outward demeanor. Henry Ward said of his sister who was his best friend and playmate that she was always "owling about."

Despite her agitation of soul, Harriet's mind remained clear enough to do good academic work and even to launch herself on some ambitious writing projects in poetry and drama. When Mary left the school in 1827 to marry a Hartford lawyer, Thomas Perkins, Catharine added Harriet to her teaching staff. Whether to help the newlyweds with their board money or to keep their own expenses down, the two teaching sisters gave up the Beecher annex to move into the Perkins house. There, according to Catharine, they found "quiet and gentility," words that were descriptive of Mary's whole personality and a continuing lifestyle that would make of her advice and her Hartford home an ongoing refuge for her often storm-tossed siblings.

As a fellow worker, Harriet closed the gap of eleven years between the sisters, and Catharine came to trust her younger sister to the point of putting eighteen-year-old Harriet in charge of the school in 1829 while she recovered from one of the nervous breakdowns that plagued the

Beechers. Taking after her father in this, as in so many other ways except in her interpretation of their shared Christianity, Catharine believed firmly in exercise as a way of warding off or getting over these episodes. The woman who had once been such an embodiment of merriment also believed in relaxing and having fun wherever and whenever possible, and Harriet has left a picture of the two of them combining these beliefs in one activity while they were working hard together in Hartford.

> Catharine and myself are riding on horseback every morning before breakfast. . . . I must tell you that I have had quite an adventure. The first time we went to ride was in the evening, and they mounted me on a perfect Bucephalus [the warhorse of Alexander the Great], and the consequence was that before Catharine was mounted I was half way out to Lord's Hill, and for the best of reasons—because my horse *would* go. I turned him and rode back to meet her, and no sooner had we got riding together than my courser set off again on a canter—and such a canter! I went up and down like an apple. From that he proceeded to run, and I went up Lord's Hill like a streak. My gentleman did not stop till he had taken me through the asylum yard to the fence on the other side, and I got down quite crestfallen. I must not omit to say that for the greater part of the way I wore my bonnet on my shoulders behind. All that night I was meditating how it was that people found pleasure in riding.
>
> At present I ride a beautiful young white horse and Catharine a ditto black one. All the difficulty is that my horse has so much of the evil spirit of emulation in him that he won't suffer Catharine's to come near him. The moment he hears the hoofs of "Tinker" behind him, he goes like all possessed, and I am forcibly reminded of that line in Horace which begins, "Jounce, jounce, jounce." Nevertheless, we have pleasant times of it.

Although they continued to reject the means of salvation in which their father so strongly believed, both Catharine and Harriet regarded themselves as Christians. Both became active in Dr. Hawes's church as they would have been in their father's in Litchfield or Boston. True to her own self-evaluation when she was wrestling with the question of original sin, Catharine had developed an ever stronger belief in a fair God who had given human beings an innate ability to be good along with a temptation to be bad. In this light, moral behavior—for which the Ten Commandments was a God-given guide—could be as saving as belief.

But above all human beings were called to live lives of self-sacrificing love through Christ's death on the cross. Catharine and Harriet taught their pupils morality by means of Bible readings and worship along with their academic work, and at one point Catharine even organized a town-wide revival. She saw in the education of young women who would go out into the world as teachers and mothers an opportunity to reform and uplift a whole society; the schoolroom could be more powerful than the pulpit. That Harriet absorbed much of her sister's thinking was apparent in a letter she wrote to Catharine during her brief reign as the school's headmistress: "This morning I delivered a long speech on 'modes of exerting moral influence,' showing the ways in which an evil influence is unknowingly exerted and the way in which each and all can exert a good one. The right spirit is daily increasing."

The sisters had early given up on Henry Ward. After a term, he was shipped off to another school in Connecticut before being taken with the rest of the family to Boston. There he was enrolled in the Boston Latin School, where he made some academic progress, but he still suffered from spiritual torment, heightened when the last of his older brothers, George, was able to go through the conversion experience at Yale, an experience that eluded Henry Ward and left him in fear of damnation. He escaped his family and himself by getting involved with the street games of the gangs that divided young Boston boys into Salem Streeters and Prince Streeters, North Enders and South Enders. One such game was a form of follow the leader that could start with as many as twenty boys, as in this vivid account by Henry Ward:

> Called to the head of the column, I plunged down Margaret's Lane, up Price and Back, up toward Copp's Hill, reducing my followers, by sheer exhaustion, one-half. A brick house was going up; into it I dashed, ran up the ladder, walked along the floor-joists, and let myself down by a rope attached to a guy on the front. Only six or seven could follow. A large mortar-bed lay near by, I dashed into that, wading through the slush. Five came out the other side with me. Tough five! They followed me into a shop, right back into the adjacent parlor, out at a side-door, though some of the last got the yard-stick well laid on by the indignant shop keeper, and the last one came out dripping from a pail of water which a woman flung after the "nasty varmints," as she styled us. Many other feats did we, but in vain. The five would stick. I remember that a large part of Copp's Hill had been dug down for filling the "Causeway," leaving a precipitous face—

well, say, fifty feet high to the eyes, but, if measured, perhaps twenty feet. Ascending the hill, I drew near the verge, a little hesitant to venture the plunge. But to confess that I dare not do *anything* would be disgraceful, and so, with but a moment's pause, I jumped for a little crumbling foothold half-way down, and off from that, as soon as on it, to the bottom, which I reached in a heap, with dirt and stones and two boys following after! Not stopping to rub my shins, rejoicing that only two were left and desperate, I took my way to the near wharf where "Billy Gray's" ships used to be, climbed the side, ran along the deck, up the bowsprit, far out, and then, with a spring, off into deep water! Down, down, down we went, and seemed likely to go on forever. At length the descent stopped, and we rose again to the surface—O joy!—to see the two boys standing on the bowsprit! They did not dare! That day's work established our reputation! We know how Alexander felt! Caesar and Napoleon can tell us nothing new about the glories of victory!

Without the woods and hills around Litchfield for roaming, Henry Ward took to the water. He enjoyed teaching younger boys to swim. His method was simple: He would take them to the edge of the wharf and "say to them, 'Jump, and I will take care of you.' Jump they did, and I did take care of them—principally by making them take care of themselves. With a little encouragement and a little touch, now and then, they would keep themselves up." He later claimed that this taught him that when people are brought to extremities where only God could save them and told to jump, God would never let them sink. In a different lesson from swimming, Henry Ward lost his nerve halfway across the Charles River. "It was a great feat to swim across, and one that I never accomplished, for having that fear I swam back, forgetting that it was just as far to one side as the other! Many persons carry themselves far across the stream of difficulty, and then, on meeting some impediment and check, swim back again, whereas the same effort, the same thought and feeling, would carry them to the other side."

Bored by studies and fascinated by the sea, Henry Ward at age fourteen decided to run away from home and find a berth aboard one of the many vessels in Boston Harbor. He went so far as to gather together the things he might need with him and write a note to brother Charles declaring his intentions. In the note he said he would try to get their father's permission, but would leave without it if necessary. Then he cannily left the note where Lyman was sure to find it. The ploy worked well. After thinking the matter over for a few days, Lyman casually asked Henry Ward to help him saw wood. As Beecher told his biographers, he knew that it was an invitation for a man-to-man talk, and he was not surprised when his father said, "It's almost time to be thinking what you are going to do. Have you ever thought?"

"Yes—I want to go to sea."

"To sea! Of all things! Well, well! After all, why not? Of course you don't want to be a common sailor. You want to get into the Navy?"

"Yes, sir, that's what I want."

"But not merely as a common sailor, I suppose?"

"No, sir; I want to be a midshipman, and after that a commodore."

"I see. Well, Henry, in order for that, you know, you must begin a course of mathematics and study navigation and all that."

"Yes, sir; I'm ready."

"Well, then, I will send you up to Amherst next week, to Mt. Pleasant, and then you'll begin your preparatory studies, and if you are well prepared I presume I can make interest to get you an appointment."

The Mt. Pleasant Institution at Amherst, Massachusetts, was a new venture, but it had good equipment; a low tuition; and, from Lyman's point of view, a laudable objective—the training of ministers. It is doubtful that fourteen-year-old Henry Ward knew that his father was setting something of a trap for him, because he went off to Amherst willingly. There is no record that he ever again wanted to go to sea. That form of rebellion would be left to a half brother, James, the last of the children sired by Lyman Beecher; James was born in Boston shortly after Henry Ward took up his studies at Mt. Pleasant.

For the senior Beechers, their Boston venture started out on a high note. In June 1826 Harriet wrote to her family in Maine. "I am happy to say that we are beginning to be really comfortable. I know not how a minister can desire any thing better than to preach the Gospel in Boston. The four younger children are with us. The girls are at Hartford, established as a family, with Aunt Esther at their head. Edward and George are at New Haven, William at Andover. My husband's health is pretty good. He has some dyspepsia at times, but it always leaves him on the Sabbath. He preaches a good deal and with much encouragement.

"There is a secret history of Boston which is very interesting—the history of minds and moral influence. Of this we have learned some already, and shall, probably, much more. We are at the North End, to which at first I felt reluctant. Mr. Beecher is enthusiastic in regard to this situation. This soil was pressed by the feet of Pilgrims, and watered by their tears, and consecrated by their prayers. Here are the tombs, and here are their children who are to be brought back to the fold of Christ. Their wanderings and dispersions are lamentable, their captivity long and dark, but God will turn it, we hope, and reclaim these churches, this dust and ruin shall live again."

Lyman was sicker than his wife apparently liked to admit, and his ailment would be redefined as depression. At about the same time, William, home on a visit, wrote to Edward: "Father was quite unwell with dyspepsia. I never knew him more cast down. He took a chair, and turned it down before the fire and laid down. 'Ah, William,' said he, 'I'm done over! I'm done over!' Mother told him he had often thought so before, and yet in two days had been nearly well again. 'Yes, but I never was so low before. It's all over with me!'" Lyman did finally fight back with the remedy that had worked before. The city was no place for farming or hunting or fishing, but he devised his own aids to exercise. He would not only cut his own wood but that of his neighbors, and he installed a number of gymnastic devices in his backyard such as parallel bars, a single bar, a ladder, and a climbing rope. People who associated dignity and decorum with ministers were at first astonished to see their pastor hanging upside down on the bars or scrambling monkeylike up the rope. Not to miss a beat when the weather was inclement, he had dumped into the cellar a large load of sand, which he would shovel from one side to the other. Shortly after he was installed in Boston, Lyman arranged to have his son Edward called to the pastorate of the Park Street Church. Edward not only kept a personal watch on his father's health but also helped him maintain it by joining him in gymnastics or sand shoveling while they discussed strategy for undoing the damage that the Unitarians were doing to the Christian faith in that old Pilgrim city.

By September, Lyman could write to Catharine:

> Yours of the 6th came duly, and awakened many recollections. I was not, however, sick when you was laid in my arms, but young, and fresh, and well. It was a year from that time that I was invaded by sickness. Since then, with a constitution part of iron and part of miry clay, I have been permitted, for the most part, to preach and labor in my vocation, and to see a family of beloved and affectionate children rise up around me, some of whom, with my most beloved Roxana, are not, while most of them remain to be my crown and my comfort to this day. I am a man of many obligations daily multiplying. I can neither speak of them nor feel

them to their extent. In your life and prosperity I rejoice, being, after Aunt Esther, my nearest contemporary among the ancients of early days. William, Edward, Mary, George and Harriet, all in their time and place, have come to be my most affectionate companions and fellow-helpers. If earthly good could fill the soul, mine might be running over; and, as it is, my consolations are neither few nor small.

This letter would suggest that Lyman was no longer in the grip of fear for his children's future fate. Along with friends on the Yale Divinity School faculty, Lyman had aligned himself with what was called the New School among Calvinist theologians. Like Jonathan Edwards before them, they supported free agency—a belief that, although human beings were born sinners, they were free to recognize and acknowledge their sinful nature and seek forgiveness rather than doomed to await a lightning bolt from God to awaken them. Although this left the doctrine of original sin intact, it raised doubt about predestination. At times Lyman was so carried away by his human sympathies that he would denounce infant damnation as well. Adherents of the Old School of Calvinists who asked Beecher to come to Boston because they had heard he was such a defender of the true faith were sometimes confused by his off-the-cuff, offbeat sermons. Lyman's views on social issues also could be enigmatic. Arriving in Boston at the same time as Lyman Beecher was a young man named William Lloyd Garrison, who would one day be as famous as Lyman's own children, and he joined Lyman's church because he had heard of Lyman's abhorrence of slavery. He became disillusioned by his pastor's unwillingness to embrace abolitionism. Beecher clung to the belief that the evil institution would die a natural death if it could be prevented from spreading to the territories in the West that were rapidly turning themselves into states.

As an admirer of Napoleon and a supporter of the defunct Federalist Party, which favored strong central government, Lyman Beecher saw more immediate threats than slavery to the supposedly united states during his Boston ministry. The deaths of both John Adams and Thomas Jefferson on July 4, 1826, while celebrations of the fiftieth anniversary of the Declaration of Independence were in progress, could be seen as a symbolic happenstance, as the end of a promising beginning. Lifelong political adversaries, men who in their thinking and persons embodied America's two different climates and cultures, they had nevertheless been able to work together for a greater good through the Revolution and the founding of a constitutional republic that was the hope of the world. As things developed, it seemed likely that they took their kind of statesmanship into the grave with them. Serious trouble between North and South started over tariff legislation, a question of money, rather than slavery, a question of morality. The North wanted to protect clothing manufacturers with a tariff on British woolens, and the South wanted to keep its best market for cotton, in Britain, wealthy and happy. In this contest, South Carolina's Calhoun, then vice president, broke a tie in the Senate to defeat the first proposed tariff on wool imports. When a compromise bill, including a tax on woolens, called the "Tariff of Abominations," got through Congress and was signed by President Adams, Vice President Calhoun wrote an anonymous tract in protest that set forth a doctrine of nullification—the right of any state to disobey a federal law it considered unconstitutional. Nullification came up again in the next go-around when senators from the South and the West argued against a resolution introduced by a senator from Connecticut to inquire into the sale of cheap western land that was allegedly drawing young artisans away from New England and boosting the cost of labor. This turned into a constitutional debate that Daniel Webster, spokesman for the North, won with a ringing address ending in "Liberty *and* Union, now and forever, one and inseparable!" But the land remained cheap, and the stream of New Englanders flowing westward in search of new lives as well as new lands was swelling to a flood.

Although powerless to exert much influence in debates based on money, Lyman could feel that he was being effective in the moral arena when the American Temperance Society was founded in Boston early in 1826; the movement he had started years before in Connecticut was going national. But he soon suffered a setback in another of his crusades. The talk that there had been some sort of corrupt deal between Henry Clay and John Quincy Adams to give Adams the presidency over General Jackson would not die down. When John Randolph alluded to it in a Senate debate by saying that Adams and Clay were a "combination of the Puritan and the black leg," Clay challenged him to a duel. The engagement was fought without bloodshed, but the fact that two men of such distinction should resort to a duel was a distressing indication that Lyman's initiative in putting an end to that abomination still had a long way to go.

When Jackson, a dueler himself, did defeat Adams for the presidency in 1828, he brought to Washington a truly scandal-ridden government in the eyes of a man with Lyman's convictions. The duel in which Jackson had killed a man was caused by remarks the man made about the gen-

eral's marriage to a woman whose first marriage had not been dissolved—
an illegal and highly irregular if not downright sinful connection. The
kind of people to whom Jackson appealed was clear when his drunken
followers made a shambles of the White House while celebrating his
inaugural. That was no surprise to anyone who knew that Jackson owed
his victory to the support of Martin Van Buren, the leader of what was
called the Albany Regency and New York City's Tammany Hall, which
controlled the votes of all the riffraff and immigrants. Now, as a member
of the cabinet as secretary of state, Van Buren was persuading the president to use the spoils system he had started in New York by firing honest
public servants and giving their jobs to party loyalists. But Jackson was
a national hero for beating the British at New Orleans in 1815, driving
the Spanish out of Florida, and chasing the Indians west out of the good
cotton-growing lands, and he did seem to be as sincere about holding the
Union together when his toast at a dinner celebrating Jefferson's birthday
in 1830 was "Our Federal Union—it must be preserved!" as his vice president, Calhoun, seemed to be scary in his responding toast to "The
Union—next to our liberty, the most dear!" About all one could do in
such uncertain times was to pray for God's guidance.

The migration from New England to the West was far from limited to
adventurers or people down on their luck. Almost any American with a
concern for the nation's future gave thought to how he or she might contribute to the development of that great region with limitless potential.
This call of the West was particularly strong in the educational and religious communities to which the Beechers belonged. The first Beecher to
respond to the call was Edward, the family intellectual. People who
respected his academic record at Yale asked him to go to Jacksonville,
Illinois, and become the first president of Illinois College, which they
were starting. The timing of this flattering offer in 1830 could not have
been better. Edward had shown every intention of settling down as pastor of Boston's Park Street Church by marrying Isabella Porter Jones, a
distant relative of his stepmother, and siring a son who was unfortunately
what they called "a congenital idiot." But the more they heard their new,
young pastor preach, the more restless many members of his congregation
became. He lacked the verbal eloquence of his father and—worse—seemingly the conviction as well. A deep thinker, Edward could not stop
wrestling with the questions that his sister Catharine posed about original sin. He did believe that human beings were sinners at birth, but he
could not believe that their condition was the will of a God who was just
and merciful. He tried to keep his developing doubts to himself, but some

of them must have spilled over into sermons, since agitation had begun for his dismissal on the grounds of "defective preaching." For Edward, going west was as much an escape from embarrassing failure as an acceptance of a new challenge.

The fact that his shadow and confidant Edward was already headed west may have had something to do with the enthusiasm with which Lyman greeted a similar invitation from Lane Seminary in Cincinnati. Unlike Edward, he was responding only to the pull, with no accelerating push behind him. In fact, his church had burned down, and his congregation was giving him full financial and moral support in rebuilding. Nevertheless, when a friend told him about a probable proposition from Lane, his positive reaction was so strong that he would recall it years later to his biographers: "I had felt and thought, and labored a great deal about raising up ministers, and the idea that I might be called to teach the best mode of preaching to the young ministry of the broad West flashed through my mind like lightning. I went home, and ran in, and found Esther alone in the sitting-room. I was in such a state of emotion and excitement I could not speak, and she was frightened. At last I told her. It was the greatest thought that ever entered my soul, it filled it, and displaced every thing else."

It remains a wonder that Lyman was able to exert enough control over his runaway impulse to take an exploratory trip to Cincinnati before taking on the job at Lane. He took Catharine, who was bored with her school now that she had it up and running well, along as companion and adviser; he had a good hunch that she might want to move with the rest of the family. Any Beecher back in Boston or Hartford who learned from Catharine's letter to Harriet that this restless pair had picked out the site for a new home on their third day in town would have started packing.

5

"Oh, good Lord!
Can we go through this?"

WHEN WILLIAM HENRY HARRISON DIED just a month after being inaugurated as the ninth president of the United States, it was a shock to the whole nation and a matter of personal grief to many of the inhabitants of Indianapolis, Indiana. A jovial, outgoing man who made friends wherever he alighted, Harrison was well remembered in the capital of a state he had helped to create while serving as the first governor of the Indiana Territory. So it was fitting that there be as large a gathering to pay tribute to the old soldier-politician as a population of four thousand could muster on a sad day in April 1841. It was an occasion that called for the presiding presence of Governor Samuel Bigger, but many in the crowd wondered about the selection of the other orator on the platform. He was the youngest, newest minister in town, the pastor of a place of worship on which the paint had hardly dried, the Second Presbyterian Church. His name, according to the program, was Henry Ward Beecher.

Beecher's youth was not a subject for comment, and even his unkempt appearance—pants tucked into mud-splattered boots, stringy hair awry—went without notice. The winning of the West was largely a young man's game. Harrison himself had been about the same age as Beecher—twenty-seven—when he was appointed governor. As for dress, active men in a town that turned into a sea of mud with every spring rain had no use for finery. And shortly after this young man opened his mouth to speak, there were few doubters left in the crowd as to his right to be their spokesman. However newly arrived in Indianapolis, Beecher was no stranger to the late president and his family, who made their home on a farm they had acquired before the turn of the century at North Bend, Ohio, outside Cincinnati. As a Presbyterian and clerk of the County Court of Common Pleas in Cincinnati, his last post before running for the White House, Harrison was well acquainted with the many Beechers who seemed to be into everything in Cincinnati. Young Beecher shed a few tears and drew more from his listeners when he told them how Mrs. Harrison had come to the aid of an impoverished young preacher and his wife, Eunice, when they began housekeeping with gifts of cherished items from the Harrisons' own first housekeeping venture—a bureau, brass andirons, and shovel and tongs—forty years before. Sounding a broader note, Henry Ward, a Whig himself, praised the general for his Christian character, his broad experience, and his sound Whig policies, which would rescue the nation from the moral laxity and deep depression into which the Democratic administrations of Jackson and Van Buren had plunged it.

Back in 1832, in the year that the Beechers left New England with high hopes and plans for putting a sound Puritan foundation under the country's rapid expansion in the West, the people kept Jackson in power with such a strong endorsement of his first four years that he was being called "King Andrew." The Beechers regretted that a man so unprincipled as to shake the government up over a snub to a woman with a past like the notorious Peggy Eaton had been given nearly unbridled powers, but they were then too absorbed in their own affairs to give much thought to the consequences. The logistics of their move must have taxed the patience and resources of father Lyman to the limit. With him on the trip were his sister Esther; wife, Harriet, with her three young children—Isabella, ten, Thomas, eight, and James, four; daughter Harriet; and son George, who was leaving Yale to finish his ministerial studies under his father's tutelage at Lane. Fortunately for the move, Mary was well established in Hartford, Edward was settling into his new position in Illinois, and Henry Ward and Charles were in college—at Amherst and Bowdoin, respectively. What William might do remained to be seen. For thirty years the family had been bedeviled by the question "What do we do with William?" The oldest son and the only one not to attend college, William so far had drifted from job to job until he decided to be a minister and spend a term at Andover Seminary. Using all of his influence with his colleagues, Lyman got a committee of ministers in Boston to license William to preach in 1830 and then placed him in a small church in Newport, Rhode Island. But by this year of change for everybody, William, equipped with a wife and baby, had already moved on to a pastorate in Middletown, Connecticut, and was talking alarmingly of joining the rest of the Beechers in their mission to win the West, since the pastor he had replaced in Middletown had announced his intention of returning. Everybody agreed that William was cursed with bad luck for no known reason.

En route to Ohio, Lyman treated his family to stays in New York City and Philadelphia, where they were split up to accept the hospitality of good church people and cut down on hotel bills. While they took in the sights, he busied himself raising the large sum of twenty thousand dollars, which he needed to lure a young man named Calvin Stowe away from his professorship of languages at Dartmouth College to become professor of biblical literature at Lane Seminary. Stowe would be bringing with him a pretty young wife, Eliza Tyler, daughter of Darmouth's president, an Old School Calvinist with whom New School Lyman had friendly theological differences. At Philadelphia they were crammed into stagecoaches for a slow and rugged progression over the Pennsylvania mountains to Wheeling, still a Virginia town, where they hoped to board a riverboat to Cincinnati. George lightened the tedium of the trip by leading them in singing hymns and, with the help of the younger children, flinging religious tracts to astonished onlookers along the way—"peppering the land with moral influence," as Harriet would wryly describe this activity. Impatient as ever, Lyman made the mistake of hiring a private coach at Harrisburg. Because the driver evidently was saving money on the quality of his horses, that leg of the journey took them eight days instead of the two days that sufficed for the regular mail coach. But Providence may have been leading them after all, for they learned in Wheeling that Cincinnati was in the grip of one of its frequent cholera epidemics, and they had to wait in Wheeling for two weeks before they could move on—by stage bouncing painfully over corduroy roads paved with logs instead of by boat. On November 14, 1832, the Beechers finally reached their destination.

If it hadn't been for reports from the Foote brothers and their closer pioneering relatives, Catharine and Lyman, these migrants from long-settled New England would have been in for a surprise amounting to a shock. Instead of a wilderness stocked with Indians, they found themselves in a bustling city that had become the entrepôt for the whole westward migration. So much construction was under way that it was hard to tell whether the city was in the process of being built or torn down. In only thirty years, the population of Ohio had jumped from fifty thousand to more than a million souls and was continuing to rise so rapidly in Cincinnati that some fourteen hundred new homes built in 1827 alone fell far short of the demand. Factories spitting smoke were turning out almost everything needed by man—more than two million dollars' worth of tools, furniture, paper, clothing, books, and whiskey made for export each year. To carry all this away to markets, steamboats nudged the wharves around the clock like pigs at a trough, and real pigs roamed the city's streets to clean them of garbage, just as they did in civilized New York. In an early letter to Connecticut, the Beechers reported that the youngest member of the clan, James, amused himself riding piggyback on these wandering scavengers. By the time the Beechers arrived, Cincinnati was supporting twelve newspapers, twenty-three churches, forty schools, two colleges, and a theater to match anything in the East. The city presented itself as a fertile religious and intellectual ground in which the Beechers could sow their moral seed.

While a new house was being built for Lane's president on the site at Walnut Hills that Lyman and Catharine had selected, the family lived in temporary quarters in town. Young Harriet found this house unpleasantly situated and uncomfortably crowded, but she very nearly went into raptures in her reports about the Walnut Hills place. "How I wish you could see Walnut Hills," she wrote to Georgiana May, her best friend from Hartford school days. "It is about two miles from the city, and the road to it is as picturesque as you can imagine a road to be. . . . You might ride over the same road a dozen times a day untired, for the constant variation of view caused by ascending and descending hills relieves you from all tedium. Much of the wooding is beech of a noble growth. The straight, beautiful shafts of these trees; as one looks up the cool green recesses of the woods seem as though they might form very proper columns for a Dryad temple." The two-story, L-shaped brick house was large enough to handle thirteen permanent residents, with room to squeeze in frequent guests. Sheltered inside the L was a veranda that was usable even during the rough weather of fall and winter, and Lyman's first-floor study opened onto this veranda.

The seminary was a short walk away by a woodland path. Lyman and his sons would commute to classes by foot, and the other students found their way easily and often to the president's accessible study. Lyman's door was as open to all nature as it was to students or members of his city congregation. In a letter to one of his brothers, young Tom recalled "the gun he used to keep loaded by the door ready for the pigeons that in those days came over by the million. Father would sit in his study chair deeply occupied, and set me by the cocked gun to watch for game. But he would hear the roar of wings as soon as I, and, with remarkable jumps for a divinity doctor, would get out the door, have his shot at the birds, and then go back to his pen." Harriet once ably summed up the Beecher ménage at Walnut Hills as "a continual high tide of life and animation."

Next to Walnut Hills, the most important place in Cincinnati for Catharine and Harriet was the parlor of their Uncle Samuel's spacious house at Third and Vine Streets downtown. Regular meetings of the Semi-Colon Club, a gathering of leading lights in the intellectual, religious, civic, and business life of the city, were held in that room. Papers by members were read and discussed as well as issues of the day; music was played for entertainment; refreshments, including "ardent spirits" for those so minded, were served. Participating members included women of accomplishment, and it is probable that one subject of discussion in the year that the Beecher daughters joined the club was a newly published book, *Domestic Manners of the Americans,* by a much-traveled English woman named Frances Trollope.

Possibly embittered by the failure of enterprises that she had launched during her stay in Cincinnati, Mrs. Trollope wrote of its society:

> Whatever may be the talents of the persons who meet together in society, the very shape, form, and arrangement of the meeting is sufficient to paralyze conversation. The women invariably herd together at one part of the room, and the men at the other, but, in justice to Cincinnati, I must acknowledge that this arrangement is by no means peculiar to that city, or to the western side of the Alleghenies. Sometimes a small attempt at music produces a partial reunion; a few of the most daring youths, animated by the consciousness of curled hair and smart waistcoats, approach the piano-forte, and begin to mutter a little to the half-grown pretty things, who are comparing with another "how many quarters music they have had." When the mansion is of sufficient dignity to have two drawing-rooms, the piano, the little ladies, and the slender gentlemen are left to themselves, and on such occasions the sound of laughter is often heard to issue from among them. But the fate of the more dignified personages, who are left in the other room, is extremely dismal. The gentlemen spit, talk of elections and the price of produce, and spit again. The ladies look at each other's dresses till they know every pin by heart; talk of Parson Somebody's last sermon on the day of judgment, of Dr. Totherbody's new pills for dyspepsia until the "tea" is announced when they all console themselves together for whatever they may

have suffered in keeping awake, by taking more tea, coffee, hot cake and custard, hoe cake, johnny cake, waffle cake, and dodger cake, pickled peaches, and preserved cucumbers, ham, turkey, hung beef, apple sauce, and pickled oysters than ever were prepared in any other country of the known world. After this massive meal is over, they return to the drawing-room, and it always appeared to me that they remained together as long as they could bear it, and then they rise en masse, cloak, bonnet, shawl, and exit.

Undoubtedly, members of the Semi-Colon Club would have dismissed Trollope's view of Cincinnati social life as "sour grapes," as were many of her other comments on a nation where a true democracy was upsetting to a person used to Britain's class-conscious society. In fact, Semi-Colon meetings often gave members the inspiration and support for activities of benefit to the whole community and even the nation. It was, for instance, one source of the backing that Catharine Beecher needed to launch her Western Female Institute now that Harriet was there to give her a hand. Although there were a number of existing girls' schools, Catharine was confident that she had something new to offer on the basis of a book that she had self-published in 1831 titled *The Elements of Mental and Moral Philosophy*. It was based on her experience in Hartford with combining moral instruction with subjects such as Latin and Greek and science and mathematics, usually reserved for boys' educations. In one subject, geography, she found existing material deficient and produced a book of her own in collaboration with Harriet. Although Harriet actually wrote the book, it carried only Catharine's name in the thought that it would be better received as the work of an already published author. Catharine's work brought her the attention and friendship of William McGuffey, a professor at Miami University in Oxford, Ohio, who would do the same thing for English instruction with his "readers," which would be used almost universally for generations.

As an admiring younger sister, Harriet accepted without fuss the slight of having her work on geography anonymous. It was in keeping with her looks and deportment. Very small—"decidedly undersized," as one person who knew her put it—she was also shy. In company she preferred to be silent, to look and listen and absorb what went on around her, rather than to shine. In intimate company, she could be voluble and witty and even cruel in the imitations she gave of other people. She had too much of the large Beecher nose to be considered pretty, but the expressive animation of her face and luminous eyes could be arresting.

People were always amazed at what stuck in the mind of this little woman who had been sitting off in a corner with a dreamy look on her face. One witness to this phenomenon was a friend who took Harriet across the river during her first summer in Cincinnati for a week's visit to a family on a slaveholding plantation. In one of her silent moods, Harriet was so self-absorbed as to make her friend wonder whether she was ill or simply ungracious, and it would be all of twenty years before she saw the fruit of Harriet's acute observations ripen in her work. This self-effacing attitude caused Harriet to submit her first paper—allegedly a work of fiction—to the Semi-Colon Club anonymously.

Papers were delivered to the club by an appointed male reader rather than the author, a practice appreciated by most of the female members, including the Beecher sisters, at a time when public speaking by women in mixed company was generally frowned upon. Even Catharine, a large and assertive woman, who had inherited her father's missionary zeal and self-confidence, would seek out a male friend or acquaintance to give voice to her thinking. She and Harriet were certainly aware of their father's views on the subject. However much slack he cut for his daughters in terms of arguing their cases privately, he wrote in a letter berating a fellow minister for letting women speak publicly that "a greater evil, next to the loss of conscience and chastity, could not befall the female sex. No well educated female can put herself up, or be put up, to the point of public prayer, without the loss of some portion at least of that female delicacy, which is above all price." Harriet clung to her female delicacy while her thinly disguised profile, warts and all, of Lyman's uncle Lot Benton was read. But when another member of the club, Judge James Hall, editor of the *Western Monthly Magazine,* flushed out the author's identity and asked that the piece be submitted to his publication's fiction contest, Harriet agreed. She not only won the contest but also, more important, the fifty-dollar prize that went with it. It was her first indication that her dream of making a living by writing fiction instead of by teaching could actually come true, and the story's appearance with her byline in an issue of November 1833, just a year after her arrival in Cincinnati, would turn out to be a historic date in the annals of American literature.

While his father and sisters were forging ahead on their new careers in the West, nineteen-year-old Henry Ward Beecher, left alone at Amherst, was stepping out from their shadows into the light of his own sunny personality. In later years he would attribute at least a generous part of his speaking and learning difficulty to competing on an uneven playing field with such articulate and naturally talented siblings as Catharine, Edward, George, and Harriet. He would attribute recovery from his speech defect to John Lovell, a teacher of elocution at Mt. Pleasant, where he prepared for Amherst. A hard taskmaster, Lovell drilled the boy until his speech turned fluent enough to allow him to appear in school plays and earn applause instead of laughter. By the time he got to college, Henry Ward was able to become one of Amherst's most admired debaters as well as "chiefest among their football kickers." His natural love of nature earned him the presidency of Amherst's Society of Natural History, but his disinterest in heavy subjects such as Latin, Greek, and mathematics kept him from earning academic honors. He made friends easily, and his disrespectful attitude toward school authorities ingratiated him with the student body generally. A practical prankster, he once sawed the legs of the only guest chair in his room so short that when a tall tutor arrived for a solemn conference he had to peer up at Henry Ward through a spread of knees higher than his head. When a professor argued that he needed mathematics as a discipline to his mind, Henry Ward saucily told him, "If that's all, I shan't go to class anymore. My mind gets enough discipline inventing excuses for not being there."

Despite an acquisition of outward skill and confidence, Henry Ward could still be very miserable and uncertain of himself inwardly. In both school and college, he struggled as hard as he had in Litchfield with his inability to have the kind of feelings he thought he needed to experience a proper conversion. He had serious doubts as to whether he was an authentic Christian even as he publicly claimed to be one. Nevertheless, his growing fluency of speech caused him to think about becoming a minister like his older brothers, and he would write to Edward and Harriet in that vein, larding his letters with pious comment and complaints about the un-Christian behavior of other students. In his personal relationships, his need to love and be loved would generally get the better of his yearning to be a good Christian. Henry always felt free to confess to Harriet without fear of reprisal, and once, after writing to her about the shocking language his classmates used, he admitted, "When I mix with the boys I do talk and act unworthy of a disciple of Christ."

Having been raised in a family always short of money, Henry Ward tried to spare his father as much of the $40 a term tuition and $1.50 a week board as he could. He managed to get teaching positions in nearby rural schools to earn money during vacations and saved money by rather dramatic gestures such as walking the hundred miles to visit his family while they were still in Boston. It was thus no feat to walk half that distance to West Sutton, Massachusetts, with a classmate, Ebenezer Bullard, and another Amherst friend to spend spring holidays at the Bullard home. There he met Eunice, one of Ebenezer's eight siblings. Statuesque and handsome, articulate and self-assured and, at nineteen, a year older than Henry Ward, she had already taught school for three terms and was planning to spend the next winter studying Latin at an aunt's home in Whitinsville. She found her brother's friend Henry Ward amusing if a bit juvenile and "exceedingly homely." Henry Ward found Eunice a lot like his admired older sisters and felt comfortable with her. She would be the kind of capable woman to have by his side if he joined his family to become a missionary out in the Wild West, as he intended to do. With his own kind of self-assurance when it came to charming people, Henry Ward made plans to see a lot more of Eunice Bullard by finding a winter teaching job near Whitinsville and arranging to board in the same house with Eunice.

Neither Eunice nor her parents suspected Henry Ward's motives. When they heard of his plan, Dr. Bullard, a country physician of the purest Puritan heritage, thought that it would be a fine thing, since Henry Ward could help Eunice with her Latin. But on the evening of the January day in 1832 when he moved into his new quarters, Henry Ward turned the Latin studies into courtship by asking Eunice to conjugate the Latin word for love— *amo*—and giving her a note that read, "Will you go with me as a missionary to the West?" Her answer was positive enough that Henry Ward rode to West Sutton the next Sunday to ask for her hand. Her surprised and displeased father exclaimed, "Why, you are a couple of babies!" Henry Ward tried to assure the Bullards that he and Eunice had talked the matter over and were willing to wait for each other until he had finished his studies and found a position. Whether he realized it or not, Henry Ward was facing the same problem that his father had dealt with in two courtships—the reluctance of parents in comfortable circumstances to see a daughter try to live in the genteel poverty to which ministers were condemned. To allay their fears, the young man took every opportunity to demonstrate the talent he counted on to carry him far. Evenings he gave well-attended and well-received talks on religion in a Whitinsville church, and Eunice was able to report back to her parents that he spoke flawlessly. A lecture he delivered near Amherst that spring earned him five dollars, out of which he was able to buy a religious book as a present to Eunice. On the Fourth of July he gave a temperance lecture in Brattleboro, Vermont, for the comparatively hefty fee of ten dollars. To put the money to better uses he pocketed the cost of transportation by walking all the way. He fed his own craving by acquiring the works of the British orator Edmund Burke, and used the last dollar to buy a plain gold band as an engagement ring for Eunice. His performance won the approval of Dr. Bullard, who predicted that his son-in-law-to-be would "make his mark in the world."

The Beecher contingent had a year of grace in which to enjoy the warm embrace of the movers and shakers of Cincinnati's social and civic life and the pleasures of their scenic retreat at Walnut Hills. Things even went well for "William the Unlucky," as he was known among his siblings. Soon after William's arrival at Walnut Hills, Lyman was able to find a pastorate for him in a new church being organized in Putnam, Ohio. Calvin Stowe, whom he had lured away from Dartmouth, although only thirty-one and younger than some of his students, gave weight to the Lane faculty as well as to the discussions at the Semi-Colon gatherings, to which he escorted young Harriet. Both Harriets were so strongly attracted to Stowe's bride, Eliza, that she became an adopted Beecher, a sister and daughter within the family. But the story would soon be different in the case of another new arrival to the Lane community. About the same age as Calvin, Theodore Weld was already a national figure for his fiery lectures and organizational activities within the growing temperance and abolition movements. Inspired by William Lloyd Garrison, who had left Lyman's Boston congregation to found and publish the abolitionist paper *Liberator*, Weld had joined the Tappan brothers, wealthy and pious silk merchants in New York, to start the American Anti-Slavery Society. Like Garrison, Weld was scornful of Lyman Beecher's position on the slavery issue—a belief that the practice was so evil and outdated that it would die of itself if its spread could be arrested and the freed slaves returned to Africa through colonization, a position also held by a young Illinois lawyer named Abraham Lincoln. As the financial angel of Lane Seminary, Arthur Tappan arranged to send Weld to Cincinnati to be professor of sacred rhetoric and oratory without consulting President Beecher. From the moment Weld arrived on campus in early 1834, trouble was in the air.

For most white Americans in the North as well as in the South during the 1830s, abolition was anathema. This was particularly true in border states such as Ohio and Kentucky, where there was always a lively and lucrative trade in progress and a free and easy exchange of people among the white populations. Rich Kentuckians, for instance, might summer in the hills around Cincinnati and bring slaves into the free state to serve them. Abolition would smash the well-rooted lives of millions on both sides of the divide to smithereens in a stroke, like a lightning bolt demolishing a large and ancient oak tree instead of letting the diseased branch wither away. Sensing the public mood, as their trade demanded of them, leading politicians such as Webster of free Massachusetts and Clay of slave Kentucky began to seek compromises to mollify the extreme abolitionists of the North and the secessionists of the South. Even autocratic King Andrew compromised by asking Congress to authorize the U.S. Post Office to stop delivery of abolitionist propaganda throughout the South to, as he said, prevent insurrection by the followers of his once vice president and now senator from South Carolina, John Calhoun. The ministers who didn't find justification for slavery in the Bible tried at least to separate the sinners from the sin and put their faith in eradicating the latter by reforming the former.

In the view of Theodore Weld, no true Christian aspiring to spread the Word would tolerate either the sin or the sinners another minute. Living among the students, many from the South, at Lane, he proved to be a charismatic leader—"a genius" according to Lyman, who would have no reason to praise him. He impressed his students as much by his character as by his reasoning. When cholera invaded the school, Weld nursed the sick and comforted the dying for ten sleepless nights and days. Weld was not one to argue the essential humanity of black people in the abstract. During the summer recess of 1834, while President Beecher was in the East raising funds, Weld led the fifty or so students still on campus into the black ghetto of Cincinnati to socialize with the inhabitants, most free but some escaped slaves in hiding. Once encouraged by these visits, Weld's students staged a picnic on Lane grounds at which young black women were among the guests. This enraged another professor in residence, who complained to the trustees. This body of conservative businessmen was thoroughly alarmed, and they issued orders banning from the campus any socialization with blacks or even discussion of matters not related to theology. Beecher did not take the student agitation too seriously. Indeed, he admired the zeal and sincerity of Weld and his disciples and felt that they would make good servants of God once study and maturity calmed them down. "If you want to teach colored schools, I can fill your pockets with money," he wrote to Weld. "But if you will visit in colored families, and walk with them in the streets, you will be overwhelmed."

In the end, it was Beecher who was overwhelmed. When the trustees fired a professor sympathetic to the students and threatened to expel Weld just before the beginning of the fall term in October, the students were outraged. Beecher hurried back to try to work out a compromise but failed. Weld and some fifty students walked out, and all but ten of them were enticed into attending a new educational institution, being formed at Oberlin. This left Lane virtually without a student body and on the brink of extinction. Beecher hit the road again in search of students rather than funds. He managed to recruit enough young men to keep the school going. Among them was Henry Ward Beecher, who had graduated from Amherst that June. Harriet demonstrated the unusually tight bond between herself and her favorite brother by making the long trip to Amherst alone—the only Beecher to attend the ceremonies. Within the next year, George went on to assume a pastorate at Batavia, New York, but Charles arrived after graduating from Bowdoin to take up the slack.

There are nice snatches in the Beecher records of Henry Ward and Charles walking to classes together through the woods while singing their heads off. Possibly from fiddling Lyman, Charles inherited a true musical talent, and Henry Ward could at least carry a tune. One of his sisters remembers and recorded the goose-bumping thrill of hearing six-year-old James's soaring soprano on an occasion when he tagged along after his harmonizing brothers. But there was an event in that woodland when Henry Ward was alone that lifted his spirits far higher than music ever could do. Although he was making his way dutifully through the studies that would qualify him to become a minister, he was still deeply troubled by doubts, still unable to relate emotionally to the God of his father. But then one day, as he would later recall,

> I was walking near Lane Seminary (where I studied theology without hope), and I was working over a lesson that I was to hear recited. The idea dawned upon me, not that there had been a covenant formed between God and his Son, but that Christ revealed the nature of God, whose very soul was curative, and who brought himself and his living holiness to me, because I needed it so much and not because I was so deserving. That instant the clouds rose and the whole heaven was radiant, and I exclaimed, "I have found God." It was the first time I had found him. *Good*, his name was; and I went like one crazed up and down through the fields, half crying, half laughing, singing and praying and shouting like a good Methodist.

From that moment on, Henry Ward Beecher would never lose the God he had found, a God who would inspire him to proclaim a gospel of love.

The very sensitive Charles was not as fortunate as his older brother. He did share with Henry Ward the doubts that made it impossible for him to experience a conversion acceptable to his father. More of an intellectual than Henry Ward, Charles let his meditations on theological writings such as those of Jonathan Edwards lead him to adopt a gloomy, pessimistic fatalism. Undoubtedly, an unrequited love for an attractive young woman in his father's congregation in Cincinnati and observing what was happening to the people around him at Lane and Walnut Hills in that year of 1835 had a lot to do with his increasingly dark outlook. The events of that year would raise in any caring mind the unanswerable question Why do bad things happen to good people?

Although the first Beechers to visit Cincinnati had been told that Walnut Hills was so healthy that people had to leave it to get sick, this turned out to be an early example of real-estate hyperbole. The waves of cholera and ague that regularly rolled over the city and many other pioneer settlements in the West inundated the seminary community as well. Survivors testified to the extreme discomfort of these maladies—intestinal distress, alternating chills and fever, debilitating weakness—that made death loom as a welcome release. Early in that unhappy year, Calvin Stowe's young wife, Eliza, contracted cholera, and Lyman's sister Esther and wife, Harriet, watched over her sufferings caringly. In poor health and a depressed state of mind ever since leaving Boston, Harriet Porter Beecher wrote this account of losing the one person who let some light into her life:

> Esther was with her that day constantly. The next morning we found no hope of recovery left. She was struggling with death when I entered: her brows were knit, and a deadly paleness was gathering fast, with distressing movements and convulsive throes. I thought, "O Lord God! Can we go through this?" Mr. Stowe said, "Oh, my love, remember, remember: 'The Lord is my Shepherd, I shall not want; he leads me in green pastures, beside the still waters; these comforts have delighted my soul.'" She broke out, "Oh, how delightful!" Her whole countenance brightened and gleamed. She waved her hands with joy, saying, "Oh, glory! There is not room enough to receive it!" She continued in this state until she sunk into a sleep-like state from which I suppose she had no more consciousness.

As it turned out, Eliza's death was something of a dress rehearsal for Harriet Porter Beecher's own death from consumption on August 10,

1835. "With morbid facility, her mind had received and retained the somber hues of grief, and she shivered as she entered amid the clouds of the dark valley of the shadow of death; nor could she at first find her Savior there," Lyman wrote of the event. "Yet, as her end drew nigh, amid acute and protracted sufferings, she was enabled to say, 'Thou art with me; Thy rod and Thy staff, they comfort me.' In her last moments the veil was lifted, and the glories of the celestial city seemed to meet her view, and the sounds of celestial minstrelsy to strike her ear. 'Music!' she exclaimed, 'music!' Can you not hear it? Beautiful music! Oh, sing! sing!' Thus the darkest hour was just before dawn; and though her weeping endured for a night, joy came in the morning. She fell asleep in Jesus."

During his wife's decline and death, Lyman was engaged in a furious theological battle with an Old School Calvinist, Joshua Lacy Wilson, pastor of Cincinnati's First Presbyterian Church. Although Congregationalists and Presbyterians had agreed to a Plan of Union in 1801 that empowered pastors to move from one body to another, Wilson, afraid that New School Beecher would taint the minds of his seminary students and draw worshipers away from Wilson's own church, claimed that Beecher was no Presbyterian. He filed heresy charges against Beecher that resulted in a trial before the Presbytery. By granting human beings free agency, according to Wilson, Beecher and his New School cohorts were flying in the face of the seventeenth-century Westminster Confession of Faith and denying such doctrines as original sin and the complete supremacy of God. For Beecher, the trial was something like a sporting event in which he could take pleasure by exercising his debating talents—"I felt easy. I had as much lawyer about me as Wilson, and more. I never got into a corner, and he never got out"—and do good by talking about his own beliefs. His confidence was justified; he was acquitted by a 23 to 12 vote. An aroused Wilson appealed the verdict to the Synod, and another trial was scheduled before that body's next meeting, in Dayton.

Lyman enlisted Henry Ward, the oldest of his sons at home, as his spear-carrier for all of these contests. The effect of these trials on the twenty-two-year-old minister in the making may be their most important and lasting result. Having seen how well his father did at Presbytery, Henry approached the Dayton trial with irreverent good humor, as this rare glimpse he left with us would indicate:

> As I emerged from my room, the doctor was standing in his study doorway, a book under each arm, with a third in his hands, in which he was searching for quotations. In an hour and a half

all his papers were to be collected (and from whence!), books assorted, breakfast eaten, clothes packed, and horse harnessed.

After a hasty meal he goes upstairs, opens every drawer, and paws over all the papers, leaving them in confusion, and down stairs again to the drawers in his study, which are treated in like manner. He fills his arms with books, and papers, and sermons, and straightway seems to forget what he wanted them for, for he falls to assorting them vigorously *de novo*.

Eight o'clock, and not half ready. Boat starts at nine.

"Where's my Burton?"

"Father I have found *The Spirit of the Pilgrims*."

"Don't want it. Where did I put that paper of extracts? Can't you make out another? Where did I lay my opening notes? Here, Henry, put this book in the carriage. Stop! Give it to me. Let's see—run upstairs for my Register. No, No! I've brought it down."

Half past eight. Not ready. Three miles to go. Horse not up.

At length the doctor completes his assortment of books and papers, packs, or rather stuffs his clothes into a carpet bag—no key to lock it—ties the handles and leaves it gaping.

At length we are ready to start. A trunk tumbles out of one side as Thomas tumbles in the other. I reverse the order—tumble Tom out, the trunk in. At length we all are aboard, and father drives out of the yard, holding the reins in one hand, shaking hands with a student with the other, giving Charles directions with his mouth—at least that part not occupied with an apple, for, since apples were plenty, he has made it his practice to drive with one rein in the right hand and the other in the left, with an apple in each, biting them alternately, thus raising and lowering the reins like threads on a loom. Away we go . . . the carriage bouncing and bounding over the stones, father, alternately telling Tom how to get the harness mended, and showing me the true doctrine of original sin. Hurra! We thunder alongside the boat just in time.

Arrived at Dayton, Henry Ward got his first look at such a large gathering of Presbyterian ministers and elders. He was not impressed. Although he saw such good qualities as "firmness (in many cases deepening into obstinacy), kindheartedness, and honesty" in the faces of the clergymen, he looked in vain for "deep thought seen in the eye or lineaments—for lofty expression—for the enthusiasm of genius—for that expression which comes from communion with great thoughts, with the higher feelings of poetry and religion, and even of speculation." As for the elders, he concluded that "for leadership the soberest men are chosen, and as stupidity is usually graced with more gravity than good sense, the body of the elders are not quite so acute in look as the higher class of working men." Despite the unimpressive character of the gathering, Lyman was once more exonerated—but this time with a condition. He was told to publish the arguments he had made to the Synod, and the resulting tract, *Views in Theology,* stirred up so much criticism from Old School adherents all over the country that an embittered Lyman Beecher complained, "They took burning arrows dipped in gall, and shot them over into the Presbyterian camp. They rifled the graves of my dead friends, out of their ashes to evoke spectral accusations against us." A more embittered Wilson once again appealed the decision to the Presbyterian General Assembly, which was not scheduled to meet until the next year.

No matter how tough the going, the Beechers always had each other as a source of strength and cheer and, not infrequently, criticism. Their relationships could be troubled at times but seldom trivial. Their letters dealt more with the state of their souls or the fate of the nation than with the weather. A good example is a letter dated March 18, 1835, from twenty-four-year-old Harriet, who was visiting in Hartford, to Henry Ward in Walnut Hills. She begins by telling her brother about a literary party where the talk among the young people had more to do with romance than poetry. Commenting on how happy a recently engaged Mr. Howe looked, a Mr. Pomeroy told Harriet that it reminded him of a time in his school days when he had kept an apple tucked away in a corner of his desk. Whenever he got a scolding he would say to himself, "I don't care, there is that apple in my desk yet." Pomeroy went on to say, "So there is Howe—no matter to him if Miss A is walking with Mr. B—or Miss G is flirting with Mr. C—there is one person here thinking of him yet." This sparked some deep thinking on Harriet's part about the nature of both human and divine love and whether the love of Jesus could be the apple in her desk. Then she let Henry Ward in on her soul searching:

> In examining my own feelings, I find that my desire for affection and confidence, was actually becoming stronger than my desire to please my Saviour—I am never in any danger of that sort of carefulness which reproves of the saying "what shall I eat & what shall I drink & wherewithal shall I be clothed?" in regard to *affection*—When I find myself more interested in thinking of the love, that is only given for a solace to this momentary life, than

I am in those things that prepare myself and others for eternity, I think it is time to stop & regain my self control—& that I shall try to do.—That was the reason I went into company tonight, I thought I should seek different scenes this week, that by awakening my social feelings and varying my objects of interest, I may prevent my mind from dwelling too much on *itself*, its wants and feelings—There is selfishness even in human love,—if it becomes absorbing—& with me it is always liable to become so—Now, my dear you will understand & approve what I am trying to do & I am sure you will wish to have me,—& you will not think that I love *you* less because I love my Saviour more—One thing that I have always loved in others is that disposition which leads them to be conscientious for their friends—I think Perkins [her sister Mary's husband] is such a one & I always loved that trait in his character—I am conscious of so much weakness and wavering myself that I feel inexpressibly grateful to any one who will help me to do right—& you my dear brother can do this, & I hope you will—you know of course how much power you have over me, & make such a use of it as will save me from unhappiness & sin as far as you can.

Do you pray for me?—Many say pray for me, as mere form but I say it with much feeling,—you would love me with a different & holier love, if you thought of me as a child of the Saviour, & one in danger, & needing help. But I speak as if you did not do it—you do doubtless—but pray for me earnestly—Your own sister H.

Like his father, Edward had to go East on fund-raising trips for his college and could only sympathize by letter about some of the unfortunate events taking place at Walnut Hills in that year of 1835. Aware of the pain that his father must be suffering after the death of his wife and in the throes of defending himself before Presbytery, Edward had an inspiration as he planned his return to the West in September. He would arrange for a gift that would lift his father's spirits like no other. The nature and reception of this gift were recorded by an eyewitness—a Harvard graduate named George Hastings, who was attending Lane with Henry Ward and Charles and who often was in and out of the Beecher home. As later published in a Boston newspaper, he wrote:

Long before Edward came out here the doctor tried to have a family meeting, but did not succeed. The children were too scattered.

Two were in Connecticut, some in Massachusetts, and one in Rhode Island. That, I believe, was five years ago. But—now just think of it!—there has been a family gathering in Ohio! When Edward returned, he brought Mary from Hartford. William came down from Putnam, Ohio; George from Batavia, New York; Catharine and Harriet were here already, Henry and Charles at home too, besides Isabella, Thomas, and James. These eleven! The first time they all ever met together! Mary had never seen James, and she had seen Thomas only once.

Such a time as they had! The old doctor was almost transported with joy. The affair had been under negotiation for some time. He returned from Dayton late one Saturday evening. The next morning they, for the first time, assembled in the parlor. There were more tears than words. The doctor attempted to pray, but could scarcely speak. His full heart poured itself out in a flood of weeping. He could not go on. Edward continued, and each one, in his turn, uttered some sentences of thanksgiving. They then began at the head and related their fortunes. After special prayer, all joined hands and sang Old Hundred to these words: "From all who dwell below the skies."

Edward preached in his father's pulpit in the morning. William in the afternoon and George in the evening. The family occupied the three front pews on the broad aisle. Monday morning they assembled, and, after reading and prayers, in which all joined, they formed a circle. The doctor stood in the middle and gave them a thrilling speech. He then went round, and gave them each a kiss. They had a happy dinner.

Presents flowed in from all quarters. During the afternoon the home was filled with company, each bringing an offering. When left alone at evening they had a general examination of all their characters. The shafts of wit flew amain, the doctor being struck in several places, he was, however, expert enough to hit most of them in turn. From the uproar of the general battle, all must have been wounded. Tuesday morning saw them together again, drawn up in a straight line for the inspection of the king of happy men. After receiving particular instructions, they formed into a circle. The doctor made a long and affecting speech. He felt that he stood for the last time in the middle of all his children, and each word fell with the weight of a patriarch's. He embraced them once more in all the tenderness of his big heart.

Each took of all a farewell kiss. With joined hands they joined in a hymn. A prayer was offered, and, finally, the parting blessing was spoken. Thus ended a meeting which can only be rivaled in that blessed home where the ransomed of the Lord, after weary pilgrimage, shall join in the praise of the Lamb. May they all be there!

Truly the crown of old men is their children.

For the Beechers there was a bright dawning to the year 1836 when Harriet married Calvin Stowe on January 6. They were drawn together by mutual mourning over the death of Eliza and a sharing of intellectual interests. Nine years older than his bride, pudgy and balding, careless in dress and manners, Stowe was nothing like the suitor whom a girl addicted to romantic fiction and poetry would be likely to choose. Apart from his appearance, Stowe was totally lacking in the vitality and athletic ability of her father and brothers, the men Harriet most admired. But he had a formidable and fascinating intellect, a sense of humor, and a deep and enlightened faith in the kind of kindly God whom all of the young Beechers were beginning to embrace. Stowe was an omnivorous reader who had turned himself into a linguist—Hebrew, Latin, Greek, Arabic, German, Italian, French—because he liked to feed on books in their original language. The fascinating part of his mind had to do with the many strange visions he had encountered as a small boy growing up in an impoverished family in Maine and his insistence as an adult on the reality of the creatures who had appeared to him. A highly imaginative Harriet was enthralled by the tales he told of his visions at the Semi-Colon Club, and she would certainly have been impressed by his already widely known scholarly achievements. But a letter Harriet wrote to her friend Georgiana just before her nearly private wedding at home bears witness that she was no giddy girl head over heels in love: "Well, my dear G. about half an hour more and your old friend, companion, schoolmate, sister, etc., will cease to be Hatty Beecher and change to nobody knows who. My dear, you are engaged, and pledged in a year or two to encounter a similar fate, and do you wish to know how you shall feel? Well, my dear, I have been dreading and dreading the time, and lying awake all last week wondering how I should live through this overwhelming crisis, and lo! it has come, and I feel *nothing at all*."

Except for the fact that she and her Calvin did become legally man and wife, Harriet was faced with a situation eerily similar to that of her sister Catharine so many years before. Plans for Calvin Stowe to take an extended European trip had been made before plans for a marriage. He was to visit biblical scholars in England and on the Continent and to buy books for Lane's library. In addition, the state of Ohio commissioned him to look at education generally in the countries he visited and return with a report on good ideas that could be adapted to American schools. Since there was not enough money for Harriet to accompany her new husband, they soon would be parted. Knowing how Harriet felt, Calvin promised her a trip back to New England to visit relatives and friends and see him off on his voyage. But before the appointed time arrived, even that short trip was no longer a possibility. Harriet's condition was mute evidence of a marriage that was more than companionate, and she could not risk the rough rides a trip would entail. The Stowes did, however, have one short journey together shortly after their wedding, when they spent a few days as guests at General Harrison's palatial home on a bluff above the Ohio River at North Bend. A small Harrison grandchild named Ben also was in residence then, but none of the party could have imagined that there were two future presidents of the United States and an internationally famous author among them. Harrison's nomination for the presidency the year before by an anti-Masonic party was not taken seriously, what with a man like Webster among the potential Whig candidates and the very slim chance that any Whig would have against King Andrew's handpicked Democrat successor, Martin Van Buren, come the voting in December.

When Calvin departed, Harriet closed the faculty house assigned to them and moved back into the Beecher residence at Walnut Hills. Experiencing her first pregnancy, she wanted the security of having a competent older woman such as Aunt Esther on hand. Catharine was away in the East on an exploratory mission to raise funds and recruit teachers for the new schools being formed in the West. She had turned over operation of her Western Female Institute to Mary Dutton, a colleague from Hartford days. George was off in Batavia learning how to run a church. Fortunately, he seemed confident enough to rise above the efforts of Dr. Wilson to use him for another attack on what he thought of as Beecher heresy. Harriet had sat in when the Presbytery was examining George with Dr. Wilson as chief inquisitor, and, like Henry before her, was half amused and half horrified by the proceedings. She wrote that her "blood boiled" when she saw George squirming to answer questions such as: "Mr. Beecher, do you think that men are punished for the guilt of Adam's first sin?" Although Wilson argued that George was not a Christian and "would never see the gates of eternal bliss," Lyman's impassioned defense of his son carried the day. Now Lyman was off to Philadelphia to defend himself once more against Wilson's charges at the General Assembly. Even with Henry Ward and Charles and Harriet Porter's three children in residence, there was plenty of room in the Walnut Hills house for Harriet.

Henry Ward was not going to Philadelphia with his father not only because he would be the man of the house at Walnut Hills but also because the editor of the *Journal*, who was going with Lyman as a delegate, needed somebody to fill in for him. To be chosen for that duty had to be a gratifying boost to the sometime faltering ego of a twenty-three-year-old seminary student. There was a great deal happening in both city and country that would require good reporting and comment from any publication worth its price. All spring the major news had been the fierce battles in Texas with the tragic loss of the Alamo and the massacre of hundreds of Texans at Goliad redeemed finally by a glorious victory at San Jacinto, where General Sam Houston's men routed a superior Mexican force, crying "Remember the Alamo!" as they charged. Even with all that drama in progress, the smoldering slavery issue was never out of the news. In the House of Representatives, John Quincy Adams denounced a resolution tabling all petitions about slavery as a "gag rule." And, of course, there was argument about extending slavery's reach if the Republic of Texas, which Houston and Stephen Austin and their followers were forming, ever became a state. In July of 1836 all of this paled in significance to the young *Journal* editor when racial conflict and rioting broke out in Cincinnati over the slavery question.

Ironically, it was the arrival in town of a disciple of Theodore Weld, whose revolt had nearly put Lane Seminary out of business, that resulted in some of the worst riots. The disciple was James G. Birney, a native of Kentucky and a Princeton graduate who had established himself as a cotton planter and attorney in Huntsville, Alabama. Being a Presbyterian elder who found it hard to reconcile slavery with his religion, Birney became active in the Colonization Society, but it was not until he heard a lecture by Weld in Huntsville that he was converted to the cause of abolition. He sold his slaves and gave up his home and profession to devote himself to the cause by publishing a weekly called *The Philanthropist*. When he picked Cincinnati as the right place to publish, his timing could not have been worse. The leading lights of the city had always done business with the South, and in that summer of 1836 they were firming up plans to build a railroad down through the Carolinas to the coast, based on the rapid development of the steam locomotive since the first American model, *Best Friend of Charleston*, was put on the rails in 1830. They wanted no part of what they disdained as an "abolitionist rag."

A committee headed by a deacon in Lyman Beecher's church, Ohio Supreme Court judge Jacob Bunet, which included Uncle John Foote, warned Birney that publishing would incite reprisals from a mob. Birney published anyway, and, inspired by the committee's tacit approval, a mob of "young men of the better class" broke into the printing shop of Quaker Achilles Pugh on Main Street, smashed the press, and threw the pieces in the river. Then they headed for Franklin House, where Birney was supposed to be living. More destruction and possible bloodshed were prevented by a courageous twenty-eight-year-old lawyer named Salmon P. Chase, who, though himself a member of the "better class" and attorney for several local banks, barred the door of the hotel with his own body and persuaded the mob that Birney was not there. This produced enough of a lull that the mayor was able to recruit a volunteer police force, and Henry Ward signed up. As recorded in a journal she was keeping for Calvin, Harriet found her brother in the kitchen pouring melted lead into a mold and asked him, "What on earth are you doing, Henry?"

"Making bullets to kill men with," he said.

"For a day or two we did not know but there would actually be war to the knife as threatened by the mob, and we really saw Henry depart with his pistols with daily alarm, only we were all too full of patriotism not to have sent every brother we had rather than not have had the principles of freedom and order defended."

It was a defense of these principles rather than an attack on the institution of slavery that became the *Journal's* editorial stance. Henry had Harriet write a letter to the paper, signed Franklin, that sided with Birney by pointing out that keeping him from publishing was contrary to the American belief in freedom of the press and the right to hold an unpopular opinion. Publicly Henry and Harriet were playing the game as safely as Lyman did. In her private journal, however, Harriet wrote, "For my part, I can easily see how such proceedings may make converts to abolitionism for already my sympathies are strongly enlisted for Mr. Birney, and I hope he will stand his ground and assert his rights. The office is fire-proof and enclosed by high walls. I wish he would man it with armed men and see what can be done. If I were a man, I would go, for one, and take good care of at least one window." Rather than become a martyr, Birney did leave town to carry on his crusade elsewhere and by other means. Henry Ward was brave enough to point out in an editorial that this was no solution to an enduring problem, because the Cincinnati riots were "flame jets which never come unpursued by the earthquake."

The city had quieted down by the time Lyman returned in August. He did not come alone. After once more being exonerated of heresy charges by the Presbyterian General Assembly in Philadelphia, he had visited his happy hunting ground in Boston and found yet another wife, a widow named Lydia Jackson, who had been a member of his congregation. With her were two of her own young children, Margaret and Joseph. Walnut Hills was once again a crowded household into which Harriet delivered twin girls in September. She named them Eliza Tyler Stowe and Isabella Beecher Stowe, but when Calvin finally got back to Cincinnati in January 1838, after his grand tour, he insisted on changing Isabella to Harriet Beecher Stowe. Calvin collected accolades for the quality of the books and the ideas—such as dividing schools into elementary, grammar, and high school grades—that he brought back and the interest of the stories he had to tell, but the year of his homecoming would turn out to be a year of hard times for the whole family and, indeed, the entire nation.

Because the Whig votes were divided, Martin Van Buren had squeaked through to victory in an election that he might wish he had never won. He had been Andrew Jackson's closest associate and adviser, but the old soldier ignored Van Buren's advice on monetary policy when he took federal funds out of the Second Bank of the United States and distributed them to state banks that were quickly dubbed his "pet banks." This brought on a fever of speculation, which Jackson then tried to cure with a specie circular directing that payments for public lands had to be made in specie, which, in turn, began soaking up gold and silver like a sponge. The nation was in a financial crisis by the time Van Buren moved into the White House, and the failure of financial houses in London, the world's financial capital, led to the worst depression that the new nation had ever experienced. The Beechers were soon made painfully aware of the ailing economy when a bank manager rode out to Walnut Hills to inform Lyman that his draft on a New York account maintained by the Tappans for his salary had been denied. Along with a host of other seemingly sound businesses, the Tappans' silk concern had gone bankrupt. People in America's financial capital were presented with an arresting symbol of the sad state of affairs when the new granite building of the banking house of I. and L. Joseph at Wall and Exchange Streets in New York City collapsed in a shower of stone and glass for no apparent reason on Monday, March 6, 1837.

In spite of death and depression, life goes on, and there were a number of important beginnings in the Beecher family. Up in Batavia, George met and married a girl from a wealthy family, named Sarah Buckingham. Possibly because he was on safe ground that far north, he also became the first member of the Beecher family to go all out in opposition to slavery by joining the Anti-Slavery Society. Graduated from Lane that spring, Henry Ward accepted a call to a Presbyterian church in Lawrenceburg, just across the line in Indiana, with twenty members, nineteen of whom were women. The American Home Mission Society would cover most of his four-hundred-dollar annual salary. Thus employed, Henry Ward went back East and married the woman who had waited patiently for four years. Eunice brought no money with her. When the couple arrived back in Lawrenceburg, Henry Ward had only sixty-eight cents in his pocket. To raise cash, Eunice sold a new cloak for thirty dollars. They rented two filthy rooms above a livery stable for forty dollars a year and furnished them with cast-off pieces from family and friends, such as the gifts from the Harrisons. For shelves they used the boxes in which Henry Ward had packed the books he had been acquiring ever since he had earned that first lecture fee. By the time of his marriage book buying had become a form of vice for Henry, which led to another vice, deception, as he volubly acknowledged to his biographers:

> Alas! where is human nature so weak as in a book store? . . . Talk of Wall Street and financing! No subtle manager or broker ever saw through a maze of financial embarrassments half so quick as a poor book buyer sees his way clear to pay for what he *must* have. Why, he will economize; he will dispense with this and that; he will retrench here and there; he will save by various expedients hitherto untried; he will put spurs on both heels of his industry; and then, besides all this, he will *somehow* get along when the time for payment comes! Ah! this Somehow! That word is as big as a whole world, and is stuffed with all the vagaries and fantasies that Fancy ever bred on Hope.
>
> Moreover, buying books before you can pay for them promotes caution. You don't feel quite at liberty to take them home. You are married. Your wife keeps an account book. She knows to a penny what you can and what you cannot afford. She has no "speculation" in *her eyes*. Plain figures make desperate work with airy "*somehow.*" It is a matter of no small skill and experience to get your books home, and in their places, undiscovered. Perhaps the blundering express brings them to the door just at evening. "What is it, my dear?" she says to you. "Oh, nothing—a few books that I cannot do without." That smile! A true housewife that loves her husband can smile a whole arithmetic at him in one look! Of course, she insists in the kindest way, on sympathizing with you, in your library acquisition. She cuts the strings of

the bundle (and of your heart), and out comes the whole story. You have bought a whole set of costly English books, full bound in calf, extra gilt! You are caught. And feel very much as if bound in calf yourself, extra gilt, and admirably lettered.

Now, this must not happen frequently. The books must be smuggled home. Let them be sent to some near place. Then, when your wife has a headache, or is out making a call, or has lain down, run the books across the frontier and threshold, hastily undo them, stop only for one loving glance as you put them away in the closet, or behind other books on the shelf, or on the topmost shelf. Clear away the twine and wrapping paper and every suspicious circumstance. Be very careful not to be too kind. That often brings on detection. Only the other day we heard it said somewhere: "Why, how good you have been lately! I am really afraid that you have been carrying on mischief secretly." Our heart smote us. It was a fact. That very day we had bought a few books which "we could not do without." After a while, you can bring out one volume, accidentally, and leave it on the table. "Why, my dear, *what* a beautiful book? Where *did* you borrow it?" You glance over the newspaper, with the quietest tone you can command: *"That?* Oh! That is *mine.* Have you not seen it before? It has been in the house this two months." And you rush on with anecdote and incident and point out the binding, and that peculiar trick of gilding, and everything else you can think of; but it will not do— you cannot rub out that roguish, arithmetical smile. People may talk about the equality of the sexes! They are not equal. The silent smile of a sensible, loving woman will vanquish ten men. Of course you repent, and in time form a habit of repenting.

Excited by the challenges of his first pastorate, warmed by the intimacies of early marriage and living by means of *somehow,* Henry Ward was entering into what he would later recall as one of the happiest times of his life. His spirit was evident in the letter he wrote to his brother George about his appearance before the Oxford Presbytery, an Old School body of Scotch Presbyterians who would decide whether he had a right to preach under their aegis. After a sixty-mile ride on horseback during which he nearly drowned while fording a swollen river, he

presented my papers. Father Craigh was appointed to squeak the questions. They examined me to their hearts' content. Elders opened their mouths, gave their noses a fresh blowing, fixed their spectacles and hitched forward in their seats. The ministers clinched their confessions of faith with desperate fervor and looked unutterably orthodox, while . . . a few friendly ones looked a little nervous, not knowing how the youth would stand fire. There he sat, the young candidate begotten of a heretic, nursed at Lane, but with such a name and parentage and education, what remarkable modesty, extraordinary meekness, and how deferential to the eminently acute questioners who sat gazing upon the prodigy! . . . Having predetermined that I should be hot and full of confidence, it was somewhat awkward, truly, to find such gentleness and teachableness!

Then came the examination: "Will the mon tell us in what relation Adam stood to his posterity?" "In the relation of a federal head." "What do you mean by a federal head?" "A head with whom God made a covenant for all his posterity." Then the questions grew on all the knotty points. Still the wonder grew, for the more the lad was examined the more incorrigibly orthodox did he grow until they began to fear he was "a leetle" too orthodox on some points. The vote on receiving me was unanimous! Well, they slept upon it. Next day, while settling the time of my ordination, Prof. McArthur of Oxford, moved to postpone the business to take up some resolutions. In the first they sincerely adhered to the Old School Pby. Assembly; second, required that all licentiates and candidates under their care do the same such. I declined acknowledging it to be true.

After apparently bluffing his way through the examination, Henry Ward suddenly turned into the heretic that the examiners had expected to find. Baffled by his response, they agreed to let him preach for six months while he thought about the matter. When he declined that offer, too, they returned his papers and told him that the pulpit of his church was vacant. Henry Ward rode home, described his experience to his congregation in his Sunday sermon, and asked them to decide at a Wednesday evening meeting what to do. By a unanimous vote, they elected to withdraw from Oxford and become an independent Presbyterian church. It gave the young minister an enormous jolt of confidence, and he would freely admit that "I had very little theology—that is to say, it slipped away from me. I knew it but it did not do me any good. It was like an armor which has lost its buckles and would not stick on. But I had one vivid point—the realization of the love of God in Jesus Christ."

While Henry Ward was exuberantly launching his career in Lawrence-burg, most of the other Beechers found themselves trying to stay afloat in troubled waters. Lyman and his new wife, who was fortunately an ener-getic and thrifty person, were faced with making do on the inadequate income from his church alone. Quite apart from the loss of the Tappan support, Lane's entering class had shrunk to some fifteen scholars, and it was highly questionable whether the salaries of faculty members such as Calvin Stowe could be paid in full, or at all. Back in her old room at Walnut Hills, Catharine had to preside over the closing of her school, which had been providing her only income. The growing depression was one cause of this failure. Uncle Samuel Foote was only one of the men of the class whose daughters would attend such a school to go belly-up and lose almost everything, including his home, which brought an end to the Semi-Colon Club. Other causes were Catharine's own unwillingness to give of her time and effort to the school as well as her increasingly abra-sive personality, which was alienating still-solvent members of that class such as prosperous Nathaniel Wright. Not only did Catharine engage in unwanted theological arguments with Wright, an elder in her father's church and father of the girl for whom brother Charles was pining, but also Lyman angered Wright by berating him for holding dances in his house and thereby endangering the morals of young people. So needy was Catharine that she risked her good relationship with her favorite sister by seizing all the assets of the school and ignoring the claims of Harriet and their colleague Mary Dutton. Catharine did manage to publish two more works that resulted in controversy rather than in riches. One, called *Letters on the Difficulties of Religion*, was an attempt to build a bridge between Old School and New School Presbyterians and between Presbyterians and other mainline Protestant denominations on the basis of leading a moral life. Readers unwilling or unable to follow her reasoning called it "Miss Beecher's Difficulties." The other bore a forbidding title, *Essay on Slavery and Abolitionism with Reference to the Duty of American Females*. In the form of a letter to Angelina Grimké, one of two sisters reared on a southern plantation, who had come North to preach abolition of slavery and full citizenship and social activism for women, Catharine took the cautionary Beecher line of promoting colonization for slaves, and she urged women to exert a moral influence on society through teaching children and persuading the men in their lives to act morally instead of the women themselves becoming active in civic affairs.

What with jobs and families, most of Catharine's brothers and sisters could not take her detached, intellectual view of the issues of the day.

Harriet and Calvin had moved back with the twins and some servants into their faculty house. Among their servants was a young black girl who presented herself as being legally free. One day she returned from town and rushed to Harriet with the news that she was a runaway from Kentucky and that her master was in town looking for her. She begged the Stowes to save her. Harriet had been aware that there was an illegal avenue of escape for people like her servant girl since 1834 when she, her father, and Calvin Stowe had been guests of the Reverend Rankin in Ripley during a meeting of the Presbyterian Synod. The Rankin house was on a bluff overlooking the river and Kentucky beyond. Every night their host put a lighted lantern in the window. Assuming from their talk that his Presbyterian guests would be sympathetic, Rankin revealed that his house was a station on the Underground Railroad to Canada. By word of mouth, the news passed around the slave population across the river that they would be on their way to safety if they could reach his light. Rankin had great admiration for the courage of the refugees, and he told his visitors the story of a young Negro woman who had managed to cross an ice-filled river with a baby in her arms to reach his house. There were people like Rankin everywhere, and the Stowes had heard of a farmer named John Van Zandt who had sold his lands and slaves in Kentucky and started over again on a place twelve miles north on the Montgomery turnpike, where he took in runaways without question and either hid them or passed them along as circumstances dictated. When the distraught servant spilled out her story, the Stowes did not hesitate. Calvin and Charles Beecher, who happened to be visiting them, loaded pistols, hitched up the carriage, and drove the girl through the night to the Van Zandt farm, where she was hidden until her pursuers gave up their search.

In that depressed summer, there was no money in the Stowe household for a vacation. Still getting used to taking care of the twins and pregnant again, Harriet felt a need to get away from the gloomy atmosphere generated by failing enterprises. With Catharine along to help with the babies, she took advantage of a standing invitation from brother William and his wife, Katherine, to visit their home in Putnam. If she had hoped to escape dealing with the ever more disturbing question of what should be done about slavery, she had made the wrong move. Like George, William was deserting the safety of the colonization camp for the front lines of the abolitionists. Catharine must have been provoked to argument by one of William's female friends, who was following the lead of the Grimké sisters, but Harriet was stimulated to thought, as her letter to Calvin reveals:

The good people here, you know, are about half Abolitionists. A lady who takes a leading part in the female society in this place, yesterday called and brought Catharine the proceedings of the Female Anti-Slavery Convention.

I should think them about as ultra as to measures as anything that had been attempted, though I am glad to see a better spirit than marks such proceedings generally.

Today I read some in Mr. Birney's *Philanthropist*. Abolition being the fashion here, it is natural to look at its papers.

It does seem to me that there needs to be an *intermediate* society. If not, as light increases, all the excesses of the abolition party will not prevent humane and conscientious men from joining it.

Pray, what is there in Cincinnati to satisfy one whose mind is awakened on this subject? No one can have the system of slavery brought before him without an irrepressible desire to *do* something, and what is there to be done?

Doing something about the slavery issue could be dangerous, and as that upsetting year drew to a close, the Cincinnati contingent of the Beecher family was rudely awakened to this possibility when news filtered down to them that brother Edward may have been killed in such an attempt. The event that rang an alarm bell throughout the nation was the death of the Reverend Elijah Lovejoy, publisher of an abolitionist paper, *Observer*, in Alton, Illinois, on the night of November 7, 1837. The whole Beecher family knew that Edward and Lovejoy had become good friends since they first met at the commencement ceremonies of Edward's Illinois College in 1835. Edward had, in fact, been responsible for persuading Lovejoy in 1836 to move his publication across the Mississippi from St. Louis, where threats to his life from proslavery forces had grown too strong to ignore. At the Presbyterian General Assembly in Philadelphia in the summer of 1837, Edward publicly sided with Lovejoy and other New School men in the bitter debate with Old School adherents, partly on the grounds that New School believers were too active in their opposition to slavery. That fall there were contentious meetings in Illinois, some of them arranged by Edward, at which both men spoke. One meeting was packed by members of the Colonization Society, led by a visiting slavery apologist, the Reverend Joel Parker, from New Orleans. In a vain effort to find a middle ground between such views and his own, Edward drew up a "Declaration of Sentiments," which held that slavery was a sin but that the sin was "organic" in that the community could be held guilty rather than the individual slaveholder prevented by circumstances from freeing his slaves even if he desired to do so.

Three times during Lovejoy's first year of operation in Alton, irate and often drunken mobs threw his press into the river, and three times supporters replaced it. When a fourth replacement was needed, it was decided to conduct the operation in secret in the dead of night, and Edward Beecher was on hand at three o'clock on the morning of November 7 to help move the press from the wharf to a stone warehouse nearby. The job done and the press apparently safely in place, Beecher went home at dawn with Lovejoy, shared a prayer and breakfast with the family, and took off for his duties at the college in Jacksonville. But the family did not hear of Edward's safety for agonizing hours. All they knew during that time was that Lovejoy fell dead with five bullets in his body and that others were killed and wounded during a shoot-out with an angry mob at the warehouse that evening. Edward would assuage his guilt at not being by his friend's side for the fight by writing *Narrative of Riots at Alton,* his strongest indictment of slavery and of "that bloody, thousand-headed, murderous tyrant, the mob."

Except for Edward, the slavery problem was not yet uppermost in the minds of most Beechers in 1838. The birth in January of a son named Henry Ellis plunged Harriet deeper into the consuming concerns of motherhood and household management. To help her, Calvin's mother was imported from Maine, and an English nursemaid named Anna was hired. All this assistance, which required little more in compensation than room and board, did not relieve her from the daily grind. She pictured a typical day in a letter to her old friend Georgiana:

> I waked up about half-after-four and thought, "Bless me, how light it is! I must . . . wake up Mina, for breakfast must be had at six o'clock this morning." So out of bed I jump and seize the tongs and pound, pound over poor Mina's sleepy head, charitably allowing her about half an hour to get waked up in—that being the quantum of time it takes me, or used to. Well, then, baby wakes—qua, qua, qua—so I give him his breakfast, dozing meanwhile and soliloquizing as follows: "Now I must not forget to tell Mr. Stowe about the starch and dried apples"—doze—"ah, um, dear me! why doesn't Mina get up? I don't hear her"—doze—"ah, um,—I wonder if Mina has soap enough! I think there were two bars on Saturday"—doze again—I wake again. "Dear me, broad daylight!

I must go down and see if Mina is getting breakfast." Up I jump and up wake baby. "Now, little boy, be good and let mother dress, because she is in a hurry." I get my frock half on and baby by that time has kicked himself down off his pillow, and is crying and fisting the bed-clothes in great order. I stop with one sleeve off and one on to settle matters with him. Having placed him bolt upright and gone all up and down the chamber bare foot to get pillows and blankets to prop him up, I finish putting on frock and hurry down to satisfy myself . . . that the breakfast is in progress. . . .

After morning prayers and breakfast during which there was consultation with Calvin who, in the custom of the day, did the family marketing, Harriet was back in the nursery, where the account continues:

I . . . start to cut some little dresses . . . when Master Henry makes a doleful lip and falls to crying with might and main. I catch him up and turning around see one of the sisters flourishing the things out of my workbox in fine style. Moving it away and looking to the other side, I see the second little mischief seated by the hearth chewing coals and scraping up ashes with great apparent relish. Grandmother lays hold upon her and charitably offers to endeavor to quiet baby while I go on with my work. I set at it again . . . when I see the twins on the point of quarreling with each other. Number one pushes number two over. Number two screams: that frightens baby, and he joins in. I call number one a naughty girl, take the persecuted one in my arms, and endeavor to comfort her. . . . Meanwhile number one makes her way to the slop jar and forthwith proceeds to wash her apron in it. Grandmother drags her away, and sets the jar up out of her reach. By and by the nurse comes up from her sweeping. I commit the children to her, and finish cutting out the frocks.

But let this suffice, for of such details as these are all my days made up. Indeed, my dear, I am but a mere drudge with a few ideas beyond babies and housekeeping. As for thought, reflections and sentiments, good lack! good lack!

Well, Georgy, this marriage is—yes, I will speak well of it, after all, for when I stop and think. . . . I must say that I think myself a fortunate woman both in husband and children. My children I would not change for all the ease, leisure, and pleasure I could have without them.

Harriet's assessment of the still-new marriage has to be regarded as remarkable in view of Calvin's reaction to the deepening economic crisis. Always a man given to hypochondria and blue moods, he very nearly fell apart when there were no new students signing up for the 1838 beginner's class at Lane and only ten left in the classes above. He would alternately pace the floor at home and rave that a man with his reputation ought to leave this sinking enterprise or he would simply take to his bed and wallow in misery. By contrast, Lyman's reaction was to take to the road once again and beat the bushes for students. He had enough success to keep the seminary's doors open and hang on to his best professor and admired son-in-law. Although she was also prone to debilitating ailments and bouts of depression, Harriet had inherited from both parental families a tendency to action in adversity. An example of maternal heritage was irrepressible Uncle Samuel Foote, who sold his mansion for what he could get for it, used the proceeds to remodel some downtown properties left empty by bankrupt tenants for his own living quarters, and started a new business that had a bright future precisely because of the economic disaster—selling insurance. To do something about her own family's finances in view of her husband's helpless attitude, Harriet studied the popular periodicals, many of them religiously oriented, and started supplying them with moral and sentimental tales and essays. She sold enough for small sums to pay the help, which let her devote about three hours of those hectic days to writing. She was modest about her ability and honest about her motives in a letter to Mary Dutton, who had gone back to Connecticut after the school shut down: "If you see my name coming out everywhere, you may be sure of one thing—that I do it for pay. I have determined not to be a domestic slave."

Almost impervious to all that was happening around him in the family and the nation was Charles. At age twenty-three, he was a romantically miserable young man. Tall and lean with a slightly apologetic stoop, he had a long, thin face, a scholar's dome, and kind eyes. Unable to shake the doubts that his theological studies had raised, he felt that he could not follow his brothers through a conversion necessary to becoming a minister. He had read as much or more romantic literature as theological tracts and was drawn more to Goethe's Werther and Byron's Childe Harold than to biblical figures and stern Calvinist divines. In his own family, he saw himself as a tragic outsider, an image darkened by popular Mary Wright's rejection of his advances. He wanted to get away as far as possible from a depressing environment in which his inability to conform put him constantly at odds with his siblings and father. He wanted to find an exotic place in keeping with his romantic dreams. From the river travelers he heard of the warm climate, the colorful mixture of peoples and languages, the European atmosphere of New Orleans. He would go there and try to turn his love of, and talent for, music into the means of living.

At a time when so many other things were going wrong in Lyman Beecher's life, the defection of this son who was not yet saved, according to his lights, was hard to take. The parting was very emotional, as Charles later described it: "'My son,' he said, with quivering lip, 'eternity is long!' and with a glance of anguish and a grasp of the hand, he turned away." In New Orleans, Charles soon discovered that he could not live on music and took a job in a countinghouse that required him to travel through the countryside collecting debts. He was temperamentally unsuited to the job and poured out his anguish in letters to his teenage half stepsister Isabella. He hated what he learned of poverty and slavery and the motivation of his fellow workers to make "cursed Money! Money! Money!" He consoled himself to some degree by serving as a church organist and writing poetry, one example of which was published in a local paper that found its way to Walnut Hills and nearly broke his father's heart. Although lacking much merit as poetry, Charles's lament was a classic cry of romantic, love-starved youth:

> Oh, must I live a lonely one,
> Unloved upon the thronged earth,
> Without a home beneath the sun,
> Far from the land that gave me birth!
>
> Alone— alone I wander on,
> An exile in a dreary land,
> The friends that knew me once are gone,
> Not one is left of all their band.
>
> I look upon the boiling tide
> Of traffic fierce, that ebbs and flows,
> With chill disgust and shrinking pride
> That heartfelt misery only knows.
>
> Where is the buoyancy of youth,
> The high, indomitable will,
> The vision keen, the thirst for truth,
> The passions wild, unearthly thrill?

Oh, where are all the bounding hopes
And visions bright that were my own
When fancy at her will could ope
The golden doors to Beauty's throne?

My mother! Whither art thou fled?
Seest thou these tears that for thee flow?
Or, in the realms of shadowy dead,
Knowest thou no more of mortal woe?

In that still realm of twilight gloom
Hast thou reserved no place for me?
Haste—haste, oh mother, give me room,
I come—I come at length to thee!

This poem inspired an impassioned response from Lyman. Especially upset by his son's claim that he had no friends, he informed Charles that the family was "united in a weekly concert of prayer" for him and added that "amid your melancholy complainings and despondencies, and my own tremulous susceptibilities, I seem to hear the reply of the Bishop of Hippo to the mother of Augustine, who came beseeching him to pray for her skeptical son—'Depart, good woman,' said he, 'the child of so many prayers cannot be lost!'" And as to the reference to Roxana, who had become in memory a saint within the family, Lyman wrote:

Your address to your mother is overwhelming me. That you should address her *in doubt* whether she now adores as an angel amid the resplendent joys and glories of heaven, or is bereft of consciousness amid the shadowy dead by annihilation, and that you should implore her personified dust to give you quickly a place in her realms of twilight gloom, as if resolved to follow her—did I not regard it as a poetical amplification, I should be terrified—petrified. Oh, my dear Charles, would to God that this blessed mother could look upon you as in life, as in my dreams since her death, she has looked and smiled upon me in my despondencies and sorrows—that she might speak to your troubled soul as she was wont to speak to mine, in the language of wisdom, and meek submission, and unutterable kindness—it would stay your maladies, revive your spirit, fill up your dreary void of desolation, and make your life, as she did mine, as full of enjoyment as can appertain to the lot of mortals.

Isabella, grown into the most physically attractive of Lyman's daughters, was the confidante not only of Charles but of her younger brother

Tom as well. Possibly to lighten the load on Walnut Hills but more likely to let her learn the womanly graces from her sister, Mary Perkins, the most conventional of Lyman's daughters, Isabella was sent East to live with the Perkins family in Hartford. Although only fourteen, Tom was sent to a newly established college in Marietta, Ohio, where he was apparently as unhappy as Charles in New Orleans. On May 30, 1838, Tom wrote a surprisingly adult, four-page letter to Isabella in the East from his brother William's home in Putnam. The news was that Tom had left Marietta and was awaiting reaction to his move from Lyman, who was attending the Presbyterian General Assembly in Philadelphia. "At the same time I wrote to father, I wrote a letter to Marietta, wishing my room mate to send my trunk (which is now weeks ago)," he informed sister Belle, "but he (I suppose by the command of Prof Maxwell) has not yet sent it. And I am determined not to go back there, if I can help it, for they are trying to force me back, for want of clothes, but brother William says that they'll have to exhaust the store here before they can get me back, for want of clothes." From this passage, William, the unlucky, would seem to have a heart bigger than his head.

Whatever Lyman might think about Tom's rebellion in leaving school, he certainly would have been comforted by another matter the boy shared with his sister:

> You can feel now, as I do about brother James, for think now, out of the sons & daughters of father, amounting to twenty seven James is the only one who is still irreligious, let us then concentrate our whole prayer on him that soon he too may feel the comforts of religion. I have often doubted within myself whether I was doing right in hoping that I was Christian without making a public profession & now I feel more about it than I ever did before, for now it is most a year since I became converted, yes more than a year, & as yet I have made no profession. I know not how God will look upon it but it is certain that I feel that I am doing wrong in thus withholding my little influence from the cause of Christ.

Belle also would have been comforted when Tom wrote that

> they talk a great deal about you, here at Putnam, & tell me that I look just like you, but you cannot tell how much I want to see you. Just think now—we have not seen each other for two years and a half, you, the only own sister that I have, although Maggie [stepsister from Lydia] seemed to me the same as one, for I never saw a girl whom I loved at so short a notice as sincerely as I do

her, & to use a common term—"I am desperately in love"—not the genus of love which that expression is usually taken to mean but that sort of brotherly love which I have in a higher degree for you.

While she was in Hartford, Isabella's beauty and the kind of intelligent caring and interest that prompted confessions from her brothers charmed John Hooker, scion of an old and well-established Connecticut family. An exchange of letters in 1839 after Isabella moved back to Walnut Hills reveals that Mary Perkins approved of Hooker's attentions and the fact that his evident feelings were reciprocated. The young man was teetering between becoming a lawyer like Mary's husband or a minister like Isabella's brothers. The subject was discussed in Walnut Hills, and Catharine weighed in heavily on the side of the ministry with a letter sent directly to Hooker:

Bell is formed by nature to *take the lead*—she will every year learn more and more of her power to *influence others* since she has been home with father and learned his plans of influence in his parish—she has unconsciously and without any worry or responsibility been extending a great influence. Father has been greatly perplexed by fashionable amusements among his young people. She has come among them and can do and will do more than father or anyone else could do to stay the evil. . . . She is growing fast in piety—in power of intellect—in power of controlling other minds. What will you find for her to do? . . . I do not want to see a woman of her talents and power put out of her place as *a leader*. She is formed for a minister's wife as much as you are for a minister. . . . If you decide to be a lawyer I shall not be very much disappointed or troubled for tho' I shall think you and Bell will in consequence be less useful and of course less happy, still I shall esteem it as the will of God that so it should be.

Mary could hardly tolerate that kind of advice, and she wrote to Isabella:

Yesterday Mr. Hooker spent most of the day with us and we discussed the question of his changing his profession in its length and breadth. . . . From all I saw and heard it was very evident to my mind that if he changes, it will be to *please you* and not from a conviction that he is called of God to enter the sacred office . . . I know him better than father or Catharine does, and perhaps as well as you do. . . . It seems to me that you are all running wild on this subject—pray bring common sense to bear and take some view of society and its various wants and claims besides the ministerial view. . . . Dear Sister I have left the subject of your health last tho not least in my view. You look only on the bright side of the picture and so does father and Catharine. If I tho't you would *ever* have strength and health I would not say a word—but I do not believe that you *will ever* be a strong and healthy woman. You may be comfortably well, so that you can attend to the duties of your family, educate your children and be very useful and happy if you do not have the duties and responsibilities hanging about you that you have no strength to perform. Think of your own dear mother, as well qualified by education and piety as you, and with a better prospect of health, after marriage her health gave way, her spirits sunk, and she was ever mourning that she appeared so useless to herself to be. I do not believe if she were living she would advise the change. . . . I think it would be *utter madness* for you to marry a minister and I wonder at father and Catharine and Harriet that they should think of such a thing when your health is in such a state. I am sure the *indications* of Providence are very strong that you ought not to be a *minister's wife*. I have given you a preachment but do *think well*. I wish you were here. I know you don't—but if Kate sets herself to make Hooker a minister I greatly fear that she will succeed. She is never afraid of consequences and always thinks things will be just as she wishes them to be. Write to me as soon as you get this and oh that you could relieve my mind of the anxieties I feel for you.

Mary probably should have suggested that Isabella go to Henry Ward's wife, Eunice, for advice. For Eunice, the honeymoon was over almost before it began. Despite living in shabby quarters with hand-me-down furniture, they could not live on Henry Ward's salary and had to start borrowing from relatives. Almost as soon as nature would allow, Eunice was saddled with an unwanted pregnancy. "It would be no great trial to me— and release me from a load of responsibility, which I felt unfit to sustain, should the baby be born stillborn," she confessed to George's wife, Sarah.

It was generally acknowledged that the three children born to Lyman Beecher's wife Harriet Porter inherited their mother's good looks, but one of them at least claimed that they also inherited from her a touch of madness.

A nationally known crusader for women's rights for four decades, Isabella Beecher Hooker was famed for her ladylike behavior but also for her outspoken opinions, such as "Oh, I am proud of my sex—I am so glad men have had to have mothers as well as fathers. Though you wouldn't suspect it from history or current literature."

1846 — We shall all be changed. — 1887

Although he shocked his fellow ministers and some of his fellow citizens of Elmira, New York, with his unclerical manners and habits, the Reverend Thomas Beecher built the nation's first, very successful "institutional church." Cursed with the "blues," as were most of his siblings, Tom had a saving sense of humor, as demonstrated in this card he created and captioned himself.

The youngest of the tribe, James Beecher led the most colorful, most tragic life—a wild youth, an officer on clipper ships, a missionary to China, the general in command of the first Union regiment recruited from ex-slaves, and a hermit preacher, all ending in madness and suicide.

111

But a daughter named Harriet Eliza arrived in May 1838, to Henry Ward's delight. He did his part in trying to help his wife by lugging water upstairs from the backyard well, cutting wood for the fires, and even changing diapers, but he left Eunice alone far too much to ease the burden of her spirit. Eunice could not in good conscience fault her husband for neglect, because he regarded it as part of his calling to be out and about and associating with the unchurched people of the town when he was not in the pulpit. But it was galling to Eunice that he enjoyed it so much.

Using his warm personality and cheerful optimism to befriend the men fishing along the riverbank or lingering around the cracker barrel in a store may have been a more effective way of spreading his new gospel of love than preaching. One of the few strong stands he took in the pulpit was to preach temperance in a town where making whiskey was its most lucrative enterprise and drinking it one of its few pleasures. This upset a good many citizens, one of whom was a neighbor. As Henry Ward would recall, he was "a very profane man, who was counted ugly. I understood that he had said some very bitter things of me. I went right over to his store, and sat down on the counter to talk with him. I happened in often—day in and day out. My errand was to make him like me. I did make him like me—and all the children too and when I left, two or three years later, it was his house that was opened to me and all my family for the week after I gave up my room. And to the day of his death I do not believe the old man could mention my name without crying."

On another issue that might have riled the citizens of Lawrenceburg, Henry Ward followed in his father's footsteps. He let his feelings about slavery show by hosting a meeting of the Colonization Society in his church, but he expressed strong doubts about abolition as the right solution to the problem. As to theology in his sermons, Henry Ward said, "As a man chops straw and mixes it with Indian meal in order to distend the stomach of the ox that eats it, so I chopped a little of the orthodox theology, that I might sprinkle it with the meal of the Lord Jesus Christ." No record was kept of souls saved or members added to his small congregation by his preaching, but the young man was enough of a presence that word of him reached the ears of Samuel Merrill, president of the State Bank in Indianapolis, who was organizing a New School congregation. On a business trip to Lawrenceburg in May 1839, he listened to Henry Ward preach and persuaded him to give a trial sermon in Indianapolis, which resulted in a call to be the founding minister of yet another Presbyterian church at what seemed to be an ample salary of eight hundred dollars a year. The hope in Eunice's mind, as they went about the difficult process of moving, was only that life in the capital would somehow be easier. Nobody, least of all the Beechers themselves, could have predicted that in fewer than two years Henry Ward would be called on to help bury a president of the United States.

6

"I will write something. I will if I live."

ON THIS COMMUNION SUNDAY in February 1851, Harriet could hardly wait to slide into the Stowe family's pew 23 at the First Parish Church in New Brunswick, Maine. She was glad to be there for a reason that she might not want to share with her ministerial brothers except, perhaps, Tom. It was the only time of the week and the only place in town where she could really rest for an hour or more. With Calvin out at Lane to teach for the winter term, the whole management of the household and family was weighing heavily on her shoulders. However big it was, the old rented house on Federal Street that she shared with six children and a couple of servants granted her no peace or privacy. "There is actually not a place where I can lie down and take a nap without being disturbed," she complained in a letter to Calvin. "Overhead is the school-room, next door is the dining-room, and the girls practice there two hours a day. If I lock my door and lie down, some one is sure to be rattling the latch before fifteen minutes have passed." On Sundays, however, she could leave the baby at home in a nursemaid's arms and count on the fact that the fear of God would keep the older children ranged along the pew beside her relatively calm and quiet. On most occasions the familiar liturgy and even the sermon would not engage her mind but rather serve like the swish of sea on sand as a soothing background to her own private thoughts. There was always a chance that one or more of these thoughts would inspire a story or an essay and always a feeling that there would be an element of the divine in an inspiration that arrived unbidden during worship.

Since these Sunday daydreams were usually pleasant and uplifting, the vision that rose before her eyes on this wintry New England morning was a shocking surprise. She seemed to be somewhere in the sunny South, a benign natural setting that made the ugly human drama unfolding in her mind more terrible. While a white man in plantation hat and riding boots stood by to watch, two strong young men, their bare ebony torsos ashine with sweat, were turning the back of a white-haired old black man into a mass of bloody flesh with heavy whips. Harriet knew that she was watching slaves beat a slave under orders, and the revulsion that she felt was nearly unbearable as she heard the old man cry out to God to have mercy on his tormentors who "know not what they do." And then she heard another voice sounding more of Jesus' words: "Inasmuch as ye have done it unto one of the least of these my brethren, ye have done it unto me." Although she tried to shake off this vision, Harriet was compelled to go on watching until the old man's battered body went limp and the look of agony on his face gave way to the radiant smile of a soul glimpsing the promised land. It was all that Harriet could do to keep from crying aloud and frightening her children and the other innocent churchgoers around her.

Feeling that the vision was very special, a divine message of some sort, Harriet said nothing of it on the walk home; somehow it might dissipate in the telling. She knew she had to write it down. She was a study in silence throughout the family dinner. As soon as it was over, she fled to her room and locked the door, hoping for more than fifteen minutes of solitude this time. If there had come a knock, she might not have heard it as she sat at her desk and copied words that seemed to sound from somewhere outside her as fast as she could move her pen. When she ran out of white paper, she did not dare to risk taking the time and breaking her concentration to search for more; she just tore the brown wrapping paper off a package into pieces and wrote on them. Once she had the experience preserved in ink, she wanted to share it. She ran down and gathered the children together in the parlor and read it to them. They wept as her words evoked the same awful scene in their minds, and she allowed herself to weep with them. Thirteen-year-old Henry could understand the import of her story, and he spoke for them all when he said, "Oh, Ma, slavery is the most cruel thing in the world!"

It was, of course, the message that her vision was meant to convey. She was glad that her children could be enthralled and moved by her rendering of it, but she was not sure what else, if anything, could be done with it. She had become a thoroughly professional writer with a popular book of short stories, *The Mayflower: or, Sketches of Scenes and Characters Among the Descendants of the Pilgrims,* to her credit as well as regular appearances in nationally circulated periodicals. Quite apart from the likelihood that many readers would be repulsed by the bloody violence of her vision and many more outraged by its implications, it was from the writer's point of view only a fragment of a tale without plot or character that could not stand alone. Rather reluctantly, Harriet shoved the mismatched sheets of paper away in a drawer and tried to put her mind on more promising material that might make up the two- to three-hundred-dollar shortfall between Calvin's income and the family's expenditures that she anticipated for this year.

Looking back, Harriet would have to acknowledge that it always had been thus, almost from the first day of their marriage. The depression that began in 1837 lingered on through a decade for the inhabitants of Walnut Hills and Lane Seminary. While the Stowe family and its wants kept growing larger, there were years when Lane could pay Calvin only half of his supposed twelve-hundred-dollar salary. Harriet fell back on taking in boarders, a survival strategy her mother had so often used. By adding to the problems, duties, and vexations of housekeeping, this strategy was counterproductive for Harriet's writing efforts, which she once described as "rowing against wind and tide." A friend, who tried to make things easier for Harriet by taking dictation, wrote an account of one writing session that took place at the kitchen table while a young black girl in training named Mina bustled about and a baby gurgled in a cradle at their feet:

> "I'm ready to write," said I. "The last sentence was: 'What is this life to one who has suffered as I have?' What next?"
>
> "Shall I put in the brown or the white bread first?" said Mina.
>
> "The brown first," said Harriet.
>
> "What is this life to one who has suffered as I have?" I repeated.
>
> Harriet brushed the flour off her apron and sat down for a moment to muse. Then she dictated as follows:
>
> "Under the breaking of my heart I have borne up. I have borne up under all that tries a woman—but this thought—oh, Henry!"
>
> "Ma'am, shall I put the ginger into this pumpkin?" queried Mina.
>
> "No, you may let that alone just now," replied Harriet. She then proceeded:

"I know my duty to my children. I see the hour must come. You must take them, Henry; they are my last earthly comfort."

"Ma'am, what shall I do with the egg shells and all this truck here?" interrupted Mina.

"Put them in the pail by you," answered Harriet.

"They are my last earthly comfort," said I. "What next?"

She continued to dictate:

"You must take them away. It may be—perhaps it must be—that I shall soon follow, but the breaking heart of a wife pleads, 'a little longer, a little longer.'"

"How much longer must the ginger bread stay in?" inquired Mina.

"Five minutes," said Harriet.

"A little longer, a little longer," I repeated in a dolorous tone and we burst into a laugh.

Calvin must have given ear to this or similar sessions in passing. He had to be as impressed with Harriet's persistence as he was gratified by her earnings. When, in 1842, she went East to visit Mary Perkins in Hartford while making arrangements for publication of her first book, Calvin wrote:

My dear, you must be a literary person. It is so written in the book of fate. Make all your calculations accordingly. Get a good stock of health and brush up your mind. Drop the E. out of your name. [Her name was Harriet Elizabeth.] It only incumbers it and interferes with the flow and euphony. Write yourself fully Harriet Beecher Stowe, which is a name euphonious, blowing and full of meaning. Then, my word for it, your husband will lift up his head in the gate and your children will rise up and call you blessed. And now, my dear wife, I want you to come home as quick as you can. The fact is that I cannot live without you and if we were not so prodigious poor I would come for you at once.

In that letter expressing an understanding and support for her ambition and a loving need for her person lies the secret of Calvin's hold on Harriet despite their differences in personality and lifestyle. The extent of the mental stimulation and equality in their relationship was unusual for their time—or, perhaps, for any time.

Harriet's shadow Henry Ward was not as lucky in love as his sister. The move to Indianapolis did little to improve Eunice's health or spirits.

She had been told, possibly by Henry Ward, that she would find no malaria in the capital, as there was in Lawrenceberg. But as soon as she entered the Merrill house, where they were being hosted until they could find a place of their own, she was told that three of the children were then in bed with malaria and that one of the city's wealthiest households was constantly visited with "chills and fever." When the Beechers did move, it was to a cottage so small that Eunice reported in a complaining letter that she had to "make the bed on one side first, then go out on the verandah, raise a window, reach in and make the bed on the other side." There they both came down with "chills," as Eunice had feared. Weariness with housework, repeated bouts with illness, and another unwanted pregnancy so changed Eunice that when Henry took his wife and little Hattie back to Massachusetts for a health-restoring visit with her parents, they did not recognize her; they thought that she was an ailing middle-aged woman come to seek Dr. Bullard's help. It is understandable that an early visitor to the cottage on Indianapolis's Market Street described Eunice as "a rather discontented woman, complaining constantly of chills and the unhealthy nature of the town."

Although his wife's condition of mind and body was a nagging worry for Henry Ward, he did not let it get him down. In a thinly fictionalized account of their Indianapolis lives, Eunice wrote of their contrasting natures: "She had not his healthful elasticity of spirit and natural mirthfulness, or hopeful way of looking upon life. She did not see the 'silver lining' which was always visible to his eyes 'through every cloud.'" She was also coming to grips with the nature of the neglect that had ended the honeymoon. In another passage from that same autobiographical novel, *From Dawn to Daylight, or The Simple Story of a Western Home,* she revealed both her understanding of the matter and the suffering it caused her:

> Ah, this unintentional selfishness so common to literary and public men, has caused more domestic unhappiness than aught else save intemperance. They have so many things to perplex and harass them—they are wearied with anxious thought for the good of their people, or by close research and investigation upon literary subjects, and the mind must rest, or change entirely the current of thought. They do not, by any means, intend to neglect their home treasures, and are not conscious that they do. But new acquaintances are gradually formed—a word must be given to this one, a few moments to that, or just a step to glance at the curiosity till all leisure time has flown, and the public servant

must return to duties which require his undivided attention, and, perhaps, not one word or look has been saved for home. If, after many such experiences, the wife ventures a timid remonstrance, a sharp rebuke may be the reply, no doubt, repented as soon as uttered, but the conscience is easily silenced by, "Well, I did not mean to speak so impatiently; but she is unreasonable. She should not forget that a public man has duties, in the way of trifling attentions to those interested in him, and—and—well, I'll be more careful in future." But conscience thus silenced, does not long ward off other, and more severe rebuffs, and it takes but a few years of such teaching to make a wife *fear* as well as *love*, and, if sometimes wearied of longing for a few loving words, sick, and overburdened with many cares, her sense of right and justice overcome both fear and love, and she speaks plain *truths*—such as a *wife* can never *safely*, venture upon—most likely she increases the evil instead of remedying it. Oh! *why* need this *ever* be so, when deep in the heart of both, burns a love stronger than death?

However lost on his wife, Henry Ward's outgoing personality brought him almost instant success in Indianapolis. The congregation that had been meeting in an upper room at a seminary grew so rapidly that, within a year, they built a church to Beecher's own rather radical design. He did not want a pulpit hung high on a wall—"a swallow's nest"—but a simple dais as in a schoolroom that would allow more intimate contact with the audience and give them a friendlier image of their pastor. Eunice seemed almost jealous in acknowledging her husband's professional skills and popularity with his flock, but she was bitter about their treatment of him when she discovered that the promised eight hundred dollars in salary was not always paid in full and did not keep them from falling farther into debt. "There was wealth in abundance among their new people. The money they wasted on parties and frivolous amusements every few weeks, would have comfortably supported their pastor's family a year, and given his wife an opportunity to rest and regain her strength," she wrote in her novel. For the most part, Beecher's siblings overlooked or ignored Eunice's complaints. Instead they observed and took pride in his evident success, as Isabella reported after an early visit to Indianapolis: "I think he is going somewhat in father's track and will perhaps one day come somewhere near his eminence."

Like Henry Ward, Isabella brought a measure of pride to the Beecher clan when she married the handsome and well-connected—a direct descendant of the founder of Hartford—John Hooker on August 5, 1841.

She was nineteen, and he was six years older. The great debate as to his career had been decided in favor of the law after he obligingly tried Yale Divinity School for a term. He had opened an office in the village of Farmington, a few miles from Hartford. Because he had strained his eyes with too much study, Hooker had taken time off during his undergraduate years at Yale to ship out before the mast, as many other young men of his time, notably Herman Melville and Richard Henry Dana, were wont to do. On his voyages to the Mediterranean and the Far East, he passed the tests of physical courage during a skirmish with pirates and moral fortitude by resisting the temptation to use the foul language and indulge in the illicit pleasures of his shipmates. Hooker was a truly gentle man and so wildly in love with the beautiful Belle that he actually welcomed her physical frailties as opportunities to show his devotion and was yielding to that trait in her character that Catharine had identified as leadership.

Long before the wedding, Hooker had ample warning from Isabella herself as to how she expected him to treat her. It was in a letter written during a visit with the William Beechers in Batavia, New York, where William had taken over a pastorate that George had given up because of recurring health problems. Isabella had apparently been making a summer vacation for herself by staying a while with a number of siblings and observing their marriages closely in anticipation of her own. Before reaching Batavia, she had already spent time with Henry Ward and Eunice in Indianapolis and at Rochester, where a partially recovered George was again trying to occupy a pulpit. With George and Sarah she had "a most labored discussion of the relative position of a wife—to her husband—her duty of submission &c" in which she took the position that ministers kept unfairly stressing the duty of wives, while those of husbands were taken for granted. She felt that William had "a fear—which he—alas—has too much reason to indulge—of the happiness of married life" for Isabella. So did she, as she informed Hooker:

> I have—for some moments in looking at the families of some even of my brothers and sisters—felt misgivings—many and great—but then—I feel that there is a radical defect in their plan—one which can be avoided—they did not start rightly—they did not each in the commencement of married life—and before it in the freshness of affection—resolve upon self-denial—self-sacrifice—a consideration of the other's feelings as much as their own—besides this—naturally and palpably unsuitable dispositions, have in the case before me unfitted the individuals for their happiness or usefulness in this world—Dearest can it be so

with us—I cannot believe it possible—if I did I would love you as a brother—a friend—but never otherwise—if I thot my married life would be such as I have seen established in my own family—I never could bring myself to fulfill an engagement, otherwise delightful.

Hooker's response to all that must have been satisfactory. But he got another jolt almost at the altar when Isabella protested the unfairness of the marriage vows that asked the woman but not the man to promise obedience. Isabella was just warming up to the subject, as her husband would soon discover. Few clients dropped by the office of the newly minted lawyer, and for the first year or so of their marriage Isabella would sit there and knit or sew while John continued his education—and hers—by reading the law aloud. When she discovered during the reading of Blackstone's *Commentaries* what little standing wives had in the eyes of the law—even whipping was considered permissible in some instances—she was incensed. This knowledge convinced her that she had been right in talking him into an agreement during their engagement that "if either of us found we had made a mistake we were at liberty to choose elsewhere"—an agreement that her more conventional family and friends found shocking.

One of Roxana's sons who might have approved any arrangement favorable to Isabella would be her pen pal Charles, who so doted on her beauty that he once wrote her: "I presume Mary and Kate and Hatty will all dawn upon our darkness; a perfect constellation of everything but—beauty—Nature could not afford much more than was necessary to complete one specimen as yourself, Bell . . . and that is why the rest are so 'expressive' but 'plain.'" By the time of Isabella's wedding, Charles had given up on his romantic dreams, married Sarah Coffin, a faithful girlfriend from college days in New England, fathered a child, and returned to the fold as an all-around assistant at and music director of Henry Ward's Indianapolis church. Playing the organ himself and conducting the choir, Charles made such impressive music, both sacred and classical, that the church earned a statewide reputation as a cultural as well as a religious center. Although not yet blessed with a conversion that he considered essential to becoming a minister, Charles did feel qualified to relieve Henry Ward of the job of running the Sunday school. The addition of Charles to the church staff was especially appreciated by adolescent girls in the congregation, two of whom—Julia Merrill and Betty Bates—already had an undisguised crush on their pastor. Charles was handsomer than his brother, and his artistic leanings along with rather dark rumors of a runaway past made him an equally romantic figure in the girls' eyes.

In the early 1840s, while the careers of most young Beechers were just beginning to show promise, the oldest sibling, Catharine, arrived full blown on the national scene with the publication of a book titled *Treatise on Domestic Economy*. Since Catharine was the only one of the adult Beechers who remained unmarried and without a home of her own, there was an element of irony in her achieving instant fame by telling other women how to run their households. But, in fact, it was her homelessness that gave her the insight and knowledge to write a book of such sound common sense and usefulness to her audience of homemakers that it was running through printing after printing, year after year. Having given up her school, Catharine had had the time, interest, and incentive to spend long visits in the homes of friends and siblings throughout the Midwest and New England. In that process she observed and analyzed the practical aspects of different styles of homemaking, much as sister Isabella had done with the psychological aspects of marriages. Even as she wandered about, Catharine considered a room in her father's Walnut Hills house as home base. But in 1842 she wrote an angry letter to her then stepmother Lydia that indicated a serious rift between them. She warned that it could become a public matter and an embarrassment to Lyman if word got around that she and Aunt Esther—who also was "making herself scarce"—were not made welcome in Walnut Hills, as they always had been in the past. Whether the tension in his household had anything to do with it or not, Lyman was most enthusiastic in supporting Catharine's plan for the summer of 1843. She would set out in her own buggy for a leisurely trip eastward to visit relatives and friends and try to generate enthusiasm and funds for an organization to recruit teachers for new western schools.

Catharine headed for Chillicothe, Ohio, where George had alighted after a third nervous breakdown had prompted him to leave Rochester and find a smaller, quieter parish to tend. There was a manic-depressive streak in all of the Beechers, but it was proving to be more debilitating in George than in most of the others. When manic, he could be the best of company, as he had been during the family's first trying trip West. He was brilliant and burned far too brightly for his own good. A perfectionist, he was constantly disappointed by his own performance as a soul saver, and his efforts to do more and better—and especially to *be better*—would end in periods when he could barely function. He was given to strong convictions, and it was typical of his nature to become the first abolitionist in the Beecher family. Like all Beecher men, he did find some relief in exercising and outdoor activities such as hunting, fishing, and gardening. One of the reasons why Catharine set out for Chillicothe that summer was George's contribution to a family circular letter: "DEAR BROTH-ERS AND SISTERS, all hail!—I only wish I had you all here, and every room in my house stowed full. When, think you, Henry and Charles, shall I see your faces here? Can you not come, one or both, this summer? Our house is completed, except a little painting, and will be ready for everybody that will come in two weeks, so make haste!"

What happened after Catharine's arrival in Chillicothe on a hot summer evening is graphically detailed in Harriet's circular letter to the family dated July 4, 1843. It is a long letter, hastily written and full of emotion of the moment, that reveals Harriet's continuing personal strug-gle with death and doubt. But the family's shared, sustaining faith, the binding and motivating force on which she relied to turn tragedy into tri-umph for them all, comes through in excerpts from Harriet's report:

Dear Brothers & Sisters all:

In an hour of deep sorrow, I turn to you that I may mingle my grief with yours—a heavy blow has fallen upon us—one of our number has been in a moment taken from our eyes—never on earth to be restored to us—Our dear brother George is now no longer a chevalier among us—his fight is over—& blessed be God, that we may say with confidant hope, his crown is won— Sister Catharine arrived at Chillicothe on Friday evening just before family prayers, & found all in unusual health & prosper-ity—George had come in from his Friday lecture and seemed in very cheerful spirits—The next morning July 1 he arose before light & went to market & brought home his marketing & about breakfast time he was missing—The servant went into the garden to seek him & found him lying on the ground with his double barreled gun in his hand—apparently the charge had passed through his cheek & up through the top of his head which was shattered—This all that any one knows of the circumstances & manner of his death—It is supposed that he fired one barrel on the birds that were disturbing his trees & that after scattering the flock he was preparing to recharge the barrel & was blowing the smoke out for that purpose when some accident sprung the lock of the other barrel—It is all conjecture however—It is only evi-dent from the wound that death must have been as instantaneous as lightning—It is very remarkable that the evening before George had in his meeting dealt very particularly on the shortness of life & stated that for some unaccountable reason the feeling was strong in his own mind that he had but a short time to live—the last words that many of his church ever heard him speak. . . .

Poor Sarah—the first that she saw of him that morning was his lifeless bleeding form on the sofa—I am told that she seemed entirely stunned—kneeling beside him with his hand in hers in heartless despair till she was at last forcibly carried into another room—The intelligence was immediately spread—The supreme court then in session held a recess and passed resolutions of sympathy—A coroner's inquest was held—at the suggestion of some of his friends—& early in the afternoon funeral services were attended in his church. . . . I need not say amid mourning—About five the same after noon Catharine & Sarah, attended by ten or twelve of George's most intimate friends & church members, started to convey the body to Putnam designing to travel all night—These particulars were brought by a Mr. Douglas of Chillicothe, a friend of George's tho not connected with his society—they are all we have yet received—Catharine is I suppose unable to write, & will be, perhaps, for some time—I am very apprehensive for the effect both on her & Sarah—whether in her present state of health she Sarah will be able to rise under such a stroke is to me doubtful—Mr. Douglas told us that George had just got delightfully settled in his new house & his garden, on which he has worked very hard this year in beautiful order—and now house & garden—all are deserted—I presume to be inhabited by the family no more—for I think Sarah probably will never feel a wish to return to them—perhaps it will pass into the hands of strangers—

Poor Sarah will feel doubly desolate in returning to her home, when more than ever she will feel the want of a mother—It seemed providential that Catharine should have got there just in time to be with her. . . . The poor girl has no father or mother & no one among her uncles at Putnam who can give her that christian consolation—you must write to her my dear brothers and sisters all of you—I dreamed last night that Henry and I were in Putnam doing what we could to alleviate her distress—I trust Father will come home that way for he now, better than any man living, could console & sympathize with her—Is there any of us . . . prepared for such a parting—without a moment of warn- ing—a word of commission—a sign—a look—a farewell—Why is it when we know that our Redeemer liveth and believe truly that the departed one shall rise again, that even now he is with the glorified spirit of our mother in heaven that I can only weep and mourn & feel so sick at heart—I thought I knew the entire emptiness of this world & why is it so distressing to see one more proof of what I knew before! . . .

For what then shall I turn to you my brothers!—Are your homes more secure than the one that has just been swept away— I have seen you but a few weeks since living, cheerful, strong & full of life—one day—& all may be over—where your pleasant mailings invited me so often to turn in thought & dwell on them in hope and love, may be only a blank desert, from which every green thing has withered—I fear we have too much in this world to love—& that we love it too well—How precious have been the gifts of the Lord unto us—what a father!—and he still lives— how many pleasant hours have we brothers & sisters spent together!— and still hoped to spend—We have seen death entering other families & clothing them in mourning, but he has not entered our dwelling—One after another has grown to manhood & woman- hood and developed talents for usefulness with which we have re- joiced—& now the stroke that has fallen upon others has reached us—Our circle has begun to break up—who shall say where it shall stop?

Nothing is firm but Christ—In Him united, we cannot die for has he not said so? He that believeth in me tho he were dead yet shall he live & whoso liveth and believeth in me shall never die!—He is not dead but sleepeth—The weapons of his warfare, the scene of his service are only changed—but "within the veil"—mysterious thrilling expression!—he has joined the great company of those who are "ministering spirits sent forth to min- ister to those who shall be heirs of salvation"—He shall not return to us but is it not better for us to return to him—If he has left desolate an earthly house where he had hoped from time to time to have received us still have we not an invitation to join him in a house with many mansions where our Father, our Brother, our Redeemer, will unite us—Oh that I could fully feel this & that this illusion which makes it seem so much better to hold communion in the flesh might be dispelled! For two or three years past I have noticed the increasing earnestness & devotion with which George has made it an object to subdue himself entirely to Christ—He has striven not as one who beateth the air, & now—*it is done*—perfection is won, sin hath no more dominion over him.

Dear Brother James, let this voice call you once more to give yourself unto God—Get about it as you would anything else— read, pray, enquire your duty. Resolve to do it & God will not be wanting on his part—Brothers all—how may this loss be made up except by our so improving it that it may be our gain—Dear brothers, sisters, who is to be called next?—Are we ready—Have we put on the Lord Jesus? Are we all waiting with our lamps burning—I could write more for my heart is full—Let us pray for each other—let us draw closer the bonds of love—& pray also for our Father that the Lord may deal gently with him in this new trial—With dearest love, I am your affectionate sister H.

Except for Catharine, Lyman and his nine other living children were as shocked and aggrieved as Harriet when the news about George reached them at different times and in different places. Henry Ward was particularly disturbed by the possibility of suicide—held to be a sin in most interpretations of the Christian canon—until the coroner came up with a ruling of accidental death and his own recollection confirmed Harriet's account of George's careless habit of blowing the smoke away from a spent barrel. Whatever Henry Ward was able to talk himself into believing, the preponderance of evidence when the case was more fully examined weighed heavily on the side of suicide, as Harriet had clearly indicated. If any other Beecher understood what really went on out there in George's orchard that morning, it would have been Catharine. George's struggle for perfection, his frustrating efforts to come to terms with Lyman's harsh doctrine, his bouts of depression evoked bitter memories of her own similar experiences, and his end was too close to what could have been hers for comfort. Her way of handling her own feelings was to go through all of George's papers, as she had done with those of Professor Fisher, and cull out all the positive material that would make it impossible for any God worthy of belief to consign George to a sinner's fate. In this case, the professionalism that Catharine had developed over the years enabled her to put the material into a memorial publication, *The Biographical Remains of Rev. George Beecher*, which emphasized George's efforts to overcome illnesses and failures so that his story would "awaken hope and encouragement in all who, amid similar embarrassments, are pressing forward to the mark for the prize of their high calling."

Understandably, Lyman was devastated by the news of George's death, but he overlooked the implications of a possible suicide and expressed confidence that his son, who "was ripening fast in holiness," was "with his mother, the glorified in heaven." That same year, as if in compensation for the loss of George, Lyman got the good news from Henry Ward that Charles had undergone a conversion during a revival and was "safe" and ready to preach. Since Henry Ward's church could not afford to pay Charles for the services he was rendering, this last of Roxana's sons to comply with her deathbed wish was struggling to get along on handouts from more affluent siblings and fees for music lessons. Thus when Samuel Merrill told Henry Ward that there was an Old School Presbyterian church in Fort Wayne, Indiana, in which a number of members were unhappy, Henry Ward seized on what he saw as an opportunity for Charles. Going to Fort Wayne himself, he recruited enough of the disgruntled members— sixteen women and three men—to form a new church, with Charles as its pastor. As in Henry Ward's own beginning, Charles would get help from the Home Missionary Society. Converted or not, Charles was far from orthodox—or "rather original," as he admitted—and soon was in trouble for being "anything but sound in faith." An alarmed Henry Ward warned him by letter to stick to "mouldy orthodoxy" until he had won over his flock, and Lyman hastened to be present at Charles's ordination to give him the same advice in the flesh. His flare for the dramatic not extinguished by age, seventy-year-old Lyman arrived in Fort Wayne on a frothing steed spattered with mud after a twenty-hour ride over wilderness roads in order not to travel on the Sabbath. Undoubtedly that effort gave weight to his message, and Charles took it to heart enough to pacify his critics.

The mid-1840s were uneasy years for the nation and most of the Beechers. In 1844 a little-known southern politician, James K. Polk, who earned the dubious distinction of being the first "dark horse" candidate for the presidency, won the Democratic nomination—largely because Martin Van Buren, on the comeback trail, opposed the annexation of Texas— and then won the election, largely because the vote for the Whig candidate, the nation's most famous politician, Henry Clay, was split by the abolitionist James G. Birney, running on the Liberty Party ticket. Polk favored annexation of Texas, California, and Oregon, and a newspaperman coined the phrase "manifest destiny" to describe this policy of expansion.

Because he had pledged to serve only one term, Polk moved at once to launch the military maneuvers and skirmishes on the Mexican border that would lead to war, and he supported the efforts of John C. Frémont and North American settlers to wrest California from Mexican hands. Meanwhile, Secretary of State James Buchanan negotiated with England for a favorable border in the Oregon region. Although supported by most Americans, expansion exacerbated the differences between North and South over the future of slavery. As slavery had contributed to a rift in the Presbyterian Church, it caused both the Baptists and the Methodists to break apart into northern and southern conferences in these years. In New England, the cradle of Puritanism, a newly born secular culture more threatening to orthodoxy than the stain of slavery was stirring. Through their writings and lectures on the lyceum circuit, Ralph Waldo Emerson and his fellow Transcendentalists such as Margaret Fuller, Bronson Alcott, Nathaniel Hawthorne, and Henry David Thoreau were spreading a message of high-minded, rational thinking on both personal and public morality, in competition with the pulpit. Immigration was swelling the ranks of the Roman Catholics and Jews, and dissident groups such as Mormons and Shakers and members of a number of utopian communities were thriving.

With the rapid changes in the culture and composition of the society around them, it is understandable that the younger the Beecher, the more trouble he or she had with reconciling life experiences with the doctrinaire view of their dynamic father. Thomas seems to have developed his doubts and disagreements after an early conversion rather than the other way around, as in the case of Charles. No romantic, Tom had an affinity for mechanics and science instead of literature and theology, and a talent for working with his hands equal to Charles's talent for performing music. Tom also had a sharp eye for people's pretensions, as revealed in a letter dated December 15, 1843, from Walnut Hills to Isabella:

> Yesterday was thanksgiving & we had a sermon from father in the second Church & a dinner from mother in the back parlor, both of them first rate in their way. We had 16 at the table which was well supplied & to which we did justice I think, about according to desert. The only practical effect I perceived was that we were wondrous witty when we begun—& very good natured when we got done—which test I esteem an experimentum crucis of a good dinner. Notwithstanding that it is thanksgiving season

we have much illness here & in town. Harriet is just getting over an attack of the quinsey which still requires the "sober muffler" for the chin . . . while Mr. Stowe has just relapsed into a bad cold, which he would fain make us esteem a serious illness. . . . Our own particular family are all well as usual. Catharine is weak & nervous—& requiring much attention, she walks on crutches still & I suppose will for some time to come. Margaret is a little ailing as all young ladies are, nowadays, & Joe is sick every morning about getting up time; neither of their complaints are very alarming. . . . Father . . . seems well & cheerful & as vigorously funny & lively as I ever knew him to be. He fiddles & writes & lectures. . . . I got a letter from Charles today, he is just recovering from a long attack (8 weeks) of billious fever, which has left him little flesh & much appetite. . . . Eunice's health is as poor as usual: i.e., so poor that she "can't live long" & yet so good, that she is out washing—ironing, drawing water, blacking boots— darning socks &c. She is to me, a standing wonder both mentally & physically. Sarah Coffin is a real treasure for Charles & Jim— words cannot tell her worth, & as for Jim himself—you may rest contented, notwithstanding his pathetic letter to you, over which I laughed heartily, when I read it. He is contented, as much as a boy can be, who longs continually for change; he gets along well with his studies & loves his brothers warmly, save when duty forces them to cross him. I have said but little about myself for as yet I have neither definite plans nor definite views—nor definite compensations for the present. I am at present just earning my board & clothes by constant & tedious labor, of a kind, not at all consonant with my tastes. So I am bluey—& dispondent very often & I feel as tho' such a useless being—& lazy withal—had better not be, than be; now this feeling instead of inspiring resolution to study & work does in my case do nothing but weigh me down with shame at my state.

When this letter was written, Tom was at home writing six hours a day for his father and spending another two hours hearing his stepbrother Joe Jackson recite. He had finished a disillusioning period as a student in brother Edward's Illinois College. Elated at first by the opportunity to be with this older, much-admired brother, Tom soon found Edward's obsession with theological questions—Edward was then deeply involved in writing a book to elucidate a new theory of creation growing out of wrestling with doubts about original sin—and prissy attitudes about proper behavior—Edward, acting as president, once suspended Tom from college for unspecified "disorders tending to disturb the worship of God in chapel"—so incomprehensible and intolerable that he wrote: "I say without fear or hesitation that if religion were to make *me* another *Edward*— I say God deliver me from being pious." From observations within the church and even his own family, he doubted the value of religion itself— "a system whose lights and glory appear to me so slim and faulty." Only the times he spent in Indianapolis with Henry Ward kept Tom from giving up on the faith altogether. This older brother chopped even less of the straw of theology into his sermon mixture than he had in Lawrenceburg, and out of the pulpit he carried on a vigorous life in which he and Tom "raised sweet potatoes weighing five pounds each, banked up celery till it was nearly three feet tall, white and crisp, picked blackberries as big as my thumb; and hunted squirrels, rabbits and smaller game." If there was one other experience of future value that Tom took away from his college years, it was acquaintance with a young Illinois lawyer named Abraham Lincoln. As he would tell it later, "Abraham Lincoln wasn't considered good enough to associate with a Beecher in those days, but I took a chance, and it didn't hurt me."

In the Beecher mind, Lincoln would have been a cut above the people with whom James, the youngest Beecher, associated. James was the only one who could really be called "wild," the only one standing in need of prayer, according to Harriet's letter about George's death. To see that he kept better company may have been one of the reasons why he was also shipped off to Indianapolis to spend time in the accommodating house that Henry Ward and Eunice built with some money from her father's estate. They were still poor enough or thrifty enough that Henry Ward felt he had to paint it himself, and he surrounded it with gardens that he personally tended. Throughout the mid-1840s, the Henry Ward Beecher home became a lively center for Bullards as well as Beechers. One brother, Dr. Robert Bullard and his family, moved up from New Orleans, where they had befriended Charles, to establish a practice, and another brother, Oliver, moved into the Beecher household. Guests found themselves in the house of a man who was more than a preacher; he was a personage. His *Seven Lectures to Young Men*, a book made up of talks he gave on how to avoid vividly described moral pitfalls such as gambling, drunkenness, and prostitution, had started selling well across the country. As unpaid editor of the *Indiana Farmer and Gardener*, he was an early environmentalist whose articles were reprinted in newspapers everywhere, including Horace Greeley's new *New York Herald Tribune*.

One guest who was particularly grateful for Henry Ward's hospitality was sister Harriet, who spent a month in his Indianapolis home in the summer of 1844. Harriet and Calvin were entering a period in their lives when brother Tom's acute observation that she suffered from real illnesses while Calvin enjoyed pretended ones would plague them to the point of threatening their marriage. At Henry Ward's house Harriet enjoyed days so quiet that she could "hear the clock tick" and so free of required activity that all she had to do was sit down to meals on time. She and Henry Ward talked long into the nights about everything under the sun, including the new fad of mesmerism, which he demonstrated to her delight by putting her into a trance several times. Calvin must have wondered whether she was being serious or playful when she wrote home that she was thinking of breaking up their "connection" and opening a school in Indianapolis. She reported that she was sick of the "boarding business," which was "too noisy & disquieting & harassing," and added, "I have forgotten almost the faces of my children—all the perplexing details of home, and almost that I am a married woman."

But, of course, Harriet did go home, and within days of her arrival in Cincinnati was writing back to Henry Ward a litany of the vexations she had encountered. One of her boarders, "a Spanish lady," gave birth in her house without benefit of a physician. A neighboring faculty wife acted as "accoucheur" and Harriet as head nurse. The festering resentment between Catharine and their stepmother had reached a point where Lydia told Lyman that she would never again live under the same roof with Catharine. When Lyman came to Harriet for advice, she gave it to him: "If this woman were *my wife!* I would say to her, 'Madam, it is *indispensable* that my daughter sick & helpless should find a home with me.' Should she reply—'Then *I* will leave'—I should answer, 'I am sorry if you feel it necessary—but I impose no restraint—you are free to go—& to return again as soon as you can bring your mind to do so.'" Lyman must have taken that advice, or some measure of it, since Catharine continued working out of Walnut Hills in forming her national organization to recruit teachers, enlisting Calvin as its titular head without pay and dragooning young Tom to be her front man and speak for her on a fund-raising tour.

Meanwhile, things went from bad to worse in the Stowe household. On June 16, 1845, Harriet described her life and her feelings about it to Calvin, who was away on a short trip:

> It is a dark, sloppy, rainy, muddy, disagreeable day, and I have been working hard (for me) all day in the kitchen, washing dishes, looking into closets, and seeing a great deal of that dark

side of domestic life which a housekeeper may who will investi-gate too curiously into minutiae in warm, damp weather, espe-cially after a girl who keeps all clean on the *outside* of cup and platter, and is very apt to make good the rest of the test in the *inside* of things.

I am sick of the smell of sour milk, and sour meat, and sour everything, and then the clothes *will* not dry, and no wet thing does, and everything smells mouldy, and altogether I feel as if I never wanted to eat again.

Your letter, which was neither sour nor mouldy, formed a very agreeable contrast to all these things, the more so for being unexpected. I am much obliged to you for it. As to my health, it gives me very little solicitude, although I am bad enough and daily grow worse, I feel no life, no energy, no appetite, or rather a growing distaste for food; in fact, I am becoming quite ethereal. Upon reflection, I perceive that it pleases my Father to keep me in the fire, for my whole situation is excessively harassing and painful. I suffer with sensible distress in the brain, as I have done more or less since my sickness last winter, a distress which some days takes from me all power of planning or executing anything, and you know that, except this poor head, my unfortunate house-hold has no mainspring, for nobody feels any kind of responsibil-ity to do a thing in time, place, or manner, except as I oversee it.

Georgiana is so excessively weak, nervous, cross, and fretful, night and day, that she takes all of Anna's strength and time with her, and then the children are, like other little sons and daugh-ters of Adam, full of all kinds of absurdity and folly.

When the brain gives out, as mine often does, and one can-not think or remember anything, then what is to be done? All common fatigue, sickness, and exhaustion is nothing to this dis-tress. Yet do I rejoice in my God and know in whom I believe, and only pray that the fire may consume the dross; as to the gold, that is imperishable. No evil can happen to me, so I fear nothing for the future and only suffer in the present tense.

Calvin was often away, raising funds for Lane or Catharine's program. Despite his devotion to intellectual pursuits and hypochondria, Calvin was a man of strong physical appetites, which he acknowledged in one of his letters to Harriet. After passing along to her what would seem to be unnecessary detail about prominent ministers in the East who were guilty of drunkenness and/or lechery, he wrote, "Bless the Lord that with all my strong relish for brandy and wine, and all my indescribable admiration and most overflowing delight in handsome young ladies, no offenses of this kind have yet been written down against me." Since Henry Ward also had passed along to her gossip about similar ministerial transgressions in Indiana, Harriet informed Calvin that she worried about whether "the Great Enemy had prevailed" against any of her brothers or him, adding, "Something seemed to ask: Is your husband any better *seeming* than so-and-so." Then she gave him some advice:

> What terrible temptations lie in the way of your sex—till now I never realized it—for tho' I did love you with an almost *insane* love before I married you I never knew yet or felt the pulsation which showed me that I could be tempted in that way—there never was a moment when I felt any thing by which you could have drawn me astray—for I loved you as I now love God—and I can conceive of no higher love—and as I have no passion—I have no jealousy—the most beautiful woman in the world could not make me jealous so long as she only *dazzled the senses*—but still my dear, you must not wonder if I want to warn you not to look or *think* too freely on womankind—if your sex would guard against the outerworks of *thought*, you would never fall.

As to her own thoughts, Harriet told Calvin that she had been reading some suggestive French novels, but they could not hurt her, since she was sick. Her claim to be passionless is to be doubted in view of her admission in one of the letters that there were times when "the old fountain rises again, warm, fresh, and full," and in view of the fact that she became pregnant almost immediately after every separation. Calvin acknowledged that his "every desire" was satisfied when he was with her. The only safe and sanctioned way of avoiding pregnancy in Beecher circles was abstinence, which may account for the many recorded separations between spouses during childbearing years. The general malaise that Harriet complained about in her letter of June 1845 did not go away. When a gift of money arrived from strangers who had heard that there was sickness in the Stowe family, Calvin insisted on using it to send Harriet to Dr. Wesselhoeft's water-cure establishment in Brattleboro, Vermont. She found the experience such a refreshing change from her harried home life that she stayed for eleven months, and her sisters Catharine and Mary joined her for part of that time.

Writing to Calvin, Harriet claimed that her only motive in staying away so long was to become a healthier and better wife and mother. Her description of a typical day at the cure is supportive of that claim:

The daily course I go through presupposes a degree of vigor beyond anything I ever had before. For this week, I have gone before breakfast to the wave-bath and let all the waves and billows roll over me till every limb ached with cold, and my hands would scarcely have feeling enough to dress me. After that I have walked till I was warm, and come home to breakfast with such an appetite! Brown bread and milk are luxuries indeed, and the only fear is that I may eat too much. At eleven comes my douche, to which I have walked in a driving rain for the last two days, and after it walked in the rain again till I was warm. (The umbrella you gave me at Natick answers finely, as well as if it were a silk one.) After dinner I roll ninepins or walk till four, then sitz-bath, and another walk till six.

Although their letters contained avowals of love, they could be almost cruelly critical of each other's faults. At one point Harriet chided Calvin for being "nervous, anxious, fretful and apprehensive of poverty" instead of trusting in Christ. "If you had studied Christ with half the energy that you have studied Luther—if you were as eager for daily inter-course with him as to devour the daily newspaper—if you loved him as much as you loved your study and your books, then would he be formed in you, the hope of glory," she wrote. At another time, exasperated with what she called his "hypo," she resorted to grim humor: "I received your most melancholy effusion, and I am sorry to find it's just so. I entirely agree and sympathize. Why didn't you engage the two tombstones—one for you and one for me?" Calvin could give as good as he got. He once presented Harriet with an invidious comparison of their natures. His anx-iety came from thoughtful and justified concern about the future, while she was foolishly and carelessly optimistic and trusting. He would lose his temper easily, but he would get over it quickly; she would brood silently and long about an offense. He was neat and she was sloppy; he would always fold the newspaper while reading it, for instance, but she would send it "sprawling on the floor."

This sort of carping had no lasting effect on their relationship. In the proper number of months after her return home, Harriet gave birth to their sixth child and third son, Samuel Charles. Soon after that, it was Calvin's turn to seek relief from household cares. He took himself off to

Brattleboro where, rather significantly, he would spend fifteen months. Writing to her school friend after he had gone, Harriet reported, "Well, Georgy, I am thirty-seven years old! I am glad of it. I like to grow old and have six children and cares endless. I wish you could see me with my flock all around me. They sum up my cares and were they gone I should ask myself, What now remains to be done? They are my work, over which I fear and tremble."

While the Stowes were trading places between home and health spa, most of their siblings were on the move as well. Rather fittingly, the first of them to set out on what was turning out to be an aborted mission to win the West was the first to turn back East. Tired of the administrative duties and fund-raising travel for the college and eager to get on with the book that he hoped would forever change Christianity, Edward accepted a call to the Salem Street Church in Boston in 1844. In the next year, the troublesome James was sent East to Dartmouth College, and the restless Tom gave up on his dream of becoming some sort of mechanic and decided to try Yale Divinity School. Catharine, the homeless, launched herself off on a peripatetic lifestyle of spending long stays in the homes of acquaintances and family all over the Midwest and Northeast while pursuing her campaign for women's education and writing her books. William, the unlucky, by now burdened with six children, was forced by disgruntled parishioners to resign his thousand-dollar-a-year sinecure in Batavia in 1844 and take on a smaller church that his father found for him in Toledo, Ohio, at eight hundred a year. In Hartford, the settled ladies Mary and Isabella were busy bearing, rearing, and even burying children, including Isabella's first, a boy.

In those mid-1840s, Henry Ward Beecher was almost too busy in the present to think about the future. In addition to presiding over a congregation that had grown from thirty-three to nearly three hundred and the Indiana Horticultural Society, he was deeply involved in the creation of the Indianapolis Benevolent Society, an institute for the deaf and mute, a school for the blind, a temperance society, and the public school system. He was constantly experimenting with new preaching techniques. One of these, which he called "taking aim," came to him after reflecting on the way the apostles preached. Instead of starting from some point in theology or some biblical text, he would talk about things that he and his audience had in common. In his first effort to take aim, he "sketched out the things we all know, and in that way I went through my 'you all knows' until I had about forty of them. When I had got through that, I turned round and brought it to bear upon them with all my might, and there were seventeen awakened under that sermon. I never felt so triumphant in my life. I cried all the way home. I said to myself, 'Now I know how to preach.'"

While learning how to preach, Henry Ward also was experimenting with what to preach. He was on safe ground when advising young men about personal morality, but he knew that he would be skating on very thin ice in dealing with questions of public morality such as slavery when one of his own elders told him, "If an Abolitionist comes here I will head a mob to put him down." In view of the stands his brothers had taken and his own gut conviction, Henry Ward knew that he could not ignore this evil and live with himself, and yet he felt that he would jeopardize the job he needed to support his family and the opportunity he had to change minds if he alienated his audience by taking an extreme position. So he would use historical or biblical events such as a father ransoming his son from the hands of Algerian pirates or the Israelites enslaved in Egypt as metaphors for American slavery, and trust his listeners to make the connection. Henry Ward remembered this strategy later in life when instructing young preachers and used fishing as a metaphor in describing it:

> You may go down to the brook under the willows and angle for trout that everybody has been trying to catch, but in vain. You go splashing and tearing along, throwing in your line, pole and all. Do you think you can catch them that way? No, indeed, you must begin afar off and quietly, if need be drawing yourself along on the grass and perhaps even on your belly, until you come where through the quivering leaves you see the flash of the sun, and then slowly and gently you throw your line so that the fly on its end falls as light as gossamer upon the placid surface of the brook. The trout will think, "That is not a bait thrown to catch me: there is nobody there," and rises to the fly, takes it,—and you take him.

In 1847, Henry Ward Beecher's style and restraint caught a much larger fish than he could then have imagined. Almost as far east as it was possible to go, in the city of Brooklyn, New York, three substantial citizens—David Hale, Henry C. Bowen, and John T. Howard—decided that the thirty-nine churches that caused their community to be known as "the city of churches" weren't enough—or, perhaps, that the existence of so many churches was proof of a rich religious soil that would nourish any new seed. But the more probable motive seems more in keeping with the go-getting times of an expanding nation just recovering from a depression and a successful war. Thriving businessmen all, the trio learned of a church property on Cranberry Street for sale and snapped it up. The property was not only a bargain as to purchase but also presumably forever, in that it was tax-free. When a new congregation was formed to replace the one that had melted away under the heat of the antislavery preaching of the old Reverend Samuel Cox, the congregation could rent the property from the owners on funds raised from pew sales for Sunday services and ticket sales for weekday lectures. To secure their investment, Hale, Bowen, and Howard wanted to find a crowd-pleasing preacher to keep the pews in demand. As in all events that come to be called providential, there was an unsuspected agent involved in the form of a New York acquaintance of Bowen's, William T. Cutler, who came back from a business trip to Indianapolis singing the praises of a minister who had already successfully started two churches at age thirty-four, was an eloquent speaker, and bore one of the most famous names in Protestantism—Beecher.

When Henry Ward got an invitation to come to New York, all expenses paid for him and his family, to address the annual meeting of the Home Missionary Society and preach at a fledgling church in Brooklyn, he was under no illusions as to the origins and purpose of the offer. He was also ready for a move to almost anywhere. Never high, Eunice's health and spirits were sinking so fast and so low that he could no longer treat her complaints lightly. Whether her illnesses were real or imagined, as his sensitive brother Tom and most of his congregation believed, the blow to her spirit delivered by the death of their fifteen-month-old son Georgie in March 1846 was not to be disputed. Henry Ward reported to Harriet, "Our people did not know *how* to sympathize. Few came while he lived; fewer yet when, on a bleak March day, we bore him through the storm, and, standing in the snow, we laid his beautiful form in his cold, white grave. Eunice was heart-broken. My home was a fountain of anguish." In her own report to Harriet, Eunice wrote, "I think you would have some trouble to recognize your sister in the thin-faced, grey-headed, toothless old woman you would find here." The sad fact reflected in Henry Ward's letter is that the congregation did not like Eunice, and the feeling was mutual. Apparently there was not much warmth involved in the admiration his congregation accorded Henry Ward either; as one of them put it, he was not "a pastor at all—only a brilliant preacher." There was substance to Eunice's later fictional account of congregational penny-pinching. In eight years the congregation had never raised Henry Ward's eight-hundred-dollar annual salary, and in some of those years even that amount was not paid—like father, like son. As a result, the Beechers were more than a year's income in debt, with no reasonable hope of paying it off.

Shrewdly, and doubtless with Edward's aid, Henry Ward arranged for appearances in Boston while he was in the East. His plan worked well. His two sermons in the New York area not only impressed the audiences but also were reported in the lay press, and his Boston performances resulted in a call to be assistant pastor at one of the city's established churches. Back in Indianapolis, he weighed two competing offers for months while Bowen bombarded him with letters—thirty in all—containing such gushy phrases as "you are our first love, the desire of our hearts." At least to Eunice, the more appealing sections of those letters guaranteed the pastor a salary of twelve hundred dollars a year, enough up-front money to clear his debts and a promise of future raises. By August, Beecher accepted the offer from what was to be called the Plymouth Church in Brooklyn, told his congregation that he leaving for the sake of his wife's health, and started settling his affairs and packing up. He sent his family on ahead and picked an October night for his own departure when nobody in Indianapolis would be aware of it. It was the day on which the first train reached the city, and there was an all-day celebration in and around the station—speeches, short sample train rides, refreshments. By nightfall, when Henry Ward showed up to be the railroad's first paying eastbound passenger, he was all alone—or almost all alone. Lying in wait to give him a sentimental good-bye were the two pretty young women—Betty Bates and Julia Merrill—whom he had once chaperoned on a long trip East and who had made of him a romantic idol ever since. For Henry Ward the event was neither historic nor romantic: "The car was no car at all—a mere ex tempore wood box and even sometimes used for hogs when without seats, but with seats, for men—of which class I (ah! me miserable!) happened to be one," he wrote. "At eleven o'clock I arrived in Madison not over proud of the glory of riding the first train from Indianapolis."

One person who might have been as happy to learn that Henry Ward was moving East as the Indianapolis girls were sad to see him go was brother Tom. By then, having found the theology at Yale as unappealing as that in brother Edward's house, Tom was pursuing a teaching career as principal of a high school in Hartford. Teaching was more appealing than preaching to Tom's practical mind. Like Catharine, he could see students improve in manners, skills, intellect, and even morals as a result of good teaching, but the salvation that was supposed to be the purpose of preaching in the austere versions of organized religion to which he had been subjected still left him cold. In Philadelphia, where he taught briefly to learn the trade, he found solace in an Episcopal church from the beauty of the ritual and music that at least stirred his senses. Learning of this, Lyman reluctantly gave Tom's experiment with Episcopalianism rather weak approval on the grounds that it had been "his mother's" denomination, quite forgetting, as he often did, that Tom's mother had been Harriet Porter and not the sainted Roxana Foote. Tom knew that the slight was unintended, but it was the sort of thing that made him and his blood brother and sister feel that they might not be true Beechers. Nevertheless, Tom loved his father, despite or because of his character quirks, and could not quite give up on hoping to please the old man by encountering some experience that would convince him to enter the ministry. In Hartford he was encouraged to find the city's leading minister, Horace Bushnell, rejecting the harsh doctrines of Calvinism to concentrate on Christian love and good works, much in the mode of brother Henry Ward and with the same show of independence from organizational strictures and structures. But the moving force in Tom's life was above all the example of Henry Ward, now enlarged and made more accessible by his call to Brooklyn. "I am so filled and led captive by an association with you that it passeth my love to woman," Tom wrote Henry Ward at about this time. "It is not because of *yourself* that I so love. But the common love we bear to Christ."

Henry Ward's presence in the East would also turn out to be a godsend for Tom's younger brother James, who was going through his own unsettling times. As he grew to manhood, James shared with his blood siblings the good looks passed down to them by Harriet Porter; he also inherited more than his share of her easily wounded spirit. Farther removed than his sister and brother from the influence of an aging and preoccupied father and, in effect, truly motherless from age seven, James had to find his own place in the scheme of things. He had shown early signs of rebellion in the company he kept in Cincinnati, and he went all out when he reached Dartmouth. How wild he actually was is questionable, although it is alleged that he indulged in ardent spirits and went absent without leave to Boston with equally wild friends. The president of Dartmouth informed Lyman that this, his last son, was rude and "impatient of discipline." Echoes of Tom's undergraduate days at Illinois sound through a letter that James wrote to his father in the fall of 1845:

My dear father
    You have doubtless on the arrival of this received another letter from the faculty with a second *supply of charges against me* such as *juggling keys in church, scraping &c* So far as the keys are

concerned I say to you as I have said to the faculty that I was entirely unconscious of having them in my hand & knew nothing of it till Prest Lord sent for me immediately after morning service. Upon entering the study I was struck with the manner of his address & was *considerably provoked* when he came out with his *grave charge*. He said—I sent for you Beecher on account of the noise & disturbance which you were the author of with a bunch of keys. I told him I have made neither noise nor disturbance. He looked mightily surprised at my flat denial & said he had understood I was the cause of the noise. I then *happened to remember* that there was a bunch of keys—shower keys—organ key & one or two others which I always carried with me & thought it possible I might have been twirling them on my fingers in service as I frequently do in my room when *not engaged in anything particular*. I then told him that I had keys constantly with me & it was possible I might have taken them out from my pocket during church but that if so it was entirely unconsciously done & without the smallest *intent of making a disturbance*. He talked a while & then said that would do for the present & I thought so too. . . . I heard nothing more of the *fuss* till Thursday night when Prest Lord requested me to call upon him immediately after tea. I was there at the time for I had much *curiosity to know what new materials for a lecture they had scratched together*—thinking that the affair of last Sunday was entirely settled. He only wished to request me to meet the faculty there in about an hour & knowing as he said my *natural brashness and impetuosity* he wished to warn me that any loss of self command might expel me from college. I met the faculty—answered more *impertinent questions* than ever were proposed to a *common* horse thief—yet through all this I kept my temper & they cannot bring up a single harsh speech against me for which *some of them are I suppose greatly disappointed*.

After my discussion, they have concluded to suspend me for three weeks & in the meantime await for further orders. My suspension is known only to about a dozen of my best friends, every one of whom regards the whole proceeding as one of the smallest acts that a faculty of a respectable college ever *descended to*. These classmates of mine sitting next to me all can testify to my *apparent unconsciousness* & they all say that during the time while I had the keys in my hand I was perfectly *sober* & that there was nothing that could show *intentional disturbance*. I should not have written anything on the subject but only awaited your answer to the communications of the faculty—if it were not that I thought you might like to know my feelings before you answer them— and besides my friends among the students who know of the transactions all desire me to write.

In no point do I condemn myself. If I was restless, it was no more than nine tenths of the students above & below suffered & as to the keys—I do positively deny any knowledge of having them in my hand. So far as the *faculty* have *influence* on *your feelings* in this procedure I am grieved—deeply grieved. Further than this I care not for they have not injured me in the least *either in character* or *standing.* . . . My standing is now good with the students & the faculty may do their worst but they cannot lower it. Do not write to me at present for I do not wish to hear from any one especially if you should be inclined to place reliance on the face which the faculty put upon the matter. *I am not in the spirit to receive advice & consolation I need not. Do not write at present.*

However Lyman managed to respond to this self-serving letter, James remained at Dartmouth, and Tom was able to write to his sisters in Hartford after visiting James in Hanover about a year later that "James . . . seems as well & more happy & contented than usual; he having just passed his soph examinations & been admitted junior. Jim is a witty— stanch fellow & if I mistake not will turn out as as well as any of us—particularly me. My heart grows to him daily & I am thankful every moment that I have had an opportunity of making him so through a visit." When James graduated in 1848, he was still not ready to pursue a churchly life. He wanted instead to go to sea. When he asked Lyman for a loan to carry out his plan, the old patriarch not only refused but also claimed that it would break his heart to lose his last son to such a life. Even Tom tried to discourage him. Only Henry Ward, remembering his own youthful dream, was sympathetic. He arranged for James to try his sea legs as crew on a coastal trader and then as a seaman aboard a clipper ship bound for Canton. James liked the activity and excitement of his life, and in the course of five years in the East India trade rose to first mate. His seagoing life coincided with the historic gold rush to California, and on a voyage in 1849 James displayed a latent Beecher sense of responsibility by being the only man to stick with his captain when the rest of the crew deserted in San Francisco.

Henry Ward's ability to find berths for James so soon after moving to Brooklyn is only one bit of evidence as to how fast he had hit the ground running. In one early revival that the brash young man from the West conducted to the consternation of his long-established fellow ministers, he added more than fifty new members to his congregation. Despite Henry Bowen's insistence on personally buying new clothing for the whole Beecher family that would be more appropriate to life in a sophisticated, eastern city than a frontier capital, the pastor himself managed to retain his informal, rumpled look in and out of the pulpit. It may have been one reason why, unlike most Protestant churches, the Plymouth Church began attracting more men than women to its services. But even conservative-minded women could not resist him, as one of them wrote: "Don't ask me what I think of him. I can't tell you for the life of me. I only know that I am intensely interested. There is a sort of fascination about the man which I should think was produced in good measure by his earnestness, his fervor, his seeming naturalness." The most convincing evidence of the community's warm reception was contained in Henry Ward's report to Harriet on the death of another child just a month after their arrival: "When Caty sickened and began her quiet march toward the once opened gate, to rejoin the brother (cherub pair), we found our house full of friends. Many of the truest, deepest hearts asked no bidding, but, with instinctive heart taught right, *lived* with us almost literally, and when her form was to go forth from us, they embowered her in flowers, winter though it seemed, and every thought and remembrance of her is sweet in its self and sweet in its suggestions."

The sharply contrasting circumstances surrounding this death with that of Georgie as well as the fact that she was bearing a new life to replace the lost one may account for less reported anguish on Eunice's part. She was gratified to find that Brooklyn was filled with New England kind of people whom she understood—or, of more comfort, who understood her. There were relatives on both sides of the family as well. Eunice's brother Oliver and his wife pulled up stakes in Cincinnati and came East in Henry Ward's wake, as if following a star, and then there was Grandma Bullard and Henry Ward's old Aunt Esther to help with the children. A Brooklyn pioneer, so long in residence that Lyman had once stayed with him en route to his East Hampton church, was Justin Foote, and he had peopled the area with a small tribe of Footes. And then there was Catharine, who had immediately recognized the Beecher house in Brooklyn as a good place to settle down and work on a book she was writing. For Henry Ward, Catharine probably repaid their hospitality amply by letting Lyman know that "I never heard any that so fully came up to my idea of 'preaching Christ.'"

Catharine used the quotation marks in her letter because she was repeating the avowal that Henry Ward made in his first sermon to "preach Christ in his personal relation to individual men." Although he said that a minister should be willing and able to deal with any subject affecting his people, including business and politics, he felt obliged to move cautiously, as he had in Indianapolis with respect to that touchiest of subjects—slavery. A good and sufficient reason for this was that one of the triumvirate backing the church, Mr. Hale, had let him know that "the antislavery agitation, conducted as it has been, has been the worst thing for the interests of religion." To make the matter even touchier for any pastor of the Plymouth Church, another of the deep-pocketed sponsors, Henry Bowen, had married into the Tappan family and therefore was strongly antislavery. When Arthur Tappan's Antislavery Society held its annual meeting, Henry managed to duck it without offending Bowen by pleading fatigue after presiding over an auction of pews in Plymouth Church that raised more than eight thousand dollars. He was not as lucky when he was chosen to represent the Congregational churches at a fund-raising meeting in the Broadway Tabernacle arranged by New York's Methodist ministers to buy the freedom of two runaway slave girls. This was shooting a ray of sunshine through the murky mists of theology, economics, and politics that clouded the slavery question to illuminate the dreadful drama of two doomed individuals—saved souls, at that, as baptized Methodists. The emotion of the moment was too much for Henry Ward's heart and head. He could not stay out of that drama, and the antislavery remarks he made were quoted in the press. It was a bad time to be caught on the wrong side of David Hale, for within weeks—on January 30, 1849—the Plymouth Church burned down.

Henry Ward calculated that it would take at least a hundred thousand dollars to replace the old church with the kind of building he wanted, and it would be impossible to raise such a sum with opposition from Hale and like-minded parishioners. But the Providence that seemed ever to rescue impulsive Beechers did it again. In mid-February Hale died, and by the beginning of the next year, Beecher's congregation would be worshiping in a structure built along the lines he had tested in Indianapolis. The totally unadorned auditorium was large enough to seat three thousand people in an arrangement that circled three sides of the platform on which the pastor would perform with no props but a chair and table; behind him was the organ and seating for a large choir. There was a significant symbolism to this uniquely Beecher building that reflected no known religious belief or rites; the remnants of Hale conservatism had been blown away with the ashes of the old church. Although the building was Beecher, the enterprise was Bowen—"I carried the subscription paper day after day and evening after evening and saw with my own eyes every subscription that was made," Bowen boasted—and would remain so until Providence acted again.

That gold fever year of 1849, when Henry Ward Beecher was raising his temple to the gospel of love; when "Old Rough and Ready" Zachary Taylor, the hero of the war with Mexico, won the White House; when Amelia Bloomer told American women that it was all right to wear pants under a suitably long tunic; when regular packets began crossing the seas between New York and Liverpool in only 33.3 days on average and a stagecoach line started carrying mail between Independence, Missouri, and Santa Fe; when Henry David Thoreau published *Civil Disobedience* to explain why he would not pay taxes to support a war that he considered unjust, Harriet Beecher Stowe was subjected to one of the greatest trials of her life in cholera-ridden Cincinnati.

Calvin was still taking the water cure in Vermont when the trouble started, and Harriet insisted that he stay there in letters that contained a daily diary of disaster. How devastating the experience was for her can be judged from just one passage in a letter that Harriet wrote to Henry Ward's wife, Eunice, in consolation for the loss of their children in Indianapolis and Brooklyn. "I have thought that even in your sorrow that it would give you pleasure to know that after ten years of trial God at length has given me a baby that I can *nurse myself*—My little Charley is large & more thriving than any child I ever had—I nurse him exclusively & with both breasts (one you know I never used before with any of my other children) & have an abundance for him & I have thought often when I felt what comfort it was to have him by my side at night & in my arms by day how greatly you were tried dear sister in losing what you had thus watched & cherished—I know dear what the aching is—which aches in spite of all that can be said or thought." A month later, at the end of July 1849, Harriet sent Calvin a journal of entries she had been making:

> July 4. All well. The meeting yesterday was very solemn and interesting. There is more or less sickness about us, but no very dangerous cases. One hundred and twenty burials from cholera alone yesterday, yet to-day we see parties bent on pleasure or

senseless carousing, while to-morrow and next day will witness a fresh harvest of death from them. How we can become accustomed to anything! A while ago ten a day dying of cholera struck terror to all hearts; but now the tide has surged up gradually until the deaths average over a hundred daily and everybody is getting accustomed to it. Gentlemen make themselves agreeable to ladies by reciting the number of deaths in this house or that. This, together with talk of funerals, cholera medicines, cholera dietetics, and chloride of lime, form the ordinary staples of conversation. Serious persons, of course, throw in moral reflections to their taste.

July 10. Yesterday little Charley was taken ill, not seriously, and at any other season I should not be alarmed. Now, however, a slight illness seems like a death sentence, and I will not dissemble that I feel from the outset very little hope. I still think it best that you should not return. By so doing you might expose yourself to a fatal incursion of disease. It is decidedly not your duty to do so.

July 12. Yesterday I carried Charley to Dr. Pulte, who spoke in such a manner as discouraged and frightened me. He mentioned dropsy on the brain as a possible result. I came home with a heavy heart, sorrowing, desolate and wishing my husband and father were here.

About one o'clock this morning Miss Stewart suddenly opened my door, crying, "Mrs. Stowe, Henry is vomiting." I was out on my feet in an instant, and lifted up my heart for help. He was, however, in a few minutes relieved. Then I turned my attention to Charley who was also suffering, put him into a wet sheet, and kept him there until he was in a profuse perspiration. He is evidently getting better and is suspiciously cross. Never was crossness in a baby more admired. Anna and I have said to each other a score of times, "How cross the little fellow is! How he does scold!"

July 15. Since I last wrote, our house has been a perfect hospital,—Charley apparently recovering, but still weak and feeble, unable to walk or play, and so miserably fretful and unhappy. Sunday Anna and I were fairly stricken down, as many others are, with no particular illness, but with such miserable prostration. I lay on the bed all day reading my hymn-book and thinking over passages of Scripture.

July 17. To-day we have been attending poor old Frankie's [an African American woman] funeral. She died yesterday morning, taken sick the day before while washing. Good, honest, trustful old soul! She was truly one who hungered and thirsted for righteousness.

Yesterday morning our poor little dog, Daisy, who had been ailing the day before, was suddenly seized with frightful spasms, and died in half an hour. Poor little affectionate thing! If I were half as good for my nature as she for hers I should be much better than I am. While we were all mourning over her the news came that Frankie was breathing her last. Hatty, Eliza, Anna, and I made her shroud yesterday, and this morning I made her cap. We have just come from her grave.

July 23. At last, my dear the hand of the Lord hath touched us. We have been watching all day by the dying bed of little Charley, who is gradually sinking. After a partial recovery from the attack I described in my last letter he continued for some days very feeble, but still we hoped for recovery. About four days ago he was taken with decided cholera, and now there is no hope of his surviving this night.

Every kindness is shown us by the neighbors. Do not return. All well be over before you could possibly get here, and the epidemic is now said by physicians to prove fatal to every new case. Bear up. Let us not faint when we are rebuked of Him. I dare not trust myself to say more, but shall write again soon.

July 26.

My Dear Husband,—At last it is over, and our dear little one is gone from us. He is now among the blessed. My Charley—my beautiful, gladsome baby, so loving, so sweet, so full of life and hope and strength—now lies shrouded, pale and cold, in the room below. Never was he anything to me but a comfort. He has been my pride and joy. Many a heartache has he cured for me. Many an anxious night have I held him in my bosom and felt the sorrow and loneliness pass out of me with the touch of his warm hands. Yet I have just seen him in his death agony, looked upon his imploring face when I could not help nor soothe nor do one thing, not one, to mitigate his cruel suffering, do nothing but pray in my anguish that he might die soon. I write as though there were no sorrow like my sorrow, yet there has been in this city, as in the land of Egypt, scarce a house without its dead. This heart-break, this anguish, has been everywhere, and when it will end God alone knows.

Charley's death and Harriet's subsequent misery built a fire under the lethargic Professor Stowe. He had been receiving offers from the East, one of which was very tempting, although it brought a salary of only a thousand a year. His alma mater, Bowdoin College, in Brunswick, Maine, wanted him to join their faculty. He accepted soon after arriving home from Vermont and assessing the damage. It took a year for the family to pull up stakes from the ground of their living for nearly two decades. Since Calvin had to make good on a commitment to Lane, it was decided that Harriet and the children go to Maine without him in the fall of 1850 to escape the pernicious Ohio climate as soon as possible. If they had not made the decision earlier, they might certainly have arrived at it in July, when the disease that took little Charley from them took the president of the United States from the country.

General Taylor's death left a final decision on a cluster of bills on the slavery question making their way through Congress to the vice president who stepped into his shoes, Millard Fillmore, from Buffalo, New York. What would soon go down in history as the Compromise of 1850 was introduced into the Senate early in the year by Henry Clay. Its important provisions would admit California to the union as a free state while strengthening the Fugitive Slave Law in deference to the South. Senator William Seward of New York opposed compromise on the grounds that there was a higher law than the Constitution demanding an end to slavery; in a speech read by a colleague, a dying Senator Calhoun of South Carolina also opposed compromise and instead demanded that the North cease all agitation about slavery and agree to its extension everywhere. In a move that surprised and sickened his northern constituents who considered him a foe of slavery on moral grounds, Daniel Webster rose to say, "I speak today for the preservation of the Union" and argued in favor of the compromise to achieve that end. Taylor was known to have been against the compromise, but when the bills passed in September, President Fillmore signed them.

By the time Harriet reached New England on her way to Maine, she found the social conversation there to be about the compromise, much as it had been about the cholera in Cincinnati. During a brief stay in Boston with brother Edward and his wife, Isabella, Harriet was bombarded with horror stories about the treatment that fugitive slaves received when they were caught. Isabella would not let it go at that and followed up with a letter to her sister-in-law in Brunswick in which she said, "Hattie, if I could use a pen as you can, I would write something to make this whole nation feel what an accursed thing slavery is." One of her children recalled that Harriet had been reading that letter aloud and when she came to that sentence, she jumped up, crumpled the letter in her hand, and said, "I will write something. I will if I live."

About a month after that, on a snowy January night in 1851, Henry Ward rode up in the cars after a speaking engagement at the Tremont Temple in Boston to visit Harriet. They talked the night away while the wind howled around the old Brunswick house. The main topic of their conversation was the Fugitive Slave Law and what could be done about it. Henry Ward came up with some plans he had for dramatizing its evil effects in church, and Harriet told him about her resolve after Isabella's prodding. "That's right, Harriet, finish it," Henry Ward said, "and I will scatter it thick as the leaves of Vallombrosa." Only weeks after receiving this encouragement from her favorite brother, Harriet experienced that strange and compelling vision in church, and she knew that there would be no rest for mind or body until she found a way to use it in a cause that was fast becoming her obsession.

7

"After all, what is a novel?"

UNTIL SNOW BEGAN FALLING FAST on that February day in 1860, Henry Ward Beecher felt aggrieved that he and his Plymouth Church had so unexpectedly been deprived of what could prove to be the opportunity of a lifetime. Since the fall of 1859, Abraham Lincoln, the Illinois lawyer who had shown such brilliance in his debates with the nation's leading Democrat, Stephen A. Douglas, had been scheduled to speak from the church's platform. It seemed appropriate that Beecher, who was prominent among the founders of the new Republican Party, would host Lincoln's first appearance before an eastern audience. New York editors such as Horace Greeley of the *Tribune*, William Cullen Bryant of the *Post*, and Henry J. Raymond of the new *New York Times* thought that a moderate like Lincoln would make a better candidate for the presidency than their own Senator William Seward, an avowed abolitionist. Beecher felt that he had been well ahead of the press in forming this opinion when his invitation for Lincoln to appear in Brooklyn had been issued and accepted, but he also felt obliged to step aside gracefully when the Young Men's Republican Union took over sponsorship of the lecture and chose Cooper Union in New York City itself as a more appropriate site.

As the snow kept falling, Beecher's ability to see silver linings took over. He realized that too many of the important people who ought to hear Lincoln speak might not be willing to take a rough ferry ride and wade through snowy streets to his church on such a night as that February 27. Could it be another instance of Providence at work? As it turned out, Beecher himself did not get to Cooper Union. Although the large auditorium there was not filled, some fifteen hundred hardy souls were on hand for an event that would be more important than they could have

149

known, and, of course, the newspapers carried full accounts of the proceedings. Undoubtedly briefed by brother Tom, Henry Ward might not have shared the surprised, even shocked, reaction of much of the audience to the man's appearance. As one eyewitness acknowledged: "When Lincoln rose to speak, I was greatly disappointed. He was tall, tall,—oh, how tall! And so angular and awkward that I had, for an instant, a feeling of pity for so ungainly a man. But his face lighted up as with an inward fire, the whole man was transfigured. I forgot his clothes, his personal appearance, and his individual peculiarities. Presently, forgetting myself, I was on my feet like the rest, yelling like a wild Indian, cheering this wonderful man." Amazingly, this was a typical reaction to a speech that Lincoln delivered like a legal brief, calling to witness the view of twenty-one Founding Fathers, a majority of the signers of the Constitution, to the effect that Congress should keep slavery from expanding into the new territories. He used few rhetorical flourishes until the end, when he appealed to the head—"Wrong as we think slavery is, we can yet afford to let it alone where it is, because that much is due to the necessity arising from its actual presence in the nation; but can we, while our vote will prevent it, allow it so spread into the National Territories, and to overrun us here in these Free States?"—and to the heart—"Let us have faith that right makes might, and in that faith, let us, to the end, dare to do our duty as we understand it."

Before Henry Ward met Lincoln in the flesh, the prospective Republican candidate for president performed in an ever more reassuring manner. During a week's trip through New England, he made speeches at more than half a dozen towns in which he expressed views on subjects other than slavery very like those that Beecher dispensed from the pulpit. At New Haven, for instance, Lincoln said, "I am glad to see that a system of labor prevails in New England under which laborers can strike when they want to, where they are not obliged to work under all circumstances, and are not tied down and obliged to labor whether you pay them or not! . . . I don't believe in a law to prevent a man from getting rich. It would do more harm than good. So while we do not propose any war upon capital, we do wish to allow the humblest man an equal chance to get rich with everybody else." The fact that Lincoln took time to visit his son Robert, who was preparing for Harvard at Phillips Exeter Academy in New Hampshire, would go down well with voters who respected a family man and with the intellectual elite who might fear that they were looking at a country bumpkin. On the Sunday after he returned to New York, Lincoln "followed the crowd," as he reported, from his lodging at Astor House across the ferry and into a seat in pew 89 in Plymouth

Church. No churchgoer or publicly professing Christian, Lincoln nevertheless wanted to hear and meet this man whose moral and political leadership he admired and would desperately need in the future if his quest for the nation's highest office proved successful.

Lincoln may have hoped on that Sunday that he would meet the preacher's even more famous sister as well. A voracious reader and possessed of a politician's sensitive finger on the public pulse, Lincoln would have been well aware that there was hardly a literate person in America—or, in fact, in the Western world—who would not immediately recognize the name of Harriet Beecher Stowe and the character she created named Uncle Tom. The resolve and activity that made both Henry Ward and Harriet people to reckon with in the mind of a man like Lincoln had their beginnings during another cold and stormy winter in 1851, when brother and sister talked a night away by the Stowe fireside in Brunswick, Maine. Although she had then determined to write something, Harriet had not been at all sure of what it should be. Some weeks after her talk with Henry Ward, Calvin came home from his stint at Lane. One day she found him literally weeping over scraps of brown paper he had found in a table drawer. They contained the scene she had written down after her vision in church. "Hattie," Calvin said, "this is the climax of that story of slavery that you promised you would write. Begin at the beginning and work up to this and you'll have your book." Already accustomed to Calvin's overly emotional reactions to her work, Harriet had to think it over for a while before she came to the conclusion that he was right. But could she afford the time that such a project would take? The state of the family finances was so bad that she had invited Catharine to come up and live with her and start a school for the numerous offspring of the whole Beecher clan to raise some money. As a professional and self-proclaimed money writer, she had another solution to her problem also worth a try. Before putting a word on paper, she sent off a letter to Gamaliel Bailey, whom she had known in Cincinnati and who was now editing an abolitionist paper in Washington, D.C., the *National Era*. Would he, she inquired, be interested in serializing a story about slave life called *Uncle Tom's Cabin, or Life Among the Lowly*, and, if so, how much would he pay for it? The figure he came back with added new substance to Harriet's growing feeling that she was fated to do this job; it was three hundred dollars, exactly the shortfall she had estimated between family income and expenditures for the year.

With Calvin's absences, either geographic or mental, Harriet was kept aware of the true state of life's practical affairs in sometimes grim, sometimes comic detail. A catch-up letter she wrote to Sarah, George

Beecher's widow, foreshadowed a novel that she hoped one day to write about the lovable and exasperating quirks of New England character. Consider only one passage from the letter, in which she deals with a plumbing problem:

> Some of my adventures are quite funny, as for example: I had in my kitchen no sink, cistern, or any other water privileges, so I bought at the cotton factory two of the great hogsheads they bring oil in, which here in Brunswick are often used for cisterns, and had them brought up in triumph to my yard, and was congratulating myself on my energy, when lo and behold! it was discovered that there was no cellar door except one in the kitchen, which was truly a strait and narrow way, down a long pair of stairs. Hereupon, as saith John Bunyan, I fell into a muse,—how to get my cisterns into my cellar. In days of chivalry I might have got a knight to make me a breach through the foundation walls, but that was not to be thought of now, and my oil hogsheads standing disconsolately in the yard seemed to reflect no great credit on my foresight. In this strait, I fell upon a real honest Yankee cooper, whom I besought, for the reputation of his craft and mine, to take my hogsheads to pieces, carry them down in staves, and set them up again, which the worthy man actually accomplished one fair summer forenoon, to the great astonishment of "us Yankees." When my man came to put up the pump, he stared very hard to see my hogsheads thus translated and standing as innocent and quiet as could be in the cellar, and then I told him, in a very mild, quiet way, that I got 'em taken to pieces and put together—just as if I had been always in the habit of doing such things. Professor Smith came down and looked very hard at them and then said, "Well, nothing can beat a willful woman."
>
> Then followed divers negotiations with a very clever, but (with reverence) somewhat lazy gentleman of jobs, who occupieth a carpenter's shop opposite mine. This same John Titcomb, my very good friend, is a character peculiar to Yankeedom. He is part owner and landlord of the house I rent and connected by birth with all the best families in town, a man of real intelligence, and good education, a great reader, and quite a thinker. Being of an ingenious turn he does painting, gilding, staining, upholstery jobs, varnishing, all in addition to his primary trade of

carpentry. But he is a man studious of ease, and fully possessed with the idea that man wants but little here below, so he boards himself in his workshop on crackers and herring, washed down with water, and spends his time working, musing, reading new publications, and taking his comfort. In all my moving and fussing Mr. Titcomb has been my right-hand man. Whenever a screw was loose, a nail to be driven, a lock mended, a pane of glass set, and these cases were manifold, he was always on hand. But my sink was no fancy job, and I believe nothing but a very particular friendship would have moved him to undertake it. So this same sink lingered in a precarious state for some weeks, and when I had *nothing else to do,* I used to call and do what I could in the way of enlisting the good man's sympathies in its behalf.

How many times I have been in and seated myself in one of the old rocking-chairs, and talked first of the news of the day, the railroad, the last proceedings in Congress, the probabilities about the millennium, and then brought the conversation by little and little around to my sink! . . . because until the sink was done, the pump could not be put up, and we couldn't have any rain-water. Sometimes my courage would quite fail me to introduce the subject, and I would talk of everything else, turn and get out of the shop, and then turn back as if a thought had just struck my mind, and say:—

"Oh, Mr. Titcomb! about that sink?"

"Yes, ma'am, I was thinking about going down street this afternoon to look out stuff for it."

"Yes, sir, if you would be good enough to get it done as soon as possible; we are in great need of it."

"I think there's no hurry. I believe we are going to have a dry time now, so that you could not catch any water, and you won't need a pump at present."

These negotiations extended from the first of June to the first of July, and at last my sink was completed. . . . Then comes a letter from my husband saying he is sick abed, and all but dead; don't ever expect to see his family again; wants to know how I shall manage, in case I am left a widow; knows we shall get in debt and never get out; wonders at my courage; thinks I am very sanguine; warns me to be prudent, as there won't be much to live on in case of his death, etc. etc., etc. I read the letter and poke it into the stove, and proceed.

Proceed Harriet did. Once she began work on her book, she fed it to the *National Era* a chapter at a time, and publication began in June 1851. It was the common practice of the times with respect to serialized fiction and a gamble by both writer and editor. Although the monthly deadline was undoubtedly a burden, it also was virtually a guarantee against writer's block or just plain loafing. In September, with the project well under way, Catharine provided a good look at what life was like in the Brunswick household in a letter to sister Mary Perkins in Hartford, which she asked her to pass along to Uncle Samuel Foote and Henry Ward for reasons made obvious in the text:

This is a very *cold* house, in a bitter *cold* climate tho' *dry and steady*. We find we cannot make the children comfortable except by a furnace which will cost $150. We must make partitions & fixtures costing some $30—We must get beds, bedding, tables, furniture &c for *five* more in the family. Wood & coal & provisions to be laid in all demand ready money. In these circumstances we need to have each pupil bring $50 to begin with. The charge for the year is Mary Dutton's *lowest* price (ie) $220 and *washings are extra* according to the number put out—We hire the washing done out of the house. We shall need to receive the rest of the payment *quarterly* as we go along.

Now you know Mr. Stowe has a monomania about *running in debt* & his mother is as bad & the only way I could make them comfortable was by *taking all the risk myself* and agreeing to foot all the bills that are not met by the salary & income from pupils. Even with this our furnace is a bugbear & all our expenses are looked on with fear & trembling. Nothing would so lighten their gloom as the view of *money in hand*—for faith is weak in the future.

The old lady has concluded to spend the winter in Natick—no remarks—

I am trying to get Uncle Tom out of the way. At 8 o'clock we are thru' with breakfast & prayers & then we send Mr. Stowe and Harriet both to *his room in the college*. There was no other way to keep her out of family cares & quietly at work & since this plan is adopted she goes ahead finely. I hope it will all be finished before the children come.

In a postscript that explains why the letter should be sent on to Uncle Samuel and Henry Ward, Catharine complained bitterly about the news that Henry Ward's daughter Hattie, and her friend, the daughter of Brooklyn neighbors, the Howards, and Uncle Samuel's daughter Hattie Foote, would not be coming to the school as promised, thus reducing sharply the anticipated income. Never modest about what she had to offer, Catharine pointed out that she and Harriet would be giving the children an education as good as the boys' school in Brunswick for a third of the annual cost. Moreover, she pointed out that Horace Mann, the most famous educator of the day, had visited them and promised to place any students they recommended in jobs paying six hundred dollars a year. She argued that she could have replaced these pupils with recruits from outside the family if she had been given enough notice. Catharine's expression of anger and points well taken came naturally to her in view of her senior position within the family, but they were increasingly resented by some of the others. Sensitive to this growing resentment of Catharine's attitudes but very grateful to her big sister for help at this time when she was most in need of it, Harriet wrote at about the same time to their father Lyman and Henry Ward in evident expectation that they might spread the word throughout the family:

> I am going to write to you with relation to Catharine's affairs— as they have become in a measure interwoven with mine. She has agreed to give me a year of her time to act conjointly with me in taking a class of our young relations and carrying on their education with that of my own children. It is a care that I should not think it right to assume without her and that I cannot support without her and it is my desire that the enterprise which she has left in the hands of others may now receive such a support from the public and or family who are a powerful part of it as to render it unnecessary for her to return to labor in that sphere. I hope you have both read Catharine's latest book [*Duty of American Women to Their Country*]. If you have not, I beg you will not let another day pass without reading it as an act of justice to yourselves and to the public. Until I read it I had no proper appreciation of her character and motives of action for this eight or ten years past. I considered her strange, nervous, visionary and to a certain extent unstable. I see now that she has been busy for eight years about *one thing*, a thing first conceived upon a sick bed when she was so sick and frail that most women would have felt that all they could hope for was to lie still and be nursed for the rest of their lives, then she conceived this plan of educating our country by means of its women and this she has steadily

pursued in weariness and painfulness in journey in peril of life and health, in watching and in prayer. A system so extensive carried on by means of correspondence all over the country, dependent on an immense number of influences and agents from Maine to Georgia and from Massachusetts to Iowa and, where one of these occurred, many, not seeing that they were only small parts of the great *whole* which was all the while moving on, have supposed that she was constantly attempting and constantly failing.

If you will look from page 152 to 155 of her last book you will see what she has accomplished and that tho' owing to Governor Slade's [former governor of Vermont who replaced Calvin Stowe as head of Catharine's national organization for a brief time] interference her Normal Institution failed in two states it is fully developed in Milwaukee and that if *our folks* now only cordially cooperate with Mr. and Mrs. Parsons, the agents, the thing may be considered as done. Catharine had earned and spent for the cause nearly five thousand dollars and she has worked as yet almost *against* even her own family for hitherto you know that we have not had full confidence in her plans, but the time has come when in my judgment there is ground and full ground for such confidence and when to neglect them any longer would be unwise and inexcusable. I repeat what I said before that altho the incidental parts and fragments of her great plan have failed and failed in cases enough to discourage any other woman yet the whole movement as a whole that she has carried on the last eight years has impressed me as a sublime specimen of that force of character which God gives to an individual now and then when he has a purpose to carry by them and which may almost be regarded as an inspiration. . . . I beg therefore, first that you will give Cates book a careful reading and rectify your own sentiments as I have mine and see just what she has been doing and then do what you can to help this Milwaukee enterprise which is just now the turning point of the whole affair.

Catharine's hope that *Uncle Tom* would be out of the way before their pupils arrived was a vain one. Begun with the thought that it could be told in three installments, the story kept growing in Harriet's imagination and on paper throughout the year of 1851, with no end in sight. Harriet was not the only busy Beecher that year. Catharine herself was publishing the book that Harriet referred to, in which she set forth the thinking behind her creation of the Milwaukee Female College and its sponsoring organization, the American Women's Educational Organization. Convinced that *Uncle Tom* was growing into a book, Catharine also began negotiating with publishers on behalf of Harriet. Retired from Lane, Lyman moved to Boston to be in familiar surroundings and near Edward. Charles also moved East, to preside over changing the First Presbyterian Church of Newark, New Jersey, into the First Congregational Church. He found himself on a rather slippery slope when the city's ministerial association let it be known that he was no longer welcome after one of his first sermons, an assault on the Fugitive Slave Law titled "The Duty of Disobedience to Wicked Laws," was published. Henry Ward, who had launched James on a seagoing career, had a hand in launching brother Tom on a ministerial career as pastor of a newly formed Congregational church in the Williamsburgh section of Brooklyn. While Harriet was using her pen, Henry Ward was using his pulpit and what had become his national outlet, the *New York Independent,* a religious paper with a circulation in the hundreds of thousands, to do his part in carrying out the resolve they had arrived at together. Although Henry Ward's increasingly antislavery columns in the *Independent* were signed only with a star, there were few readers who did not soon discover whose hand was under that star.

Henry Ward may have tried to wear the cloak of anonymity in his writing to avoid embarrassing the paper's owner, one of the founders of his church, Henry Bowen. But within the church, Henry Ward made his sympathies crystal clear. A golden opportunity to do so was the unanticipated result of his appearance at the slave auction in New York's Tabernacle. Largely because importing slaves from abroad had long been illegal, the economics of slavery had changed by the 1850s. In the more densely settled, farmed-out states such as Virginia, slaves had lost their value as laborers, but black workers remained in great, even increasing, demand in the Deep South and the Southwest and in the new territories into which slavery could be introduced. Thus, with their value rising, the breeding and rearing of slaves became an important kind of crop in the older states, and a white man who brought his beautiful slave daughter to a Virginia market was not surprised to have a trader pay twelve hundred dollars—more than the annual salary of a professor at Bowdoin—for her; she would fetch even more in the sex trade of New Orleans. In this rare instance, the trader could not bear to think about her fate. He not only offered her a chance to buy her freedom for the amount he had paid, but also he put down a hundred dollars himself and persuaded a fellow trader to match it to get the ball rolling. Well-wishers took the girl to Washington, where she was able to raise another four hundred dollars. She was only halfway there and about to give up when somebody who had seen Beecher at the Tabernacle wrote to him for help. Beecher replied that he could raise the rest if the girl could come to Brooklyn. Accepting her word of honor that she would return to Richmond if she did not get the money, her trader owner took the risk of sending her into free territory and into the hands of people known for opposing the Fugitive Slave Act.

On the first Sunday that the young woman who called herself Sarah was in Brooklyn, Henry Ward seated her in a front row close to the stage. Under a proper hat borrowed from Eunice and with her light skin she would attract little more notice from members of the congregation who filled the rest of the auditorium's three thousand seats than any other stranger. The service proceeded as usual through prayers, recitations, and hymns until it came time for the pastor's sermon. Henry Ward got up from his chair, also as usual, and walked around the table in front of him so he would have more freedom of movement during his informal delivery, scooping up a Bible as he went to read his text. He paused for a moment and looked around at the gathering as if to discern the thought behind every face before he started to read: "Then said Jesus unto them, I will ask you one thing: Is it lawful on the Sabbath day to do good, or to do evil? To save life or destroy it?"

Leaving the questions hanging in air, Henry Ward closed the book, walked over to the stairs leading down into the auditorium, held out his hand, and said, "Come up here, Sarah, and let us all see you."

Trembling with shy fright, the woman managed to make it up the stairs with the help of Beecher's hand, and he led her to an empty chair. When she was seated, he turned to face the audience, gestured toward Sarah, and said, "This is a remarkable commodity. Such as she are put into one balance and silver into the other. I reverence woman. For the sake of the love I bore my mother I hold her sacred even in the lowest position and will use every means in my power for her uplifting. What will you do now? May she read her liberty in your eyes? Shall she go free?"

Whether Sarah could read faces or not, she certainly must have heard the sniffling and some outright sobs as the ushers passed the plates across the rows and brought them forward, heaped with the necessary "silver" in paper, coin, and jewelry. A quick count of the returns allowed Beecher to put his hand on Sarah's shoulder and assure her that she now was free. At that, the congregation broke into applause, a response deemed inappropriate in orthodox worship. But Henry Ward clapped along with them and said when he could be heard: "When the old Jews went up to their solemn feasts they made the mountains round about Jerusalem ring with their shouts. I do not approve of an unholy clapping in the house of God, but when a good deed is well done, it is not wrong to give an outward expression of joy."

If the effect of an action can be judged by the criticism it draws, Henry Ward's slave auction, which he repeated whenever there was an opportunity to do so, hit a high mark. It came mostly from religious and political conservatives, often to be found in one embodiment. Those who did not charge him with committing a sacrilege or inciting rebellion claimed that he at least was indulging in unseemly sensationalism. He resorted to his frequent fishing metaphor in response: "I say he is the best fisherman who catches the most fish whatever epithets may be flung at him about the kind of bait he uses."

Although the response to the misadventures of Uncle Tom as they appeared serially in the *National Era* was unusual in the amount and intensity for a publication of such limited range, nobody could have anticipated what happened when the book came out in March 1852. The well-published Catharine had tried to interest her own established publishers—Harper & Brothers in New York and Phillips, Sampson & Company in Boston—in *Uncle Tom* to no avail; they feared that it would hurt their business in the South. But the wife of a young Boston publisher, John P. Jewett, persuaded her husband to read the serial, and he entered into negotiations with the Stowes. He presented them with an unusual choice: a 10 percent royalty on every copy sold, or a 50–50 split on profits or losses if they would underwrite half the expense of publication. With no interest or experience in matters of business, Calvin sought advice from an old Boston friend, Congressman Philip Greeley, who said after reading Jewett's proposal but without reading a word of the book, "Why, Calvin, there is really no choice here. You and Hattie have no money to gamble with. Take the 10 percent. There's no risk in that! After all, what is a novel? Even if it is successful, it's merely a flash in the pan and then it's all over—especially a novel on an unpopular subject by a woman! You tell Hattie that if she makes enough out of it to buy a new black silk dress I shall consider her very fortunate."

Calvin opted for the 10 percent on Harriet's behalf and, grateful for the advice, he took the first copy off the press and presented it to Congressman Greeley just as he was boarding a train for Washington. Greeley started reading the book immediately, and it brought such a welling up of tears that he was embarrassed to be seen weeping over a novel by other passengers in the cars. He got off the train at Springfield, Massachusetts, hired a room at a hotel for the night, and finished the book. He undoubtedly knew how wrong he had been by the time he finally reached Washington, because by then the news was out that the book had sold three thousand copies in the first day. Another shortsighted party to the project was the publisher himself. Jewett wanted Harriet to trim the tale as serialized; he would have to put it out in two volumes, and he was afraid that this would hurt sales. Harriet balked on the grounds that she had written the story just as it had come to her and did not want to tamper with it. In the event, Jewett had to keep eight power presses running night and day as he turned out edition after edition until three hundred thousand copies had been sold within the first year, while across the ocean a million and a half copies were sold in Great Britain and its colonies, and translations proliferated on the Continent. Unfortunately, neither the writer nor the American publisher profited financially from the book's wild success abroad. Nevertheless, Harriet took in ten thousand dollars in the first four months—more ready money in hand than any Beecher had ever hoped to have.

Astonished and flattered by the money and attention flooding in upon her as she must have been, Harriet did not lose the level head upon which her husband, children, and innumerable relatives and followers depended. Mrs. Howard, a wealthy Brooklyn friend of a number of Beechers, accompanied Harriet on a trip eastward from New York in June, and they made an overnight stop at the Perkins' house in Hartford. Sister Mary put them both in the same bedroom, "at Mrs. Stowe's request," according to Mrs. Howard's account of the occasion. Tired from her travels, Mrs. Howard climbed right into bed. But Harriet, seemingly in a daze, undressed slowly, scattering petticoats, stays, and stockings around as Calvin complained she did with newspapers. Once comfortable, she sank to the floor, took the pins out of her hair, and began brushing her curls. Mrs. Howard could not take her eyes off the "little girlish figure gathered in a heap" who had become the most famous writer in the world. For an almost unendurable time, Harriet remained silent, and Mrs. Howard was afraid to speak and interrupt the train of thought in a mind she had come to admire. When she finally did start to speak, Harriet told her roommate that all the publicity had caused her brother Edward to warn her that "it might induce pride and vanity and work harm to my Christian character."

Not knowing quite what to say to that, Mrs. Howard still held her tongue, and Harriet went on, "Dear soul, he need not be troubled. He doesn't know that I did not write that book."

"What? You did not write *Uncle Tom?*" Mrs. Howard said.

"No, I only put down what I saw."

"But you have never been at the South, have you?" Mrs. Howard asked.

"No, but it all came before me in visions, one after another, and I put them down in words."

As sensational as it was, Harriet's triumph was not the only event to disturb the normal tranquillity of that small academic community in Maine in 1852. At about the same time that she got back to Brunswick in June, the Democrats, meeting in Baltimore, nominated a Bowdoin graduate, Franklin Pierce, for the presidency. This selection brought no rejoicing among Beechers and their like-minded friends. Despite the fact that he was pure New England—son of a former governor of New Hampshire and Maine-educated—Pierce was what they were calling a "dough-face" Democrat, who was in favor of the Compromise of 1850 and would therefore be acceptable to the South. Pierce also had some personal problems well known in that intimate society—an overfondness for strong drink, and a difficult wife. But he did have one loyal collegemate named Nathaniel Hawthorne, who had recently published a novel called *The Scarlet Letter*, which dealt with the forbidden theme of adultery and had become the fastest best-seller on record until the arrival of *Uncle Tom's Cabin*, another novel on a forbidden subject. If Harriet had been aware of Hawthorne's view of women writers—"I wish they were forbidden to write on pain of having their faces scarified with oyster-shell"—she might have taken wicked pleasure in besting him. She certainly would have faulted Hawthorne for glorifying his old college chum in a campaign biography titled *The Life of Franklin Pierce*. When he heard of that effort in the works, the Beechers' friend Horace Mann said, "If he makes out Pierce to be a great man or a brave man, it will be the greatest work of fiction he ever wrote."

The Pierce nomination was only one of the events in 1852 that would share some of the spotlight with Harriet. Books by two other Beechers—*Views on Theology* by Lyman and *Conflict of the Ages* by Edward—also were published in that year. In the rarefied realm of theology, these works would have been more highly prized than Harriet's fiction, but publication would not have put either of these other Beechers in danger of suffering from "pride and vanity." Of the two religious works, Edward's was the more significant. It represented a quarter of a century's deep thought and impressive scholarship begun when Catharine raised with Edward her doubts about the doctrine of original sin. The conflict of the ages in Edward's view had been going on between the intuitive understanding implanted by God in human beings as to "honor and dishonor, right and

wrong," and the doctrine that all human beings were born sinners con-
signed to eternal damnation by God in punishment for Adam's fall. A
God who condemns one human being for another human being's trans-
gression was committing an act incomprehensible and unacceptable to a
mind created to understand honor and right and to the nature of a God
who would implant such an understanding in the human mind. Nevertheless, Edward believed that human beings were born with a tendency
to sin. What Edward considered a revolution in theological thought was
his concept of preexistence. God had created a world before the present
world with sinless souls who could share in his eternal life, but after the
fall of Satan and his angels they had chosen to follow Satan's evil ways
and become sinners. Instead of losing these souls for eternity, God gave
them a second chance, as it were, by letting them be reborn in a new creation, the world we all know, where they could be saved by believing in
and following the system made known through the Bible and its Christian interpreters. The evidence is that only one of Edward's ministerial
brothers—Charles—and none of his equally religious sisters ever came to
grips with his opus. Although Edward occasionally resorted to such simple metaphors as calling this world a hospital for sick souls, a few para-
graphs from his "brief summary of the whole case" clearly indicate the
difficulties he posed for even the most theologically minded readers:

> But if all men existed and sinned before this life, in another state
> of being, then it is easily conceivable, and worthy of belief, that,
> when first created, all the demands of honor and right as to their
> constitution and circumstances were fully met, and that, since in
> those circumstances, they sinned, the fault was entirely their
> own, and not at all God's. Moreover, it is easily conceivable, and
> worthy of belief, that the result of a course of sinning should be
> to leave in their minds that predisposition to sin which we, in
> common cases, designate by the name sinful habit, but which is
> in this case called original sin, which is no part of the original
> constitution of the mind, but was introduced into it by the sinner
> himself, so that for it he, and he only, is responsible, which is not
> an act, but a permanent result of previous acts, and appears as
> simply a strong predisposition, or tendency, or propensity to sin.
>
> It has also been shown to be supposable that the fall of Satan
> and his angels took place in the far-remote ages of past eternity,
> and that since their fall other spiritual beings have been seduced
> to join them in their revolt, and have come under the despotism
> of Satan, forming a vastly extended kingdom of fallen souls. It is

still further supposable that God saw fit to destroy the power of Satan and hosts by a system of disclosures, in which he should enter this kingdom, and, by a material system, regenerate and rescue from his grasp a large portion of his subjects and destroy him and the rest by these disclosures of moral power that should proceed from this work of redemption. It may be that, not only this world, but the whole existing material system, were created with reference to this end, and that this is the basis of the analogies of things material and spiritual. That for the same end the incarnation and atonement of Christ were predetermined, and the results of the whole work ordained before the foundation of the world.

Edward's siblings had no need of understanding his work, since they had already let God off the hook of being the bad guy who created them as sinners and then punished them for it. In their various ways they were trying to spread a gospel of love in which there was a caring God who suffered with people as they confronted the trials of the human condition and who gave those who obeyed his commandments and believed in his promises the courage to get through their trials and finally be rewarded with eternal life. Harriet preached this appealing gospel throughout *Uncle Tom*, and it undoubtedly was an important factor in its popularity. Like Henry Ward, Harriet acknowledged learning as much or more about the true faith from the black people she had always around her in the house than from any book or pulpit. As sales kept mounting, it developed that *Uncle Tom* was finding a good market in the South. Paying heed to her artistic as well as her moralistic voice, Harriet managed to be rather evenhanded in assessing blame for the evils of slavery. She created some characters who were decent white Southerners and some who were hypocritical or uncaring Northerners, and she postulated colonization as a solution to the problem. Ironically, ardent abolitionists were counted among the critics of Harriet's treatment, even though a host of contemporaries and most historians credit *Uncle Tom* with making the single most persuasive argument for their cause. The people who had to bear the brunt of Harriet's ire were her fellow Christians. The weapon she used in her attack on them was often the sharp knife of sarcasm, as in the following scene aboard a riverboat carrying south to the market Uncle Tom and a number of other slaves torn from their families, including a young woman named Lucy, who had lost her husband:

Dizzily she sat down. Her slack hands fell lifeless by her side. Her eyes looked straight forward, but she saw nothing. All the noise and hum of the boat, the groaning of the machinery, mingled dreamily to her bewildered ear; and the poor, dumb-stricken heart had neither cry nor tear to show for its utter misery. She was quite calm.

The trader who, considering his advantages, was almost as humane as some of our politicians, seemed to feel called on to administer such consolation as the case admitted of.

"I know this yer comes kinder hard, at first, Lucy," said he, "but such a smart, sensible gal as you are, won't give way to it. You see it's *necessary*, and can't be helped!"

"O, don't, Mas'r, don't!" said the woman, with a voice like one that is smothering.

"You're a smart wench, Lucy," he persisted, "I mean to do well by ye, and get ye a nice place down river, and you'll soon get another husband,—such a likely gal as you—"

"O! Mas'r, if you *only* won't talk to me now," said the woman, in a voice of such quick and living anguish that the trader felt that there was something at present in the case beyond his style of operation. He got up, and the woman turned away, and buried her head in her cloak.

The trader walked up and down for a time and occasionally stopped and looked at her.

"Takes it hard, rather," he soliloquized, "but quiet, tho',—let her sweat a while, she'll come right, by and by!"

Tom had watched the whole transaction from first to last, and had a perfect understanding of its results. To him, it looked like something unutterably horrible and cruel, because, poor, ignorant black soul! he had not learned to generalize, and to take enlarged views. If he had only been instructed by certain ministers of Christianity, he might have thought better of it, and seen in it an every-day incident of lawful trade, a trade which is the vital support of an institution which an American divine* [Harriet supplied the name in a footnote: Dr. Joel Parker of Philadelphia—the same Joel Parker who had come up to Illinois from New Orleans in 1837 to oppose the antislavery martyr Elijah Lovejoy and her brother Edward in debate.] tells us has *"no evils but such as are inseparable from any other relations in social and domestic life."* But Tom, as we see, being a poor, ignorant fellow, whose reading had been confined entirely to the New Testament, could not comfort and solace himself with views like these. His very soul bled within him for what seemed to him the *wrongs* of the poor suffering thing that lay like a crushed reed on the boxes, the feeling, living, bleeding, yet immortal *thing* which American state law coolly classes with the bundles, and bales, and boxes, among which she is lying.

Tom drew near, and tried to say something; but she only groaned. Honestly, and with tears running down his own cheeks, he spoke of a heart of love in the skies, of a pitying Jesus, and an eternal home; but the ear was deaf with anguish, and the palsied heart could not feel.

Night came on,—night, calm, unmoved, and glorious, shining down with her innumerable and solemn angel eyes, twinkling, beautiful, but silent. There was no speech nor language, no pitying voice or helping hand, from that distant sky. One after another, the voices of business or pleasure died away, all on the boat were sleeping, and the ripples at the prow were plainly heard. Tom stretched himself out on a box, and there, as he lay, he heard, ever and anon, a smothered sob or cry from the prostrate creature,—"O! what shall I do? O Lord! O good Lord, do help me!" and so, ever and anon, until the murmur dies away in silence.

At midnight, Tom waked, with a sudden start. Something black passed quickly by him to the side of the boat, and he heard a splash in the water. No one else saw or heard anything. He raised his head,—the woman's place was vacant! He got up, and sought about him in vain. The poor bleeding heart was still, at last, and the river rippled and dimpled just as brightly as if it had not closed above it.

At times in her book, Harriet threw away the knife and attacked with a club:

This is an age of the world when nations are trembling and convulsed. A mighty influence is abroad, surging and heaving the world, as with an earthquake. And is America safe? Every nation that carries within its bosom great and unredressed injustice has in it the elements of this last convulsion.

For what is this mighty influence thus rousing in all nations and languages those groanings that cannot be uttered, for man's freedom and equality?

O, Church of Christ, read the signs of the times! Is not this power the spirit of Him whose kingdom is yet to come and whose will to be done on earth as it is in heaven?

But who may abide the day of his appearing? "for that day shall burn as an oven: and he shall appear as a swift witness against those that oppress the hireling in his wages, the widow and the fatherless, and that *turn aside the stranger in his right*: and he shall break in pieces the oppressor."

Are not these dread words for a nation bearing in her bosom so mighty an injustice? Christians! Every time that you pray that the kingdom of Christ may come, can you forget that prophecy associates, in dread fellowship, the *day of vengeance* with the year of his redeemed?

A day of grace is yet held out to us. Both North and South have been guilty before God: and the *Christian church* has a heavy account to answer. Not by combining together, to promote injustice and cruelty, and making a common capital of sin, is this Union to be saved,—but by repentance, justice and mercy, for, not surer is the eternal law by which the millstone sinks in the ocean, than that stronger law, by which injustice and cruelty shall bring on nations the wrath of God!

As gratifying to Harriet as the public response to her book was that of prominent people and other writers at home and abroad. America's most famous and popular poet, Henry Wadsworth Longfellow, who also had been a student and teacher at Bowdoin before moving on to Harvard, wrote to Harriet: "I congratulate you most cordially upon the immense success and influence of 'Uncle Tom's Cabin.' It is one of the greatest triumphs recorded in literary history, to say nothing of the higher triumph of its moral effect," and in his own diary he noted: "At one step she had reached the top of the staircase up which the rest of us climb on our knees year after year." John Greenleaf Whittier gave Harriet "ten thousand thanks for thy immortal book," and wrote to William Lloyd Garrison: "What a glorious work Harriet Beecher Stowe has wrought. Thanks for the Fugitive Slave Law! Better would it be for slavery if that law had never been enacted; for it gave occasion for 'Uncle Tom's Cabin.'" In England, where the book sold as fast as in the States, Prince Albert read it and prevailed on Queen Victoria to read it, too; Lord Cockburn of the Queen's Privy Council said that "Uncle Tom" had "done more for humanity than was ever before accomplished by any single book of fiction," and Charles Dickens wrote in a review: "If I might find a fault in what has so charmed me, it would be that you go too far and seek to prove too much. I doubt there being any warrant for making out the African race to be a great one." The German poet Heinrich Heine, who had drifted away from religion, was prompted to go back to his Bible by the novel, admitting that he "with all my sense have come no farther than the poor ignorant Negro who has just learned to spell. Poor Tom indeed seems to have seen deeper things in the Holy Book than I." In France, novelist George Sand hailed Harriet as a "genius, as humanity feels the need of genius—the genius of goodness, not that of the man of letters, but of the saint. Yes—a saint!" Tolstoy placed *Uncle Tom's Cabin* on a level with *Les Misérables* and *A Tale of Two Cities* as moral art. One abolitionist who did appreciate Harriet's work was Garrison, who told her in a letter: "I estimate the value of anti-slavery writing by the abuse it brings. Now all the defenders of slavery have let me alone and are abusing you."

How right he was! Once the praise died down, the criticism began to be heard. Not surprisingly, one of the most serious critics and complainers was the minister she had chosen to name, Joel Parker. He howled that she had mangled the quotation she attributed to him and had taken it out of context. Her offense to Parker, if offense it was, was made to seem all the more odious because he had been a longtime colleague and sometimes friend to all the Beecher ministers. Harriet prevailed on Henry Ward to represent her in dealing with Parker. When he discovered after some research that Parker, whatever his attitude about slavery might be, could make a good case as to the inaccuracy of the quotations, Henry Ward got Harriet to write a letter of apology. It was a different matter with respect to the faceless, often nameless, critics, both North and South, who challenged Harriet's knowledge of her subject. These people had sincere economic, emotional, even religious motives for wanting their slave-enhanced way of life to continue, and they felt both the need and the right to discredit this obscure little woman who was making such damning charges. Harriet understood their point of view and was quite aware of the possibly dire consequences of her work. She did expect family and good friends like Mrs. Howard to accept at face value her claim to have been divinely inspired in the writing, but she knew that it would leave the critics unmoved. Her answer to this was to begin almost immediately on a new book, *The Key to Uncle Tom's Cabin*, in which she would detail her personal experiences with slaves and slavery—her visit to a plantation in Kentucky, her knowledge and use of the Underground Railroad, her talks with brother Charles about his New Orleans experience, her intimate acquaintance with ex-slaves in her own household, and the like—and her research into the literature on the subject.

Despite all of the congratulations and the money rolling in, Harriet had a hard time seeing herself as any kind of celebrity. Asked for her biographical information, she wrote:

> So you want to know what sort of woman I am! Well, if this is any object, you shall have statistics free of charge. To begin, then, I am a little bit of a woman,—somewhat more than forty, about as thin and dry as a pinch of snuff—never very much to look at in my best days and looking like a used up article now. . . . I was married when I was twenty-five years old to a man rich in Greek and Hebrew and Latin and Arabic, and alas, rich in nothing else. . . . But then I was abundantly furnished with wealth of another sort. I had two little curly headed twin daughters to begin with and my stock in this line has gradually increased, till I have been the mother of seven children, the most beautiful and most loved of whom lies buried near my Cincinnati residence. It was at his dying bed and at his grave that I learned what a poor slave mother may feel when her child is torn away from her.

Almost unconscious of her own fame in that first year, Harriet was in awe of fame in others. The celebrity of the hour was Jenny Lind, the "Swedish nightingale." When Lind, just finishing her triumphal tour of America with a last concert at Castle Garden, learned that Harriet was in New York, she sent her two tickets to a supposedly sold-out performance with a note praising *Uncle Tom*. It was the first concert Harriet had ever attended—a vestige of her Puritan heritage kept Harriet away from any form of theatrical entertainment, including a dramatization of her *Uncle Tom* that was on the boards within months of the book's publication— and she wrote to Calvin that it was "a bewildering dream of sweetness and beauty." She also initiated an exchange of notes with the songstress that resulted in being able to use the Lind name and a hundred-dollar gift to kick off a successful fund-raising effort to buy the freedom of several more slaves through Henry Ward's contacts.

Whether motivated by Harriet's view of him in her autobiographical letter or his own anxieties, Calvin chose those busy months after publication as a time to negotiate a better salary from Andover Theological Seminary in Andover, Massachusetts, and resign from Bowdoin. As she had in the move from Cincinnati, Harriet left her family in Brunswick and went alone to Andover to find a suitable place for them. Armed this time with money, she acquired a stone structure in which theological students had once made coffins and wheelbarrows as a form of manual training and a source of income for the seminary. Shuttling on a newly constructed railroad between Boston and Brunswick, Harriet supervised a remodeling of the stone house into a private dwelling while getting a start on her sequel to *Uncle Tom*. She was also engaged in a correspondence with antislavery forces in Great Britain that would lead to an invitation for a visit from the Stowes in the following year. Understandably, there is not much evidence that she gave any thought to the election of Franklin Pierce in the fall. It was a foregone conclusion by June, when the votes that might have gone to the Whig nominee, General Winfield Scott, were destined to be split by the Free Soil Party nominee, John P. Hale. The event that Harriet might have noted with more interest were the deaths of the two great compromisers, Henry Clay and Daniel Webster; with them gone, the odds in favor of a rift in the Union were greatly increased.

One other Beecher who profited almost directly from Harriet's fame was Catharine. Freed of the need to help support the Stowe household, Catharine went back to organizing her American Women's Educational Association, with Harriet named to her Board of Managers. Catharine was able to raise twenty thousand dollars to build the enduring Milwaukee Normal Institute. But a Beecher for whom Harriet's triumph may have been a source of annoyance rather than pride was half brother Tom. Unlike most of his siblings, Tom did not seem to think that doing anything about the institution of slavery was his business, and often being identified as the brother of Harriet or Henry Ward could be demeaning. Although he made it clear by the way he led his life and conducted his relationships that he abhorred any form of man's inhumanity to man, Tom's ingrained pessimism led him to doubt the efficacy of reformist activity above and beyond the personal level. Just at this time, in fact, Tom's focus on life was intensely personal; he was going through an absorbing and tragic romance and marriage. During his teaching time in Hartford, Tom met and fell in love with Olivia Day, the delicate and sensitive daughter of a former president of Yale. In doing so, he stepped into the middle of an intense emotional relationship between Olivia and her cousin Julia Jones, which might be illustrated by phrases from two letters that "Livy" wrote to her "Jule": "You are the home of my heart" (before her marriage) and "He is the air that I breathe, but you are the blue sky!" (after marriage). In a letter to Julia, Tom assured her that he, too, treasured the friendship that the young women enjoyed and added prophetically: "We will celebrate a triple alliance which shall yield, if not as great a theme to history, yet will make one of the three as happy as I can be."

Since the friendship between Livy and Julia involved a great deal of letter writing, a record remains of Livy's not quite successful efforts to understand Tom. Passages from some of Livy's premarital letters to Julia suggest that she was trying to convince herself as much as her friend that she was making the right choice:

> He is a strange person . . . you might easily fancy him more gentle, elegant and pleasing in his manners than he is. He can be the first at times, but it is not his habitual manner. . . . Do not be severe upon my absolute inability to describe Mr. Beecher; he is entirely beyond my ken. I could not say one thing about his character without feeling as if perhaps it was untrue and I ought to contradict it in the next sentence. . . . He does everything vigorously and well, whether it be singing, teaching, carpentering or furnace tending, but especially planning. . . . He gives himself strongly to the mood of the moment, seeing things so vividly from one point of view and then from another and giving utterance to his thoughts freely and impetuously. . . . I believe that he is truly and earnestly religious, and I trust he will come out symmetrical sometime, if he lives long enough.

After their marriage, Livy gave Julia a very telling comparison between her husband and his most famous brother: "Henry will run out into the garden and bring you an exquisite moss rose selected carefully for *you*, or give you anything or everything on the spur of the moment. But when Miss Katy Beecher wants someone to run all over New York half a dozen times to get a crutch made for her—she knows *which brother to ask*."

Tom's love for Livy seemed to be beyond expression. He apparently thought her to be too good, too delicate to undergo the pains and indignities of the human condition. When she and the child she was bearing died, he shocked his sisters by his stoic acceptance of the event and going so far as to call it "a cause of thanksgiving." To Isabella, the blood sister from whom he hoped for understanding, he wrote:

> I cannot make you see as I do without any effort—that for Livy to have lived and become a mother would have been as foul an incongruity as it would have been for *Undine* [a water nymph] to have been transformed into a steady dutch vrow, nursing her children through the measles. . . . Every day since our betrothal we have talked of death—as near to us. She supposed of *me*. I supposed of her. From no prayer was it ever absent. Our love, knew only separation and trial here. My heart has been torn for her. Hers was always anxious for me, and we walked hand in

hand in heaven—more hours than on earth. . . . I am not anxious to compel men to feel as I do. I will not pronounce it as exemplary or pious or even sane. It is simply my *fact*—after twenty six years of despair. Christ gave me *Livy*—and some mysterious elixir of *something*—so that when He took her, I rejoiced and did not weep and cannot.

If Harriet's success could be of little use to Tom, it was life-enhancing to other family members. She used some of her wealth to participate in establishing a life annuity for Lyman. Since her British hosts thought she would need a secretary for her visit, she persuaded Charles to get a leave of absence from his Newark church to go along on her projected five-month trip in April 1853. She intended to spend much of it on the Continent, having her first experience of European culture, and she thought that Charles would be the ideal companion because of his knowledgeable interest in the arts and the ability to speak French that he had acquired in New Orleans. Handsomer than the rest of her blood brothers, Charles was tall and thin and graceful with the look of a poet that might be well received in the circles she expected to frequent. Learning of the Stowe expedition through family correspondence, Sarah, George Beecher's widow; her son, George, an aspiring painter; and her wealthy brother, William Buckingham, elected to join the party on their own account. In preparation for the adventure, Harriet closed the stone house in Andover for the duration and farmed out to friends her children and the faithful dog Rover, who always attended family prayers and slept under her bed. With *The Key to Uncle Tom's Cabin* finished and off to the printer, Harriet was rewarding herself at last with a stimulating and carefree interlude.

In the British Isles, her hosts, mostly members of the aristocracy with strong antislavery sentiments, saw to it that she would have a time to remember. She was feted everywhere, royally entertained in private homes, and applauded in large gatherings where Calvin or Charles spoke for her. A highlight was a dinner laid on by the lord mayor of London. There she met and "had a few moments of very pleasant, friendly conversation" with Charles Dickens and his wife despite that rival novelist's rather tepid reception of her work. In addition to the lord mayor, Harriet was introduced to a number of political leaders, including one past and two future prime ministers but not Lord Aberdeen, then the occupant of that office. One of Harriet's main sponsors was the duchess of Sutherland, a close friend of Queen Victoria, but the queen did not receive this celebrated visitor. The slight was deliberate, as President Pierce's minister to the Court of St. James's, James Buchanan, who arrived in London on the heels of Harriet's departure, reported to the State Department: "I have learned from a high titled lady that the Queen absolutely refused to see Mrs. Stowe either at the Palace or the Duchess of Sutherland's, and that she had refused to attend the concert given at the latter place by the Black Swan, lest she might meet Mrs. Stowe there. My informant says, she remarked very sensibly that American Slavery was a question with which Great Britain has nothing to do." Perhaps there was no greater acknowledgment of the little American woman's importance than this official inattention. Calvin had to return to America from London, but Charles and Harriet enjoyed a rich, cultural feast during the European part of their journey. Harriet deliberately kept a low profile, and they did for the most part what any leisured, well-heeled tourists would do, and Harriet returned rested and eager to resume her family life in Andover in September.

Buchanan's choice of adverbs—"very sensibly"—reflected the attitude of the "doughface" Democrats from the North and proslavery men such as Jefferson Davis, the secretary of war, who had come into power with President Pierce. They did not think that the federal government should make slavery its business or, in fact, that it had a constitutional right to do so. The leading Democrat in the Senate, Stephen A. Douglas of Illinois, introduced the Kansas–Nebraska Bill in January 1854 that would leave the question of introducing slavery in these territories west of the Mississippi up to "popular sovereignty." In effect, this would nullify the Missouri Compromise. Almost immediately, antislavery forces, including the most politically involved Beechers, sprang into action. Edward started organizing Boston ministers to oppose the act, while Harriet wrote an article for the *Independent* urging women, though disenfranchised, to use their influence as wives and mothers on their voting men. Fearing that there was no choice for them in any of the existing parties, fifty opponents of Douglas's bill in Ripon, Wisconsin, met to start something they called the Republican Party. Fearing that proslavery settlers would flood into the territories to outvote their counterparts, a Massachusetts Emigrant Aid Society (later to be broadened to include all of New England) was formed to subsidize antislavery people willing to move out to the territories. None of these efforts could keep both houses of Congress from passing the bill and President Pierce from signing it. In Nebraska, voters responded by electing an antislavery legislature, but in Kansas proslavery forces won with the help of what might be described as armed mercenaries from the slave states, known as "border ruffians." It was the beginning of a seesawing exchange of power between these two groups that would go on for years and escalate into so much killing that the territory became known as "bleeding Kansas." At a meeting of the Emigrant Aid people in New Haven, Henry Ward Beecher said that "Sharpe's rifles are a greater moral agency than the Bible." At that, the group raised funds to ship twenty-five rifles to antislavery forces in Kansas, and Beecher went back to Brooklyn to persuade his church to ship twenty-five more. Thereafter, weapons sent to Kansas were called "Beecher's Bibles," and the Plymouth Church became "the Church of the Holy Bibles."

By the mid-1850s Henry Ward's ministry had become phenomenally successful but disturbingly controversial to more orthodox colleagues. As in Indiana, Beecher made changes in the rules governing Plymouth Church that virtually separated it from all other Congregational bodies. Whereas, for instance, the standard Congregational form acknowledged "the scriptures as the only infallible guide in matters of church order and discipline," Beecher's statement dropped mention of the scriptures and declared that "this church is an independent ecclesiastical body, and in matters of doctrine, order, and discipline, is answerable to no other organization." He also eliminated the Trinity from his Article of Faith and substituted belief in "one everlasting and true God." Some critics claimed that he also had substituted a performance by Beecher for "prayerful worship." Even brother Tom, who had a tendency to see the warts standing out on the faces of those he loved most, once said while filling in for Henry Ward at Plymouth Church, "All those who came here to worship Henry Ward Beecher may withdraw from the church—all who came to worship God may remain." Henry Ward was not much of a pastor in the usual sense of that word, and he left the details of running the organization to others. But as a charismatic leader, he had no trouble getting his people to buy the freedom of slaves or send rifles to Kansas. He could persuade them to go along with other changes in attitude, often lightening the matter with humor. Against all tradition, he urged the women of Plymouth Church to speak out in prayer meetings. When one of them rambled on pointlessly for too long a time, Henry Ward said as she finally sat down, "Nevertheless I believe that women should speak. We will now sing number five hundred six."

By the time of the 1856 campaign, Henry Ward was so confident of his congregation's support that he had no qualms about speaking his mind on any and every subject, including politics. Indeed, he considered it the duty of a minister to discuss and participate in civic affairs. Those fifty farsighted souls in Wisconsin had grown into a host large enough to form a major party, using the name Republican, which held its first national convention in Philadelphia and nominated John C. Frémont, the Californian hero of western exploration, for president. He would be opposed by James Buchanan, a colorless Pennsylvania politician chosen by the Democrats in hopes of capturing the large electoral vote of his state and in preference to the incumbent Pierce and aspiring Douglas, both of whose reputations were bloodied by the ongoing trouble in Kansas. Like his fellow ex-Whigs in New York, Senator Seward and editor Greeley, Henry Ward Beecher participated in the formation of the new party and took what amounted to a leave of absence from Plymouth Church—he would show up for Sunday services—to stump the state for Frémont. Henry Ward gave a three-hour address every weekday wherever he could find a crowd, and so exhausted himself that he began suffering from what he feared might prove fatal dizzy spells. Beecher also took over editorial control of the influential *Independent* by persuading owner Bowen to hire an attractive and ambitious young member of his congregation, Theodore Tilton, to press his political and religious views on its national audience. Despite Henry Ward Beecher's repeated warnings that "the election of Mr. Buchanan will be the beginning of an excitement and of a warfare such as has never been dreamed of hitherto," Pennsylvania's electoral vote did put its native son into the White House.

Except for Henry Ward, who was finding his Brooklyn platform wide enough to match his ambitions, the restless Beechers were very much on the move during the 1850s. Early in the decade, Isabella's husband, John Hooker, and his brother-in-law, Francis Gillette, bought a one-hundred-acre tract called Nook Farm just west of Hartford. Hooker and Gillette both built substantial homes, and soon Mary Beecher Perkins and her husband, Thomas, joined the colony, as did a number of other, more distant relatives. They were very early pioneers in what would become a trend in American life—the move to the suburbs. Thoroughly and respectably upper middle class in lifestyle and income, these Nook Farm settlers were nevertheless individualistic, independent thinkers whose social life consisted of lively discussion and debate as they moved freely in and out of each other's homes. Hooker was known as a "brass-mounted Abolitionist"; Gillette was a maverick given to running for office on various minority party tickets until finally in 1854 a group of these parties joined together to put him in the Senate; Perkins was such a substantial and conservative lawyer that Harriet picked him to handle her affairs when the money started rolling in. Disheartened by the poor sales and harsh criticism of his book, Edward decided in 1855 to answer the call of the West again by becoming pastor of a new church in Galesburg, Illinois, home of Knox College, and a part-time professor in a theological seminary in Chicago. Charles was never comfortable in Newark, and the community was never comfortable with him, since his sometimes strange thoughts that emerged in sermons and publications suggested that he might be "unsound." Never earning enough to support his family, Charles depended on hand-outs from richer siblings, which he repaid in service such as accompanying Harriet to Europe and preparing the music for Henry Ward's *Plymouth Collection of Hymns*. When Edward reached Galesburg, he arranged for Knox College to offer Charles a job as teacher of elocution and music, but infighting between Presbyterians and Congregationalists for control of the college caused Charles to leave after a year and return to Andover, where the family put him to work compiling Lyman's autobiography. Unlucky William moved from church to church—in one of them he had to go to court to collect back salary—until Calvin and Harriet settled him in a pastorate in North Brookfield, Massachusetts, where side income from being the town's postmaster enabled him to scrape by. Aptly, William's only known publication was a pamphlet titled *The Duty of the Church to Her Ministry*, in which he complained bitterly of the poverty in which so many congregations kept their pastors.

As unorthodox as his older half brothers—or perhaps more so—Thomas Beecher quickly got into trouble with his Williamsburgh congregation. It was conceded that he shared Henry Ward's flare for preaching, but his lack of enthusiasm for Henry Ward's antislavery stance alienated a largely abolitionist congregation. Worse, he denounced the business practices of members of his congregation whose wealth was counted on to finance the church under construction. When called before the church's council, he was so insulted by their questions that he refused to answer them, and they were so incensed by his attitude that they threatened to fire him without official notice and thus make it impossible for him to get another church. As the story goes, Tom walked out of that meeting and right into the arms of a deacon from the First Congregational Church of Elmira, New York, who had been sent to ask him to be their pastor. Tom sent off a brashly honest letter to Jarvis Langdon, the wealthy Elmira businessman heading the church's search committee. In it he asked for a fifteen-hundred-dollar annual salary and forty dollars for moving costs, and an agreement that he could leave, or the church could ask him to leave, at the end of any month without recriminations. He expressed doubts as to "whether it is possible for any church to be benefited by any services of mine as preacher and teacher" and added that he had "no ambition to found or foster or preserve a church as such. My exclusive aim is to help men as individuals to be Christians." Langdon and his associates appreciated the young man's honesty, or perhaps were moved by a single sentence: "For though I speak bold words, yet my heart is very tender and very tired and would fain rest in just some such place as Elmira." In 1854 Tom moved to Elmira and went to work.

The farthest-moving Beecher, James, came ashore after five years at sea. At first he tried going to work in a Boston business under the aegis of brother Edward, but soon found that kind of work wanting. After one of his voyages he had said, "Oh, I shall be a minister. That's my fate. Father will pray me into it!" With something of a shrug, he surrendered to that fate and entered Andover Theological Seminary. He never completed the course. When a call came for somebody to manage a bethel (a chapel for seamen) in China, James was so obviously the right person for the job that a quick ordination was arranged, and he was off again to the Far East. This time, however, he would not go alone. He had married a slightly older woman, a widow from Newburyport, Massachusetts, named Annie Morse, who had ambitions to become a writer.

When the Beechers gathered at Harriet's stone house in Andover to celebrate Lyman's eightieth birthday on October 12, 1855, James and, of course, George were the only children missing. At one point Lyman demonstrated his agility by leaping a fence at the seminary campus, and they all trooped to a studio in town to have a group portrait made by the new art of photography. This gathering was a prelude to a kind of self-examination that would continue through the process of creating Lyman's autobiography, to which all of them contributed, with Charles in charge of pulling it together. Some of the thoughts that came to Charles while he worked were recorded in a letter to Henry Ward:

> I have been studying the letters written by father & the children to Edward from 1818 to 1826. E. went to college in 1818 & all the older children were converted in that interval. I have extracted all that reveals Father's agency in reference to the great problem of the conversion of his children. It is deeply affecting. It is really one of the most solemn things I have attended to for a long time. It fills me with concern for my own children, & my great stupidity in regard to them, & above all, my unbelief in regard to their danger. *Is* eternal punishment a reality? Father thought so. He never doubted. Strike that idea out of his mind, & his whole career would be changed, his whole influence modified.

Standing, left to right, are Thomas, William, Edward, Charles, and Henry Ward. Seated, left to right, are Isabella, Catharine, Lyman, Mary, and Harriet. Taken by Mathew Brady before he became famous as the photographer of the Civil War, this picture recorded the second and last family gathering of Beechers in Amherst, Massachusetts, where the Stowes were living while Calvin was a professor at the seminary. Only George, who had died, and James, who was running a seamen's bethel in China, are missing. It is said that a spry eighty-year-old Lyman leaped over a fence on his way to or from the studio where the picture was taken.

He never could write to E, "If I could but see one of my children *out of danger,* I think I should experience a joy hitherto unknown." What *danger* if he believed in no future endless ruin? Yet Isabella & Mary I fear reject father's belief on that point, & Hatty's mind is I fear shaken—do *you* believe in it? Do you really believe that the wicked will exist forever, and continue forever in sin? The only point on which my mind recoils is, on the question of their endless *existence. If* they exist, I can conceive that they might be unchangeably wicked, & of course miserable. But do you believe this? How can we affect *our* children as Father did us, if we have not the same concern for them, the same sense of their awful danger?

I am not satisfied with my own state & fear that I have no real communion with God—and yet have no life to struggle for any. My soul seems cold as death—and I have not strength enough to pray or strive. And yet, I feel a kind of settled resolution not to waste my life. I feel a kind of *resignation* to be and do whatever God appoints. If He decides for me to come here, I will try to be faithful to my charge, if not, I am about to seek some small society either in N.E. or in Kansas—and try to be a faithful minister.

My heart is much affected by the early *unity* of the family contrasted with our present isolation. I don't know as the thing can be mended for we had not felt then the divisive force of our own strong but undeveloped natures, and the equally divisive force of diverse careers and fortunes in life. Yet I think we might in some respects do better.

I have been deeply touched for *Catharine* on reading over her early letters. I wish you could read them. All before & after her engagement with Fisher, & his death. All her deep & painful struggles in religious matters for years. How she has suffered; how she has been tried! And yet the character she shows is a very interesting one—I mean in her letters. Now I know she has peculiarities that repel some from her. And yet it seems sad to me to see her cast out as it were from the family circle by Mary, & Hatty, & you—not that she is really cast out—but—something *virtually* pretty near it. Yet she is sincere, & kind, & benevolent—That is she seems to have been so—both by natural impulse & on principle. Cannot she be made to feel more of the warm sympathy of fraternal affection in her loneliness?

And cannot we strive to renew & revive the affection of early years, between all the members of the family? I do not love to be cut off from *you* as I am—never to hear from you, except by newspapers—I long to have *all* of father's children—as far as circumstances will allow, working nearer together, instead of farther asunder—How shall we achieve it? Let us resolve to try—Let us revive the old family circular, and not leave ourselves to pass years with scarce a word exchanged. Above all, I wish *you* would write to me a good letter to help me in things spiritual.

Possibly because of his mission on behalf of the whole family, Charles was not included in the party that Harriet assembled for her second trip to Europe in the summer of 1856. She was again in need of a vacation after finishing another novel, *Dred: A Tale of the Great Dismal Swamp*. At the suggestion of her publisher, she again addressed the problem of slavery, but from a different angle. She wanted to show how the evil institution affected the lives of white owners. In this instance, more than in *Uncle Tom*, she was true to her own description of a novel: "A novel is now understood to be a parable—a story told in illustration of a truth or fact." She was writing in a year when the death and violence in her book was a reflection of the truth or fact to be found in the daily news. One event only thinly disguised in *Dred* was the cowardly caning of Massachusetts' antislavery senator Charles Sumner at his desk by a young proslavery congressman from South Carolina. As for mayhem and murder in the struggle over slavery, the abolitionist fanatic John Brown provided a gory instance when he slaughtered five proslavery people in Kansas. *Dred* was not greeted with the applause and critical acclaim accorded to *Uncle Tom's Cabin* and was, in fact, vilified by religious conservatives for the attack that she again launched at timid clergymen. But the book sold well, and Harriet revealed her pride in being a money writer in a letter to Calvin boasting of a hundred thousand sales in four weeks and adding: "After all, who cares what critics say?"

Harriet's children were growing up, and it was time to introduce them to the world. She took her eighteen-year-old twin daughters, Harriet and Eliza, whom she planned to leave in a European school to brush up on language and culture, and her oldest son, Henry. At sixteen he was tall, athletic, and handsome—a throwback to some of her brothers instead of taking after a shrimp like her or his soft, round, bearded father Calvin, whom Harriet affectionately called her "rabbi." Henry was a favorite child, as his namesake was a favorite brother, and the chemistry between Harriet and this son was good. Calvin would be with them until he had to go back to his teaching job, and Henry would have to leave them in time to enter Dartmouth. To be sure of a companion for the rest of the trip, Harriet persuaded Mary Perkins to be part of the party. Early on, they enjoyed an experience denied them on their first visit to England, as described by Calvin in a letter home: "Yesterday we had just the very pleasantest interview with the Queen that ever was. None of the formal, drawing-room, breathless receptions, but just an accidental done-on-purpose meeting at a railway station, while on our way to Scotland. The Queen seemed really delighted to see my wife, and remarkably glad to see me for her sake. She pointed us out to Prince Albert, who made two most gracious bows to my wife and two to me, while the four royal children stared their big blue eyes almost out looking at the little authoress of 'Uncle Tom's Cabin.' Colonel Grey handed the Queen, with my wife's compliments, a copy of the new book. She took one volume herself and handed the other to Prince Albert, and they were soon both very busy reading."

A more significant event in terms of Harriet's past and future lives was getting to know Lady Byron, the widow of the poet whose work had lightened with romance Harriet's Calvinist childhood. Harriet did not expect to like this woman, because her coldness had allegedly caused Byron to pursue his notoriously sinful ways. But she found Lady Byron, in her sixties and ill, to be a warmhearted person who had devoted her life to quiet acts of charity. The rapport between the women was so strong and unexpected that Harriet ended her first note to Lady Byron with these words: "I love you, my dear friend, as never before, with an intense feeling I cannot express. God bless you!" Lady Byron had shown her regard for Harriet by insisting on being alone with her after a luncheon party and sharing with her a matter she had kept secret all the years since Byron's death in 1824—their marriage had been broken up by Byron's incestuous relationship with Augusta Leigh, his half sister. In an instant what had been a nasty rumor was turned into a horrid fact for Harriet. Lady Byron said that the reason for discussing this with Harriet was her fear that the editors of a new edition of Byron's work would again lay the blame for his bad behavior on her, and she felt that the time might have come to go public with her side of the story. Incensed by the fact that her new friend had been a martyr to her husband's reputation for so long, Harriet agreed. But when she revealed what had been said behind closed doors to her sister Mary, who also had been at the luncheon, she got a good dose of Beecher caution from the most conservative—and some said, most levelheaded—member of the tribe. Mary argued that Lady Byron's motives would be misjudged if she spoke out while she was still alive, that justice would be better served by taking up the case after her death. In a few future meetings and continuing correspondence, Harriet apparently convinced Lady Byron of this point of view and implied that she would be her posthumous defender.

For the rest of the trip, Harriet and Mary turned into tourists. Since most of her family was on the other side of the Atlantic, Harriet devoted her talent to some of the liveliest travel writing of the day, as is evident in these excerpts from her account of their trip from Marseilles to Rome by steamer and carriage:

> About eleven o'clock, as I had just tranquilly laid down in my berth, I was roused by a grating crash, accompanied by a shock that shook the whole ship, and followed by a general rush on deck, trampling, scuffling, and cries. I rushed to the door and saw all the gentlemen hurrying on their clothes and getting confusedly toward the stairway. I went back to Mary, and we put on our things in silence, and, as soon as we could got into the upper saloon. It was an hour before we learned anything certainly, except that we had run into another vessel. The fate of the Arctic came to us both, but we did not mention it to each other; indeed, a quieter, more silent company you would not often see. . . . As it was, we turned aside and the shock came on a paddle-wheel, which was broken by it, for when, after two hours' delay, we tried to start and had gone a little way, there was another crash and the paddle-wheel fell down. You may be sure we did little sleeping that night. It was an inexpressible desolation to think that we might never again see those we loved. No one knows how much one thinks, and how rapidly, in such hours.
>
> We went limping along with one broken limb till the next day, about eleven, when we reached Civita Vecchia, where . . . Mary and I, and a Dr. Edison from Philadelphia, with his son Alfred, took a carriage to Rome, but they gave us a miserable thing that looked as if it had been made soon after the deluge. About eight o'clock at night, on a lonely stretch of road, the wheel came off. We got out, and our postilions stood silently regarding matters. None of us could speak Italian, they could not speak French, but the driver at last conveyed the idea that for five francs he could get a man to come and mend the wheel. The

five francs were promised, and he untackled a horse and rode off. Mary and I walked up and down the dark, desolate road, occasionally reminding each other that we were on classic ground, and laughing at the oddity of our lonely, starlight promenade. After a while our driver came back. Tag, Rag and Bobtail at his heels. . . . They put a bit of rotten timber under to pry the carriage up. Fortunately, it did not break . . . till after the wheel was on. Then a new train of thought was suggested. How was it to be kept on? Evidently they had not thought in that direction, for they had brought neither hammer, nor nail, nor tool of any kind, and therefore they looked first at the wheel, then at each other, and then at us. The doctor now produced a little gimlet, with the help of which the broken fragments of the former linchpin were pushed out, and the way was cleared for a new one. Then they began knocking a fence to pieces to get out nails, but none could be found to fit. At last another ambassador was sent back for nails. While we were thus waiting . . . an interesting little episode here occurred. It was raining, and Mary and I proposed, as the wheel was now on, to take our seats. We had no sooner done so than the horses were taken with a sudden fit of animation and ran off with us in the most vivacious manner, Tag, Rag, and Co. shouting in the rear. Some heaps of stone a little in advance presented an interesting prospect by way of terminus. However, the horses were luckily captured before the wheel was off again, and our ambassador being now returned, we were set right and again proceeded.

At every post where we changed horses and drivers, we had a pitched battle with the driver for more money than we had been told was the regular rate, and the carriage was surrounded with a perfect mob of ragged, shock-headed, black-eyed people, whose words all ended in "ino," and who raved and ranted at us till finally we paid much more than we ought, to get rid of them. At the gates of Rome the official, after looking at our passports, coolly told the doctor that if we had a mind to pay him five francs we could go in without further disturbances, but if not he would keep the baggage till morning. This form of statement had the recommendation of such precision and neatness of expressing that we paid him forthwith, and into Rome we dashed at two o'clock in the morning of the 9th of February, 1857, in a drizzling rain.

We drove to the Hotel d'Angleterre,—it was full—and ditto to four or five others, and in the last effort our refractory wheel came off again, and we all got out into the street. About a dozen lean, ragged "corbies," who are called porters and who are always lying in wait for travelers pounced upon us. They took down our baggage in a twinkling, and putting it all into the street surrounded it, and chattered over it, while M. and I stood in the rain and received first lessons in Italian. . . . A young man came by and addressed us in English. How cheering! We begged him, at least, to lend us his Italian to call another carriage, and he did so. A carriage which was passing was luckily secured, and Mary and I, with all our store of boxes and little parcels, were placed in it out of the rain, at least. Here we sat while the doctor from time to time returned from his wanderings to tell us he could find no place. . . . When at last the doctor announced lodgings found, we followed in rather an uncertain frame of mind.

We alighted at a dirty stone passage, smelling of cats and onions, damp, cold, and earthy, we went up a stone stairway, and at last were ushered into two very decent chambers. . . . The "corbies" all followed us,—black-haired, black-browed, ragged, and clamorous as ever. They insisted that we should pay the pretty little sum of twenty francs, or four dollars, for bringing our trunks about twenty steps. The doctor modestly but firmly declined to be thus imposed upon, and then ensued a general "chatteration," one and all fell into attitudes, and the "inos" and "issimos" rolled freely. "For pity sake get them off," we said; so we made a truce for ten francs, but still they clamored, forced their way even into our bedroom, and were only repulsed by a loud and combined volley of "No, no, noes!" which we all set up at once, upon which they retreated. . . . Our hostess was a little French woman, and that reassured us. I examined the room . . . and resolved to avail myself without fear of the invitation of a very clean, white bed, where I slept till morning without dreaming.

The trials of the trip were forgotten by the time that Harriet arrived home in good spirits in June. She was disappointed that young Henry, busy with examinations at Dartmouth, was not on hand to greet her. She thought of taking his younger brother Fred up to Hanover to visit Henry, but she discovered that another destination was in order. Fred had started to use alcohol to cope with teenage anxieties of an undersized, rather sickly, middle child in an overachieving family. To outsiders it might seem a paradox that alcohol abuse should surface in a family famous for preaching temperance for half a century. But temperance was something of a relative term in a hard-drinking society. The variety and strength of America's ardent spirits were so celebrated that Sir Richard Burton, the British explorer and author who had sampled the exotic delights of Africa and the Middle East, decided to accept an invitation from an American officer he had met in Aden, Lieutenant John Steinhauser, to drink their way through the United States and noted this prospectus in his journal: "I'll drink mint-juleps, brandy-mashes, whisky-skies, gin-sling, cocktail sherry cobblers, rum-salads, streaks of lightning, morning-glory. It'll be a most interesting experiment. I want to see whether after a life of 3 or 4 months, I can drink myself to the level of the aborigines." Although he expressed pride in not disgracing himself when he reported to Harriet what other pastors did, Calvin acknowledged a taste for alcohol that may well have been exercised, however discreetly. Harriet left a written record of her daily use of the substance after her work brought her into more sophisticated circles. When she felt faint during a visit to her publisher's office, he poured her a glass of champagne that seemed to do her so much good that he later sent her some bottles of Catawba wine. She found that beverage bracing as well and ordered a dozen more bottles. In a note to daughter Hattie, one of the twins who helped with managing the household, she instructed her to put the wine in the dining room closet where she could get at it to pour herself a "portion" after breakfast and before her afternoon walk. Not to be misunderstood, she added that "the *stimulus* will be used up in active out-of-door exercise which will strengthen my general health." Henry Ward also mentions a stash of Catawba wine in one of his houses, and one of the many ways by which Thomas Beecher shocked the pious citizens of Elmira was his practice of keeping his own mug at a favorite tavern, where he would drop in regularly for a beer.

It may have been Tom's open and frequent use of the "stimulus" as well as his comparative youth that made Harriet think that he would be understanding of Fred's problem. Tom had gained stature in his sisters' eyes in January 1857 when he married Julia Jones, the energetic and sensible cousin of his first wife, Livy. "We were made one first in love of Livy, and then in grief for her," he said, and Harriet undoubtedly heard an echo of her own romance and marriage in which Eliza Tyler, Calvin's first wife, was the initial connection and a remaining presence. Tom and Julia were boarding in Dr. Gleason's water cure establishment in Elmira, and Fred might profit from a health regimen that had done Harriet so much good. Whatever her reasons for doing so, Harriet's putting Fred into Tom's hands was the beginning of a common practice among Beechers whenever somebody needed tough love. Tom was a man who practiced what he preached—that what you do to and for others rather than what you believe is the test of a Christian.

While Harriet was delivering Fred to Tom, she got a telegram on July 9 with the devastating news that her beloved Henry had drowned while swimming in the Connecticut River near Dartmouth. Harriet rushed back to Andover, where she found the stone house filled with shocked and grieving collegemates wanting to tell her how popular Henry had been. One boy, who lived in the same boardinghouse, said he had noticed a seal ring on Henry's finger at lunch on the day of the drowning and exclaimed, "How beautiful that ring is!" As he got up to head for the river, Henry said, "Yes, and best of all, it was my mother's gift to me." It was a story that would help her bear the weight of sorrow, because it meant that he knew that she loved him. But did God love him? He had written to her after going home from Europe, "I may not be what the world calls a Christian, but I will live such a life as a Christian ought to live." By that statement alone, he would not be what a Calvinist called a Christian, and a lingering remnant of her father's certitude about damnation for the unconverted caused Harriet anguish. She poured it out in a letter to Catharine, who had wrestled with similar demons after Professor Fisher's drowning:

> If ever I was conscious of an attack of the Devil trying to separate me from the love of Christ, it was for some days after the terrible news came. I was in a state of great physical weakness, most agonizing, and unable to control my thoughts. Distressing doubts as to Henry's spiritual state were rudely thrust upon my soul. It was as if a voice had said to me: "You trusted in God, did you? You believed that He loved you! You had perfect confidence that he would never take your child till the work of grace was mature! Now he has hurried him into eternity without a moment's warning, without preparation, and where is he?" I saw at last that these thoughts were dishonorable to God, and that it was my duty to resist them, and to assume and steadily maintain that Jesus in love had taken my dear one to his bosom. Since then the Enemy has left me in peace.

As she had done before and would do again, Harriet turned to work to keep her mind off her sorrow. This time she wanted to use her fictional talent to deal with the issues raised by her personal tragedy rather than those of the nation, even though the antislavery forces suffered a severe setback through the U.S. Supreme Court's ruling in the case of *Dred Scott v. Sanford*. The Court ruled in effect that the Missouri Compromise of 1820 was unconstitutional and held that Congress has no right to deprive citizens of their property—a slave being property—anywhere in the nation. Thus Scott, who had sued for his freedom on the grounds that his master had taken him from Missouri into the free state of Illinois, would remain in bondage. Harriet decided to let *Uncle Tom* and her own *Dred* stand for what she thought of treating black human beings as property. In the novel she called *The Minister's Wooing*, her concern was with the pain that harsh Calvinism could cause people. In a central scene, Harriet pictures Candace—"a powerfully built, majestic black woman, corpulent, heavy with a swinging majesty of motion like that of a ship in a ground-swell"—trying to comfort her employer, a Calvinist, who has just learned that her unconverted sailor son has been lost at sea and is presumably subject to eternal damnation. Understandably, the woman is weeping and railing against God, and Candace says:

> Now, honey, I knows our Doctor's [the local pastor] a mighty good man, an' larned—an' in fair weather I ha'n't no 'bejection to yer hearin' all about dese yer great and mighty tings he's got to say. But, honey, dey won' do for you now, sick folks mus'n't have strong meat, an' times like dese dat jes a'n't but one ting to come to, an' dat ar's *Jesus*. Tell ye, honey, ye can't live no other way now. Don't ye 'member how He looked on His mother when she stood faintin' and tremblin' under de cross, jes like you? He knows all about mothers' hearts. He won't break yours. It was jes' 'cause He know'd we'd come into straits like dis yer, dat he went through all dese tings,—Him, de Lord o' Glory! Is dis Him you was talkin' about?—Him you can't love? Look at Him, an' see if you can't. Look an' see what He is!—don't ask no questions, and don't go to no reasonin's—jes look at *Him*, hangin' dar, so sweet and patient, on de cross! All dey could do couldn't stop His lovin' 'em, He prayed for 'em wid all de breath He had. Dar's a God you can love, a'n't dar? Candace loves Him—poor, ole, foolish, black, wicked Candace,—and she knows He loves her.

Harriet could not resist taking swipes at behavior and views she found wanting in other religious and moral matters. She poured the acid of sarcasm on one aspect of slavery. The story is set in Newport before 1808 when, according to Harriet, sailing in the slave trade was the town's most profitable business. After one trip on a slaver, a character named George "declared that the gold made in it was distilled from human blood, from mothers' tears, from the agonies and dying groans of gasping, suffocating men and women, and that it would scar and blister the soul of him that touched it. In short, he talked as whole-souled, impractical fellows are apt to talk about what respectable people do. Nobody had ever instructed him that a slave ship, with a procession of expectant sharks in its wake, is a missionary institution, by which closely packed heathens are brought over to enjoy the light of the gospel." She gave a glancing blow to the anti-Catholicism that Lyman and to a lesser extent her theologically concerned brothers Edward and Charles preached. Her heroine, Mary, a little Puritan, and a French woman, a devout Catholic, find themselves "melting together in that embrace of love and sorrow, joined in the great communion of suffering." Mary's sorrow comes from her fears as to both the earthly and heavenly fate of the supposedly drowned young sailor, and the French woman's from being deceived and deserted by a fictionalized Aaron Burr, clearly a stand-in for Lord Byron in that he was a brilliant, charismatic charmer with a Calvinist background—grandfather Jonathan Edwards—who allegedly became a lecherous womanizer.

Once more, Harriet felt entitled to treat herself to a trip abroad after the novel was finished in 1859. In one respect at least things had improved on the home front. Tom had straightened out young Fred by sending him to a remote spa when he found him associating with the wrong kind of young men in Elmira. Fred returned to Andover abstinent and ambitious to study medicine at Harvard, where Harriet arranged for her good friend Dr. Oliver Wendell Holmes, author, physician, and anatomy professor, to keep an eye on him. With the twins along, Harriet spent most of her time in Florence, although she found herself impressed and moved by the Holy Week ceremonies at the Vatican in Rome and by the romance and scenery of the Amalfi coast and Capri. While in Florence she met James Field, who would become her Boston publisher, and his young wife, Annie, who would become her best friend and correspondent. She also turned an acquaintanceship into a fast friendship with Robert and Elizabeth Barrett Browning. Quite apart from literature, Harriet and the British poetess shared an interest in spiritualism that seemed to be gaining more adherents by the day. Harriet was skeptical about its more popular forms—"circles and spiritual jugglery"—and concerned about a conflict with her Christian beliefs. But in Florence she met a very religious woman from Boston who also was a medium and began receiving "very strong impressions from the spiritual world" while she was with her. As their correspondence suggests, she began to have more understanding of and appreciation for the strange and fascinating visitations that Calvin had been having all his life. Neither of them had quite recovered from the death of their son Henry. Although Harriet felt near to him when she was with the medium in Florence, she took issue with Calvin's report that a guitar vibrating at the touch of an unseen hand in the stone house in Andover was a sign of Henry's spiritual presence. "I cannot, however, think that Henry strikes the guitar—that must be Eliza," she wrote. "Her spirit has ever seemed to cling to that mode of manifestation, and if you would keep it in your sleeping room, no doubt you would hear from it oftener." She evidently interrupted her letter to visit her medium friend. While she was there, and in the presence of three other people, sounds of strumming came from a Florentine guitar hung so high on the wall that none of them could have reached it. "Now that is strange," the medium told her. "I asked last night that if any spirit was present with us when you came today, that it would try to touch that guitar." In her postscript reporting the incident to Calvin, Harriet added, "We marveled, and I remembered the guitar at home."

Before Harriet got home herself, she heard of the political storm that was brewing across the Atlantic. She was encouraged that Henry Ward was plunging into the fray from the pulpit and in print to support this man Abraham Lincoln, who had been nominated by the new Republican Party. If his actions suited his reasonable words, there was still a faint hope of keeping peace in the land.

8

"This war is killing me."

THE FUNERAL TRAIN BEARING THE BODIES of America's slain president and his eleven-year-old son, Willie, who died in the White House during the worst year of the long Civil War, chugged out of the Baltimore & Ohio Station in Washington, D.C., at 8:00 A.M. on Friday, April 21, 1865. The train would be retracing in easy stages the 1,654-mile route that Abraham Lincoln had taken from his home in Springfield, Illinois, to the nation's capital a fraction over four years earlier. Known as *The Lincoln Special,* it was being hauled by an engine with a large portrait of President Lincoln mounted over the cow catcher. Along with the bodies, the cars, draped with funeral garlands, carried some three hundred mourning dignitaries, but the people most intimately affected by the assassination were not among them. Only a week had gone by since Mary Todd Lincoln had been sitting beside the president at Ford's Theater, her hand in his as they laughed together at the comedy on the stage, when a shot rang out and his bloodied head dropped into her lap. So shattered were Mrs. Lincoln's nerves that she could not bear to leave her sheltering White House room to take part in any of the public expressions of grief, and her living sons, Robert and Tad, were keeping their mother company in her sorrow. The absence of the little family would not be noted as thousands upon thousands of people, hats off and handkerchiefs in hand, lined the tracks to watch the train crawl by or crowded into the public halls of major cities to view the familiar, fatherly figure at rest in peace at last—three hundred thousand in Philadelphia alone, waiting five hours in a line three miles long to file through Independence Hall for a reverential glimpse of their fallen leader on Sunday, April 23.

In preparation for the train's arrival in New York the next day, Henry Ward Beecher, back from Charleston, made of its journey a metaphor for the way that victory had turned this prairie lawyer into a man for the ages. Inspired by a congregation at Plymouth Church that overflowed the pews into aisle seats, climbed onto windowsills, and huddled outside by open doors and windows to catch whatever words they could, Beecher came up with a passage of extempore free verse that caught the mood of the moment so well that it would be widely reprinted at the time and long requoted by historians:

> Pass on, thou that has overcome! Your sorrows, oh people, are his peace! Your bells and band and muffled drums, sound triumph in his ear. Wail and weep here; God made it echo joy and triumph there. Pass on!
>
> Four years ago, oh Illinois, we took from your midst an untried man, and from among the people. We return him to you a mighty conqueror. Not thine anymore, but the nation's, not ours, but the world's.
>
> Give him place, oh, ye prairies! In the midst of this great continent his dust shall rest, a sacred treasure to myriads who shall pilgrim to that shrine to kindle anew their zeal and patriotism.
>
> Ye winds that move over the mighty places of the West, chant his requiem! Ye people, behold a martyr whose blood, as so many articulate words, pleads for fidelity, for law, for liberty!

The voice of another and very different man with a Brooklyn background sounded a similar theme. Walt Whitman spent more time in theaters and bars than he did in churches, but he was interested in the fact that "the new theologies bring forward man." These new theologies seemed to be at the root of the sermons a young man in his own neighborhood was preaching, and he wrote at one point, "It is only fair to say of Beecher that he was not a minister. There was so much of him man that there was little left of him to be minister." As for Beecher, he found Whitman's revolutionary book of poetry, *Leaves of Grass*, fascinating and took to quoting lines such as "I find letters from God dropt in the street, and every one is sign'd by God." Indeed, according to Whitman, people who had just come from hearing Beecher would tell the poet that "his whole sermon was you, you, you, from top to toe." It is clear that these two men of a new age thought very much alike, and it is not surprising to hear an echo of Beecher in a stanza from one of Whitman's poems about that dreadful April, "When Lilacs Last in the Dooryard Bloom'd":

Coffin that passes through lanes and streets,
Through day and night with the great cloud darkening the land,
With the pomp of the inloop'd flags, with the cities draped in
  black,
With the show of the States themselves as of crape-veil'd
  women standing,
With processions long and winding and the flambeaus of the
  night,
With the countless torches lit, with the silent sea of faces and
  the unbared heads,
With the waiting depot, the arriving coffin, and the sombre
  faces,
With dirges through the night, with the thousand voices rising
  strong and solemn,
With all the mournful voices of the dirges pour'd around the
  coffin,
The dim-lit churches and the shuddering organs—where amid
  these you journey,
With the tolling tolling bells perpetual clang,
Here, coffin that slowly passes,
I give you my sprig of lilac.

Whitman would be only one of the five hundred thousand people in
New York shuffling past the open coffin of the dead Lincoln in City Hall
who would remember Lincoln as they last saw him in February 1861,
when he paused briefly in the city en route to take up the heavy burdens
of a nation coming apart. President-elect or no, Lincoln was not well
liked in New York, where only 35 percent of the voters had cast a ballot
for him and where the mayor, Fernando Wood, was openly proposing
that New York City secede from the Union. As a newspaperman aware of
the sentiment in the city, who was fortunate enough to have a good view
from the top of an omnibus, Whitman watched with a kind of horror as
Lincoln, conspicuous with his height and high silk hat, climbed out of a
hack into the middle of a hostile, silent crowd. Whitman imagined that
"many an assassin's knife and pistol lurk'd in hip or breast pocket there,
ready, as soon as break and riot came." But Lincoln turned his back to
the crowd and walked slowly up the steps to the door of Astor House,
turned again, and coolly studied the gathering before disappearing into
the hotel. The man's evident courage gave Whitman and doubtless many
other onlookers hope for the future.

It had not been the national crisis awaiting Lincoln's arrival in Washington that persuaded James Chaplin Beecher to leave his post in China in 1861 and return to enlist in the Union Army; it was an unfolding personal tragedy. In 1859 his Annie, the aspiring author, had left him to go back to the States, where she hoped to sell a book about their experiences in the Orient and to recover from an illness to which no Beecher liked to give a name: alcoholism. As it had been with Harriet's son, so it would be with Annie. She was tucked under the wing of brother Tom in Elmira, where she could take advantage of Dr. Gleason's water cure, but surviving scraps of her rather anguished correspondence suggest that she first bounced around from Beecher to Beecher. It is clear from these letters in the spring and summer of her return that she was not welcome in at least one household.

To the Hookers at Nook Farm she wrote:

My dear friends—Be comforted and of good cheer, and all will be explained. Eunice *beats all nature*, but I cannot say to you what I would for it is only by the utmost skill that I can get this to you. She telegraphed to Tom, and has probably to Edward and Henry for we hear nothing from Fred. This will only prolong my absence from Jim, as I will never leave under such circumstances. Never. I am waiting for Henry in great *torture* though I still retain my senses for a wonder. There is no more necessity for John [Hooker] than the President. Sarah is too much dismayed poor child to answer your letters even would Eunice consent. Tell Kate that with cold and chills I am too miserable to get out or prepare the papers of which we conversed while I was in Hartford. Because I was not able to pay the wash bill which the man was willing to let stand until I could get out, she declared I had no money in Chelsea that Henry must pay my passage back to China and God knows what all. Through this howling which doubtless is good for my soul, I am cool and have answered her not a word. I have not named one of my private matters to her because I know she would make a handle of it to injure James. I have not forgotten the $5. Yours in haste, Annie.

Again to the Hookers:

Brooklyn, April 25. My dearest Isabella, how good—how excellent—how generous you were to write and love your Annie still, when you thought her appetites were stronger than her reason. God bless you dear—Jim's own sister! I have had, and shall prob-

ably have an awful time of it, but God reigns though the Devil is trying to. Have you received a note from me? Eunice has prohibited the sending a note or message so that I have been in a dilemma of the most *excruciating* kind. *Now* I am at father's [Lyman had moved from Boston to Brooklyn to be near Henry Ward] and will *die* here before things shall remain as they have been. I cannot explain until Henry has been informed of the steps I have been compelled to take. To remain under Eunice's roof longer was *insupportable*. Pray that my deliverance may come soon and that I may be led to believe in the mercy of that God who from darkness bringeth wonderful light. You will always be close to my heart dear Isabella on account of your *unselfishness*. Mother sends love father is asleep. Answer *immediately*.
A. E. Beecher.

Annie was finally delivered into Tom's hands, and a letter she wrote from Elmira to Charles Beecher contains more than a dollop of *in vino veritas*:

July 8/59. My dear Charles, I am hastening you will perceive to let you know just how I am, and what Mr. Loomis has frightened you about or Belle Hooker or somebody. I did not wish him—Mr. Loomis—to know aught of the troubles at Henry's, nor why I cannot have a home in Brooklyn except among strangers. Mother would accommodate me but you know her house is *full*. Loomis wrote that he wished to become more acquainted with me before I left and suggested my making a visit. I sent him word that I should like to board there a few weeks while I was correcting a few of my proof sheets but that he had better say nothing about it not even to Tom for there was only one chance in a hundred of my coming. Please ease Belle and Kate and yourself on this head.

My book will *not* contain anything about future punishment as I am convinced it is *not* true, but am too much of a coward or too *ignorant*—which is as bad if not worse to meddle with the matter. Common sense leads me to the conclusions I have formed and I am day by day learning to comprehend God. I tell you Charles to believe—to *realize* what you teach and profess to believe would *craze* me. The day is rolling on fast when that hideous and appalling doctrine will have faded away—and men will comprehend that why the Creator wishes to keep them from *sin* is that it bites and *stings* us to death even in this world. My book contains only playful letters—anecdotes gathered up during my three years absence.

I shall state things however just as they are and you can believe or not just as you choose. I shall not leave Elmira until Tom says go! Mrs. Gleason wonders how I have done as well as I have done. If you expect me to become humble enough to love my enemies including *Eunice* you will be disappointed. I should think *you* had suffered enough from her to know a little what I passed through.

You say Tom's *theory* is not as good as yours but his practice better. O Charles! That theory that makes a man unselfish and self-denying is Christ's theory and I want no better. Julia and Tom have saved me I do believe from insanity. I tell you my dear brother I *need* love—tenderness—soothing attentions and most of the time I have had them at Elmira. I could live and die here with Tom and Julia if Jim were here too. But that cannot be. He owns his little church—is working hard—and doing well. You would be relieved dear Charles could you *see* me—but you now read all that I write with jaundiced eyes.

I have just received a letter from Lieutenant Clary of the U.S. Ship of war Minnesota inviting me to visit his sisters in Springfield. I think much of his friendship as he is a southern man and that ship was manned by southern officers bitterly opposed to *Beechers*.

Believe me Charles when I repeat that I love you and all of your family too well to be angry with them for making what I really should consider "impudent speeches" from any other persons. Since I have found *Eunice* is about to publish a book I have almost concluded to "take off" without giving the world my delectable "letters from the East." Tom likes Eunice so *do not think he influences me*. I *feel* that I despise her.

Do not say Tom is a Universalist and influences me on that point. He is a believer in eternal punishment or at least he does not think as I do. I *love* him, and I also respect him, but I should cease to respect myself if I *could* be swayed this way and the other by even the Beechers. No, Charles, I have looked this matter over until I *know* I will cease to love God when I believe in any Hell worse than this World. Men suffer too much on account of their own sins here to be tortured hereafter. Either they sink to eternal rest at death or rise to the very bosom of celestial joy. I *know* it, and when I fall into it, it is awful sorrow to me. I pity everybody even Eunice. Perhaps she is crazy. I was informed that she was about to publish "Western doings." I hope she won't take it into her head to amuse the public with "Brooklyn doings." Write soon—immediately—and send this letter without fail to Belle Hooker. Your Annie in haste.

Isabella Hooker was right in the middle of this developing drama involving her blood brothers, and she found it fascinating in a horrible sort of way. "The complications of Jim's troubles is beyond anything that novels relate," she once wrote. Despite the fact that husband John did well enough as a lawyer to keep her and her children in considerable comfort at Nook Farm and shed some reflected glory on her as wife of a respected public official—lifelong reporter of the state Supreme Court and one-term representative in the state legislature—and promoter of good causes such as abolition and women's rights, Isabella was increasingly restless and disappointed with the course of her life. Gifted with a good mind, she was always resentful of having had so little formal education and jealous of the accomplishments and what she saw as the independence of her half sisters Catharine and Harriet. Catharine's predictions as to Isabella's health turned out to be right on the mark, and she complained of just about every female trouble in the book—excessive menstrual flow, displaced uterus, headaches, back pain, nasal polyps, and a "diseased nervous system" leading to periods of mental confusion. Despite having help, she found the chores of motherhood and housekeeping trying and distasteful. When it all seemed too much for her with the coming on of menopause in the spring of 1860, Isabella went to Elmira for a five-month stay at the Gleason establishment, where Mrs. Gleason, who had medical training, could treat her gynecological problems and brother Tom could minister to her spirit.

She wrote almost daily letters home in which she described her medical treatments to John in rather gruesome detail and conveyed other messages slyly, such as this one in a letter to one of her daughters: "Tell papa that Mrs. Gleason says—that my sleeping late in the morning, is the one thing that has saved him from having a *nervous*, *fidgety*, perhaps even *crazy* wife. She highly approves my past practice in this and most other respects." Despite her ailments, Isabella displayed the kind of high spirits and self-confidence that Catharine had said would make her a leader. She was quite conscious of her beauty—and more, as she wrote to John:

> It is funny, how, every where I go—I have run on the credit of my relations—no where, but at home can I lay claim to a particle of individuality—to any distinction of goodness, smartness or anything else whatever. . . . It becomes more and more evident to me—that I have great power of personal influence—Family name goes a great way no doubt—but here is magnetism of heart, and eye and voice, that is quite individual—oh, how I wish I might exert this on a broad scale, to sweep people along in the right path—Approbativeness—real love of admiration is as strong perhaps as in the days of childhood and youth—But benevolence is uppermost, I am quite sure of that—and thank God for the assurance. I truly wish I knew how much one might enjoy of the personal tribute that follows successful effort—without becoming selfish—or even self conscious and vainglorious.

Isabella moved in Elmira's best social circles, reporting Sundays spent at the home of Jarvis Langdon, the town's wealthiest citizen. In a move that would have interesting consequences, she persuaded the Langdons to let their daughter Livy, who was about the age of Isabella's Mary, become her roommate at Gleason's because the girl was "living on her nerves instead of her muscles." Isabella would not let her female troubles interfere with a romantic interlude, and she proposed a conjugal visit to John:

> If I stay into August as I am certain I ought to, (on account of my monthly period coming just the last of July—or first of Aug. and I must have treatment after that, before leaving finally) it would break up these two months most charmingly to have you here a few days—and I *know*—yes certainly know—that we could have such a good time . . . and your health would be so much improved that you would go home—and not think of the small four weeks that must pass, before I should follow you. . . . In confidence also—and best of all—I asked dear loving Mrs. Gleason—whether I might make you most heartily welcome—and could do so, without detriment to health—and she said—yes—without hesitation—and wished you could come by all means—She would secure our room to us, unmolested and do everything she could to make your visit pleasant.

It is not clear whether Isabella crossed paths with her sister-in-law Annie also sheltering at Elmira, but she did receive a long letter from brother Jim, still maintaining his bethel in Hong Kong Harbor. Not surprisingly in view of Annie's departure a year before, he complained of loneliness to the point where "my noble loving dog . . . is the best friend I have in China." He expressed doubts about his work because "I don't think my mind is so elastic as it once was and in consequence my preaching is neither effective or very acceptable." Like Annie, he was running into people who had no use for Beechers: "I get sundry harsh words occasionally because so unfortunate as to be Henry's & Hattie's brother . . . a crime which is surely no fault of mine since at the time I was born they were both respectable young people and how could I know what they would be when they should grow up." But the poignant part of the letter had to do with Annie:

> I'm glad you did not write before, concerning my dear wife, & glad that from only one I should hear what for the time being almost broke my heart. What has happened was not unexpected by me, but when it came I was no better able to bear it. . . . However, let it pass. Only once has Mr. Loomis written me before upon the subject. What I have said to him and to my much loved brother Tom I have now to say to my beloved sister Isabel. Whatever may have taken place in the past three years of sorrow, and hopelessness, yet I testify to the love and devotion of my dear wife, and never has my love changed. What she was to me when I first loved her, she is now, and always will be. If I have suffered, she has suffered more, for it was the thought that her fearful weakness was breaking my heart, which gave her greater agony than even her own danger of destruction. The past is past, however. With regard to the future, I only pray and love. Perhaps sometime I may hope.

Although Jim wrote that he would rejoice in Annie's return, his own future in China was so uncertain that he thought it would be better for her to remain at home. By the time Jim came back to the States in 1861, Annie had been committed to an asylum, from which she periodically escaped. Her behavior baffled, exasperated, and embarrassed Tom. When she was wandering drunk in the streets of Elmira, he feared that she would end up at the infamous Haights Hotel and become "somebody's mistress or everybody's." But when it turned out that she had sought refuge in a respectable private home instead, he had to confess to Isabella: "Bad woman I think her. But I have not supposed that 'bad' and adulterous were interchangeable terms. I repeat to you what I said to Henry—Annie loves Jim in every fibre of her being. She is coarse, *amorous*, sensual, in her love—but I verily believe and so does Jim—*faithful*. She has adulterous thoughts and I have been sorely tempted to declare her an overt sinner. But I cannot in honor." Arriving about the time that Lincoln was calling for volunteers in response to the fall of Fort Sumter, finding Annie in such a state that they could not be together and being without employment or prospects, Jim followed the lead of other Beechers and enlisted as chaplain to a regiment being raised in Brooklyn. He soon switched to active service when his background as a seaman familiar with weapons and the handling of men qualified him for a commission in the 141st New York Volunteers.

Although, like Tom, James was not on record as having any particular passion for getting rid of slavery, he must have found the enthusiasm for battle among most of his siblings and their families contagious. From the echo of the first shot, Henry Ward turned his Plymouth Church into a source of funds and supplies, including clothing, weapons, and even mail service for the troops. He paid for equipping one regiment out of his own pocket, and when his underage son Henry asked permission to enlist, he said, "If you don't, I'll disown you." Fred, the son Harriet thought was safely involved with medical studies at Harvard, tried first to become a military surgeon and, failing that, enlisted as a foot soldier in the Massachusetts Volunteer Infantry. Another Fred, Charles's son, joined up in Georgetown, Massachusetts, where his father had become pastor of the Congregational Church. Henry Ward told his congregation: "My oldest son is in the army, and shall I read with trembling anxiety the account of every battle to see if he is slain? I gave him to the Lord, and I shall not take him back and I will not worry and fret myself about him. I will trust in God though He slay not only him but me also." Harriet wrote in the *Independent* that "this is a cause to die for, and—thanks be to God!—our young men embrace it as a bride and are ready to die." The young men went literally singing off to war, as in Andover, where ninety seminarians formed a unit they called the Havelock Grays and belted out a newly minted song—"John Brown's Body Lies A-mould'ring in the Grave"—as they drilled on the commons in front of the Stowes' stone house.

On June 11 Harriet wrote to Calvin from the Beecher home at 124 Columbia Heights in Brooklyn:

> Yesterday noon Henry came in, saying that the Commonwealth with the First Regiment on board, had just sailed by. Immediately

I was of course eager to get to Jersey City to see Fred. Sister Eunice said she would go with me, and in a few minutes she and I were in a carriage, driving towards the Fulton Ferry. Upon reaching Jersey City we found that the boys were dining in the depot, an immense building with many tracks and platforms. It has a great cast-iron gallery just under the roof, apparently placed there with prophetic instinct of these times. There was a crowd of people pressing against the grated doors, which were locked, but through which we could see the soldiers. It was with great difficulty that we were at last permitted to go inside, and that object seemed to be greatly aided by a bit of printed satin that some man gave Mr. Scoville [Henry Ward's son-in-law].

When we were in, a vast area of gray caps and blue overcoats was presented. The boys were eating, drinking, smoking, talking, singing, and laughing. Company A was reported to be here, there, and everywhere. At last S. spied Fred in the distance, and went leaping across the tracks toward him. Immediately afterwards a blue-overcoated figure bristling with knapsack and haversack, and looking like as assortment of packages, came rushing toward us.

Fred was overjoyed, you may be sure, and my first impulse was to wipe his face with my handkerchief before I kissed him. He was in high spirits, in spite of the weight of blue overcoat, knapsack, etc. that he would formerly have declared intolerable for half an hour. I gave him my handkerchief and Eunice gave him hers, with a sheer motherly instinct that is so strong within her, and then we filled his haversack with oranges.

We stayed with Fred about two hours, during which time the gallery was filled with people, cheering and waving their handkerchiefs. Every now and then the band played inspiriting airs, in which the soldiers joined with hearty voices. While some of the companies sang, others were drilled, and all seemed to be having a general jollification. The meal that had been provided was plentiful, and consisted of coffee, lemonade, sandwiches, etc. . . .

We parted from Fred at the door. He said he felt lonesome enough Saturday evening at the Common in Boston, where everybody was taking leave of somebody, and he seemed to be the only one without a friend, but that this interview made up for it all.

I also saw young Henry. Like Fred he is mysteriously changed, and wears an expression of gravity and care. So our boys come to manhood in a day. Now I am watching anxiously for the evening paper to tell me that the regiment has reached Washington in safety.

In the middle of the next month, the singing stopped and the fighting began at the First Battle of Bull Run in Virginia, during which the shocked and scared volunteers of the Union Army were routed by supposedly overpowered Confederate forces. On both sides of the Mason-Dixon line, watching anxiously for the paper would become a daily ritual not so much to see the results of often inconclusive battles as to scan the lists of the fallen for the names of loved ones. Through 1861 and into 1862, news from the front tended to be better for the South than the North. The people who thought that the purpose of the war was freeing the slaves were heartened when Union general John C. Frémont imposed martial law on Missouri and emancipated the slaves of secessionists in late August. But three days later Lincoln disappointed some of his most ardent followers by countermanding the orders, to keep the border states on his side, and transferring Frémont to other duties. Henry Ward Beecher crossed over to the city to pay homage to the deposed abolitionist hero when Frémont was staying at Astor House on leave, and the general in turn crossed over to Brooklyn to receive a warm welcome at Plymouth Church. Beecher's ties to Frémont were based on more than politics. So close were the Beechers to John T. Howard, one of the church's founding triumvirate, and Mrs. Howard's family, the Raymonds, that Eunice nursed little Henry Ward Beecher Howard with her own breast. A wealthy investor, Howard had been associated with Frémont in a gold mining venture and was often at the colorful Californian's St. Louis headquarters, where Howard's son, Jack, and nephew, Ros Raymond, served as uniformed aides. The disgruntled Raymond's fuming over Lincoln's incompetence and foot dragging on the slavery question was a strong influence on Beecher's thought in the early stages of the war.

If Howard provided Henry Ward with ammunition to fire at the administration in Washington, the other living member of the triumvirate, Henry C. Bowen, gave him the big gun to use it. With many of his enterprises failing as a result of the war, Bowen wanted to strengthen his best remaining asset, *The Independent*. Thanks to its talented young managing editor, Theodore Tilton, it was said to be the world's most profitable religious journal and second only to the *New York Herald* among national secular papers in profitability. Nevertheless, Bowen decided that it was time to call in Henry Ward's debt to him by asking the minister to come out from under his star and become the paper's editor, with the thought that the Beecher name would boost circulation. Beecher, who wanted to influence national policy in any way he could, welcomed the assignment, and felt he could count on young Tilton to make the additional workload bearable. Although ambitious to occupy the editor's chair himself, Tilton could hardly object to working under Beecher, who was responsible for placing him in his increasingly remunerative job in the first place and who was, in his own words, "my minister, teacher, father, brother, friend, companion."

Shortly after the new editorial alignment at *The Independent*, Tilton had an unexpected opportunity to put his boss and mentor deeply in debt to him. Beecher's son Henry was serving in the headquarters of the Army of the Potomac, which was "a combination of barroom and brothel," according to a highly placed Washington insider. In one or the other of these establishments, young Beecher was involved in a brawl and was forced to resign his commission. It is due to Tilton's charm and brashness that the Beechers did not suffer public humiliation at the time and that history does not record the exact nature or location of the young man's offense. Tilton got on a train and headed for Washington as soon as Henry Ward told him the bad news. Arrived in the capital, Tilton went directly to Simon Cameron's house. The then secretary of war was expecting luncheon guests, but so engaging was Tilton's personality that the secretary had a place set for him at the table, where the witty, well-informed New York editor became the main entertainment. When the other guests had departed, Tilton had no trouble convincing Cameron to sign a paper giving young Henry Beecher a new commission in the regular army. Whether to nail the matter down securely or to further impress his boss, Tilton took the paper directly to the White House and secured Lincoln's signature as well. Henry Ward was "exquisitely" grateful for what Tilton had done, but Eunice was not. The mother in her saw in the disgrace of her son a chance to keep him out of harm's way for the duration. So furious was Eunice at Tilton for his interference that he never again dared step foot in the Beecher house when she was at home.

Throughout the first half of 1862, when spit-and-polish General George B. McClellan's large, well-trained, well-equipped army kept faltering and falling back on the verge of victory, when Lincoln kept issuing statements to the effect that the purpose of the war was to put down rebellion rather than to free the slaves, Henry Ward Beecher raged in his editorials. Sample snatches give the flavor of his attacks: "Neither Mr. Lincoln nor his Cabinet have proved leaders. . . . Our armies have been managed as if they were a body of nurses in a foundling hospital. . . . Let it be known that the Nation wasted away by an incurable consumption of Central Imbecility. . . . The government cannot any longer avoid choosing the issue that had been made up and thrust upon it—*freedom or slavery.*" Henry Ward got no argument from his managing editor, Tilton, who had a young man's passion for radical reform, but got what must have been a surprising letter written in their separate hands by his sisters Mary and Harriet.

Mary:

> I don't know as you will thank me for what I want to say to you—& perhaps you will not read it—no matter—it will relieve me to write it. I am very near explosion & must open the safety valve—I have read your leaders in the Independent every week for some months past—with great pain—all that you say may be true, I can't disprove it, but what possible good is to be gained by saying what destroys all confidence in the administration & in the commanders of our army—at a time when we need all the elasticity, all the vigor & courage that mortal man can feel—you are doing all you can to discourage & weaken—you made every man's heart lead in his bosom—I never in all my life under any circumstances felt so utterly heartless & helpless as after reading one of your articles & I am ready to ask with old Sojourner Truth [the name that a slave named Isabella took when she got her freedom and became a lecturer for the rights of both blacks and women and so intimate with Beechers that she showed up at Harriet's stone house during Lyman's eightieth-birthday party], "Is God dead?" If I look through your glass I see nothing but imbecility, anarchy & the most intolerable selfishness and wickedness that was ever developed & if this is all true—the sooner this form of government ends the better—for surely nothing worse can rise upon its ruins—your desponding Mary.

Harriet, the doer, did not just wring her hands like Mary, but she did suggest that Henry Ward was doing more harm than good, and told him in part:

> That the administration ought to have its measures criticized I freely grant, but I am not able to see of what practical use will be some things that you say—for ex. that the President is a man destitute of a single capacity for leadership—that he has no steady plan but does from time to time what this or that person advises

him to—That kind of criticism is *hopeless* as far as its effects go—it is merely proving to a crew in a storm that the man who can hold the helm is drunk or imbecile. . . . The general tone of your articles is deeply discouraging to that very class whose demoralization & division would be most hopeless defeat for us. . . . Your evident championship of Frémont (you know that we all are his friends) has been spoken of by some as injuring the effects of some of the best things you have said—People lay down the paper & say, "Oh . . . he's a Frémont man—that's what's the matter with him."

Harriet granted that Frémont and McClellan were being abused, but she suggested that Henry Ward go down to Washington and "see with your own eyes, talk with Chase [secretary of the treasury and their very old friend from Cincinnati who did so much to help quell the riots there] & Seward & Lincoln & see if you can't throw out a few notes of encouragement. . . . Will you go to Washington with me in a week or two? I will go if you will."

In that year of 1862, which was so frustrating to Northern hopes, there was at least one Beecher who would not have agreed with Harriet's willingness to give General McClellan the benefit of the doubt. At age thirty-eight, Thomas Beecher took a leave from his Elmira church and signed on as chaplain to the 141st New York Volunteers. It has to be seen as a surprising and quixotic act, since Tom was the only Beecher who had never expressed moral outrage over the institution of slavery and its adherents. But his younger brother James was a lieutenant colonel in that regiment, and James was desperately unhappy. He was torn between his duty to do right by his hopelessly addicted wife, Annie, and his feelings for a wholesome young woman named Frankie Johnson, whom he had met through his Connecticut relatives. Aside from a mutual physical attraction, James and Frankie were both dealing with lost loves—in Frankie's case an engagement to James's nephew, Frederick Perkins, broken off by her family's interference—and in need of new ones. Beecher-wise, James felt himself to be odd man out in an organizational structure where he had to follow often irrational orders from inept or venal superiors. Like the president himself, James chafed about wasting time and playing politics within the headquarters of an army that did not seem to be going anywhere. Nothing could be more in keeping with Tom Beecher's character than to have enlisted simply to be near and helpful to his distressed brother and, just possibly, to experience enough of war firsthand to be a better pastor to his flock. Whatever his motives in getting him there, Tom's customary wide-eyed—some would say cynical—view of human behavior led him to conclusions about McClellan's command that may well have changed history.

As a chaplain, Tom Beecher would have been open to confidences from his fellow officers and enlisted men that they would not have dared to share with line officers. During the four months of Tom's service, the standoff between McClellan and Lincoln had become a major factor in the fortunes of war in the East. A West Point graduate and hero of the war with Mexico, McClellan had a reputation for intelligence and thoroughness throughout the military establishment and even in civilian life, where he had been an executive of the Illinois Central Railroad. Having been one of the lawyers for the railroad, Lincoln would have been aware of McClellan's reputed abilities when he placed him in command. Initially it was a good choice, because McClellan proved to be a genius not only at turning thousands of raw recruits into a disciplined army but also in earning the admiration and loyalty of his men. Proud of the army he created, McClellan became its protector as well as its leader. He dreaded defeat and deliberately ignored the president's war orders on the grounds that he either did not have enough men or the right equipment to obey them. McClellan evidently thought that he could get away with this behavior because he was aware that Lincoln was a minority president and that there probably were a similar percentage of copperheads, as Southern sympathizers were called, and Democrats within the army as in the general population. Being somewhat neutral himself, chaplain Tom was able to present a sympathetic ear to these disloyal elements and soon was convinced of a plot afoot to imprison Lincoln and his cabinet and install McClellan as head of a military government. Tom was able to make use of his long-ago willingness to associate with an interesting but socially inferior young Illinois lawyer and gain a private audience with the man in the White House. Because of the confidentiality involved, Tom would never reveal to anybody what passed between the two men at that interview, but shortly thereafter McClellan was at last relieved of command.

At some point during the same stretch of time when Lincoln was dealing with rising impatience within the civilian population that editors such as Horace Greeley and Henry Ward Beecher were trying to fan into flame, there was another secret meeting between Lincoln and a Beecher, according to family legend. It is a credible story as reported by Lyman Beecher Stowe in his book *Saints, Sinners, and Beechers:*

> One dark and stormy night in 1862, late in the evening, a very
> tall man muffled in a great cloak rang the bell of the Beechers'

house. Mrs. Beecher opened the door. The tall stranger asked to see Mr. Beecher on a matter of great urgency but declined to give his name. Mrs. Beecher was afraid to let him in. Her husband's life had often been threatened since the Kansas troubles. Leaving the caller in the rain she went up-stairs and told her husband. He insisted on seeing the stranger who was then shown to the study on the top floor. For hours Mrs. Beecher heard the two men in earnest conversation and finally she heard the familiar cadences of her husband's voice in prayer. After something like four hours Beecher himself let the man out. The next morning when his wife asked him who the stranger was he merely smiled. He did not tell her until after the assassination that the strange caller was President Lincoln.

This story has been affirmed and denied by an approximately equal number of reliable persons. Since it seems to be reasonably well established that at the time alleged the President was in New York conferring with some of his generals I am disposed to believe it. It seems to accord with both Lincoln's informality and his shrewd sense that he should have sought opportunity for an undisclosed talk with such a powerful molder of public opinion. And certainly Beecher's attitude toward the President and his policies grew from then on constantly more understanding until they came into complete agreement.

The fact that Henry Ward did not feel the need of accompanying Harriet to Washington in that late fall of 1862 could be another affirmation of the Brooklyn meeting with Lincoln. Instead of Henry Ward, Harriet took with her one of her twins, Hatty, her twelve-year-old son Charlie, and her sister Isabella. In some respects Isabella was more involved with the war effort than Harriet, who had been spending much of her time turning out two novels—a tale of an old New England community called *The Pearl of Orr's Island*, which Theodore Tilton commissioned to run first as a serial in *The Independent*; and *Agnes of Sorrento*, a Renaissance romance inspired by her travels in Italy and run in the *Atlantic* by James Fields. After her course of self-examination in Elmira, Isabella Hooker had a form of epiphany in Hartford. A nineteen-year-old Quaker abolitionist named Anna Dickinson, who had shocked proper society by stumping for Lincoln's election, came to the Connecticut capital to speak on behalf of her antislavery crusade. She so impressed the Hookers that they took her home for the night. During an all-night talkfest, Anna persuaded Isabella that women not only have a right, but also a duty, to speak out and told her all about the leaders of the feminist movement, Elizabeth Cady Stanton and Susan B. Anthony. Inspired by this woman young enough to be her daughter, Isabella's first effort to make her leadership personality felt outside the home was in work for the Women's Sanitary Commission, which did so much to bring medical service to the troops. Disappointed as most of her siblings by the president's seeming timidity on the slavery question, she bombarded the White House with letters and was as eager as Harriet to find out if Lincoln really was serious about his announced intention to issue the Emancipation Proclamation on January 1, 1863. But Isabella had an important personal mission in Washington as well: she wanted to see brothers Tom and James and find out through personal contact how Jim was bearing up under his load of remorse and guilt over Annie.

The visit with Tom went very well—a sumptuous meal in his tent in an encampment outside Washington. There was no cause for alarm either in a fortuitous encounter with James. They were awakened from naps in their hotel by the beat of drums and tramping feet and rushed to the window just in time to see James, handsomer than ever in his dress uniform, ride by with his regiment. James saluted the ladies with his sword and came back with some fellow officers, all in high spirits, for a visit when the march was over. Isabella was a bit put off that she could not provoke James into talking about politics, but then neither of her blood brothers seemed to care that much about the affairs of state. Trading a bit on her reputation to call on his superior officers, Harriet managed to get a forty-eight-hour leave for son Fred, who had been commissioned a lieutenant, put on some weight, and acquired a better-looking uniform. She whisked Fred off to the hotel, where she had booked a room for him next to hers, and held a small family reunion. "Imagine a quiet little parlor with a bright coal fire and the gaslight burning above a centre-table, about which Hatty, Fred and I are seated," she wrote to Calvin. "Fred is as happy as happy can be with mother and sister once more." Harriet found Fred "as loving and affectionate as a boy can be" and quoted him as saying of the interlude, "Oh! this pays for a year and a half of fighting and hard work." But Harriet did not leave it at that. Learning that Fred was eager to see action, she wrote letters that brought him a promotion to captain and transfer to the staff of a front-line general.

That was not the only effective letter writing that Harriet would do while in Washington. She had never responded to a document signed by half a million women called "The Affectionate and Christian Address of Many Thousands of Women of Great Britain and Ireland to Their Sisters, the Women of the United States of America," which had been sent to her after her first visit to Britain. It urged American women to use their influence to end the crime of slavery. In view of the aid being given the Confederacy by Britain despite an official policy of hands-off neutrality with respect to the conflict in America, Harriet wanted to reply to the "The Affectionate and Christian Address" for publication, hopefully in England, where she was still a best-selling author as well as in America, but she first wanted to be absolutely sure that the Emancipation Proclamation would be issued as promised. The only person who could give her that assurance was "Father Abraham," as she called him in one of her letters. Senator Henry Wilson of her then home state of Massachusetts arranged for a presidential audience, and on a cold November day Harriet and her party were ushered into what Isabella described as a drab room in the White House, where they waited rather nervously for Lincoln to appear. Despite all that they had read and heard about him, Isabella was not quite prepared for the "rough, scrubby, black-brown, withered, dull-eyed object" who shambled into the room. It was almost laughable to watch this tall, awkward man bend over tiny, momentarily tongue-tied Harriet to take her hand.

"So this is the little lady who started this big war," Lincoln said by way of putting her at ease.

Lincoln led his visitors over to a coal fire, spitting and spluttering in its grate. Warming his own hands above it, he said, "I do love a fire in a room. I suppose it's because we always had one to home."

Then they sat and talked for about an hour. Whether by request or their own sensitivity, Harriet and Isabella apparently felt obligated to leave no record of the substantive part of their conversation, but both gave evidence later that they had been convinced of Lincoln's intention to go through with emancipation and his approval of Harriet's projected reply to the British women. They also came away with sympathy and understanding for the enormity of Lincoln's task and his devotion to it. Harriet did record one exchange along these lines when she asked Lincoln how he ever had time to dine, and he replied, "I don't exactly, as you say, *dine*. I just browse around a little, now and then." But the remark that would come back to haunt them later was Lincoln's answer to a question as to how long the war might last: "I shall never live to see peace. This war is killing me."

For the young people looking on, the event was more entertaining than solemn. They were bemused by what they considered Lincoln's backwoods manners and speech. As soon as they were out of the White

House, Charlie asked his mother, "Why does the President say 'to home' instead of 'at home'?" Not wanting the boy to lose respect for a man whom she now truly admired, she quoted St. Paul: "Though I be rude in speech yet not in knowledge; but we have been thoroughly made manifest among you in all things." It is not known whether Harriet should be included in daughter Hatty's account of the event to her twin, Eliza. Her letter reflected the possibly understandable snobbery of a young woman just back from European schooling. She described the whole affair as so amusing that they could barely get through it without exploding and claimed that they "perfectly screamed" with laughter as soon as they were back in their hotel room.

If Harriet did allow herself to relax and join briefly in that laughter, she made up for it by sitting right down to finish her reply to the British women. She reminded them that theirs had been a voice from across the water encouraging the elimination of slavery eight years before and then unsheathed her sharp weapon of sarcasm to describe the voice she was hearing now that war was under way:

> We have heard on the high seas the voice of a war-steamer, built for a man-stealing Confederacy, with English gold, in an English dockyard, going out of an English harbor, manned by English sailors, with the full knowledge of English government officers, in defiance of the Queen's proclamation of neutrality! So far has English sympathy overflowed. We have heard of other steamers, iron-clad, designed to furnish to a slavery-defending Confederacy their only lack,—a navy for the high seas. We have heard that the British Evangelical Alliance refuses to express sympathy with a liberating party, when requested to do so by the French Evangelical Alliance. We find in English religious newspapers all those sad degrees in the downward-sliding scale of defending and apologizing for slaveholders and slaveholding, with which we have so many years contended in our own country. We find the President's Proclamation of Emancipation spoken of in those papers only as an incitement to servile insurrection. Nay, more,—we find in your papers, from thoughtful men, the admission of the rapid decline of anti-slavery sentiments in England.

In her best purple prose, Harriet told of hearing a thousand escaped slaves at a Washington encampment sing "that strange rhythmical chant which is now forbidden to be sung on Southern plantations—the psalm of this modern exodus—which combines the barbaric fire of the Marseillaise with the religious fervor of the old Hebrew prophet—'Oh, Go down Moses, way down into Egypt's Land.'" Harriet closed with a direct appeal to British women "as sisters, as wives, and as mothers, to raise your voices to your fellow-citizens, and your prayers to God for the removal of this affliction and disgrace from the Christian world."

When the sisters headed home from Washington, they could not have known that the long-anticipated Emancipation Proclamation only weeks away would mark the watershed of the century for both the nation and the family. On January 10, 1863, Lyman, the Beecher family patriarch, died in the home on Willow Street, Brooklyn, where he had been living through seven years of a long, gentle decline in energy and awareness. His chief pleasure during that time was attending the services and meetings in Henry Ward's Plymouth Church. Whether he failed to comprehend his son's departure from the harsh Calvinist doctrine to which he still clung, or whether he decided to condone it, he was proud of Henry Ward's ability to fill a three-thousand-seat auditorium and once admitted, "Thought I could preach until I heard Henry." He retained the wit and humor that had made his seemingly impossible demands bearable by those who knew him best. When Harriet told him during one of his lucid moments that he was "a very handsome old man," he quipped, "Tell me something new." Despite the glorious vision of heaven he had offered other believers, he was not eager to get there himself. In the last speech he gave at Plymouth Church, he said, "If God should tell me that I *might* choose—that is, if God said that it was *his* will that I *should* choose whether to die and go to heaven, or to begin my life over again and work once more, *I would enlist again in a minute.*" In the event, Lyman had his own "glorious vision of heaven," according to what he told one of his daughters a day before he died, and his last whispered words to his wife were those from a hymn, "Jesus, lover of my soul, Let me to thy bosom fly!"

When the family gathered in Brooklyn to be at the crowded funeral services in Plymouth Church, there was rejoicing rather than sorrow: "At family prayer, which was family *praise*, singing being our chief occupation, there was an unpremeditated outburst of memories of the most beautiful and touching character. We feel that our dear father is not taken from us, but given back to us again," as one of the children wrote. Only two of Lyman's ten living children were unable to attend the ceremonies. Under wartime conditions, Edward was not able to make the long trip east from Galesburg. For all of them, but especially for Isabella and Tom, the absence of James would strike the one note of true sorrow. It would be Isabella's responsibility to go from the graveside of her father to the bedside of her brother in a Washington hospital.

James had not been wounded in battle. Beecher-like, he broke down under the accumulated weight of the seemingly insoluble problems and frustrations that he had been encountering since his return from China. From the beginning, he had to cope with the embarrassment of near poverty. Correspondence with Eunice and Henry Ward in the late fall of 1861 is evidence of how this disturbed him. More than half of his first army check went to acquiring a "horse and fixtures" and the rest to paying for "poor Annie's" asylum. To get on with his life, he had Henry Ward cosign a $200 loan from the Metropolitan Bank in New York. When he got to Washington and realized that he could not pay the loan off by the due date, James gave a fellow officer who was going to New York to tend to his thriving civilian business $10 to take up the note at the bank on the understanding that James would pay him the $200 out of his next regimental paycheck in January 1862. So James was as shocked as his sister-in-law must have been to get a tart message from Eunice about the note, saying that "it has been again matured for some weeks and the sheriff came here today to sue your brother for it." It had to have been something of a last straw for Eunice, who had quite obviously had her fill of Annie, and a huge embarrassment for James. He wrote hasty letters to both Eunice and Henry Ward explaining the circumstances and informing his brother that he would send an advance on his pay of $150 by "Adams Express" and asking a loan of $50 to cover the balance. Preacher or no, James undoubtedly thought of a good many harsh words to bestow on the officer who had let him down. Perhaps trivial in itself, this incident is illustrative of the dynamics in the Beecher family and may well have had considerable bearing on the switch that James made from chaplain to a higher-ranking, better-paying commission in another regiment.

The appearance that James had presented to Isabella and Harriet of being a happy camper was a sham. His anxieties grew so great that Tom wrote, "To hear of his suicide would not surprise me at any time. Annie is a shirt of Nessus [a centaur Hercules had to kill to save his marriage] clinging to Jim." Possibly because of his involvement with the plot on Lincoln, Tom informed Isabella in early 1863 that he was afraid of losing his own sanity and that he was going back to Elmira. He thought that he could do no more for James, who was so involved in regimental politics that he would have been court-martialed if his colonel had not been relieved of command first. In effect, Tom handed James over to Isabella.

She rushed to Washington and reported back to her husband that James, overworked as a result of the troubles in the regiment, had started taking drugs—chloroform to try to sleep, morphine supplied by the surgeon—until he landed in the hospital "broken down and out of his head." In a misguided effort to cheer him, the doctors had Annie sent down and put them in a room together. This "capped the whole," Isabella wrote. "Jim loathes her—her breath is pestilence itself, and he could not endure it, so he came here, after sending her back to Elmira." With all of her leadership qualities on display, Isabella marched into the office of Secretary of War Edwin M. Stanton, a friend to a number of Beechers, and arranged for an honorable discharge for James on the grounds of ill health, and she took him up to a Dr. Taylor's sanitarium in New York.

Once she had James relieved of the duties that had been depressing him, Isabella began proposing a divorce to relieve him of the anxiety Annie imposed on him as well. Tom would not go along with the idea and warned, "Be careful not to subpoena me as witness for while I loathe the woman, I cannot in truth and honor think Jim entitled to a divorce." With all the tough love that Tom gave both Annie and James, he never suspended judgment and once called their troubles "long delayed retribution" for their behavior. He advised Isabella not to baby James and confessed that "if his courage fail, I'll pity him but never love him as I like to love the patient ones who bear their crosses well—till all is finished." The patience Tom had in mind was waiting until Annie's addiction took its inevitable toll. Meanwhile, Tom did what he could to alleviate matters—for instance, writing to James on March 25, 1863:

> In today's Advertiser appears a modest caution not to trust Annie on your account—signed by you as per your letter to Dr. Gleason. For political purposes there is an anti-Beecher copperhead stir just beginning in town here. I am strong enough to handle it. It begins with an attack on Henry—& his lecture. It will go on with innuendos about me—& this necessity of publishing Annie—will bring round her some anti-Beecher fellows—who will glory in helping on her tongueiness. You, keep away & keep quiet & continue in dry-dock, refitting. Don't know anything—don't hear anything. Don't read & don't write anything. I am all right—hearty & happy—You be the same—but for the present you must not come to Elmira.

Within a month, James Beecher was no longer in need of patience; his Annie died of delirium tremens.

Now able to pursue his relationship with Frankie Johnson openly and in good conscience, James recovered rapidly, and he reenlisted with a new rank of full colonel in what was beginning to look like a new war. Having lost patience with stalemate and incompetence, Lincoln began switching generals. After Ambrose Burnside, who had replaced McClellan, lost a costly battle to General Robert E. Lee's forces at Fredericksburg, Virginia—twelve thousand Union casualties to five thousand Confederate—Lincoln put Joseph Hooker in command of the Army of the Potomac. One general he kept in place was a virtually unknown figure with an undistinguished record in military and civilian life and a reputed fondness for ardent spirits by the name of Ulysses S. Grant, whose troops were making progress in a grinding campaign to open the Mississippi River to federal traffic. In the wake of the Emancipation Proclamation, the Union War Department decided to recruit escaping slaves in the South. It was considered a tricky and difficult experiment, since little was known as to the true loyalty of these people, and it was widely believed that "the nigger won't fight." For reasons unrecorded, James Beecher was given this job, and in May, a month after Annie's death, he began working at it in New Bern, North Carolina. Only five weeks later he could write from Headquarters, First North Carolina Colored Volunteers, to "My dear Frankie" at her home in Guilford, Connecticut:

> My Regt is organized, equipped and tolerably drilled. . . . Everybody is surprised who sees the boys for they do improve wonderfully. In four weeks more, if wanted, we will be most happy to pay attention to any rebels who may need attention. I have heard from Tom that my former Regt wherein I suffered so much has gone down as I supposed it would. Oh if they only would have let me I could have made a good regiment of it, but I couldn't work against everybody. The major has resigned and the officers are equally on the spoils. Yet after all I am not sorry for that experience terrible as it was. It led the way to this work. It brought me back to humble, trembling reliance in Christ, the stronger that it is so humble. It has made a new man of me in many respects. Besides all this, all has assured me of the love of a true little woman—faithful through good report and bad report.

While Colonel Beecher was whipping his regiment into shape throughout that spring and summer for service under fire, his siblings and their families were dealing with a variety of equally difficult challenges. For Harriet it would be another uprooting of the family. Calvin Stowe decided to retire from the faculty of Andover Seminary at the end of the spring term in 1863 to work on a book about the Bible that he had long been contemplating. Harriet looked on it as an opportunity to return to her own roots in Connecticut. Mary and Isabella were firmly anchored on the outskirts of Hartford, and there was still land available in a grove beside the Park River, where she and her school chum Georgiana May used to find refuge. Even though the city was creeping in around the spot, Harriet bought four and a half acres and began construction of an elaborate eight-gabled house graced with wide verandas and adorned with gingerbread. As she had done in moving from Brunswick to Andover, she shuttled between Andover and Hartford to supervise construction. For months it kept her mind off the harrowing news from the battlefronts, where there were more casualties in every engagement—ten thousand on each side during another Union defeat at Chancellorsville, for one—as she indicated in a letter to her friend Annie Fields:

> Can I begin to tell you what it is to begin to keep house in an unfinished home and place, dependent upon a carpenter, a plumber, a mason, a bell-hanger, who come and go at their own sweet will, breaking in, making all sorts of chips, dust, dirt, going off in the midst leaving all standing,—reappearing at uncertain intervals and making more dust, chips, and dirt. One parlor and my library have thus risen piecemeal by disturbances and convulsions. They are now almost done, and the last box of books is almost unpacked, but my head aches so with the past confusion that I cannot get up any feeling of rest. I can't enjoy—can't feel a minute to sit down and say, "It is done."
>
> The fountain plays, the plants flourish, and our front hall minus the stair railing looks beautifully; my pictures are all hung in parlor and library, and yet I feel so unsettled. Well, in a month perhaps I shall get my brains right side up.

But in a month the news from a place in Pennsylvania called Gettysburg would send her brains reeling in another direction. Although word that the Army of the Potomac under another new general, George Meade, had routed Lee's invading forces brought general joy to the North, it brought consternation to the Stowe home. A Captain Fred Stowe was listed among the wounded. A letter from a chaplain informed them that a fragment of a shell entered his right ear but that he was "quiet and cheerful, longs to see some member of his family." A cousin of Fred's, Robert Beecher, did see him and telegraphed that Fred would soon be sent home. That was not good enough for Calvin, who was already worried about Fred as the result of a letter earlier in the spring in which Fred confessed that he was again in trouble with alcohol. Calvin set out to find his son and had the kind of tragicomic experience that seemed to befall him whenever he risked any form of action. At the Springfield railroad station, he was set upon by pickpockets who robbed him of more than a hundred dollars and so shook him up that he was ill and forced to return home. Harriet pulled the same strings that she had used to get her son into harm's way to get him out of it by a medical discharge. When he did arrive home, he soon confirmed his father's worst fears.

Fred Stowe was not the only family casualty at Gettysburg. The other Fred, Charles's son, serving as a lieutenant in the battle, was far more gravely wounded. It would be hard to imagine a worse time for such news to arrive in Georgetown. Charles had been no happier there than he was in New Orleans and in some of his other pastorates. The pay was not enough to support his family, and he had to borrow from wealthier relatives such as the Hookers. In a letter thanking Isabella for money, he told her that he had sold his violin because he did not have time enough to practice for the kind of music he liked to perform. He likened his life as a pastor to being "ground on a great grindstone, to be bought and held as a slave of every darned fool in the village," and he went so far as to claim, "I am crucified with Christ." For a man in that mood, charges of heresy brought against him by twenty-seven members of his congregation must have been nearly unbearable. They objected to his somewhat eccentric views on matters such as preexistence—he shared Edward's— and spiritualism—he had an open mind about it not unlike the Stowes' and Isabella's and that of the First Lady of the land, who believed that she was in touch with the spirit of son Willie after his death in the White House that year. Thus, in July 1863, Charles was on trial before a Congregational council, and Edward had come from Galesburg to help in his defense. As soon as he heard about his son's wound, Charles wanted to drop the trial and rush to Gettysburg, but his wife, Sarah—the "treasure," according to Tom—insisted on going instead and found her Fred lying in a barn with an abscessed wound so serious that she had to nurse him for two months.

With a special soft spot in her heart for her companion of carefree days in Europe and a searing scorn for the Old School believers who had been harassing her father and brothers for thirty years, Harriet joined Edward's defense of Charles. She wrote to influential clerics such as Dr. Leonard Bacon of Yale, who had delivered the eulogy at Lyman's funeral, and asked for their aid. As she told Bacon, Charles was gifted with a wide-ranging imagination and liked to "explore and revel in the celestial statistics and geography in years before the world was" with the result that "certain moles and bats pick up fragments of these things and pore over them as heresies." The "moles and bats" won the first round, and Charles was convicted, but the majority of his flock stood by him. Edward and Charles published *The Result Tested*, explaining their position, and a higher body eventually set aside the council's verdict.

Henry Ward Beecher did not join in his younger brother's defense, because he was not available. By mid-1863 he was in danger of a Beecher-style breakdown as a result of his multiple activities, including editorship of the *Independent*. As he had done in the past and would do in the future, Henry Ward accepted an offer from his congregation to underwrite a vacation of several months—this time abroad—and then turned over the editor's chair to his young friend and colleague Theodore Tilton. Henry Ward was in Europe during the troubles in his extended family that summer, but he was unexpectedly running into troubles of his own. To recharge his battery of vitality, he elected to go alone and escape all the usual demands on his time and attention. For just a while he hoped to leave responsibility for family, friends, the church, and even the fate of the nation in other hands. It was a vain hope. As soon as he set foot in Great Britain in June, he was shocked to observe at firsthand the extent and intensity of sentiment in favor of the Confederate cause. Thanks to Harriet's earlier presence and still current popularity in the mother country, the Beecher name and fame as antislavery advocates were well established, and Henry Ward was immediately urged by British people who shared their views to speak out on behalf of the Union. At first he begged off because of his need for rest, and he left for a leisurely tour of the Continent. Quite apart from the state of his health, he thought that an effort to change the mind-set of what he regarded as misguided and misinformed people who felt that their personal fortunes depended on a Southern victory would be futile. Although the Emancipation Proclamation had provided an argument in favor of supporting the Union on moral grounds, it was not until news of the July victories at Gettysburg and Vicksburg reached him that Henry Ward felt that he could confidently argue his case on the grounds of self-interest as well; the British would have to do business with the winning side. Thus armed, he advised his contacts in Britain that he would be willing to address a series of meetings in October.

Deliberately, Beecher's sponsors chose sites for his appearances where he would encounter the greatest resistance—Manchester, Liverpool, Glasgow, Edinburgh, London—where labor and capital alike were suffering losses. Never in all of his experience had Henry Ward encountered such hostile audiences. Liverpool was the worst of them all. There had been threats to his life if he came to speak, and, according to his account, "There were men in the galleries and boxes who came armed, and some bold men on our side went up into those boxes and drew their knives and pistols and said to those young bloods, 'The first man that fires here will rue it.'" It took Beecher an hour and a half of thrust and parry with the crowd until he could begin his speech. Even then he "sometimes felt like a shipmaster attempting to preach on board of a ship through a speaking trumpet with a tornado on the sea and a mutiny among the men." At every stop, however, Beecher eventually left the stage with applause ringing in his ears and was able to read a favorable account of the event in the next morning's papers.

As might be imagined, Beecher was called on to handle a number of difficult and potentially embarrassing questions, particularly in the matter of race relations. His skill in doing so comes through in excerpts from his remarks at a farewell breakfast in Manchester (brackets as in original):

> I will turn to that letter in one of your local papers . . . containing those three questions, which the writer says have never received straightforward answers. I will endeavor to show you what a straightforward answer is. The first question is, "Do colored persons ever attend your church in Brooklyn?" Yes, by scores and hundreds. [*Cheers.*] Second, "If so, where do they sit?" Wherever they can get a seat. [*Cheers and laughter.*] Allow me to say that our church will hold but three thousand, and it is extremely difficult for any one to get a seat. I have said humorously in expostulating with our people, that they are sometimes impatient of having so little use of their own pews, for which they pay an inordinate rent, "Gentlemen, you know very well when you rent pews here what it means; you pay three hundred dollars for a pew for the sake of sitting in the aisle, and you knew it when you bought your pew." It is expressly stipulated that if a man is not in his pew to occupy it within a certain number of minutes before the service begins, he forfeits his right to sit there. . . . Well, when our own pewholders have to hustle for their own seats, because strangers may come an hour beforehand, when this has been going on for sixteen continuous years—if you ask me whether we take colored people by platoons, and walk them up and seat them on the platform—why, no, we don't treat them

any better than white folks. [*Loud laughter and cheers.*] We treat them just *as* we do white folks. [*Cheers.*] Now, let me say this: I have never exerted any direct influence on this subject; it has only been the Christian feeling and good sense of my own parishioners that have led them to determine their line of action towards colored people within the body of the church. . . . Third, "Have you ever seen any (that is, colored people) amongst your congregation; and would they be allowed to sit in any pew of your church or intermingle with your white hearers?" If my people were like the man who wrote this letter, they would not be permitted to sit a moment there. [*Cheers.*] This is not a mere jibe. I will tell you in a moment why I make this remark. But I have seen them, not once or twice, or fifty, but hundreds of times. I tell you the truth, gentlemen, though we are not better than hundreds of other churches. We have been led by acquiescence in those great truths preached in Plymouth Church—that man is not what he is on account of title, education, or wealth, but because God made him and loves him, and God will redeem him in immortality and glory. [*Cheers.*] And that broad ground has led us to feel insensibly, more and more, that a man in the house of God is to be treated as we would treat that man on the threshold of judgment day. . . .

The close of the letter containing these questions is as follows: "I could multiply instances to almost any extent of brutality towards colored people in the North, and of kindness and indulgence towards them in the South, which I witnessed during a long and protracted tour through the States. Though my original antipathy to slavery was never eradicated, I came to this conclusion,—that a Slave in the South was a far gayer and happier creature than a free black in the North." There you have it. Ah! there never was a serpent yet that was taught to speak in human language that first or last the sibilation did not come out. Whenever I find a man undertake to tell me, that any human creature, considered in the totality that makes up a man, in his body and soul—in his loves, independence and purities—in his relation to time and eternity—is a better man in slavery than he is out of it, I say, "Thou son of the devil, get thee behind me." [*Loud cheering.*] On the other side, let me say pointedly, that the treatment of the blacks in the North was bad—that we imbibed prejudice from the South—that the poison of slavery in every fiber of our body wrought out bad laws and usages; *nevertheless, the party now predominate throughout the North, though once a small minority, has fought up against that prejudice and wrong, until at last it is in ascendancy: and Englishmen are asked now to strike us, who have been martyrs for freedom, because of the prejudices which came from the men who are now in rebellion.* [*Great cheering.*] And I avow, there is a good deal of work yet to be done. We do not appear before you as a saintlike people; we are, just like you, in the midst of struggles where all sorts of influences are in combination. We have fought so far with complete success—thanks to God; but it is not done yet. There are many things we need to change, and are trying to change. All we ask is, that when our faces are as it were turned toward Jerusalem, you will not stop us. [*Loud cheers.*]

All of Henry Ward's stenographically recorded addresses in Britain contain the italicized notations of *cheers* and sometimes *laughter*, indicative of how he won the sympathy of his audiences after gaining their attention. With a touch of humor, Henry Ward used his reception at a London hotel as a metaphor for the effect of his efforts: "When I first went to London I stopped at the 'Golden Cross,' and they put me in a little back room right under the rafters. When I came back from the Continent, there had been considerable said, and they received me more politely at the 'Golden Cross,' and put me in a third-story front room. On the third visit, I was received by the landlord and his servants in white aprons, and was bowed in and put in the second story, and had a front parlor and bedroom and everything beautiful." By no means sure that he would have such success, Henry Ward had done a lot of praying before each speech, and just before leaving for home, he wrote to Tilton:

My dear Theodore . . . I am a noisy spectacle, and seem to thousands, as one employing merely worldly implements, and acting under secular motives. But should I die, on sea or land, I wanted to say to you, who have been so near and dear to me, that in God's own very truth, *"the life that I have lived in the flesh, I have lived by faith in the son of God."* I wanted to leave it with someone to say for me, that it was not in natural gifts, nor in great opportunities, nor in personal ambition, that I have been able to endure and labour. But that the secret of my outward life has been an inward, complete, and all-possessing faith of God's truth, and God's own self, *"working in me to will and to do, of His own good pleasure."*

Beecher's British speeches were widely reported and widely praised in the United States. In an article for the *Atlantic Monthly*, Oliver Wendell Holmes called his effort "a more remarkable embassy than any envoy who had represented us in Europe since Franklin pleaded the cause of the young Republic at the Court of Versailles." Lincoln himself read all of the addresses and told his cabinet that "if the war was ever fought to a successful issue there would be but one man—Beecher—to raise the flag at Fort Sumter, for without Beecher in England there might have been no flag to raise," according to biographer Emmanuel Hertz. Family chronicler Lyman Beecher Stowe reported meeting New York Supreme Court justice Roger A. Pryor, who had served on General Lee's staff many years earlier. "He told me," Stowe wrote, "that it had been the opinion of General Lee and the members of his staff that had it not been for *Uncle Tom's Cabin* and Henry Ward Beecher's speeches in the British Isles the Confederacy could have secured the recognition of Great Britain and France with all that would have meant to them in both moral and material aid." Whatever effect they had on the course of the war, Henry Ward's speeches established him as a firm friend of the administration and opened doors in Washington for him.

Shortly after his return to Brooklyn, Henry Ward received a handwritten letter from Secretary of the Treasury Salmon P. Chase, urging him to come to Washington as a guest in his home. It is a revealing document in that Chase, a radical Republican with strong abolitionist views, tells of his differences with the president over the exceptions in the Emancipation Proclamation [it did not apply to slave states loyal to the Union and portions of states in rebellion under Union occupation] but notes that he, Chase, must be "thankful for skimmed milk when cream is not to be had." Chase must have felt that Beecher would lend a sympathetic ear to his complaints because of their cooperation in antislavery matters during their Cincinnati days in the 1830s and because of Beecher's support for General Frémont, who would in 1864 accept the nomination of the hastily formed Radical Republican Party to run for the presidency. Chase's differences with Lincoln would result in his resignation from the cabinet, but Lincoln's political savvy would result in his appointment as chief justice of the U.S. Supreme Court after the election was over. Henry Ward doubtless took advantage of his old friend's offer of hospitality, but it is to be doubted that he weighed in on the dispute with Lincoln. Judging by Beecher's recorded visits to the capital in 1864, the door where he sought the warmest welcome was the one that opened onto the portico of the White House.

Whether by intent or happenstance, Henry Ward was inside the White House when it became known that Congress had passed the Thirteenth Amendment to the Constitution, which, when ratified by the states, would end slavery everywhere in a reunited nation. A crowd gathered at the White House to cheer Lincoln, and the Great Emancipator appeared at a window with the Reverend Mr. Henry Ward Beecher at his side to acknowledge their approval. Hearing on another occasion that Lincoln was sending emissaries through the lines to discuss terms of peace with Confederate representatives, an alarmed Henry Ward rushed to Washington to argue the president into waiting for victory now that Sherman was slicing the South in half and Grant was battering Lee just miles from Richmond. Beecher would write of that visit to the White House:

> We were alone in his receiving room. His hair was "every way for Sunday." It looked as though it was an abandoned stubble-field. He had on slippers and his vest was what was called "going free." He looked wearied and when he sat down in a chair looked as though every limb wanted to drop off his body. And I said to him: "Mr. Lincoln, I come to you to know whether the public interest will permit you to explain to me what this Southern commission means." Well, he listened very patiently and looked up to the ceiling for a few moments and said: "Well, I am almost of a mind to show you all the documents."
>
> "Well, Mr. Lincoln, I should like to see them if it is proper." He went to his little secretary and came and handed me a little card as long as my finger and an inch wide and on that was written:—
>
> "You will pass the bearer through the lines" (or something to that effect).
>
> "There," he said, "is all there is of it. Now Blair thinks something can be done, but I don't, but I have no objection to have him try. He has no authority whatever but to go and see what he can do."
>
> "Well," said I, "you have lifted a great burden off my mind."

Lincoln would soon have occasion to lift another burden from Henry Ward's mind: the need to have a questionable favor granted for a friend to whom he considered himself in deep debt. Two New York newspapers opposed to the administration—the *World* and the *Journal of Commerce*—printed on May 18, 1864, an alleged executive proclamation calling for a draft of four hundred thousand additional troops and a day of fasting and prayer just when Grant's forces were bogged down in the Wilderness campaign. Fortunately, the editors of the other New York papers detected false notes in the document's wording and held it for verification. It was a hoax intended to cause panic on the stock market and inflate the price of gold, and it might have had that result if all the city's papers had used it. Lincoln himself and Secretary of State Seward proclaimed the proclamation a forgery, and orders went out to Major General John A. Dix in New York to close the offending papers and arrest their editors and publishers. On investigation, it was discovered that a young newspaperman named Joseph Howard, working with some brokers in a position to cash in on the rise in gold, was responsible for the forgery. Howard was hustled off to a cell in Fort Lafayette, and Lincoln ordered General Dix to let the offending papers begin publishing again. Young Howard was the son of the Howard who was one of the two living members of the trinity who founded Plymouth Church. As noted earlier, the Howards were among the Beechers' closest friends, and they would have been aware of how Theodore Tilton had extricated Beecher's son from embarrassment and possible punishment. The minister was in no position to pose as holier than thou, even if he wished to do so. He went directly to Lincoln as Tilton had done and was able to carry a signed order for Joseph Howard's release over to another good friend in power, Secretary of War Stanton.

Lincoln's wisdom in letting a rascal off the hook as a favor to one of the nation's most effective communicators was very apparent. In that election year of 1864, both Henry Ward and Harriet made early contributions to Lincoln's cause with strong statements about his character. In a speech in Philadelphia, Henry Ward rather oddly stressed the president's humble origins and ungainly appearance as proof that he was one of the common people and a symbol of democracy's virtue in that he had "shown the world that successful government is not the mystery that only a privileged few can enact." Although Harriet struck a similar note in the beginning of an article for the magazine *Watchman and Reflector,* she paradoxically took off in a nearly poetic flight to describe the president's *uncommon* characteristics:

> Lincoln's strength is of a peculiar kind; it is not aggressive so much as passive, and among passive things it is like the strength not so much of a stone buttress as of a wire cable. It is strength swaying to every influence, yielding on this side and on that to popular needs, yet tenaciously and inflexibly bound to carry its great end; and probably by no other kind of strength could our

national ship have drawn safely thus far during the tossing and tempests which beset her way. Surrounded by all sorts of conflicting claims, by traitors, by half-hearted, timid men, by Border State men and Free State men, by radical Abolitionists and Conservatives, he has listened to all, weighed the words of all, waited, observed, yielded now here and now there, but in the main kept one inflexible, honest purpose, and drawn the national ship through.

Harriet herself was trying to draw the Stowe family ship through rather choppy waters by writing articles on a wide variety of subjects as fast as she could. She had to make up for Calvin's lost income and cover her own extravagances in building the Hartford house. There were off-again, on-again costs of treating Fred—a sea voyage with his father, an asylum—since he kept falling off the wagon, likely a very literal experience for an inebriate at the time. The house cost more than planned when it had to be rushed to completion for a June 1864 marriage of daughter Georgiana to an Episcopal clergyman. That Stowe wedding amounted to raising a flag to let everybody know that the Stowe ship was sailing under different religious colors. It all started in Andover in 1862 when one of the twins, Hatty, began showing symptoms of going through a religious crisis similar to the one her Aunt Catharine had experienced at about the same age. Quick to spot it, Catharine described their niece to brother Henry Ward as one of the "lambs of the fold, who are torn and wounded by the thorns of Calvinism." Catharine did not find this surprising in view of Hatty's exposure to teachers from Andover Seminary, uncles such as Edward and Charles, and even a mother who was overly emotional in her religious attitudes. To Catharine's eye, Hatty took after her blood grandmother Roxana; she was *"Footish"* and *"undemonstrative"* in temperament: "That *emotive* experience toward Christ which her mother exhibits does not suit her taste or nature any more than it did Uncle Samuel's and mine," Catharine informed Henry. "She *can't* feel so and *don't wish* to." After something of a struggle to make sure that her daughters would *"be in earnest* to religion," Harriet encouraged all three of them to be confirmed in the Episcopal Church along with their Aunt Catharine. When they moved to Hartford, Harriet bought a pew in St. John's Church, and Fred, hoping it might help him conquer his addiction, also was confirmed with "no great ecstatic joy." Although she never officially switched allegiance from her Congregational/Presbyterian affiliation, Harriet had good memories of the Episcopal service from her childhood times at Nutplains and went to church with her children since "to have my children with me in the fold of Christ, to unite with them in the sacrament has been the thing of all others I have longed for."

Of all the lambs "wounded by the thorns of Calvinism," the one who suffered most may have been the sensitive musician Charles, who had to duck his head to hide the tears brought on by his father's harsh sermons when he was a small boy. Unlike most of his siblings, who simply drifted off to munch on more appetizing theological fare, Charles persisted in trying to chew up the thorns and digest them. The result was a book he published in 1864 titled *Redeemer and Redeemed* and intended to explain, among other things, the atonement, or why Jesus had to die on the cross. If the book had been published before his heresy trial, the charge might have been changed to insanity. To account for the existence of evil and sin in a world created by a good and loving God, he used his brother Edward's preexistence theory as a given and argued that for no known reason evil entered the mind of the angel Lucifer, who became the Devil, the leader of an ongoing rebellion against God. To bring his message home to readers, Charles used the Civil War as an analogy in several places, as, for instance: "There are those who would regard the Devil as a mere abstraction, an allegory, a fable. But they might as reasonably call Mr. Davis an abstraction, or slavery an allegory. Rebellion and despotism are not such abstractions in human experience as to justify the turning of the originator of all rebellion and despotism into a myth. The existence of Jehovah is no more clearly revealed in the Bible and in nature than the existence of Satan."

This Devil's source of power is death, a descent into hell, according to Charles. But a believer like his siblings in a merciful and loving God, Charles could not depict hell as a fiery furnace but as a separation from the glorious reunion with the Creator in the heaven of prerebellion. Again he used the Civil War analogy: "Should the chiefs of the rebellion in this land be finally seized, and condemned to hard labor among felons, we can imagine how they would look back on the time before the rebellion, when they were loyal, when they trod the floors of Congress, and when their eloquence shook the Senate, and their wisdom contributed to shape the legislation of a vast continental empire! But now that the rebellion is crushed and they are convicts, eloquence is not for them, statesmanship and jurisprudence, the lofty and ennobling aims of legislation and government, the exhilarating excitements of public affairs,—all are theirs no more. They move with the chain-gang, and break stones on the road. They see men, once their inferiors, thunder along in state, engrossed in those high affairs that they so well remember, casting a glance of mingled pity and abhorrence as they pass; and, stung to the soul, they continue their degrading toil till night remands them to their cell."

How does God fight the rebellion in the gospel according to Charles? He tries to win back Lucifer's followers by compassionate means, the only ones available to his character as a loving God. Several times he sends his "only begotten son" to earth to appear to leaders such as David and the prophets and as an Old Testament character called Melchisidec to show human beings the way to salvation. Frustrated by Lucifer's continuing power over men's minds, he finally turns his son—or mediator—into the man Jesus. By his suffering and death at the hands of Lucifer's forces, his descent into hell, and his resurrection, Jesus overcomes death and ends Lucifer's power over those who follow him. Throughout, Charles emphasizes self-sacrifice, so dramatically symbolized by the cross, as the essence of God's love. And what about the thorny question of human beings who have no opportunity to hear the Word? Charles solves this one as Edward solved original sin by postulating a postexistence in which they would have a second chance, as it were.

Like the earlier words of Edward, Charles's book did not cause much of a stir, even within the family. It is probable that they looked on it as a poetic flight of fancy to which Charles was addicted. But they would have agreed with his depiction of God's nature as loving and of self-sacrifice as essential to salvation, a central theme in the writings of Catharine and Harriet, the sermons of Henry Ward, and the actions of "tough love" Tom. However they expressed it in their words or exhibited it in their actions, the fundamental motivation of all the sons and daughters of old Lyman Beecher was the effort to get right with God, as they understood that process. From his correspondence it is clear that this was as true for the one actual warrior among them, James, as for his brothers in their safe sanctuaries.

The relationship to older famous siblings that James found questionable in Hong Kong turned out to be of considerable value when he arrived in New Bern to organize a black regiment. Among the slaves who escaped when General Burnside captured the Outer Banks and most of the coastal ports of North Carolina was a man named William Henry Singleton. At New Bern, where he made a living as a servant to white Union officers, Singleton rented the A.M.E. Zion church and began recruiting his fellow ex-slaves into a regiment that he tried to put into fighting trim by drilling once a week with corn stalks for weapons. By the time James Beecher arrived on the scene, Singleton was working with a thousand men who desperately wanted to be bearing real arms. The only salient fact about the colonel who came to give them guns in Singleton's *Recollections of My Slavery Days* is that he was "a brother of Henry Ward Beecher, that great champion of our race." The Beecher reputation would have given Singleton and his recruits good expectations as to the sympathies of their new commander, and Singleton's preparations would have made James's job a great deal easier than anticipated. Singleton seems to have been satisfied with his reward: "I was appointed Sergeant of Company G, being the first colored man to be accepted into the federal service and the only colored man that furnished the government a thousand men in the Civil War."

By midsummer 1863, the First North Carolina Colored Volunteers were encamped on Folly Island, their sector of the siege of Charleston, South Carolina. In his letters to Frankie, James is very high on the morale of his men, who are "better disciplined than any N.Y. regiment I have yet seen" but very pessimistic about the campaign, since Union forces "are no nearer to taking Charleston than we were six months ago. No doubt Gen. Gilmore is an excellent officer but there is a screw loose somewhere. The enemy meanwhile are building two batteries to our one." He took Frankie on a tour of the front: "The sharp shooters of both sides are perched in all sorts of nondescript holes & firing through cracks in every direction. It is one continual pop-pop and a man cant show half his head without getting a ball through it. I saw one poor fellow shot right through the heart. I detest this little sneaking way of fighting." He let her know the trials of camping: "We have poor food and no cooking utensils. My kitchen furniture consists of 1 coffee pot, 1 sauce pan and two shovels to fry pork & flap jacks in. . . . My bed consists of four stakes and a board across, a rubber pouch & wool blanket. It's a little rough on the bones—especially when one is losing flesh at rate of 2 lbs per week."

Soldiers at war have forever needed to unburden themselves of fears and frustrations to somebody, and for James this somebody was Frankie. They had obviously reached some sort of understanding before James took off for New Bern, but James was still conducting a courtship by letter along with reporting on his activities and concerns about his command. He wanted Frankie to know all about him beginning with the fact that he was a motherless child who "might have been a better man had mine lived. . . . And yet had mother lived, she might have had many an anxious hour which she had escaped." He warned her that he was not likely to achieve either fame or fortune: "But when it comes to money matters, I'm all in the wind. I have never saved a dollar, have wasted very few and am none the better off than at twenty one. So as to the custom in prospective English marriages I state my prospects with a kind of assurance that you know all about it before." He said that he had learned a lesson from the breakdown of the previous winter. It was not caused by "the fact that I had used more or less of stimulants" but by the fact that "there is a certain amount of tense application which keeps one in prime working order—that beyond this brains wont work." Taking this lesson to heart, he had recently avoided a similar breakdown. "The moment this came to me," he wrote, "I just dropped everything—I said to my good Saviour, 'Ive done my best—Ive plead for my men, Ive worked through thick and thin to keep my regiment from demoralization & to prove myself worthy of my position—Ive used every ability given to me nor counted my life dear—and now come I to Thee'—And from that day to this, Ive worked just as hard, but worried not a bit."

James was nearly devastated when he got what he called "scolding letters" from Frankie and sister Isabella. They accused him of dwelling too much on his own problems and worries instead of providing Frankie with "written loving words." James was very hurt by this. If he had come across them, he could have responded succinctly by quoting the words of Richard Lovelace in *To Lucasia on Going to the Wars*: "I could not love thee, dear, so much, Lov'd I not honor more." James struggled to say the same thing as he wrote: "When you first gave me your love, in response to mine it came soothingly it is true for I needed it—and it did its work for I rested in it—You know I did. The time comes near when I can ask you to take my name and share my home—to be mine & mine only and on this threshold of a new life, do you think I can look coolly on my work the result of which success and honor & a wife or disappointment and failure and loneliness. For, Frankie, though Ive no objections to go up to love—Ill never make love come down to me."

In a nearly literal sense, James went up to love early in the year 1864, when he was granted a leave, a good part of which was spent in Washington scrounging men and supplies for his regiment. He would regret that he was not on hand to lead the regiment, renamed the Thirty-fifth United States Colored Troops, during its first battle, at Olustee, Florida. The men rewarded his faith in them. Although the regiment took 230 casualties, it stood fast in guarding the line of retreat for the rest of the federal forces. James did not regret the time he was able to spend with Frankie, during which they firmed up plans for a spring wedding if and when he could get another leave and come to claim her at her Guilford home. That form of happy ending was not to be. Leave from his command, now headquartered in Jacksonville, Florida, proved elusive for James. Fortunately for them both, Frankie was young, strong, and confident. In defiance of convention and her own family's wishes, she spent months working every possible angle to go down and marry James wherever she could find him. The problem was getting a pass from the War Department to go into the battle zone. Frankie had help from both Beechers and Footes, to whom she also was related, and at one point Henry Ward and his friend Howard plotted to smuggle her aboard one of the regular steamers to Hilton Head. When this failed because she could not get to New York on time, Frankie went to Washington in June, and the same Senator Wilson who had eased Harriet into the White House opened the doors of Secretary Stanton's office to her. She wrote of the occasion to James:

> Sec. Stanton was standing at his desk with a line of waiting men round the room. One woman beside. Mr. Stanton was splendid— treated me with the respect & kindness that he would his most valued friend—read my paper spoke gently & with sympathy— said he approved of my going—wanted I should go & approved my personal conduct in the matter—it was that of a spirited, true hearted woman—but just now orders had been sent to Florida that he might not tell me about that made it impossible for me to go just yet—in a fortnight if I would have the subject again brought before him he would *probably* be able to give me a pass. So don't try to come for me but hope on.

Hope was richly rewarded on July 18, 1864, when Frankie and James finally met up in Jacksonville and that evening were married in the headquarters of General William Birney in a ceremony that she described in a letter to her mother:

> Ah, dear friends, if you could all have been present at that little military wedding at seven o'clock last evening, my happiness would have been complete. I have never read in fact or fiction of a wedding more unique and romantic, yet so touching and so solemn. Imagine two large parlors thrown into one, with long windows and moonlit verandas at either end; in place of the usual elegant furnishings, see tables and desks strewn with dispatches and writing materials; behold the glowing western sky without, and the picturesque groups of colored people looking in

from the piazzas at the unusual sight. Within the four young men in the full dress uniform of a general's staff; a handsome colonel also waits, and a minister in clerical dress. A few moments—and then a fine looking, gray-haired general with sash and star brings in upon his arm a little woman in half bridal attire, and gives this woman to be married to this colonel. . . . Then they salute the bride, and she receives the kisses with the feeling that they represent the good wishes and blessings of all her dearest friends. Then came the wedding supper, also unlike any other; and then while we sat in the moonlight on the broad upper piazza, the well-trained band of the 7th U.S. gave us a serenade that might well make us believe that sorrow and sin had left the earth forever.

As a colonel's wife, Frankie was entitled to quite a few amenities—a nice house with servants inside and a constant guard at the door, horses to ride and cows to provide fresh milk, the best available food, and solicitous attention from junior officers and their wives. Judging from her letters, there were guests of both sexes at table for every meal, horseback rides in the afternoons, and sessions of whist in the evenings. The only missing element in an idyllic life for a new bride was the bridegroom, so often away with his troops. These separations resulted in a remarkable exchange of letters that reveal a warm and mutually supportive relationship. Being a brisk and busy optimist, Frankie was able to deflect the often gloomy outpourings from James, a depressive brooder, by her accounts of the kind of daily doings that were reassuring evidence of a normal and happy home life awaiting him.

Since she was now a Beecher, however newly minted, Frankie also found time for good works—in particular teaching the largely illiterate black troops to read and write in one-on-one sessions. James would have been most appreciative of this activity, since the morale of his men and the attitude of the other white officers toward them was of greatest concern to him. "There is now no doubt that all of my wounded men left on the field at Olustee were bayoneted in cold blood," he reported to Frankie. "It is said to have been done by some South Carolina troops. . . . You may judge this does not make me feel peculiarly happy—especially when the new man come to relieve Gen Seymour while he pities the poor *loyal Floridians* who suffer so much from the effects of the war don't see anything particularly out of the way in this. Says he has no doubt my wounded were murdered but that its 'very hard to restrain men when their blood is up.'" It was this sort of thing rather than the hardship of camp or fear of death—"I'd rather fight a battle any day than make a Quarterly Ordnance Return"—that bedeviled James to the point of writing to Frankie that "aggravations of this life have interfered greatly with my own spiritual life. I have no enthusiasm of love to Christ, no elevation of character, no soul life whatever save what your coming has awakened." Realizing from many confessions of this sort the depth of her husband's need for her made Frankie happy just to be there for him whenever he could come to her.

But personal soul searching was only part of Colonel Beecher's correspondence. His verbal descriptions of incidents in the strange and dangerous business in which he was engaged preserve their immediacy like snapshots in a photo album.

There were good days:

> Sunday P.M. Today is like some pleasant dream. The weather is beautiful beyond comparison & my camp is a picture in itself. All the streets lined with evergreens & arched at the head & foot. A glorious spreading tree overhanging my tent. I had usual service this morning. Just now the effect is strange enough. Four or five squads are singing. Some in the wild plantation songs of the olden times. Some in new tunes. Yet the whole makes a kind of harmony which fills the air & seems to echo all through the trees. My good friend & Surgeon Marcy is reading Uncle Toms Cabin to an admiring group in the next tent & then rich laughing comes in so splendidly that I wish Hattie could look in even at this late day to see how Uncle Tom can be enjoyed.

There were comic days: "I like my boys right well. Gen Seymour was taken aback by the enemy fighting behind trees. So four or five Regts are picked out to drill in Indian fashion. Mine is one & you would think us perfectly mad to see us dashing through the woods, yelling & dodging & firing from behind logs & all sorts of things."

There were deadly days:

> Officers Hosp Ward 6, Beaufort S.C. Dec 2nd '64—My beloved— Im grateful for life spared though very sorrowful at being on my back. We had a hard fight under great disadvantages. There was only one road and thick jungle on either side & the enemy had 2 guns right sweeping the road. I was 5th Regt & was ordered up to move through the thicket along the right of the road, flank

the battery and charge it. I did so but the enemy ran the guns off & I came right in front of a strong earth work that nobody knew anything about. A round shot killed poor old Gray [his horse]. I left him and pressed on at head of my column. A round shot struck me across both legs above the knees & upset me. I found no bone broken & pushed on. Then the boys opened fire without orders, and then the bushes were so thick that the companies were getting mixed. I halted and reformed the companies. Then got orders to move to left of the earth work & try to carry it. I led off by the left flank & the boys starting finely & singing with "follow de colonel." It was a perfect jungle all laced with grape vines & when I got on the left of the earth work and closed up I found that another regiment had moved right through mine & cut it off so that I only had about 20 men. We could see the rebel gunners heads. I told the boys to fire on them & raise a yell, hoping to make them think we had a force on their flank. We fired and shouted and got a volley or two in return. A rascally bullet hit me just below the groin & ranged down nearly through my thigh. Then I went back with my twenty to the road again—found 35th83rd54th men all mixed together. Went to work to clear up though the fire of the enemy was very hot. Got hit here with a spent ball in left hand. In course of an hour got the companies all right & in order. Firing ceased at dark & we held our ground. I was so stiff that I couldn't get along so I shook hands with Col Willard who did splendidly all day & wasn't touched and Dr. Marcy helped me back & then I was sent to the boat & here I am, stiff and helpless but not dangerously hurt, only grieving that I couldn't take the battery.

Resourceful Frankie wrangled her way up to Beaufort, where she was taken on as a nurse at the hospital and was able to find board in a nearby home. She nursed James until he was well enough to rejoin his regiment on February 18, 1865, the day when General Sherman's troops occupied Charleston. But the war was not quite over for Colonel Beecher's men. On February 19 James wrote to Frankie:

We have skimmed the county thus far. It grieves me to see such splendid houses and furniture burnt up. But we cant take it along, and up they go—Tonight the whole horizon is lighted up splendidly—No less than four grand conflagrations going on at once—I shall get to be a regular brigand. We are only 10 miles from Charleston but I don't think we will go there—Probably will have to scour this district for some days. Have seen no regular troops. Am occasionally fired on by bush whackers. Marcy is well & invaluable to me. Tonight I have 20 horses, 21 oxen, 1 two horse carriage &c &c—and chickens enough to start a farm yard. Q.M. Terry & Dr. Marcy are the best leaders for raiding parties I have. Personally I have only stolen 3 horses, one cart and a Methodist minister—who begged hard for the horses, but I told him he & his brother ministers by their preaching had forced me to leave the pulpit & take to fighting and do not only take his horses but burn his house if it came on my line of march.

I love you Frankie dear—While burning houses and stealing horses & every pretty piece of furniture that goes to ashes reminds me how I wish it was in our house—These planters have lived most luxuriously—but they have to rough it now.

It would be nearly a month before James led his regiment into the city. In the meantime, nervy Frankie had gone into Charleston as part of General Gilmore's party, found a place to live in a deserted mansion with a family of former slaves, and begun work as principal pro tem of a public school with thirty teachers and six hundred pupils. She was proving herself to be the perfect wife for the general her husband would soon become. The war-crossed lovers would be together at last, with Frankie working at James's side as he took on the task of trying to fulfill the last wishes of his martyred commander in chief to "bind up the nation's wounds."

9

"Wait—wait—singing songs in the night"

HER ADMIRERS CALLED HER the most prominent woman in America. Her critics devised names for her that were largely unprintable in her day. She was so well known that newspapers saved a lot of type in the countless columns they ran about her doings by referring to her simply as "the Woodhull." Her notoriety by whatever name—she called herself Victoria Claflin Woodhull—made mandatory a headlined account on September 18, 1876, of an event that would normally have been overlooked as a private matter. The Woodhull was granted a divorce from her almost equally notorious husband, Colonel James H. Blood, whose name she never took, on the grounds of his adultery. Readers who had followed the couple's highly publicized careers or who had known them personally were greatly astonished to note a provision in the decree that permitted the Woodhull to marry again and denied that privilege to the colonel. The divorce with all of its implications was in keeping with the character of the first woman to run for the office of president of the United States and with the mood of a nation going through its Centennial year of independence.

Both the Woodhull in the act of discarding her husband and the nation at its great celebration in Philadelphia that summer seemed to be turning away from a dark past to face what promised to be a brighter future. Despite ten years of uneasy peace, the wounds of war were still festering. The difficult transition from slavery to freedom throughout the South was being marked by episodes of violence. A prosperity jump-

232

started by the economic stimulus of war was being dampened by depression. The bright stars of the war hero in the White House were tarnishing in the acid of scandals reaching up to his vice president's chair and into his own office in the person of his private secretary. Instead of saluting icons of a glorious past, the crowds at the Centennial Exposition rather symbolically swarmed into the Machinery Hall, where recent inventions such as the telephone, typewriter, and refrigerator car that would at least make life easier were on display. The telephone was, in fact, so new that it had first functioned only two months before, when its inventor, Alexander Graham Bell, was able to send a voice summons to his assistant in the next room through a wire: "Mr. Watson, come here. I want you." As for the Woodhull, a practitioner and proponent of free love as well as women's suffrage, a vision of Jesus that had come to her while she was briefly serving time in New York's Ludlow Prison was causing her to repudiate much of her past in favor of a new life and message.

In a speech just weeks after her divorce, the Woodhull began claiming religious inspiration rather than a belief in social freedom as the basis for her attitudes about relations between the sexes. She told her audience in a Boston theater,

> People call me a free lover. The first time I ever heard the words "free love" mentioned was at a Methodist church. The minister was holding one of those protracted meetings, and telling everybody to come forward to the mourners' bench where the love of God was free to all. Then for the first time the idea that this was true, struck me to fruition. God is love and love is God. Who dares to tell me tonight that the love of God is not as free to me as it is to you! On the one side is pure undefiled love; on the other is the abominable force lust. I appealed for the former and my appeal has closed the halls of Boston to me for four years. Your abominable lust I abhor, and God's intelligent love I adore.

To some ears these words might have had the same ring as those from the mouth of the nation's most famous preacher, Henry Ward Beecher. But to no ears would those words have struck a sourer note than Beecher's and those of most of his extended family. That this woman who had been instrumental in putting the Beechers through years of terrible trial dared to pose as some kind of messenger from God was blasphemy to them.

The twists and turns that would eventually lead to a crossing of paths between such strikingly different human beings in their public manifestations as Henry Ward Beecher and Victoria Claflin Woodhull had begun immediately after the war, with political disagreement between Beecher and his protégé Theodore Tilton. Henry Ward believed in lenient treatment for the defeated South, as proposed by Lincoln and seconded by his successor, Andrew Johnson. In an early letter to the new president, Henry Ward wrote: "I feel confident that God has raised you up to complete the great regeneration of the South, which war has begun. At that stage of the work at which we are now aimed, I am persuaded that your views and sentiments are eminently sound and wise." Evidently Henry Ward expressed this view to Harriet, too, as revealed in a letter she wrote to a friend in England early in 1866:

> We have a president honestly seeking to do right, and if he fails in knowing just what right is, it is because he is a man born and reared in a slave State, and acted on by many influences which we cannot rightly estimate unless we were in his place. My brother Henry has talked with him earnestly and confidentially, and has faith in him as an earnest, good man seeking to do right. Henry takes the ground that it is unwise and impolitic to endeavor to force Negro suffrage on the South at the point of a bayonet. His policy would be, to hold over the Negro the protection of our Freedman's Bureau until the great laws of free labor shall begin to draw the master and servant together, to endeavor to soothe and conciliate, and win to act with us, a party composed of the really good men at the South.

The trouble started a little later that same year, when Henry Ward chose to make public a version of these views through an open letter. He was viciously attacked by Radical Republicans through most of the papers of the North, including the *Independent*, edited by Tilton. How could a founder of the Republican Party support a Democrat like Johnson? How could a minister and advocate of temperance stand by a man who was publicly profane and drunk? How could a nearly lifelong opponent of slavery now advise what amounted to leaving the fate of freed blacks in the hands of their oppressors? And on, and on. Henry Ward was able to shrug off the general criticism and even that of Tilton, who was given to reckless emotionalism. But when his sainted older brother Edward out in Illinois published a disavowal of his views, Henry Ward blew his top. "When I stood almost alone, my church in my absence, full of excitement and all my ministerial brethren, with a few honorable exceptions either aloof or in clamour against me, the whole religious press well nigh denouncing me and the political press furious, it would seem as if common affection, would have withheld an attack from my own household and that there could be in this universal uproar against me, on all hands, no such fear that truth would go by default as should justify a brother in rushing to the front to strike me" was only one such passage in the letter he wrote to Edward, but he ended it by saying that he felt "more love for you than for any of my brothers" and that "this very love and looking up, made your assault in the circumstances harder to bear but has not changed my love, or disturbed my confidence in your love." The stir created by the public expression of Henry Ward's views caused Harriet to write him privately that he seemed to be taking his opinions from the old governing class in the South who wanted to govern again whereas "it may be the design of God to set aside this old aristocracy in the reorganization of society at the south and to bring up the *common people* as in New England." In addition, she felt that Henry Ward had not taken into account the fact that "*the conquerors are sore with suffering*—too sore to be reasonable."

If he had had time to pay attention to the political wrangles going on up North, brother James might have provided Henry Ward with at least one ally in the family. As the general in charge of a subdistrict of the military district of Charleston, South Carolina, James was responsible for reconstruction in an area ninety miles square and the offshore islands of Edisto, Wadmalaw, Johns, and James, in which there were two sizable towns and some six hundred plantations. Having learned literally to love his black troops, James was in sympathy with the needs and aspirations of the newly freed people, but he was also aware of how much they had to learn to handle their freedom successfully, and he was faced with the many practical problems of getting some sort of sustaining economy going in his devastated district as fast as possible. Almost instinctively, James adopted Henry Ward's approach of establishing an equable working relationship between whites and their former slaves in the hope that it would prove the basis for a viable free society. The instrument he used was a labor contract between plantation owners and ex-slaves. He described his work in a letter to Isabella early in 1866:

> A perfect chaos was anticipated, so I started in December and addressed public meetings of white and freed people in various parts of my district. My motto was "Fair work for fair wages." In consequence by the middle of February 300 contracts were made, and before the end of the month the whole mainland of my command was in complete order. No loafers, white or black, were allowed, and only ninety whites and eighty colored persons were

receiving rations, and these were entirely women and children. Then I inspected thoroughly the sea islands of my command which were held in special charge of the [Freedmen's] Bureau. Affairs there had become so demoralized that I was obliged to move a force upon the island and disband the so-called local police and thus preserve order. This was done to the entire satisfaction of the Major-General Commanding (Sickles). Then the Government began to restore plantations to the original owners, and the question of contract came up. I found here an entirely different class of people from those I had instructed on the mainland. Their worst feelings of bitterness and laziness had been encouraged, carpet baggers had speculated among them, and the Government had been swindled by improper issue of ration tickets, until no white man could go upon the island except at the risk of his life. I quietly sent a guard with orders to arrest any officer of less rank than myself who should issue a ration on the islands of my command. . . . I set the people at work on all the plantations where the owners were not on hand, and made order that the owner of every restored plantation should first offer to his own people a fair contract which they should accept or leave the place to give [an opportunity] for others to come in. This [so impressed] General Sickles that he made [the command] throughout his department. This has been a labor requiring intense study, hard riding, and no small amount of patience. But it has "paid."

Perhaps unfortunately for the future of reconstruction, General Beecher was relieved of his duties and command when the Thirty-fifth United States Colored Troops was mustered out of service in June 1866. If James's discharge was a loss to the country, it was a boon to his brother Tom. James and Frankie packed up and went to Elmira just in time to take over Tom's church, while his older brother indulged a typical Beecher case of the blues by going off alone on a nine-month round-trip by sea to San Francisco, pausing in places where he could earn money by joining a construction crew. Tom's tendency to fall into depression was reflected in letters dating back to his teen years, but in none more so than one he wrote to console Henry Ward's son-in-law on the death of a child:

My theory of the universe and of this world is one that no amount of pounding or bruising can ever make your buoyant and loving heart accept. To me the death of your little boy chimes in with a unison of evil. I say it was bad. It was wrong. It was of the devil who has the power of death. I hate him, and I hate his works, and I hate this world. It is a world where Jesus could not live, my Livy couldn't nor your boy. They all died too soon. 99 in every 100 die too soon. Death has passed upon all. This is a gloomy world. I give it up. I have no part in it. I wont plan—I wont hope—I wont fear. I will only endeavor to keep from its evil, bind up its gashes, shine into its darkness, prophesy heaven and wait—wait—singing songs in the night.

Small wonder that optimistic Henry Ward once said, "I always get the blues when I go toward Elmira."

Alice, one of Isabella's daughters, had a long visit with her Aunt Julia while Tom was gone. Although James and Frankie boarded at the Gleason health establishment across the way, Alice saw a lot of them, and she informed her mother that James also seemed to be "blue" because he felt inadequate to fill his brother's shoes in the pulpit even though everybody else appreciated his sermons and lectures. Nevertheless, he took on the additional work of pastor to a rural church in nearby Christian Hollow, where energetic Frankie pitched in to run a Sunday school and conduct prayer meetings. Alice was quite impressed with both of her outgoing aunts and the general atmosphere they created. She reported that Frankie was always kissing James, who remained as "unresponsive and monosyllabic as ever." Glad to have James and Frankie back in the fold, Catharine wrote a letter on New Year's Day 1867 to them and Julia. She said that she was trying to start a family circular letter that might come to them from Edward and warned that "if it does come—please send it *to me*—instead of to Henry as directed. I fear it would *stop there* in the mass of material that goes to his box." Catharine promised to have the letter end at Henry's finally and then added a cheerful personal note: "I have a delightful home where I board in the city—where I can see friends every day—ride the cars &c. So I am spending a very pleasant winter—my health perfectly good & no walking sticks needed—for which I am duly thankful I hope."

If the circular ever did make the rounds, the entries from most of the siblings in the next few years would have justified Tom's gloomy view of life. Still struggling with son Fred's alcoholism, Harriet seized on what seemed like a godsend when Fred came home from socializing in a bar with a story he had heard from three young veterans. Raised on stony Connecticut farms, they were so impressed with the lush land and long growing season in Florida where they had been sent as soldiers that they pooled their service pay and rented a thousand-acre place called Laurel

Grove Plantation on St. John's River near Jacksonville. They soon ran out of funds and returned home hoping to find financial backing for their enterprise. Harriet offered to put up the money if they would take Fred on as superintendent of the project. The Stowes hoped that the combination of responsibility and a job requiring physical activity would enable Fred to control his drinking. But in spreading news of her investment around the family through a letter to Charles, Harriet explained it as an opportunity to help the "poor people whose cause in words I have tried to plead," since they would be employing ex-slaves.

With no major project of her own through 1866 and 1867, Harriet devoted a good deal of effort to prodding and scheming to get Calvin to finish the book he had retired to write. Once much of the manuscript was in hand, she wrote to her friends the Fields, who had promised to publish it, that she would be bringing the material and Calvin to Boston and warned that "in regard to Mr. Stowe, you must not scare him off by grimly declaring that you must have the *whole manuscript complete* before you set the printer to work. You must take the three-quarters he brings you and at least make believe begin printing, and he will immediately go to work and finish up the whole; otherwise, what with lectures and the original sin of laziness, it will all be indefinitely postponed. I want to make a crisis that he shall feel that *now* is the accepted time, and that this must be finished first and foremost." The ruse worked. Calvin's *Origin and History of the Books of the Bible* came out in 1867 and resulted in an unanticipated sale that earned ten thousand dollars in royalties and went a long way toward justifying Harriet's admiration and abiding faith in her partner. Harriet had a harder time convincing an unenthusiastic Fields to publish a book of verse she had written titled *Religious Poems* in that same year, and it was not one of her winners.

In the spring of 1867 Harriet went down to Florida to inspect Laurel Grove and see how Fred was doing. Although not impressed with Laurel Grove, where they were trying to grow cotton—a judgment that bore bitter fruit in the eventual loss of ten thousand dollars—she fell in love with a property with a grove expected to yield seventy-five thousand oranges a year at Mandarin, across the river. She wrote a glowing account of it to Charles in a letter trying to persuade him to consider joining her in acquiring property there and even in becoming an Episcopalian so he could serve as pastor to the chapels she planned to build along the river. However Charles might have reacted to the suggestion under normal circumstances, any thought of it was driven out of his mind that summer by a triple tragedy. His two youngest children—Essie, fifteen, and Hattie, twelve—went boating with their twenty-year-old cousin, Edward's son,

Albert, on a pond near their Georgetown home. Like a bolt of lightning from a clear blue sky, word came to Charles and Sarah that the boat had overturned, and the three young people had vanished. They rushed to the pond, where they saw men already diving in search of their children. Sarah collapsed in a dead faint, but Charles joined the divers. He could see nothing in the murky depths, and neighbors led him away with a revived and anguished Sarah as soon as he surfaced. Charles would record it as a kind of saving miracle that the girls appeared to be enjoying a peaceful sleep when their bodies were at last recovered, and their faith enabled the parents to create an atmosphere so heavenly at the time of the funeral that Isabella reported finding it "hard to breathe earthly air at all."

Writing to Henry Ward, who did not receive word in time to be at the funeral, Charles told him that "Jesus the Lord has sustained us in an unexpected and wonderful manner—pouring out a tide of love and happiness through my spirit at a time that my heart was as if pierced with a sword. . . . This has produced a tenderness all over this community, a softness of heart—among all & even those who have been most opposed to me—that it seems a time most propitious to putting in the seed." Charles wanted Henry Ward to take advantage of the situation and stage a revival of at least a week in Georgetown. Even though brother William and Calvin Stowe were both going to preach for him, Charles argued that no one "could do so much to break the spell laid on us & burst the bonds fettering our development as you. This is what the church needs & I need. The revival of religion here, and the gathering in of the precious harvest—would do more to comfort Sarah & me than anything else. The state of Christ's cause here lies heavily on my heart—and kills my joy almost. Think, dear brother, whether for *once* you will not make an exception in our favor and come away from your wider, more important field, for a season to do what so needs to be done here."

Edward and his wife, Isabella, accepted the tragedy in much the same spirit as Charles and Sarah. Responding to a letter of sympathy from James, Isabella wrote, "The shock was stunning awful at first—& we were staggered by it. It was truly as you say 'a *strange* sorrow,' we were ready to faint when thus rebuked of the Lord—But we have been enabled to say, 'Thy will be done,' we know the Lord doeth all things well—and we are trying to be cheerful & happy, & and we are learning to do without the bright beautiful one, who was the sunshine of our home." Edward wrote James that "you too have been called to learn in the school of sorrow & what you say of its refining power is true. Not that all who suffer are improved by it, but that when used by the Saviour it purifies & refines, teaching faith & patience, submission & obedience. Indeed it is spoken as an essential part of Christian training." In response to Albert's death, he said that "it remains to us to serve God more earnestly in our shortening life, till we are united to him in that better world." One of the ways by which Edward was trying to serve the Lord that year was to keep his famous brother Henry Ward from straying off the path of true faith. Like Catharine and Charles, whose plea went unanswered, Edward was often exasperated by trying to get through to the man with an overflowing mailbox and a wide field to cover. He began one letter taking issue with Henry Ward's views with this line: "I am discouraged in ever writing to you, because you never answer me."

Early in 1867 Edward expressed concern about what he called "trials of faith." He was especially upset by a student in the Chicago theological school where he taught who became so "skeptical & unsettled" that he quit the ministry after reading Herbert Spencer, the British philosopher and apostle of evolution whose body of work was often called social Darwinism. "When I was in your house last," Edward recalled, "I saw & read a volume of essays by Herbert Spencer, you asking me what I thought of it? I replied, it leads to the denial of a personal God which is virtual atheism." By December of that year, Edward had read a great deal more of Spencer and was thoroughly alarmed, as were a group of Chicago Congregationalists meeting with publisher Henry Bowen from Brooklyn to discuss the editorial content of the *Independent* as edited by Theodore Tilton. Observing that Tilton had "publicly disowned some of the essential elements of the evangelical system" such as "that Christ died for our sins according to scriptures" and having been informed that Tilton's editorial policy was approved by Henry Ward, Edward warned:

> You & Tilton will be in collision with the greater portion of the Congregational body. . . . If things come to this issue, you will not be able to uphold Tilton but he will sink you. I fear Tilton more & more. His advice to young men to read Emerson's essays & especially Herbert Spencer's first principles as "awakeners" is dangerous & may be ruinous. One is a teacher of pantheism & the other denies the personality of God, & reduces him to an unknown & unknowable force, & makes all things, even the emotions, & choices of men to be evolutions of it and all religions, also fetishism, paganism &c to be evolutions of it, & to have warrant in it. He does not believe in miracles, or Christianity & yet Mr. Tilton is advising young men to read him as an awakener. He is one of the most dangerous writers of the age. It

takes great energy in a well developed Christian to escape his unsettling power & things are fast drifting, not merely to a rejection of Christianity, but to a virtual scientific atheism, under his influence & that of others of the same school.

This letter did provoke an instant reply from Henry Ward—a hastily scribbled document that looked like an explosion in ink. He said, in part:

It is nearly four years since I withdrew from the management of the Independent, and a year and a half since I withdrew from the arrangement by which my sermons were to be published in it. Since that time I have not been to the office, nor had the slightest connection of any kind with it, nor have I been consulted about its affairs, nor am I in any manner, directly or indirectly, concerned with the paper. Nor am I an advisor of its content. On the other hand, it is well known that I am in positive antagonism with the whole general drift of the paper. Mr. Bowen will scarcely recognize me in the street, and feels bitterly my withdrawal from all part or lot in the paper. . . .

Theodore Tilton and I are personally friends. In matters of public policy we differ. He also is a member of my church. But, he has come to that period of life in which he breaks away from the traditions which he has received from me & others, to form his own opinions—I do not know what ground he now rests upon. From several circumstances I am led to believe that it is an Embellished Naturalism. . . . I do not regard him as . . . especially precise in his religious philosophy. But whatever he holds or rejects, he does it on his own personal responsibility. Meanwhile, no other man in America has had his views so thoroughly published as I have. My most incidental remarks are culled, my lecture room familial talks are reported, my sermons are weekly printed in Methodist, Baptist & Congregational papers, in papers without ecclesiastical connections, & in secular newspapers. I live out of doors without walls or roof. . . . I am an old man— Tilton a young man—The question is not whether I agree with him, but how far he agrees with me! There, spread before millions is my testimony to the essential elements of Christianity. There is my life work, in building up Christian influences—It is . . . as definite & tangible as the Pyramids of Egypt.

The rift between him and Tilton was wider than Henry Ward knew or was willing to acknowledge, ironically because of the minister's growing relationship with Tilton's wife, Elizabeth, and their children. He had known the petite, pretty, dark-haired Elizabeth since she was a child in Plymouth Church Sunday school and handsome Theodore—the "blond poet," as he was sometimes called—since, as a bright youth newly over from the city, he became such a worshipful member of the church that he began recording all of Henry Ward's sermons and talks in shorthand. In 1855 the Tiltons became, in Beecher's words, "one of the finest couples I ever married." From then on, as his mentor and sometime boss, Beecher spent a lot of time with Tilton at work in the offices of the *Independent* and at play, when they would shop together in Manhattan's finest stores for the gems that Beecher collected and kept in his pockets to fondle as a form of pacifier when he was overwrought and for the artworks and furnishings they both acquired to adorn their Brooklyn homes. He was more of a surrogate father to Elizabeth, baptizing the children and stopping by to talk over any problems she might have, spiritual or otherwise. By 1867 Tilton was riding high professionally as a nationally known editor and speaker who was augmenting his income by going on the lecture circuit from fall to spring. Not wanting Lib, as they called her, to be lonely during his trips, he urged Beecher to put her high on his list for pastoral calls, saying, "There is one little woman down at my house who loves you more than you have any idea of."

Calling on Lib Tilton was more than a ministerial duty for Henry Ward. One of the reasons why he was often too busy to respond to the calls of his siblings in 1867 was the time-consuming effort he was putting into writing a novel. He and Lib often talked about what each was reading, and he had discovered that she was a connoisseur of novels. He took to reading passages of the book he was calling *Norwood: or, Village Life in New England* to her as he composed them and asking for her opinion. The practice was a compliment to her and a comfort to him in more ways than one. In addition to the pleasure of playing to an admiring and appreciative audience of one, Beecher found the whole atmosphere of the Tilton home relaxing. In one of her letters to her husband on tour, Lib wrote, "Mr. B called Saturday. He came tired and gloomy, but he said I had the most calming and peaceful influence over him, more so than any one he ever knew. I believe he loves you. We talked of you. He brought me two pretty flowers in pots, and said as he went out, 'What a pretty house this is; I wish I lived here.'"

The Beechers' three-story brownstone town house at 124 Columbia Heights was only a mile from the Tiltons' two-story home at 174 Livingston Street, no stretch for a man who once had walked a hundred miles round-trip to call on the girl who became his wife. The Beechers could look out on the East River, but the Tiltons only had to walk a block to reach the shops on Fulton Street. The first floor of the Beecher house was given over to a large parlor, where Henry Ward worked and greeted all comers who wanted to see him from two to four on weekday afternoons. Except for a shiny grand piano, the furniture was nondescript and worn, according to a visiting journalist. Everywhere the eye tried to rest it would come upon the fruits of Henry Ward's shopping sprees—pictures of some kind covering nearly every inch of wall space; ornamental objects of every size, shape, subject, and texture crowding the tables and a shelf that ran around the walls; gilt-edged volumes gleaming from a large bookcase; at one time three oriental rugs, one on top of the other, gracing the floor because the master of the house could not resist buying them but had nowhere else to put them. The Tilton house was equally cluttered. "Sofas and ottomans were strewn about in luxurious careless-ness," creating, in the words of another journalist, "comfort and ease in everything." Paintings reflected both the interest and the vanity of the owners. Tilton had arranged for his friend the artist William Page to paint portraits of Henry Ward Beecher, William Shakespeare, and Jesus, for whose likeness Tilton himself sat as model. In contrast to the Beecher house, there was no public traffic, although it was a favorite gathering place for invited guests from literary, artistic, and political circles, espe-cially when Tilton was at home. Rather clearly, the calming effect the place had on Henry Ward had more to do with the presence and nature of Lib Tilton than her surroundings. The order of march on Columbia Heights was set by a much older woman with no time for fiction and hardened by life into a figure called behind her back by her husband's parishioners "The Griffin," a fabled animal half eagle and half lion.

Lib Tilton's published correspondence with Theodore reveals her great concern over the estrangement between the two most important men in her life. Apparently she knew all about the disagreement over the contents of the Independent that prompted the exchange between Edward and Henry Ward. In alluding to that she wrote, "I can never rest satisfied until you both see eye to eye and love one another as you once did." She may have been given some hope of reconciliation since the two men were at least nominally allied in the pursuit of one cause: women's suf-frage. Theodore was the organizer and Henry Ward the titular head of the Equal Rights Organization, which was hoping to secure the same rights for women as blacks with the Fourteenth Amendment to the Con-stitution, granting freedmen citizenship going through the legislative process. Lib tried to be very open about seeing Beecher. "Pardon me if so many of my letters are filled with accounts of the pastor's visits. It is because I would have you know all that fills my thoughts that I write so frequently of him. Yesterday he made us very happy. It was Saturday. He came about 11:30 A.M., bringing flowers, as usual. After visiting with me twenty minutes, he said, 'I am hungry to see your children.' 'Are you really?' I said, 'then come up directly and see them.' I had set apart this day for doll dressing, as I had not time before Christmas. So he followed me upstairs, where, for one full hour, he chatted and played with them delightfully." Apparently a jealous Theodore reacted unfavorably to accounts like this, since Lib felt obliged to write, "About eleven o'clock today, Mr. B called. Now, beloved, let not even the shadow of a *shadow* fall on your dear heart because of this, now, henceforth or forever. He cannot by *any possibility* be much to me, since I have known you." And on another occasion, "Darling, we must both cultivate our self-respect by being what we seem—then will be fulfilled my ideal marriage—to you and you only a wife—but contact of the body with no other—while then a pure friendship with *many* may be enjoyed, ennobling us. Let us have not even a shadow of doubt of each other—tho' all the world are weak yet will *we* be strong."

Whatever else they might lead to, Henry Ward's visits with Lib apparently helped him to bring out his only work of fiction in 1868. As a novelist, he was no competition for his sister. *Norwood* is notably lacking in narrative thrust, and the characters are simply mouthpieces for Henry Ward's philosophical and theological views. Spokesman for the author is a physician, Dr. Wentworth, and his dialogues with the very orthodox village pastor, Dr. Buell, suggest the kind of talks Henry Ward wished he could have had with his father. The flavor of the book comes through this scene, in which the two men are discussing where God may be found:

Dr. Buell: "I find God in Christ the Saviour. I seek him in prayer, in meditation, and in His Word."

Dr. Wentworth: "Thus do I also. But not so only. . . . Dr. Buell, do you believe the Scriptures? Do you believe that those very heavens above your head declare the glory of God, or only that they *did* four thousand years ago? 'The earth is the Lord's and the fullness thereof, the world and they that dwell therein!'—now, today, here in this field—yonder, over that meadow, just as much as in Palestine. . . . Do you think that I can *believe* this universal presence of God—in the sun, in the season, in the sea and on the mountains, in tree and herb, in the clouds and storm, in summer and harvest, in the city among men and in the wilderness, yet suppose that Nature has nothing more for the soul than the catalogue of scientific names and a recitation of the order in which phenomena happen? Is there nothing of God in flowers, in forests, in birds, in insects, in my poor garden, in yonder valley, along the mountain flank, in those thunder-heads looming up white over the horizon yonder? Or is all this only meaningless matter? When my wife speaks to me, is it only sound—wind? or is it a movement of air upon my ear, that conveys to my heart deep meanings? And is Nature mere phenomena? or is it God's phenomena, meant to convey something deeper than the body catches—something for the soul? Why, then, should you, a minister of God, hunt through books for God, and stand in pity of me, who use the Bible as I would a Botany—which does not contain living plants, but only word-descriptions of them. If I would see the plant itself, I must go out of the book to nature. And the Bible cannot contain the truth itself, only the word forms, the lettered symbols of truth. God does not live in a book. Man does not live in a book. Love, Faith, Joy, Hope, do not, cannot live in a book. For the living truth, we must go outside of the Bible which is but to religion what a Botany is to gardens, meadows, and all their flowers! I am not ashamed to own that I feel as if some sort of positive relationship existed between me and every living thing. A spice bush, a clump of wild azaleas, a bed of trailing arbutus, a patch of eye-brights, a log covered with green moss,—these all seem to be of my family kin. The spiders, too, the crickets, the field-mice, and all the swarms of birds, the worm—that as a child I was taught to abhor—are of God's family and mine. Since I accepted the New Testament, all the world has become my Bible. My Saviour is everywhere—in the book and out of the book. I see Him in nature, in human life, in my own experience as well as in the recorded fragments of His own history. I live in a Bible. . . . But it is an unbound book! It is wider than that I can reach its bounds. It is enough for me that I believe when it is said, "All things were made by Him, and without Him was not anything made that was made."

Henry Ward's appreciation and knowledge of nature is his greatest gift to the reader from *Norwood*. Because his detailed descriptions of its sights and sounds are both educational and inspirational, the reader is tempted to become more aware of the living world around him or her.

Probably due to the author's name recognition, the book sold surprisingly well. Henry Ward was a hands-on person in his relationship to nature, and with his income rising as fast as his reputation—he was making some forty thousand dollars a year—he bought a farm at Peekskill, New York, to which he would escape during the week as often as possible. With the help of a resident farmer, he grew prize-winning vegetables as he had in Indianapolis and was able to use his good judgment of horseflesh to acquire fast mounts. He was at the farm in August 1868 when little Paul Tilton died of cholera, the third of their children to die. Off lecturing, Theodore could not return in time to be with Lib, and Henry Ward had to console her when he came down to conduct the funeral. Still grieving in October, Lib heard that Henry Ward would be coming down again from Peekskill to speak at a rally for General Grant, who had been nominated by the Republicans for the presidency. She was so impressed by Henry Ward's performance that she went to his home the next day to congratulate him and doubtless to absorb more sympathy for her loss. She found him alone, since his family was still in the country, and whatever passed between them caused her to make an enigmatic entry in her diary for October 10: "A Day Memorable."

In giving up treasured time in the country to speak for Grant, Henry Ward was responding to the call of duty rather than desire. During the 1856 campaign for Frémont, he had overextended himself and developed symptoms that made him think he was "going to have apoplexy or paralysis or something of the kind." The symptoms had persisted off and on through the years since then. Several times during a sermon he would have fallen to the floor if he had not grabbed the table; on other occasions he thought he was going to drop dead in the street. "If I had consulted a physician, his first advice would have been, 'You must stop work,'" Henry Ward told his biographers. "But I was in such a situation that I could not stop work. I read the best medical books on symptoms of nervous prostration, and overwork, and paralysis, and formed my own judgment of the case. The three points I marked were: I must have good digestion, good sleep, and I must go on working. These three things were to be reconciled, and in regard to my diet, stimulants, and medicines I made the most thorough and searching trial, and, as the result, managed my body so that I could get the most work out of it without essentially impairing it." Important to this body management were the days he could spend in Peekskill; the weeks during hay fever season when he stayed at the Twin Mountain House in New Hampshire; and the occasional long leaves he took, such as his trip to Europe and Great Britain during the war. But the work did go on, and he regarded participation in the political process as an essential part of that work. "Complaint is often made of ministers . . . that they meddle with things that they do not understand," he told his congregation. "I think they do, too, when they preach theology. There is an amazing deal of 'wisdom' that will be called 'rubbish' one of these days. But when ministers meddle with practical life, with ethical questions and relations, they are meddling with just what they do understand—or ought to. If they do not understand these things, they have failed to prepare themselves for one of the most important functions to which they address themselves as ministers."

Henry Ward regarded governance in a democracy as involving ethical questions with which he was obliged to concern himself and never more so than in 1867 and 1868, when the continuing standoff between Congress and the president over Reconstruction threatened to undo all that the bloody war should have done for the country. Throughout 1867 the Radical Republicans kept passing and repassing over Johnson's veto legislation to give Congress and therefore the federal government rather than the states control over granting citizenship and voting rights to blacks. This resulted in military occupation of the South and an influx of unscrupulous carpetbaggers from the North. Whites reacted by forming organizations to intimidate blacks such as the Ku Klux Klan, which became what was called the "Invisible Empire of the South." Congress also tried to gain almost complete control over the executive with the Tenure of Office Act, which would require the president to get Senate approval before removing any members of his cabinet. Considering the act unconstitutional and a deliberate thumb in his eye, Johnson fired Secretary of War Stanton, a Radical Republican, and replaced him with Grant, who was then commander in chief of the army. There ensued a form of musical chairs when Grant vacated the office and returned to his command, and Stanton returned to his office, only to have Johnson appoint yet another replacement. In early 1868 the House used Johnson's supposed violation of the Tenure of Office Act along with some other charges to impeach him, but a surprise switch in the Senate by Radical Republican Edmund G. Ross of Kansas was enough to set aside the House verdict by a single vote. As an admirer of Grant's role in the war and as a staunch moderate Republican, Henry Ward believed that Grant stood a far better chance of cleaning up the mess in Washington than the Democrats' nominee, Governor Horatio Seymour of New York, who had been branded a wartime copperhead by his opponents. A majority of voters agreed with Henry Ward; Grant won in a landslide.

In late December 1867 a personality who would lighten the lives of Beechers for the rest of the century debarked from *Quaker City* in the port of New York. He was a young newspaperman named Samuel Clemens, who had signed the letters he wrote for American newspapers during a long and extensive trip abroad "Mark Twain." The Langdons and their daughter Olivia came down from Elmira to meet their returning son Charles, a shipmate who had befriended the writer. Having seen her picture during the trip, Sam Clemens was eager for the meeting with Charles's sister, which took place on New Year's Day 1868. At the same time he met Isabella Beecher Hooker and her daughter Alice, who had come to the city on the cars to visit with their old friends the Langdons. It was something of a coincidence that Clemens was almost literally holding in his hand a letter from Elisha Bliss, Jr., of the American Publishing Company in Hartford, who wanted to make a book of his letters. But it was no coincidence that Isabella took her new find over to Columbia Heights in Brooklyn on January 5 to impress the literary lights of her own family, Henry Ward, Harriet, and Catharine, all gathered there. Citing his considerable experience in publishing, Henry Ward did young Clemens a favor by advising him to drive a hard bargain with Bliss. Clemens went back with the Langdons for a visit in Elmira and then to Hartford to stay with the Hookers while conducting his business. In a letter dated January 25, 1868, to Alta California, he called Hartford "the handsomest town I have ever seen" and reported: "What country it is! At the hospitable mansion at which I am a guest, I have to smoke surreptitiously when all are in bed, to save my reputation, and then draw suspicion upon the cat when the family detect the unfamiliar odor. I never was so absolutely proper in the broad light of day in my life as I have been for the last day or two. So far I am safe, but I am sorry to say that the cat has lost caste."

In the next few years, the greater Beecher family would experience a real need for a lightening of their lives. "I don't know of any who could so well as you adopt the language of the scriptures, 'all thy waves have gone over me'—Stroke upon stroke falls upon you—blows, too, which strike the very heart center," Henry Ward Beecher wrote to Charles and Sarah on September 26, 1868. The occasion was a news account and telegram Henry Ward received from General Sheridan reporting the death of Lieutenant Frederick Beecher in a fight with Indians in Colorado. It was a little more than a year after the drowning deaths of Fred's two younger sisters. Despite severe wounds at Gettysburg, Fred had stayed in the army and was serving with the Forsyth Scouts in an action that would be called the Battle of Beecher Island and marked by a monument to Fred, whose commander wrote of him, "Not an officer of his acquaintance but has a sore heart at the loss of a comrade so loved for his many manly & military virtues." In his reply to Henry Ward, Charles raised a version of that unanswerable question as to why bad things happen to good people when he said, "There is something strange about Fred's history—his trials so severe—& his death so painful—yet his character so faultless, his disposition so mild, unselfish, almost feminine in its delicacy—One would not have thought that he needed such an ordeal." Although Harriet at first thought that Charles's "hold on life is broken" by this new tragedy, he would write to James a month later: "I wish you could be with us when his remains come home, to be laid by the side of his sisters—Altho' it is a house of sadness, yet it is not a house of unhappiness—Those that were with us last year at the funeral of Essie and Hattie were lifted up & seemed brought near Heaven. Our hearts were united in love—and the dividing influences of the world seemed to die away. . . . We are comforted by the thought that in the society of the dear ones he so mourned—& in the presence of Saviour—he has found rest and blessedness."

In a sense Fred's death meant an end to war for the Beecher clan just as one of President Johnson's last acts in December—proclaiming general amnesty to all parties involved in the rebellion—meant an end to war for the nation. But the Fourteenth and Fifteenth Amendments and other forms of Reconstruction legislation were raising an issue that would turn into a new cause for a number of Beechers. Women were conspicuous for their absence in the granting of suffrage and other rights to newly freed blacks. The first National Women's Suffrage Convention, meeting in Washington in January 1869, took the position on the Fifteenth Amendment that "a man's government is worse than a *white* man's government, because in proportion as you increase the tyrants, you make the condition of the disenfranchised class more hopeless and degraded." Despite this determined start to a movement, women were by no means united, either in the nation or in a large extended family like the Beechers, as to the rights they desired and the means of getting them. That spring the Equal Rights Association split into a conservative group headquartered in Boston called American Woman Suffrage Association, with Henry Ward Beecher as president, and the more militant, New York–based, all-female National Woman Suffrage Association. Isabella Beecher Hooker, who had become personally friendly with the already famous women's rights crusaders Susan B. Anthony and Elizabeth Cady Stanton, joined their

New York group. She tried to bring Harriet along with her as a contributor to their magazine *The Revolution,* but Harriet backed out when they
refused to give the magazine a less radical name.

Never one to keep silent, Harriet started to write for the paper of the
Boston contingent, *Woman's Journal,* instead. She also agreed to share
the byline on a publication by sister Catharine that year titled *The American Woman's Home.* After devoting nearly half a century to promoting
education and independence for women, Catharine surprisingly opposed
women's suffrage and involvement in political and civic affairs. In this
book she gave her definition of the proper role for a woman: "The family
state then, is the aptest earthly illustration of the heavenly kingdom, and
in it woman is its chief minister. Her great mission is self-denial, in training its members to self-sacrificing labors for the ignorant and weak: if not
her own children, then the neglected children of her Father in heaven.
She is to rear all under her care to lay up treasures, not on earth, but in
heaven. All the pleasures of this life end here, but those who train
immortal minds are to reap the fruit of their labor through eternal ages."
When the *Hartford Courant,* thinking she was probably in league with
Isabella, whose now outspoken views were beginning to create news,
identified Catharine as a suffragette, she wrote an indignant denial: "This
is not true of myself or of a large majority of my family and personal
friends, most of whom would regard such a measure as *an act of injustice
and oppression,* forcing conscientious women to assume the responsibilities of the civil state, when they can so imperfectly meet the many and
more important duties of the family state."

Whatever their stand on women's issues, all Beechers believed in justice per se, a belief that led the two most prominent siblings, Henry
Ward and Harriet, into activities in 1869 that caused unwanted storms of
criticism to burst over their heads. Henry Ward's sympathy was aroused
by a scandalous killing that was headlined in the news of the day. After
a Mrs. Daniel McFarland divorced her husband on the grounds of adultery on his part, she let it be known that she intended to marry a well-
known member of the *Tribune* editorial staff, Albert D. Richardson. An
enraged McFarland walked into the newspaper's office and shot Richardson. Although remarriage of a divorced person, as well as divorce itself,
were frowned on by most Christian denominations, Henry Ward felt that
her husband's transgressions gave him leave to join another minister in
conducting a deathbed marriage ceremony for Mrs. McFarland and Richardson, but it opened him up to harsh criticism from orthodox believers.

What prodded Harriet into an action that would be called at best foolish and at worst evil was a very old scandal—the shocking story that she had heard from Lady Byron.

Remembering her implied promise to the friend that she had made on her visits to England in the 1850s, Harriet felt obliged to act on it when a book titled *My Recollections of Lord Byron* by Countess Guiccioli, the poet's last mistress, was published in 1868. The countess repeated the charge that his wife's cold treatment had been the cause of Byron's exile and subsequently depraved behavior. The charge from such a source was an injustice in view of all that Harriet had learned about the matter and more than she could stand. She wrote an article for the *Atlantic Monthly* and *Macmillan's Magazine* in England that was expanded into a book, *Lady Byron Vindicated*, in 1869. For those Victorian times it contained an astonishingly frank account of what Lady Byron had told her:

> She said that, from the outset of their married life, his [Byron's] conduct towards her was strange and unaccountable, even during the first weeks after the wedding, while they were visiting her friends, and outwardly on good terms. He seemed resolved to shake her views of the family state. He tried to undermine her faith in Christianity as a rule of life by argument and by ridicule. He set before her the Continental idea of the liberty of marriage, it being a simple partnership of friendship and property, the parties to which were allowed by one another to pursue their own separate individual tastes. He told her, that, as he could not be expected to confine himself to her, neither should he expect or wish that she should confine herself to him, that she was young and pretty, and could have her lovers, and should never object, and that she must allow him the same freedom.
>
> She said that she did not comprehend to what this was tending till after they came to London, and his sister came to stay with them. At what precise time the idea of an improper connection between her husband and his sister was first forced upon her, she did not say; but she told me *how* it was done. She said that one night, in her presence, he treated his sister with a liberty which both shocked and astonished her. Seeing her amazement and alarm, he came up to her, and said, in a sneering tone, "I suppose you perceive *you* are not wanted here. Go to your own room, and leave us alone. We can amuse ourselves better without you."

She said, "I went to my room, trembling. I fell down on my knees, and prayed to my heavenly Father to have mercy on them. I thought, 'What shall I do?'"

She did not tell me what followed immediately upon this, nor how soon after she spoke on the subject with either of the parties. She first began to speak of conversations afterwards held with Lord Byron, in which he boldly avowed the connection as having existed in time past, and as one that was to continue in time to come, and implied that she must submit to it. She put it to his conscience as concerning his sister's soul, and he said that it was no sin; that it was the way the world was first peopled; the Scriptures taught that all the world descended from one pair; and how could that be unless brothers married their sisters? that, if not a sin then, it could not be a sin now.

She went on to say that when she pressed him hard with the universal sentiment of mankind as to the horror and the crime, he took another turn, and said that the horror and crime were the very attraction; that he had worn out all *ordinary* forms of sin, and that he *"longed for the stimulus of a new kind of vice."* She set before him the dread of detection; and then he became furious. *She* should never be the means of his detection, he said. She should leave him; *that* he was resolved upon; but she should always bear all the blame of the separation. In the sneering tone which was common with him, he said, "The world will believe me, and it will *not* believe you. The world has made up its mind that 'By' is a glorious boy, and the world will go for 'By,' right or wrong. Besides, I shall make it my life's object to discredit you. . . ."

I asked, "Was there a child?"

She said there was one, a daughter, who made her friends much trouble, being of a very difficult nature to manage. I had understood that at one time this daughter escaped from her friends to the Continent, and that Lady Byron assisted in efforts to recover her. Of Lady Byron's kindness both to Mrs. Leigh and the child, I had before heard."

Harriet made the argument that Lady Byron kept her silence not because of her husband's threats but because of her consideration for his sister, with whom she became friendly, and their child, as well as her own peace of mind. Harriet confessed to Lady Byron her youthful infatuation with the man and his poetry, and it was this that made Lady Byron feel that Harriet would lend a sympathetic ear to her story. Despite all that happened, Lady Byron continued to admire "By's" genius. She blamed much of his behavior and thinking on an unfortunate upbringing, which included an indigestible dose of harsh Calvinism, and, as Harriet wrote, "she seems to have remembered, that if his sins were peculiar, so were his temptations." Lady Byron was convinced that Byron had been saved at the end by the kind of loving God in whom she believed. The thrust of the book was to show that Lady Byron, though sinned against, was understanding, self-sacrificing, and forgiving as a good Christian should be, rather than the mean cause of her husband's tribulations. All things considered, Byron came off reasonably well, but the public did not read it that way.

Harriet was subject to "the most unsparing and pitiless criticism and brutal assault," according to her son. Her article and book were called obscene, and even Theodore Tilton, apologizing for having to attack a frequent contributor, wrote an editorial in the *Independent* in which he described her account as "startling in accusation, barren in proof, inaccurate in dates, infelicitous in style, and altogether ill-advised." A cartoonist pictured her climbing the statue of an idealized Byron leaving muddy handprints and footprints behind. The *Atlantic* suffered a nearly fatal cancellation of subscriptions. But one of America's most respected literary figures, Oliver Wendell Holmes, came to Harriet's defense. Not that she needed his support; Harriet, as always, felt that she was doing God's work. At a time when justice for women was becoming the burning question of the day, Harriet was providing her own kind of answer, consciously or not.

In this instance, at least, Isabella Hooker so thoroughly agreed with her sister's message that she helped her put the book together. She had done some writing herself, and in a publication called *Womanhood: Its Sanctities and Fidelities*, she attributed much of women's problems to the fact that men were endowed with an "animal passion" over which they could lose control, a theory that could well have elicited her approval of the Byron tale. But Isabella was not content with merely writing about her cause. In 1870 she put the legal savvy she had picked up while studying with her husband to good use by drafting and introducing into the Connecticut legislature a bill to give women the same property rights as their husbands, which would finally be enacted seven years later. Then she began drawing on the Beecher in her to join Susan B. Anthony on a national speaking tour. By January 1871 Isabella was well enough known and had enough confidence in herself to head a national suffrage con-vention in Washington. When she arrived in the capital, Isabella was surprised and probably not at all pleased to find the most notorious woman in the United States—Victoria Claflin Woodhull—already there and stealing much of the thunder she had hoped to create.

Still only thirty-two, Woodhull had by then lived a number of differ-ent lives. Born in near poverty but graced with physical beauty and a quick mind, Victoria and an equally attractive younger sister, Tennessee, called Tennie, grew up in a mostly fatherless and destitute household in Ohio. Dabbling in spiritualism and the occult in general, the girls started traveling throughout the Midwest in their early teens as seers, faith heal-ers, and dispensers of patent medicine. At fifteen, Victoria married Dr. Canning Woodhull, a physician who turned out to be an alcoholic and who deserted her after she bore him a retarded son and a daughter. Vic-toria divorced the doctor and made a connection with Colonel James Blood, a handsome and polished war veteran with advanced social ideas, who left his own wife and family to follow Victoria and her unmarried sister to New York. There the young women practiced their wiles as well as their healing arts on an ill and aging Commodore Cornelius Vander-bilt, who rewarded them by setting them up in business as the first and only women stockbrokers on Wall Street. With the commodore's backing they earned enough money to begin publishing *Woodhull & Claflin's Weekly,* in which they advocated women's rights, free love, and unpopu-lar political views, which included printing Karl Marx's *Communist Man-ifesto.* They supported their parents in a city apartment and acquired a house on Thirty-eighth Street. Although she married Colonel Blood as soon as he was free, Victoria invited Dr. Woodhull, down on his luck, to live with them, an act that her critics viewed as a form of sexual perver-sion and that the French called a ménage à trois.

It was altogether astonishing for proper Isabella Hooker from Nook Farm to discover that this woman—through the agency of her friend and counselor Benjamin Butler, lawyer, wartime general, and congressman from Massachusetts—had arranged to present to the Judiciary Committee of the House of Representatives a memorial arguing that the Fourteenth and Fifteenth Amendments applied to women as well as blacks on Janu-ary 11, the day Isabella's convention was to begin. This event would be another first for Woodhull, or any woman. Susan B. Anthony immedi-ately proposed that they delay opening the convention and go to hear what Woodhull had to say, but a shocked and upset Isabella and many like-minded women wanted to have nothing to do with the Claflin sisters. Isabella was a guest at the home of Senator Samuel Clarke Pomeroy of Kansas on the night of January 10, and when she discussed the matter with him he advised her that "men could never work in a political party if they stopped to investigate each member's antecedents and associates. If you are going into a fight, you must accept every help that offers." Isabella bought the good advice and went along with Anthony's proposal.

The look of the Claflin sisters was another surprise for Isabella and the other ladies of the convention. They were young and fresh-faced with no cosmetic embellishment and, in dark dresses with no ornamentation other than a single rose pinned to Victoria's waist, more conservatively dressed than most of the other women in the room. When she began to speak, Victoria seemed shy and suitably in awe of her surroundings, but she soon warmed up to her presentation until she commanded the rapt attention of the male committee members and the enthusiastic endorsement of the female audience. An instantly entranced Isabella invited Victoria to repeat her presentation to the full convention that afternoon. During a tête-à-tête of several hours, Isabella discovered that Victoria shared her interest and experience in spiritualism as well as in the politics of women's rights, and Isabella would write to friends and family that "my prevailing belief is in her innocence and purity. I have seldom been so drawn to any woman. I shall always love her and in private shall work for her redemption if she is ensnared, for I never saw more possible nobilities in a human being than her." Isabella's infatuation with Victoria cost her a number of supporters. A typical letter informed her that "it will not be agreeable to us to invite you to speak in our church. . . . I fear your influence is wrecked by this unholy alliance." But the enthusiasm that Victoria helped to engender enabled Isabella to collect thousands of signatures to a declaration of women's right to the elective franchise and an invitation to present it in person to the Senate Judiciary Committee. She acquitted herself so well that Susan Anthony called her "the soundest Constitutional lawyer in the country."

"Infused" and "inspired" by the experience, Isabella wrote to her husband that "I dare not tell you all that I see in the future." If she had been aware of a bit of byplay at the time of the House hearing, Isabella would have found the future less enticing. When he heard that Isabella Beecher Hooker might snub the Woodhull, a man in the crowd milling around the antechamber told anyone who would listen that "it would ill become these women and especially a Beecher, to talk of antecedents or to cast any smirch on Mrs. Woodhull, for I am reliably assured that Henry Ward Beecher preaches to at least twenty of his mistresses every Sunday." This was the first report that a rumor so far limited to people with intimate Brooklyn contacts had spread to the general public. This whiff of sin in holy places originated inside 174 Livingston Street, where the Tiltons' once brightly burning marriage was sinking into smoldering ashes. In her sometimes too-confessional letters, Lib wrote sentences such as these about Beecher—"Now, I think I have lived a richer, happier life since I have known him. And have you not loved me more ardently since you saw another high nature appreciated me?"—that led to confrontation and argument when Theodore came home. In addition to raising suspicions about her conduct with Beecher, Tilton began to berate Lib for an extravagance that was digging a hole so deep in their finances that even his lecture fees could not fill it. A maid reported that Tilton would often slam around the house and raise his voice and sometimes lock Lib in her room, whereas Lib would yield and agree to almost anything to keep the peace. To escape her husband's tantrums, Lib took the children and went to Schoharie, New York, for the summer of 1870. On July 3 she returned alone to Brooklyn with the apparent intention of having it out with Theodore. Exactly what passed between them in that empty, echoing house was never made known except by Theodore's claim that Lib had tearfully confessed to having improper relations with her pastor.

If he had known what was going on in the Tilton house that night, Henry Ward Beecher would not have been having such fun the next day, during an Independence Day celebration at Henry Bowen's Woodstock, Connecticut, country place. The fact that Beecher was one of the guests at the affair along with President Grant was evidence that Beecher and Bowen were on friendly terms once more despite the competition that Beecher's new magazine *Christian Union* was giving Bowen's *Independent*. The relationship was such that Beecher and Bowen ran a footrace to entertain the rest of the party. Beecher felt that he had also mended fences with Tilton and had even announced the trio's renewed cordiality at one of his Friday church meetings. That July 4th would be one of the last days that Henry Ward Beecher could live through with a merry heart and a clear mind for years to come.

Although it was understood between them during the night of confession that Theodore would forgive Lib and Henry Ward and keep the matter quiet, Theodore was "just blasted" and could not hold his tongue for more than a month. As a leader in the suffrage movement, he was in frequent contact with both Miss Anthony and Mrs. Stanton. On an August evening, Susan Anthony was visiting the Tilton home and keeping company with Lib, who was in the early stages of pregnancy, while

Theodore went out to a dinner with Mrs. Stanton at which his tongue, quite probably loosened by wine, wagged wildly. He told the whole story, calling Beecher a "damned lecherous scoundrel" in the process. His temper up, Theodore went home and provoked a quarrel with Lib so violent that Anthony stayed the night in Lib's room to protect her from possible physical assault and was rewarded with a version of the story from Lib. Conscious of Tilton's position in the movement and the large audience he provided for their views as editor of both the *Independent* and Bowen's secular Brooklyn *Union*, the two women kept what they had learned that night to themselves. Not so Lib's mother. To explain herself when she fled again to Ohio for a long visit with friends, Lib had to lay "bare my heart" to her mother. Mrs. Morse did not blame Henry Ward, whom she admired, for whatever her daughter told her; she was sure that the fault lay with her son-in-law, whom she hated to the point of once going after him with a butcher knife, an incident that resulted in her leaving the Tilton house for a place of her own nearby. When Lib returned to Brooklyn in December and the rows resumed, Lib moved to her mother's house for refuge, and Mrs. Morse asked Beecher for advice and help.

It has to be presumed that Henry Ward knew something of what was going on in the Tilton ménage, even though he apparently had not seen Lib since July. In response to Mrs. Morse's request, he asked Eunice to go with him to call on the lady. Either he was taking a calculated and daring risk, or he was totally unaware of having anything to hide from his wife. While Mrs. Morse poured out her knowledge of the affair to Mrs. Beecher in the downstairs parlor, Henry Ward went up to the bedroom where the now very pregnant and distraught Lib lay and prayed with her. Having long ago barred her own door to Tilton, Eunice was in full sympathy with Mrs. Morse's view of Theodore as the villain. As they talked it over on the way home, the Beechers decided to have Henry Ward advise Lib to separate from Tilton and arrive at a financial settlement with him. He passed the suggestion along through Mrs. Morse, but instead of taking the advice, Lib let Theodore talk her into coming home once more by promising to sleep over at the home of his good friend Frank Moulton. On December 24 Lib miscarried what she would later describe as a "love child."

By then Theodore had confided in Moulton and a few friends from the Plymouth Church, and the word of Tilton's marital problems reached the ears of his boss, Henry Bowen. Already disturbed by Tilton's editorials criticizing his friend Grant and expressing views on love and marriage not unlike those in the Claflin sisters' weekly, Bowen had removed Tilton from the editorial chair of the *Independent* but left him in charge of his secular paper at an increased salary. A rumor Bowen heard in late December that Tilton might leave his wife for another woman brought about a confrontation during which Tilton told Bowen about Lib's confession. Bowen was not as shocked as Tilton might have anticipated, since his first wife, Lucy, had made a similar confession on her deathbed not long before Beecher took off on his wartime journey to Europe. Bowen had kept that confession to himself to protect his family's reputation and Beecher's as well, since Bowen's investments in the church and various publications depended on the minister's talents and fame. But this time, because of the natures, ages, and positions in the community of the participants, it was very likely that the Tilton mess, whether true or not, would surface and render Beecher a liability instead of an asset. Bowen seized on this opportunity to use Tilton as an agent to get rid of Beecher without involving himself and persuaded Tilton to write a note to Beecher that Bowen would deliver: "I demand that for reasons which you explicitly understand, you immediately cease from the ministry of Plymouth Church, and that you quit the City of Brooklyn as a residence."

When Bowen delivered the note, Henry Ward told him that Tilton was "crazy." He went on to tell Bowen all he knew about Tilton's abuse of his wife and about his alleged adulteries. Meanwhile, Tilton prevailed on Lib, still weak and ailing from her miscarriage, to write a letter to Henry Ward acknowledging that she had told Theodore everything and implying an improper sexual relationship. Informed that Beecher did not take his request to leave town seriously, Tilton told Bowen that he would confront Henry Ward with Lib's letter, and Bowen threatened to fire him if he let Beecher know what he, Bowen, had said about him. At this point Tilton went to see his friend from college days Frank Moulton for advice. Moulton proposed a face-to-face meeting with Beecher at which Tilton could read Lib's letter. It was a bitter winter night, but Moulton offered to walk over to the church, where they knew Beecher could be found, and bring him back to the Moulton house for the confrontation. Since Moulton's wife was a faithful Plymouth Church member, Beecher knew the man slightly and did not hesitate to go with him when told that something had come up about his relationship to the Tiltons. As they slogged through the snow, an apprehensive Beecher asked Moulton what he could do and was told, "I don't know. I am not a Christian; I am a heathen; but I will try to show you how well a heathen can serve you. . . . I will try to help you."

Moulton lingered discreetly in the parlor below while Henry Ward went upstairs to see Tilton. The young man read Lib's note to Beecher and then charged his once mentor and dear friend with threatening his career through conversations with Bowen as well as alienating his wife's affections. Tilton promised to keep the matter secret for the sake of his wife, whom he held guiltless, but Henry Ward realized that the document in Tilton's hand could be damning and that the damage it could do in the wrong hands to him, his family, the church, and all the causes he promoted was incalculable. He simply refused to believe that Lib would write such a note, and Tilton challenged him to ask her about it. When he saw Beecher stagger down the stairs, Moulton thought that the blow the older man—he was fifty-seven had just received might be more than he could take, and he offered to accompany him to the Tilton house. In doing so, he was establishing himself literally as a middleman. Good-looking and affable, with experience in negotiations as a contact man for an export house in the city, Moulton was well suited for the role. Arrived at 174 Livingston Street, Moulton again held back while Henry Ward rushed up to Lib's bedroom. He found her awake but ghostly pale. She told him that, in her weakened condition, she could not resist Theodore's pressure to sign a letter he composed, claiming it would enable him to confess his own transgressions and thus clear their marriage. But she had no more will to resist writing in her own hand a statement that Beecher proposed, saying in part, "Wearied with importunities, and weakened with sickness, I gave a letter inculpating my friend, Henry Ward Beecher, under assurances that that would remove all difficulties between me and my husband. That letter I now revoke." As they walked away, Henry Ward read the note to Moulton and asked him to pass the message to Tilton. With the paper tucked in his pocket, he was able to go to his own home and fall asleep.

Henry Ward's respite was brief. The next day, Moulton sought him out to inform him that Tilton had gone home after midnight and persuaded Lib to write yet another letter, addressed to "My Dear Husband," which, in effect, charged Beecher with obtaining a statement from her under false pretenses. In view of this, Moulton asked Beecher to return Lib's letter. Although Henry Ward argued that it was his only proof that the Tiltons were making false accusations, Moulton was persuasive: returning the letter would prove Beecher's good intentions and calm the Tiltons into silence. As the shock and confusion into which the charges had thrown him had begun to wear off, Beecher felt that secrecy at almost any cost was his best hope of riding out the crisis. Moulton agreed with him, so Beecher returned the letter. Neither of them was aware that, while this exchange was going on, Bowen was firing Tilton from his job at the *Union*, in violation of their contract. Moulton heard about it from a despairing and fuming Tilton as soon as he returned from meeting Beecher. But it was not until the next day that Henry Ward got the news from Bowen at the annual New Year's Day open house that the Beechers hosted. Beecher agreed that Bowen had done the right thing until Moulton showed up at the party and took his host aside for a private talk in the minister's study.

Moulton had come to warn Henry Ward that a jobless Tilton was desperate and liable to do anything. During their argument over his employment, Bowen had told Tilton what Beecher had said about him to justify the firing. As Tilton's oldest friend, Moulton claimed to know that the rumors Henry Ward had passed along were untrue. Tilton had always been faithful to his wife. Henry Ward wanted to believe Moulton and "felt very unhappy at the contemplation of Mr. Tilton's impending disaster. I had loved him much, and at one time he had seemed like a son to me." Pacing back and forth, Henry Ward began thinking aloud and taking on himself a load of guilt for his part in the trouble that had come on his erstwhile close friends. He had been wrong in passing along what might be lies about Tilton when he should have known better; he had been wrong, as an older man, in not recognizing the extent to which he might have been arousing Lib's affections without intending to do so. All the while Moulton was taking notes, and he asked whether Beecher's sentiments could be put in the form of a letter to show to the Tiltons. Henry Ward agreed as long as it would stand as an expression of compassion for their plight rather than any admission of wrongdoing. In the end Moulton wrote a summary in his own words, and Beecher signed it. It was dated January 1, 1871, addressed to "My Dear Friend Moulton," and said:

> I ask through you Theodore Tilton's forgiveness, and I humble myself before him as I do before my God. He would have been a better man in my circumstances than I have been. . . . I will not plead for myself, I even wish I was dead, but others must live and suffer. I will die before anyone but myself shall be inculpated. All my thoughts are running toward my friends, toward the poor child lying there with her folded hands. She is guiltless, sinned against, bearing the transgressions of another. Her forgiveness I have. I humbly pray to God that he may put it into the heart of her husband to forgive me. I have trusted *Moulton* in confidence.

Thus began a year of great anxiety for Henry Ward Beecher, during which he would frequently suffer familiar symptoms of impending death that he would mention in letters and even in sermons. There were many meetings with Moulton, whom Beecher trusted completely, to plan moves in the ongoing strategy of secrecy to which all parties agreed. There was even a reconciliation with the Tiltons involving encounters so emotional that on finding Tilton at Moulton's house on one occasion Beecher kissed him on the mouth and on another occasion in Lib's bedroom, according to Beecher's own report, "I kissed him and he kissed me, and I kissed his wife and she kissed me, and I believe they kissed each other." But unknowingly the human being closest to Henry Ward, not excepting his wife, was becoming an agent of his undoing. In the summer of 1870 Harriet Beecher Stowe went into a slump that kept her from working as a result of her daughter Georgiana's coming down with a serious nervous disease and the death of her brother-in-law and most trusted business adviser, Thomas Perkins. She had committed herself to grind out two novels that would run as serials in brother Henry Ward's *Christian Union* and then be published in book form. She also needed money to finance her Florida ventures. She was by then very much an old pro, and by fall she was sending her pen flying again. She met her deadlines, and the public was reading both books—*Pink and White Tyranny* and *My Wife and I*—early in 1871. One of those readers was the Woodhull, her sister Isabella's new colleague, and this crusader for free love who had announced her intention of running for president was distinctly unhappy with what she read into Harriet's work.

For these books, Harriet had turned her critical eye on the changing and disturbing social life of postwar New York. She made no bones about using her books as pulpits. She actually told—or perhaps warned—her readers that *Pink and White Tyranny* was a story with a moral rather than a novel. The moral was that divorce is always morally wrong. Harriet was a bit more subtle with respect to *My Wife and I*. She let her characters speak for her in proclaiming what was going wrong with the women's suffrage movement. She actually mentions Miss Anthony and Mrs. Stanton by their right names, and she might as well have done so for the Woodhull and Isabella. Ironically, the most interesting and amusing character in the book is a woman variously described as a tramp or a hussy named Audacia Dangereyes, who puts out a publication called *Emancipated Woman* and aspires to run for president. Audacia makes indecent sexual advances to male characters, one of whom, the narrator and author's spokesperson, says of *Emancipated Woman,* "Every holy secret of human nature, all those subjects of which the grace and the power consists in their exquisite delicacy and tender refinement, were here handled with coarse fingers. Society assumed the aspect of a pack of breeding animals, and all its laws and institutions were to return to the mere animal basis. It was particularly annoying to me that this paper, with all its coarseness and grossness, set itself up to be the head leader of Woman's Rights, and to give it harsh clamors as the voice of woman." There was much more derogatory comment about the personality, practices, and beliefs of Harriet's stand-in for the Woodhull. Harriet was kinder to her sister—but not much. She pictures another leader of the suffrage movement as a handsome, gently reared lady named Mrs. Cerulean, of whom one of the men says, "I like to hear her talk. And if we didn't have to live in the world we do, and things weren't in any respect what they are, nothing would be nicer than to let her govern the world. But in the great rough round of business she's nothing but a pretty baby after all—nothing else in the world." Of Mrs. Cerulean's improbable relationship with Miss Dangereyes, one male character says, "'Dacia called on her with her newspaper, and conducted herself in a most sweet and winning manner, and cast herself at her feet for patronage; Mrs. Cerulean, regarding her through those glory spectacles which she usually wears, took her up immediately as a promising candidate for the latter day. Mrs. Cerulean don't see anything in 'Dacia's paper that, properly interpreted, need make any trouble, because, you see, as she says, *everything ought to be love*, everywhere, above and below, under and over, up and down, top and side and bottom, ought to be *love*, LOVE."

Harriet's needle got under Victoria Woodhull's normally thick skin, especially because the story about Harriet's brother had finally caught up with her. She had it directly from the mouth of the respectable and respected Mrs. Stanton, who had it directly from Tilton's mouth, and she decided to fight fire with fire. She wrote what was then called a "card"— an open letter to the editor—that appeared in both the *World* and the *Times* on May 22, 1871. Because she admitted to opinions different from "self-elected orthodoxy," she accused them of "endeavors to cover my life with ridicule and dishonor." She openly advocated free love "in its highest, purest sense as the only cure for immorality," but she charged her judges with being against free love while practicing it secretly. "For example, I know of one man, a public teacher of eminence, who lives in concubinage with the wife of another public teacher of almost equal eminence. All three concur in denouncing offenses against morality. . . . I shall make it my business to analyze some of these lives and will take my chances in the matter of libel suits."

Lest there be any doubt as to the lives she would analyze, the Woodhull asked Tilton to meet with her and told him bluntly that she had in mind him, his wife, and Henry Ward Beecher. This called for an emergency meeting at Moulton's house, where it was decided that Tilton should endeavor to placate the Woodhull to secure her silence. Fortunately, he was in a position to do so, since Moulton and Beecher, among others, had pooled their resources to give Tilton some employment by starting a magazine, *The Golden Age*. Tilton offered to write a biography of Woodhull for his magazine, a proposition that she could not refuse because of her need for even faintly respectable publicity to further her political career. Tilton put his heart and some more available parts of his anatomy into the project when it became clear that he and his subject both believed in practicing what they preached about free love. Woodhull told a Chicago reporter that Tilton had been her lover, and his extravagant praise for her would seem to confirm her admission. In addition to calling the Woodhull "the most divinely gifted of human souls," Tilton boldly argued in favor of her most controversial position: "On social questions her theories are similar to those taught by John Stuart Mill and Elizabeth Cady Stanton, and which are styled by some as free love doctrines, while others reject the appellation on account of its popular association with the idea of promiscuous intimacy between the sexes—the essence of her system being that marriage is of the heart and not of the law, that when love ends marriage should end with it, being dissolved by nature, and that no civil statute should outwardly bind two hearts which have been inwardly sundered." Whether Tilton's effort proved convincing to the reading public or not, it did serve to give the Brooklyn contingent a summer of silence.

With her novels out of the way and doing well—the circulation of *Christian Union* was doubled while *My Wife and I* was running—sixty-year-old Harriet, still full of drive and as needy as always, went looking for a new subject that summer. She had met a young woman, the wife of a magazine editor she knew, Thomas Bailey Aldrich. The woman's personality suggested a heroine for a novel, and Harriet invited herself to the Aldrich summer place in Portsmouth, New Hampshire, to learn more about her. When Harriet arrived hot and exhausted from her train ride, Mrs. Aldrich produced a pitcher of cold claret punch that her parched visitor downed in minutes. Harriet felt the room start spinning and collapsed on a couch, heedless of the fact that her hooped skirt flew up and revealed her well-worn boots and her flowery, ribboned garter knots. This embarrassing show placed the young hostess, who had been nervously in awe of the world-famous author, in an awkward position. Not wanting to disturb her obviously tipsy guest, Mrs. Aldrich tried to cover the exposure with a scarf, only to hear Harriet murmur, "What are you doing? Let me sleep." When her hostess explained the situation, Harriet waved her away, saying, "I won't be any properer than I have a mind to be."

One sibling who would have applauded Harriet's response was the Reverend Thomas Beecher. Returned from his long voyage in restored health, Tom was conducting an unorthodox ministry in Elmira with new vigor, to the delight of that rising literary star Samuel Clemens, a.k.a. Mark Twain. Pastor of the church founded by Jervis Langdon, Tom was elected to preside when their daughter Livy married Mark in 1870. Because the publisher who put out his best-selling *Innocents Abroad* was in Hartford, Twain took advantage of his growing Beecher connection in 1871 to rent the Nook Farm home of the Hookers, where he had once been a guest, but he spent summers in Elmira. Undoubtedly Mark worked up the courage to smoke in the Nook Farm place he rented with a clear conscience once he observed that the Reverend Tom shared that vice and another—a fondness for ardent spirits—with him. Tom Beecher lived by his own lights and had no respect for either public or clerical opinion. When a professor friend and his wife died leaving four daughters behind, Tom and Julia adopted the girls, but he would not accept more than his thirty-five hundred dollars in salary. That meant living in a kind of genteel poverty that friends and church members tried to relieve with gifts. The gesture was often futile. Noting Tom's shabby overcoat, Jervis Langdon gave him a new one. Langdon was a bit miffed to find his minister walking the streets in the old coat a few days later but not surprised by Tom's explanation. He had run into a man with no coat at all and given him the new one because he thought that the old one was too poor for a gift. When Tom's congregation grew too large for the church, he began holding services in the Opera House on Sunday nights, and in Eldridge Park on Sunday mornings in good weather. He had to prevail on the town fathers to grant an exception to the Sabbath laws so the streetcars could carry the crowds to the park services, where he preached in a very unclerical costume of white suit and white felt hat, a style that Mark Twain copied. Tom's fellow ministers were so incensed that they expelled him from their union, an action on which Mark Twain commented in a letter to the local paper: "Happy, happy world that knows at last that a little congress of congregationless clergymen, of whom it had never heard before, have crushed a famous Beecher and reduced his audiences from fifteen hundred down to fourteen hundred seventy-five with one fell blow."

Tom's sister Isabella made a tactical error when she decided to give her sister Catharine a letter of introduction to the Woodhull. Catharine thought that she could modify Woodhull's ideas on free love and marriage, and Isabella, who also found them extreme, was hopeful that she might prevail by reason of her impressive age—seventy-one that year—and reputation as a pioneer in women's education. She also was sure that when Catharine saw Victoria she would be "just as much in love with her as the rest of us are." Arrived at the Woodhull residence on East Thirty-eighth Street, Catharine found it was crowded, and the women decided to take a carriage ride in Central Park for privacy. Totally unaware of rumors about Henry Ward and always imperial in manner, Catharine lectured the Woodhull on the immorality of her beliefs until the younger woman could stand it no longer. She told Catharine that her lecture was unbecoming in view of the fact that her brother practiced what Victoria was preaching. Shocked and insulted, Catharine told the Woodhull that she would guarantee with her life that Henry Ward kept his marriage vows and added, "I will strike you for this, Victoria Woodhull. I will strike you dead!"

Catharine's first blow was an unsigned letter to a Hartford paper in that fall of 1871 requesting the governor to ban a scheduled speech by the Woodhull. Allowed to give her address nevertheless, the Woodhull delivered a counterpunch: "Miss Beecher told me . . . she would strike me. . . . I will present her with my other cheek. . . . She may profess Christ, but I hope I may exceed her in living his precepts." But Woodhull was fed up with the ridicule and the strikes from the Beecher sisters and decided to go after them in a very un-Christian manner, through Henry Ward. She did not consider whatever the minister had done with Lib Tilton a sin. On the contrary, she thought it a natural outlet for a man of his power and charisma who was married to a "Griffin." In effect, she blackmailed Beecher into a series of meetings with a note such as this, in part: "I desire to have an interview without fail. . . . Two of your sisters have gone out of their way to assail my character and purposes. . . . You doubtless know that it is in my power to strike back . . . but I do not desire to do this. I simply desire justice." The Woodhull got the impression at these meetings that Beecher secretly agreed with her views, possibly because he had met the man and found fascinating the radical social philosophy of Stephen Pearl Andrews, who, as a frequenter of the Thirty-eighth Street house, was providing the philosophical underpinning for the Claflin publication's editorial stance. With this impression in mind, the Woodhull wanted Henry Ward to come out in the open by introducing her at a November lecture for which she had hired Steinway Hall, New York's largest auditorium. Beecher got Moulton and Tilton into the act, and they advised him after talking to Woodhull to humor her, since it could be "your last chance to save yourself from complete ruin." At a meeting the day before her lecture, according to Woodhull's account, Beecher "got upon the sofa on his knees beside me, and taking my face between his hands, while the tears streamed down his cheeks, begged me to let him off" because he was "a moral coward on this subject." Woodhull responded with the threat that, if he did not appear with her, "I shall begin by telling the audience why I am alone, and why you are not with me." She said that Beecher promised to preside if he could get up his courage, and it turned into a true cliff-hanger. While three thousand people filled the auditorium, Woodhull, Moulton, and Tilton waited in the wings for Beecher. At the last minute, with no sign of Beecher, Tilton led Woodhull out and introduced her. She made no mention of Beecher.

Perhaps on account of Tilton's gesture, Beecher was given another breather until early 1872, when he was subjected to what he failed to recognize at the time as another kind of blackmail. This form of enforced compliance was orchestrated by his now "dear friend" Moulton on behalf of Moulton's dearer friend Tilton. Tilton was on a downhill slide in every aspect of his life. The *Golden Age* was losing money; without the credentials of an editorship of a thriving journal like the *Independent*, Tilton drew disappointing audiences on his lecture tour, with a resulting loss of fees. By hinting broadly at the kind of disclosures that Tilton was capable of making, Moulton managed to get Bowen to settle a year-long dispute over his breach of contract by paying Tilton seven thousand dollars. With Beecher, Moulton used Henry Ward's compassion for the Tiltons as leverage. He got Beecher to come up with a two-thousand-dollar "loan" for Tilton's domestic expenses and then, by showing him evidence of sums purportedly provided by others, a five-thousand-dollar contribution to keeping the *Golden Age* afloat. For this, Beecher had to take a mortgage out on his house and deliver the proceeds to Moulton in cash. These negotiations resulted in a curious three-part document signed by Bowen, Tilton, and Beecher in which each man expressed regret for past injurious comments about the others and promised never to resurrect them in the future. Silence was becoming expensive.

But silence did continue to reign, even within the extended Beecher family. How much Henry Ward might have discussed his plight with Edward, who had left his pastorate in the West to move to Brooklyn in 1871 and assist his younger brother both at the *Christian Union* and the church, has never been revealed. Pioneer "snowbirds," Harriet and family had begun spending winters in Florida, and she was serving the state as its first tourism promoter through articles in the *Christian Union*. She was still working on Charles to join her in Florida and on Henry Ward as well through persuading Eunice to come down for a visit at Mandarin in February 1872. In the letters exchanged between the Beechers, there isn't a hint of the Tilton affair. They contain loving salutations from both sides, and the contents speak of a long and comfortable marriage in which the partners understand and value each other's interests and virtues. Some samples:

From Eunice at a hotel in Havana where she awaited transport to Florida, February 6, 1872: "Somehow, my room is quite a favorite calling place. All are very kind—but it gives me so little time for myself to write—think or be quiet—The ladies are all very fashionable—think lots of dress attention and parties—I *don't*—so think it strange that they spend so much time—where there is no dress—no grand style—and no talk of parties balls &c—I would be thankful to be left in peace to write & read—but can't well say so when all are so kind. The truth is dearest *being your wife* subjects me to great inconvenience for though you may not know it you *are a great man* in the estimation of people here—both the guests and natives. I will submit to the inconvenience—rather than not be *your very own*." February 9, 1872: "I am up bright and early this morning, and sitting by my open window—or lattice exactly—facing the East, where the sun, not having completed his morning toilet, begins to redden the horizon—It is not, perhaps, the proper thing to be looking into his bed chamber, watching his proceedings, but then he should keep his *blinds shut* and render his operations less attractive. He seems to be getting angry—red in the face, and I shouldn't wonder if in a few moments he should rise up in his wrath and quite look me out of countenance. But I won't budge till I am compelled to anyhow."

Henry Ward from home in Brooklyn, January 30, 1872: "I was more sorry to leave you alone for the voyage than I could say, but, I hope you are so much better by this time that you are rewarded for your courage. . . . Cook wishes me to inform you that we have caught *eleven* rats, five at a time twice, & once one—Everything is going on smoothly. Mary [sister Perkins] & I are like two cats by the fire, we eat, sleep, lick our paws & rub our faces, stretch & go to sleep again in a way that befits the Castle of Indolence—I go tonight to New Haven—to begin my work [a prestigious series of lectures to students at Yale Divinity School]." March 31, 1872: "I am so happy in knowing that you are gaining in health. It has always been a shadow over the future, to fear that I should walk alone the few remaining years of my life. For, alone I shall be, if you go from me. In *jest*, we have often spoken of other connections. But, such a thing is the remotest of possibilities. Should you go, no one would ever take your place. . . . I saw Bertie [a son] at Springfield when I lectured, on Monday last. He is well—says he has given up all his bad habits, talks mournfully about his love of the weed, as if it were a habit of 40 years!— and heroically consents to sacrifice his pleasures to filial duty! It was too comical—I had written him a letter on Frank's death and put this thing very strongly. When in Boston, I got him a *good* gold watch chain, his having broken, and sent it to him, with a card, saying that it was sent to him in honor of his having a clean mouth. Between you and me, he is growing very handsome; I see few boys more killing to callow school girls."

The Mandarin where Eunice arrived for a few months' visit pleased Eunice so much that she started making plans for a place of her own and, she hoped, for Henry Ward, although the winter months were the busiest in the church calendar and the prime time for the lecture tours he counted on to cover the expenses of an expansive way of life. The charm of Mandarin was best described by the best writer in the family in a letter Harriet wrote that year to another famous woman writer, George Eliot—Mary Ann Evans—whom she had befriended in England:

> The great tidiness and culture of England here gives way to a wild and rugged savageness of beauty. Every tree bursts forth with flowers, wild vines and creepers execute delicious gambols, and weave and inter-weave in interminable labyrinths. Yet here, in the great sandy plains back of our houses, there is a constant sense of beauty in the wild, wonderful growths of nature. First of all, the pines—high as the stone pines of Italy—with long leaves, cighteen inches long through which there is a constant dreamy sound, as if of dashing waters. Then the live-oaks, narrow-leaved evergreens, which grow to enormous size, and whose branches are draped with long festoons of the gray moss. There is a great, wild park of these trees back of us, which, with the dazzling, varnished green of the new spring leaves and the swaying drapery of moss, looks like a sort of enchanted grotto. Underneath grow up hollies and ornamental flowering shrubs, and the yellow jessamine clings into and over everything with fragrant golden bells and buds, so that sometimes the foliage of a tree is wholly hidden in its embrace.
>
> This wild, wonderful, bright and vivid growth, that is all new, strange, and unknown by name to me, has a charm for me. It is the place to forget the outside world, and live in one's self. And if you were here, we would go together and gather azaleas,

and white lilies, and silver bells, and blue iris. These flowers keep me painting in a sort of madness. I have just finished a picture of white lilies that grow in the moist land by the watercourses. I am longing to begin on blue iris. . . . You should have a little room in our cottage. The history of the cottage is this: I found a hut built close to a great live-oak twenty-five feet in girth, and with over-arching boughs eighty feet up in the air, spreading like a firma-ment, and all swaying with mossy festoons. We began to live here, and gradually we improved the hut by lath, plaster, and paper. Then we threw out a wide veranda all around, for in these regions the veranda is the living-room of the house. Ours had to be built around the trunk of the tree, so that our cottage has a peculiar and original air, and seems as if it were half tree, or a something that had grown out of the tree. We added on parts and have thrown out gables and chambers, as a tree throws out new branches, till our cottage is like nobody else's, and yet we settle into it with real enjoyment. There are all sorts of queer little rooms in it, and we are accommodating at this present a family of seventeen souls. In front, the beautiful, grand St. John's stretches five miles from shore to shore, and we watch the steamboats ply-ing back and forth to the great world we are out of.

The capacity to get what amounted to a spiritual lift from the beau-ties and workings of nature around her was an attribute that Harriet and her soul mate of a sibling, Henry Ward, were fortunate enough to share. It enabled them to experience relieving moments of sheer joy in the midst of otherwise sad and anxious times. Weighing heavily on Harriet's mind and heart at the time she wrote that glowing letter was the myste-rious disappearance into the "great world" of her son Fred. Whether in Florida or Hartford, he could not keep from indulging in alcoholic binges, and he wrote to his mother in the summer of 1871 that going to sea might be the only way to avoid "falling into a sin I hate and despise but before which I seem to be powerless." He gave it a try by setting sail for San Francisco, but by the end of the year word came back to the Stowes from companions on the voyage that Fred had headed straight for a liquor store as soon as they landed and then simply vanished. The fam-ily would never hear of, or from, him again.

By the time that the "snowbirds" returned to that "great world," the lid that the Brooklyn conspirators were trying to clamp on the Beecher-Tilton scandal was rattling and popping like the tin top on a boiling pan. Despite the fact that she was the first woman in history to be nominated for the presidency—in May, by the Equal Rights Party—along with the nation's most famous black man, Frederick Douglass, as a running mate, the Woodhull was sliding downward on a slope slipperier than Tilton's. Vanderbilt had dumped the Claflin women, with the result that they had to evacuate their brokerage offices, close down the *Weekly*, leave their Murray Hill residence, and keep moving from place to place with their whole entourage as the rents came due. Worse, in view of her political aspirations, the Woodhull had a falling out with the main wing of the suffrage movement, headed by Anthony and Stanton, and her relationship with Tilton ended in a violent quarrel caused by the things she said and wrote about his good suffragette friends and by the fact that Tilton supported Horace Greeley, nominated by the Democrats, instead of her. The break with Tilton sent some chills up Brooklyn spines, since the Woodhull-Claflin combine was known to be blackmailing people with threats of exposure to cover their financial losses. They had already washed what little dirty linen they could see in Greeley's domestic life—they claimed he was what would later come to be known as a male chauvinist pig—and had named some of Greeley's employees, among them John Hay, once Lincoln's secretary and who would become a famous diplomat, as frequenters of houses of ill repute by night and authors of moral platitudes by day. There was no telling how, where, or when the Woodhull might use her information about the alleged Beecher-Tilton affair.

That Beecher was afraid of what might come up in the merry month of May, when the suffrage groups and Woodhull's convention would be in session, is apparent in a letter he wrote to sister "Belle" dated April 25, 1872. Knowing her infatuation with all of these women, he may well have had a dreadful hunch that she had heard the rumors about him, but he chose not to be specific:

> I was sorry when I met you at Bridgeport not to have had longer talk with you, about the meeting in May. I do not intend to make *any* speeches on any topic during anniversary week—Indeed I shall be out of town. I do not want you to *take any ground this year* except upon *suffrage*. You know my sympathy with you. Probably you and I are nearer together than any of our family. I can not give reasons now. I am clear—Still you follow your own judgement. I thank you for your letter. Of some things *neither talk nor will I be talked with*. For love and sympathy I am deeply thankful. The only help that can be grateful to me, or useful is *silence*, and a silencing influence on others. A day may come for converse—it is not *now*. Living or dead, my dear sister Belle *love*

me and do not talk about me, or suffer others to in your presence. God love and keep you. God keep us all! Your loving brother, H.W.B.

Despite his concerns over what might come next in the Tilton affair, other matters in his busy life enabled Henry Ward to keep his sanity throughout the spring and summer of 1872, as revealed in his correspondence with Eunice. After her return from Florida, she was either away helping to ease the death of a granddaughter or in residence at Peekskill. The country place, where Henry Ward had built a large, gingerbreaded, turreted house called Boscobil, was his escape hatch physically and mentally. The intensity of his preoccupation with it can be judged by a note he wrote that late spring to Eunice when he was unexpectedly detained in Brooklyn by church business: "If they [plants he had ordered] do come, tell Mr. Turner to finish out the row of *white-leaved* plants, he will know which—in front of geraniums,—to set out the *calceolarias* in a line *back* of the *coleus* (or red-leaved plants), and two feet distant from them, one at each space between the coleus.—The small blue flowered plants, lobelia, are to be set out in front of the white leaved plants—two feet distant from them & one foot apart in the row." In August he could be found again at the Twin Mountain House, to which vacationers from other spas were brought in on Sundays to hear him preach and where on weekdays he indulged in his favorite sport of croquet. He and Harriet, who often joined him there for a while, were so competitive that they were known to set lanterns by the wickets to keep on playing after dark. In this distracted summer of 1872 he carried his passion even further, writing Eunice: "I went last Monday with Asa Banon over to N Conway to hear Grant, & returned same day making a 70 mile ride—pretty good for a Hay Fever patient! Played croquet in rain all Saturday—without a sniff—or sneeze!"

It is to be doubted whether hearing Grant was worth the ride, because the president was a notably poor and brief speaker. That year he did not need oratory, because he was running well ahead of all competition, including the Woodhull. Her campaign and life were in a shambles by September, when she went to Boston to address the National Spiritualists' Association, of which she was president. Rumors were circulating among the delegates of the efforts she and Tennie were making to raise funds by blackmailing people. As the Woodhull stood to begin her prepared speech on the "social revolution," she "was seized by one of those overwhelming gusts of inspiration . . . taken out of myself . . . by some power stronger than I . . . to pour out into the ears of the assembly . . . the

whole story of the Beecher and Tilton scandal in Plymouth Church."
Woodhull would later say that she did not remember her speech in detail,
and the astounded reporters and editors of the New England press would
not repeat it other than to call the speech obnoxious and note that she
had slandered a clergyman. But E. A. Meriwether of the southern *Memphis Appeal* had no such scruples and reported in part: "Mrs. Woodhull's
speech poured out like a stream of flame. . . . Henry Ward Beecher suffered severely. . . . She said . . . he preached every Sunday to his mistresses, members of his church, sitting in their pews, robed in silks and
satins and high respectability! . . . She believed it her mission to show up
the shams, to uncover the hypocrisies. When she finished off Beecher,
she came back to Boston and lifted some of its editors high in the air, and
scorched them with her accusations." If the speech did not win the
White House, it did inspire her titillated audience to reelect her to the
presidency of their organization.

An uneasy silence prevailed in Brooklyn and among the Beechers
until November, a month that would forever live for them in infamy. It
began for Henry with a letter dated November 1 from Isabella in which
she told him that she had heard the whole story from Woodhull and
Stanton. She wondered if it was "true you had a philosophy of the relation of the sexes so far ahead of the times you dared not announce it,
though you consented to live by it." She was so upset by the whole thing
that, as soon as she heard the story, she had sent her sensitive husband,
John, and daughter Mary off to Europe to spare them the embarrassment
that her continuing support of her suffragette friends would cause them
in light of these revelations. But she indicated that she might be willing
to join Henry Ward in proclaiming a new social freedom and suggested
that silence about such a belief, if he held it, was his real mistake. The
next day, an issue of *Woodhull & Claflin's Weekly*, somehow revived for
the purpose, hit the streets with the headline: "THE BEECHER-TILTON
SCANDAL CASE: The Detailed Statement of the Whole Matter by
Mrs. Woodhull." The paper sold a hundred thousand copies, some going
for as much as forty dollars, and blew the rattling head right off that boiling cauldron of scandal to scorch the nation for years. Woodhull took the
same position as Isabella, or vice versa, in asserting that Henry Ward's sin
was hypocrisy rather than adultery. Indeed, she claimed that "the
immense physical potency of Mr. Beecher, and the indomitable urgency
of his great nature for the intimacy and embraces of the noble and cultured women about him, instead of being a bad thing as the world thinks
. . . is one of the noblest endowments of this truly great and representative man."

The immediate reaction of Beecher and Tilton, as advised by Moulton, was to continue holding the line on silence. This was spelled out in Henry Ward's response to Isabella on November 9:

> My dear Sister Belle, Your great heart is a refuge to those who need sympathy. But you take too serious a view. At present you will help me most; as will all my family and friends, by *Calm Silence*. These miscreants have shamelessly distorted and defiled the specks of truth there were, and they do not know about the root or stem of things on which the reality stands. God knows, God Comforts. God will defend and deliver. Never was there a case in which it might be so appropriately said "*Stand still* and see the salvation of Israel." I have no philosophy to unfold, no new theory of society. The matter has already sunk out of sight in N.Y. My own people are calm and noble. The infernal machine will have exploded in vain I think and hope. For your love, confidence and sympathy I more than thank you. You are nearer to me as sister and companion than ever, or than ever could have been without this great need. Lovingly yours, H.W.B.

So involved was she in the feminist cause and her infatuation with Woodhull that Isabella did not believe in Henry Ward's innocence. She tried to enlist her brother Tom on her side and got a predictably enigmatic response. He informed her that he wanted to stay out of the controversy, since there was no proof of Henry Ward's guilt, but added: "To allow the devil himself to be crushed for speaking the truth is unspeakably cowardly and contemptible. I respect, *as at present advised*, Mrs. Woodhull, while I abhor her philosophy. She only carries out Henry's philosophy, against which I recorded my protest twenty years ago, and parted (lovingly and achingly) from him, saying, 'We cannot work together.' . . . In my judgment Henry is following his slippery doctrines of expediency, and in his cry of progress and the nobleness of human nature has sacrificed clear, exact, ideal integrity." There was no question about the reaction of others in the family. Harriet jumped in with both feet to protect her little brother. She used all her influence to have the authorities cancel a scheduled speech in Boston that fall by Woodhull, whom she would thereafter call a witch. When later that November Isabella threatened to come down and deliver her view of the matter from Henry Ward's Plymouth Church platform, Harriet moved in with Eunice and stood guard at every service to remove her sister, by force if necessary, if she showed up. Isabella never did appear, but possibly not from fear of Harriet.

Still pressing for silence, the strategist Moulton sent Tilton to quiet Isabella. Tilton returned from visiting her at the home of a mutual friend in New York and told Moulton, "I did for the purpose of quieting her as against making the charge of adultery against him, charging her with adultery. . . . I came back and told Mr. Beecher that, and he seemed to be satisfied with it, and was delighted with it." Edward, his brother's colleague and frequent substitute at Plymouth Church, gave Isabella a hard back of the hand. He reminded her that Jesus "condemns divorce except for one cause, and denounces even looking at a woman to lust after her as adultery. Mrs. Woodhull's movement will sink in perdition all who indorse it. I fully believe he is innocent and pure . . . and I do not believe that God would thus sustain a liar, a hypocrite and a libertine, and he is all that if he is guilty."

After November 2, all attempts at secrecy were ludicrous. Although there was no major exposure in the reliable media, there was certainly much gossip. Henry Ward did stick to the tripartite agreement with Bowen and Tilton and held his tongue, but Tilton was constitutionally unable to do so. When he thought that the finger of guilt was being pointed toward him instead of Beecher by the public, he took to writing out long statements of his own position and reading them to as many as fifty different people. Beecher complained, and Moulton advised that it was good to let Tilton blow off steam by writing and then suppress the writings. Besides, Tilton was still proclaiming his wife's innocence and only charging Beecher with improper advances. As far as the general public was concerned, the scandal was kept very much alive throughout November by the stories of the in-and-out jailing of the Claflin sisters and Colonel Bood on charges based on the recently enacted Comstock Law against sending obscenity through the mail. This gave Harriet ammunition in her fighting the Woodhull's scheduled appearance in Boston in December, as she wrote to her daughters: "The vile women 'jailbirds' had the impudence to undertake to advertise that they were going to give a lecture in Music Hall. It has roused such indignation among the citizens that I am told the whole thing is to be stopped. . . . The impudence of those witches is incredible!"

At about the same time, Harriet wrote to Eunice deploring the part that Isabella and her husband, John Hooker, who had returned from Europe and was supporting her, were playing in the drama. Hooker tried to argue that Isabella was protecting Henry Ward by staying in the enemy camp and warning him of their attacks. Harriet was not buying that: "I confess to feeling more indignant with John than at Isabella, but with both I find it a hard struggle to preserve anything like Christian faith.

The Henry Ward Beecher scandal was a godsend for artists.

THE LATEST SENSATION!

THE BEECHER MINSTRELS.

1. CHORUS: Mrs. Tilton.
2. BONES: Theodore Tilton.
3. FIRST FIDDLE: Counsellor Morris.
4. BANJO: Mrs. Cady Stanton.

5. MIDDLE MAN: Frank Moulton, "Our Mutual Friend."
6. ACCORDEON: Miss Susan B. Anthony.
7. TROMBONE: General Ben Butler.
8. TAMBOURINE: Rev. Henry Ward Beecher.

9. ECCENTRIC VOCALIST: Miss Tennie C. Claflin.

BONES TILTON: Hen-ery, why am our Statements like a piece of Soap?
TAMBO BEECHER: Why am our Statements like a piece of Soap, Theodore?
BONES TILTON: 'Cause there's a heap of LIE somewhere in them!
MIDDLE MAN MOULTON: Openin' Chorus—"Write me a few more letters from home."

I try to pray that their blinded eyes may be open, that they may see and repent this evil that they have been doing & that we may have the right and Christian feeling toward them." Harriet excused Isabella more than John, whom she regarded as levelheaded, on the grounds that the Woodhull was a real witch exercising some sort of demonic power over her sister. The Hookers were virtually ostracized by Nook Farm society. Even Mary Perkins and the Stowes, who had moved from the house Harriet had built too close to town to a smaller one on Forest Street, barred their doors to them. Although they were still living in the rented Hooker home while building their own odd and magnificent establishment next to the Stowe house, the Mark Twains also refused to see their landlady.

It was not in the nature of Beechers to let the scandal keep them from fulfilling their commitments and promoting their causes. In the year 1873, the indefatigable Catharine came out with another best-seller, *Miss Beecher's Housekeeper and Health Keeper*. It had chapters such as "The Marketing and Care of Meats"—"Lobsters . . . are to be put alive into boiling water, which is the quickest and least cruel way to end their life"; "On Warming a House"—"Warming by an open fire is nearest to the natural mode of the Creator, who heats the earth and its furniture by the great central fire of heaven, and sends cool breezes for our lungs"; "Domestic Exercise"—"It is an interesting illustration of the benevolence of our Maker, that the appropriate duties of the family, uniting intellectual, social and moral with both sedentary and active pursuits, are exactly fitted to employ every faculty in healthful proportion." Unmarried though she remained, Catharine's book would have been a godsend to any new bride, with its very up-to-date and sound advice on every detail of housekeeping. While still racketing around from place to place in her seventies, Catharine took occasion to do some research on this book during a visit to her niece, Mary's daughter, Mrs. Edward Everett Hale, in Boston. Catharine made such a mess experimenting on recipes in the Hale kitchen that the help walked out. Finding an unhappy wife and daughter struggling with the unaccustomed task of making dinner when he got home that evening, Dr. Hale went up to Catharine's room, where she was happily writing, knocked on the door, and said, "Aunt Catharine, your visit is over! A hack will call for you first thing in the morning." Quite a while later Hale spotted Catharine sitting on a bench in Boston Common and tried to hurry by her unseen, but she hailed him and asked him to look at the books she had just bought. In view of what had happened her cordiality disarmed Hale, and he asked if she could visit them. "Right now!" she said and followed him home for a harmonious two-week stay. At about the same time, Catharine straightened out another host, Andrew D. White, president of Cornell. When she dropped into his office and told him that she wanted to take a course in his college, he said that courses were not open to women. She brushed that aside with "I prefer to take them with men," and then told him that she wanted to live in a convenient dormitory. "It has no accommodation for ladies," an exasperated White informed her, and she said the she had inspected the rooms and found them satisfactory and that "young men, who are of appropriate ages to be my grandsons . . . will not trouble me in the least." With that, she had her way.

Another Beecher on the move was Charles, who heeded Harriet's siren song and departed from Georgetown for Florida. He settled across the state near Tallahassee and was hired by the Northern carpetbaggers in the capital as superintendent of public instruction. He also bedeviled those friends and family he called "besnowed" with tales of an Eden abounding in fruit trees and *"Roses, Roses, Roses!"* In the winter of 1873 Eunice was able to spread her winter trip between the Stowe and Charles Beecher establishments. Once again there is a heavy exchange of correspondence between Eunice and Henry Ward, which is remarkable for having almost no mention of the scandal. With her long-standing dislike of the Tiltons and kept mostly in the dark by her husband, Eunice seems to have brushed the thing aside as just another example of Henry Ward's getting in trouble through his good-hearted trust in deplorable people. Her letters are full of Florida chitchat and yearnings and plans to acquire property there. He is flatly opposed to that idea, saying that the Peekskill place is enough for their recreation and possible retirement. And no wonder; the North remained his happy hunting ground. Besides giving the Yale lectures for another year, he reported a killing general lecture schedule by place and date in February: "Harrisburg, Pa. 17. Pittsburgh 18. Cleveland O 19. Louisville Ky 21. Cincinnati 22—(then by night to Indianapolis spending Sunday & Monday 24)—St. Louis 25, 26. Peoria Ill 27. Chicago 28. Milwaukee March 1 (back by night to Chicago for Sunday & Monday 3)—Toledo O March 4. Ann Arbor Mich. 5—Buffalo 7. & home."

Keeping such a strenuous schedule may have been Henry Ward's salvation. A surface of energy and accomplishment hid what he would call "a terrible accumulation of anxieties." In that spring of 1873, snatches of the documents exchanged among the conspirators in silence, such as the tripartite Bowen-Tilton-Beecher "covenant," began surfacing in the local press. Since he still trusted Moulton completely, Henry Ward was bewildered as to the source. But his clear-eyed sister Harriet was not. In a letter to a friend, she blamed it on "Tilton and his colluder, Frank Moulton," who "were showing all his letters & notes & concessions to Mrs. Stanton & the free love roost of harpies generally who were exulting over the scrape he was being drawn into & meaning to use it to coerce him into favoring their unclear theories & unclear leader." By June, Henry Ward notified Tilton in a note of despair that he could no longer keep a promise of silence that he had made mostly to protect the reputation of innocent Lib Tilton and her children. "I shall write for the public a statement that will bear the light of the judgment day. God will take care of me and mine. . . . I would not have you waste any more energy on a hopeless task," he advised Moulton. It was hopeless, he argued, because Tilton's mercurial personality, despite many good traits, made him *absolutely unreliable.*" Tilton was going public because he thought that the tripartite covenant painted him in the wrong light as receiving forgiveness from Beecher rather than as forgiving Beecher for his improper conduct. Moulton chided Beecher for giving up on their strategy and showing "a selfish faith in God." In the end, he persuaded Beecher to publish a card in the *Brooklyn Eagle* "exonerating Tilton from the base lies to which the tripartite covenant referred" along with another card in which Beecher told the world that the charges against him were totally untrue. These cards resulted in what he defined as a "hollow peace" with Tilton.

Gratifying as they were to his family and loyal members of the Plymouth congregation who had been urging him to speak out, these cards came too late. People convinced by the Tiltons' stories thought that his denial was worse than his alleged sin. "Wouldn't you think if God ever did strike any one dead for telling a lie, He would have struck then?" was Susan Anthony's reaction. As to Tilton, there were too many other sources of information for Beecher's card to stop the movement within the church to expel him from membership for slandering their pastor. Tilton had long since given up going to church and reverently recording in shorthand his pastor's sermons, but the expulsion was a wound to his pride and another tear in his rapidly shredding reputation. He regarded the action as unjust and probably in violation of the church's rules and promptly complained to the Reverend Richard Storrs, the minister of Brooklyn's sister Congregational Church. A little jealous of Beecher's popularity and miffed that Beecher had failed to respond to a note of sympathy written on the day that the story broke in *Woodhull & Claflin's*

Weekly, Storrs was open to reading Tilton's various written accusations and hearing whatever else he related in person. He decided that the charges were serious enough to summon in early 1874 a council of other concerned churches to examine the conduct of Plymouth Church in dealing with the matter. Since Congregational churches were traditionally independent and Beecher had early in his ministry rewritten the rules to make sure that Plymouth Church would be a law unto itself, he chose to ignore the council and blithely go about the business of conducting his annual pew sales. Despite the fact that the doings of the council made investigation of the scandal legitimate and juicy news for the press all over the country, it was counterproductive in terms of Tilton's intention to injure the church in which Bowen was heavily invested and possibly drive Beecher out of town. A Plymouth Church record showed 174 new admissions and only 34 dismissions for that year, and the council, chaired by an old friend of the Beecher family, Dr. Leonard Bacon of Yale, issued a very mild reprimand. Bacon himself had harsh words for Tilton's character and strong criticism for Henry Ward's failure to defend himself.

As ministers themselves, Henry Ward's brothers were fascinated professionally and personally with accounts of the council proceedings that they read in newspapers wherever they were. Something of a church lawyer as a result of his own trials, Charles wrote from Florida:

> Your remark as to the possible fetid odor of the council appeared
> to me quite appropriate when I saw that they had invited that
> skunk John Pike of . . . Mass. Of course, I cannot picture the
> result, in words, to which the Council may come. But should
> they yield to the machinations of Storrs . . . to advise disfellow-
> ship it will run a line of division through the churches of the
> whole country. Dr. Post warned them of this at the beginning.
> The position of Plymouth Church is the true one & for once it
> happens that truth and popular instinct coincide. The churches
> that rally on the Plymouth platform will be the churches of lib-
> erty & progress. Those that follow the lead of the Council
> (should it go wrong) will constitute an old . . . element which
> will grow more & more cantankerous as it grows more narrow
> and impotent.

Mary who, along with Charles and his wife and Eunice, was visiting at Mandarin that March, wrote to Henry Ward: "I want to tell you how much Harriet & I have you in our tho'ts—our prayers & our best love—

our first tho't in the morning—& last at night has been for you, & we rejoice exceedingly that you are carried safely thru these fiery trials by 'one who walks with you in the midst of fire' for surely Daniel & his friends were never put into a more fiery furnace than you have been in for two years past."

The exchange of letters this season between Brooklyn and Florida included a good deal of comment on the no longer secret scandal. Whether to give a true account of his own mood or to put his wife's mind at ease, Henry Ward wrote to Eunice on Saturday night, March 21, 1874:

> The Council comes off on Tuesday night, Wednesday, & Thursday. The tide of sentiment against it, is rising & has risen to an extraordinary height. The atmosphere of Brooklyn is hot against any such interference with Plymouth Church,—There are signs, too, that S[torrs] & B[udington] [pastor of a Presbyterian church who joined in calling for a council], are growing less and less confident, and it is predicted that within a year Storrs will be in the Presbyterian Church and Budington adrift. Our fold are jubilant—and the other churches are full of discontented men,—I closed my lectures at Yale on Thursday. There was much enthusiasm—in which the faculty participated fully as much as the students. The Faculty . . . drew up a highly complimentary letter, which will in due season be published. I believe that they will ask me to *take another year*. They have informally offered it already.— My health was never better—I eat, sleep soundly, and I am going to *ride* a good *deal* this Council week.

By the time the Florida contingent returned to Brooklyn, Beecher was no longer so cheerily optimistic. Disappointed and angered by the results of the council, Tilton published a long reply to their criticism of him along with what he thought would be the clincher—Beecher's "letter of contrition" written on that dark night when he had first been handed Lib's damning note. Beecher sought advice on meeting this attack from two men of high national repute as politicians and lawyers, General William Tracy and Ben Butler, the same Massachusetts congressman who had arranged the House hearing for the Woodhull. Both men were in favor of sweeping it all back under the rug again, and Tracy went so far as to threaten the Tiltons with the stick of a suit for blackmail and, that failing, to offer the carrot of a free trip to Europe to keep them quiet. Neither fear nor favor worked with Tilton, and Beecher felt obliged to take a calculated risk and appoint a six-man committee from the congregation of Plymouth Church to look into the entire affair and interview in depth everyone involved, including himself

While the investigation was going on, Henry Ward stayed at Peekskill as much as possible and let loyal Eunice keep watch in Brooklyn by attending meetings, reading the papers, and picking up gossip. When he learned that Lib Tilton would be the first person to go before the investigating committee, Henry Ward dashed off this note to his wife: "I feel deeply the sorrow of Mrs. Tilton. I can through you send to her my love, and my profound sympathy—Tell her that *the bitterness of death is past,* and that she may rest in that Divine bosom where she has so unfailingly found refuge. Her statement will be the cry of a wounded heart, a cry of mother & wife to *mothers & wives,* and it will be heard,—She never had so many friends as she has today,—Her reply *need not be long.* . . . I would to God I could lend her some of my calming & courage. I shall stand by her to the end, and shall boldly honor her before the whole nation." Lib Tilton could hardly have done better by Beecher. She told the committee flatly that she had not committed adultery with him. She explained away her confession by saying that she was "nearly out of her mind," that "a mesmeric condition was brought to bear" on her, that she "thought it would some way serve Theodore and bring peace to his household." She revealed that her apparently good marriage had long been in trouble and that Tilton "laid the cornerstone of free love and desecrated its altars . . . so that the atmosphere was not only godless but impure for my children." While Tilton tore her down, "with Mr. Beecher I had a sort of consciousness of being more. I felt myself another woman." A madly jealous Tilton scoffed at her claim of "friendship" with Beecher, saying that she had a "sensual influence over men" and that she could not distinguish between "an innocent or guilty love." Tilton, she said, was simply out to "crush" Beecher. If she had known Tilton to be the man he was proving to be now, she would not have encouraged the minister's acquaintance.

Lib's performance before the committee provoked Theodore into giving them a long and detailed account of what he now called a "criminal connection" for which his wife bore no guilt because of her innocence. He documented it with some of the written messages passing among Bowen, Beecher, Moulton, and himself and spiced it with tales of actually seeing Beecher touch his wife's legs while supposedly studying some pictures on the floor and of finding Henry Ward and Lib locked together in her bedroom when he made an unexpected appearance at home. Although the meetings were supposedly closed, reporters haunting the scene milked participants for enough detail to spread the story across the nation. William Beecher, whose disappointing career had once caused him to write to Henry Ward that "I don't think God needs me," weighed in from Chicago, where he was living in retirement with a daughter: "When Tilton's manifesto came, I felt greatly distressed not seeing how to account for the strong expressions in your letters, but I said, 'Henry never could have written them, the expressions are not at all his style.' I think they are forgeries, or are altered and so doctored as to appear worse than the reality. . . . I want to assure you of my confidence, my honour for you, my sympathy & greater love, if possible." Writing from Poughkeepsie, New York, where he was then ministering, James said that he was going camping but doubted that he would be "out of the current of scandal" even there and added: "I only want to write one line; not of counsel, for you do not need it any more than I am competent to give it. Not a mere expression of confidence which would be a sort of insult. Only this. Out-side of and independent of all that is said or done, there is to me and to others a revelation of Christian *manhood,* so new in some of its aspects that I have no words for its expression. Brother Henry will you try to understand me when I say that I thank God with daily prayer for that I am begotten of the same earthly father, for every drop of common blood which makes you my brother. I love you beyond all men living, and that with a sort of reverence I had never supposed possible toward any, short of the one perfect man whom I understand better by your help."

Armed with that kind of support as well as righteous anger over the Tilton "manifesto," Beecher finally presented himself to the committee. According to a letter Eunice wrote to their daughter, Henry Ward—"the dear guiltless simple-hearted man"—had finally seen both Tilton and Moulton in their "naked depravity and baseness," and as result "the noble old Lion roused himself . . . and holds back nothing." Beecher used all of his oratorical talents to deliver an impassioned defense of himself. Speak-ing of his pastoral visits to the Tilton home, he said that "at no interview which ever took place did anything occur which might not have occurred with perfect propriety between a brother and a sister, between a father and a child." While his "blind heedlessness and friendship" might have "beguiled her heart," he claimed that Lib Tilton had "thrust her affections on me unsought." He accused Tilton of "promiscuous immoral-ities" and of being motivated by hatred and greed. He blamed Moulton, whom he had once said was "sent by God" to help him, for taking advan-tage of his naïveté to extort financing for the *Golden Age.* He attributed his extreme statements about possibly resigning or wanting to die to an inherited "tendency to sadness, the remains in me of a positive hypo-chondria in my father and grandfather." As to the policy of silence, which even his supporters could not understand, he said, "The great interest which I had built up, the book which I was writing, my own immediate family, my brother's name, now engaged in the ministry, my sisters, the name which I hoped might live after me and be in some slight degree a source of strength and encouragement to those who should succeed me, and above all the cause for which I had devoted my life, seemed imper-iled. It seemed to me that my life work was to end abruptly . . . and in disaster."

Henry Ward was back in Peekskill when the council not unexpect-edly cleared him of all charges in its report to the congregation. His faithful watchdog in Brooklyn, Eunice, described the scene in a letter dated August 28, 1874: "It is 11:45—and I am just home from the Friday night Meeting—and such a meeting! Oh my Darling! Such a full thor-ough vindication! Such enthusiasm! Such shouts & cheers! . . . If you could have been present, you would feel that the sufferings of the past wretched years were almost paid for by the love and confidence and devotion manifested this evening." At one point, when the report exon-erating Beecher made "scorching and withering reference to Tilton and Moutlon, a voice from the large circle of reporters called out—'that's a lie'—and a fist was raised above the head." The voice belonged to Moul-ton, according to Eunice, and there were cries of "throw him out." But the chairman of the meeting called for silence and insisted that letting him stay to listen to the rest of the report might change his mind. It did not. As Eunice wrote: "For a half hour four Police stood not far from Moulton—as soon as the amen was uttered—He rose to create a distur-bance—but the police laid hold on him and carried him out. . . . The vast throng outside pressed upon him and the four police took him up bodily—tumbled him into a carriage—with the greatest difficulty beating off the crowd. . . . Moulton was under the influence of liquor it is said."

Even more outraged by the committee's findings than Moulton was Tilton, who responded by filing charges against Beecher in Brooklyn's City Court. The language of his complaint was very specific and calcu-lated to whet the public appetite for more lurid revelations when it went to trial:

> That the defendant, contriving and willfully intending to injure the plaintiff and deprive him of the comfort, society, aid and assis-tance of said Elizabeth, the wife of the plaintiff, and to alienate

and destroy her affection for him, heretofore on or about the tenth day of October, 1868, and on diverse other days and times after that day and before commencement of this action, at the house of the defendant, No. 124 Columbia Street, City of Brooklyn, and at the house of the plaintiff, No. 174 Livingston Street, City of Brooklyn, wrongfully and wickedly and without the privity or connivance of the plaintiff, debauched and carnally knew the said Elizabeth, then and ever since the wife of the plaintiff, by means whereof the affection of the said Elizabeth for the plaintiff was wholly alienated and destroyed, and by reason of the premises the plaintiff has wholly lost the comfort, society, aid and assistance of his said wife, which during all the time aforesaid he otherwise might and ought to have had and enjoyed.

As a result of this action, Eunice wrote to Henry Ward a month to the day after her jubilant account of his clearance:

Oh, if it was only me that they were tormenting—how willingly would I take the whole burden to see you joyous—light hearted and happy as of old. . . . But dear Henry—let them rage—it is all going to come right. . . . Excuse me now my darling—*Do not* grieve or let your heart be troubled for Mrs. T—She is not worth one pain from your true noble heart—Oh could I have known this web that was being woven around you seven or eight years ago—I could have shown you how little worthy she was of all this suffering. The truth is not in her—give the Devil his due Tilton is not all to blame—*it never was in her.* Forgive me love— The memory of those days before & after her statement when you wandered over the house looking so sad—is ever before me—& the knowledge of how unworthy she was of all that supporting from a heart whose delicacy, sensitiveness & noble traits she could never have fathomed—haunts me daily.

Although it may not have seemed so in Brooklyn and Peekskill, there were other events of note throughout a generally quiet nation in 1874. Hopes for better lives for working people were raised when Massachusetts passed the nation's first ten-hour workday for women and children under eighteen. There was a bright moment in Washington when President Grant's daughter, Nellie, was married in the White House to Algernon Frederick Sartoris. Dark clouds for Republicans and the Northern approach to Reconstruction gathered over the Capitol when the Democrats regained a majority in the House of Representatives for the first time since 1860. Formation of the Women's Christian Temperance Union in Cleveland and the founding of the Greenback Party to end payment in specie and bring about currency inflation reflected social and political movements that would grow for the rest of the century. Even in Nook Farm, with all of its Beecher associations, there was a minor scandal to divert attention briefly from the doings in Brooklyn. William Hooker Gillette, John and Isabella's nephew who lived nearby, took off for New York to play a one-line part in Mark Twain's dramatization of *The Gilded Age*, a novel he wrote in collaboration with Nook Farm neighbor Charles Dudley Warner. Going on the stage was considered so disreputable in a family of middle-class respectability and Puritan heritage dating back to colonial times that his absence from the native turf was attributed to "studying in New York." Young Gillette's defection had been engineered by Mark Twain himself, who liked to play mischief with respectability. He gave Gillette the part, provided him with three thousand dollars to pursue a career that would make him famous as an actor and playwright, and finally assured his reentry into the best social circles by having his performance "blessed" by the attendance of the Reverend Joseph Twitchell, pastor of Asylum Hill Congregational Church and Twain's best friend, when the play came to Hartford.

In many ways the Brooklyn proceedings intensified the disruption that the scandal was causing in the normally placid Nook Farm society. Harriet's twins had made some effort to heal the breach between families, and their mother wrote to them:

> I am glad you went ahead and got into pleasant relations with Mary and Eugene [Isabella's daughter and son-in-law] and your Aunt Isabella before I came. They have so deeply wounded my sense of all propriety and affection in the course they took about my brother that for me it would have been impossible to do it, but I am glad you could and did, and I think it will be easier for me to meet them since you have—Your aunt is like many mono-maniacs all right if the wrong string is not jarred but I fear that seeing me will jar it. I am not a person who takes offense easily—it is very difficult to offend me—but there are things which strike my *very life* and these accusations against my brother are among them. I cannot hear that subject discussed as a *possibility* open for inquiry without such an intense uprising of indignation and scorn

and anger as very few have ever seen in me these late years—but if ever I should hear those who ought to know better maundering out insinuations and doubts about him I think there will be the eruption of a volcano that has for years been supposed to be extinct—they will see *what* I am and thoroughly aroused.

Caught in the crossfire between family and friends and her trusted allies in the women's cause, Isabella was finally wounded to the quick when the "old Lion" turned on her and publicly described her as mad. She fled to Europe for an indefinite stay, leaving her husband, John, back from his own European escape, behind to carry on the fight. Unconvinced of Henry Ward's innocence, loyal to his wife, and, as a founder of the community, galled by the way the Hookers were being shunned, John tried to enlist the family pastor, Joe Twitchell, on their side. Believing that Isabella had shown the minister some papers that would convince him of Henry Ward's guilt, John called on Twitchell and was told that the purpose of Isabella's visit and documents was to prepare people in the dark such as Twitchell for her brother's inevitable downfall. Twitchell was still suspending judgment, but as he wrote of the visit: "Mr. H. said that no one of Mr. B's partizans was doing so much for love of him as Mrs. H. for she was allowing herself to rest under the charge of conspiring against him just because she feared it might work against him to clear herself (as she easily could) of his charge as it was made in the public prints last autumn. Mr. H. gave me the impression that he believed Mr. B. to be guilty."

The trial that started in January 1875 in the Brooklyn courthouse was destined to last for more than six months and generate more newspaper copy, articles, and books than any event of the century except the Civil War. The actors in that drama played to a full house every time the court was in session, and people were willing to pay up to five dollars to get a seat. The purely fascinating issue at stake was whether the most famous minister of the gospel in America was guilty of adultery, a sin in almost everybody's book. It would be bad enough if he had been caught in a bordello, but he was charged with sinning in the most respectable circumstances and in the process corrupting a devout member of his congregation young enough to be his daughter and betraying a friend of long standing whom he had once looked upon as a surrogate son. If he were found guilty, it would prove to some, as his own brother Tom suggested, that the gospel of love he preached from the pulpit was nothing but a moral quicksand. Although Henry Ward Beecher was quite evidently the star of the show, members of the supporting cast also were celebrities. In some circles, Theodore Tilton outshone his mentor. The "blond poet," as he was often described in the press, was willing to express unorthodox and even outrageous views that appealed to people who regarded themselves as free thinkers. Beecher's lead attorney, William Maxwell Evarts, had such stature after successfully defending President Johnson during his impeachment trial that he would later become a secretary of state. He would have what any newspaper reader would recognize as a worthy adversary in Tilton's lead lawyer, William A. Beach. Both of these men were supported by other able attorneys. Then, of course, people who got a seat in the courtroom would be able to watch the wronged women in the alleged crime, Lib Tilton and Eunice Beecher, whether they heard from them or not.

Lawyers drew the narrative as it had unfolded from 1868 onward out of the mouths of witnesses in exhaustive and exhausting detail. Witnesses included the principals, Beecher and Tilton; Frank Moulton and his wife, to whom Beecher had confided his feeling during the secrecy stage; and domestics from the Tilton household. Neither side felt it was wise to call Lib Tilton to the stand. But when the adversaries had rested their cases, the judge let the courtroom audience enjoy a dramatic coda to the performance by allowing Lib to arise and read a letter in which she again denied committing adultery with Beecher. Of course, the jury could not consider her letter in its deliberations. Nor could they consider all of the sidebar material, such as the exchange of letters between the Tiltons, that was published throughout the trial. The testimony raised few questions about actual events in the story. In this regard, the plaintiff seemed to fare worse than the defendant. Tilton admitted to an adulterous affair with the Woodhull, for instance, and his brutish behavior at home was well established. Beecher admitted to an overly warm friendship with Lib and foolish behavior in the effort to cover it up. Left up in the air were the interpretations the various witnesses placed on their activities and admissions. It was generally conceded that Moulton was a calm, even-handed witness, in contrast to his behavior when the church committee brought in its report. Evidently he decided to let his wife, Emma, provide the kind of testimony that his good friend Tilton needed. Aware that Emma Moulton had been a lifelong and adoring member of Beecher's congregation, almost everyone in the courtroom was surprised to hear her say things such as this: "He [Beecher] walked up and down the room in a very excited manner, with tears streaming down his cheeks, and said that he thought it was very hard, after a life of usefulness, that he should be brought to this fearful end. . . . And I said, 'I have never heard you preach since I knew the truth that I haven't felt that I was standing by an open grave. I cannot express to you the anguish and the sorrow it has caused me to know what I have of your life. I believed you since I was a girl—believed you were the only good man in this world. Now it has destroyed my faith in human nature. I don't believe in anybody.'" In the end, the jury had to decide in whom they could believe, and some excerpts from Beecher's testimony leave no doubt as to the difficulty they faced.

On cross-examination attorney Fullerton, representing Tilton, is questioning Beecher about the night when he first heard of the charges against him (text in brackets as in original document):

Q.: Now, Mr. Beecher, up to that time—up to the time of the interview with Mr. Tilton at Mr. Moulton's house—had you been aware in any way that Mrs. Tilton had an undue affection for you?

A.: No, sir.

Q.: What Mr. Tilton said to you, then, on the night of the thirtieth upon that subject, was the first intimation you had ever received from any quarter whatever, that such was the fact?

A.: I think it was. I do not recall any other hint or intimation.

Q.: And Mrs. Tilton had denied it orally and in writing to you?

A.: She had.

Q.: Did you believe it after that?

A.: I have stated to you already that I was more in a state of perplexity than of belief.

Q.: No, no; don't get us all into a state of perplexity by your wrong answer. [Laughter.] Will you be kind enough to state whether, after the denial of Mrs. Tilton of the allegation that her affections had been transferred to you, you then believed it?

A.: I state again, sir, that I was in a state of perplexity and not of belief.

Q.: Will you state whether, or not, you did believe that her affection had been transferred to you?

Mr. Evarts: He has answered it.

Mr. Fullerton: He has not answered it.

Mr. Evarts: Why not?

Mr. Fullerton: Why not? Don't ask me, or I shall give you an answer that you won't relish. He has not answered.

Mr. Evarts: You draw the witness's attention distinctly to a psychological proposition whether he had a belief, and he has answered very distinctly that he was then in a state of perplexity and not of belief. I don't know any better answer that can be made, if it is true.

Judge Neilson: It is an answer so far as it goes, but he can state whether he believed it or not.

Mr. Fullerton: Yes, sir. [To the witness.] Now, Mr. Beecher, I put the question to you again. After Mrs. Tilton had denied orally to you, and in writing, that these charges—denied the truth of these charges, revoked them all, did you believe that she had transferred her affections to you?

A.: I will state that I had both the belief and unbelief and that I fluctuated from the one to the other.

Q.: Did it not enter into your consideration whether or not her conduct in charging you with immoral practices, a charge which, if true, would work your ruin, was an evidence or not that her affection had been transferred to you?

A.: It certainly was an evidence, and yet I was not yet apprised of all the facts, I felt there was more to come out than I knew that night.

Q.: Then you suspended your judgment, did you?

A.: I suspended my judgment so far as a final judgment. At times I thought that here was the evidence that she had done it; at other times I revolted against it, and found myself moved from that conviction.

Q.: Well, you hadn't the highest regard for Theodore Tilton up to that time, had you?

A.: I cannot say that I had the *highest regard* for him.

Q.: And as between him and his wife, which did you think more likely to tell a falsehood?

A.: [Emphatically.] He.

Q.: You had a high regard for Mrs. Tilton, did you not?

A.: I did.

Q.: You had admired her Christian character up to that time?

A.: I had.

Q.: You had regarded her as a woman of truthfulness in every respect?

A.: I had.

Q.: Of exalted piety?

A.: I had.

Q.: And purity?

A.: I had.

Q.: And yet you tell me that when she told you verbally, and put it in writing, that these charges were false and that she was importuned to make them when she was sick, it did not convince you that they were untrue?

A.: She had made charges, Mr. Fullerton, and admitted it—

Q.: One moment, Mr. Beecher.

The witness [continuing]: And she now took them back.

Q.: One moment. Don't review the ground, tell me whether all these circumstances did not induce the belief in your mind that the charge which Mr. Tilton had made against you, that you have won his wife's affections, was untrue?

A.: No—and yes.

Mr. Fullerton: Let it stand that way. When did you expect to get further evidence upon that subject?

A.: I had no definite expectations as to time, sir.

The exchange between attorney Fullerton and Beecher with regard to the "letter of confession" went like this, in part:

Q.: Well, under the circumstances in which this letter was written, you might wait for him [Moulton] to put it down, probably, if you wanted him to record it. Did you not want him to record your sentiments in your language?

A.: No, I did not: that is, I should have had no objection if he could have recorded it in my language, but I did not expect that he would attempt to do it, more than to catch a figure here and there or some phrase.

Q.: Were you not very anxious that the exact state of your feelings should be conveyed to Mr. Tilton?

A.: I relied on Mr. Moulton to convey them.

Q.: Why didn't you examine the paper to see whether he had done well what he had undertaken to do?

A.: I relied upon him.

Q.: Entirely?

A.: Entirely.

Q.: Did you say anything like this [Reading.]: "I ask, through you, Theodore Tilton's forgiveness, and I humble myself before him as I do before my God"?

A.: I used, generally, a statement of this kind—that I had, for my error and wrong in the matter, humbled myself before God, and I should not be ashamed to humble myself before Theodore Tilton.

Q.: You had discovered your wrong, then . . . When had you made the discovery?

A.: In the conversation with Mr. Moulton on the night on which I went to Moulton's house, and in the subsequent—in the conversation, in some parts of it, on the night of the thirty-first, and in those—

Q.: What had been said on that subject on the night on which you went to Mr. Moulton's house?

A.: He had talked to me about Mr. Bowen, and the wrong he had done to Mr. Tilton.

Q.: What connection had you with that?

A.: I had advised it.

Q.: And then you discovered that *that* was wrong?

A.: He told me that the whole thing was false.

Q.: Did he give you any reason for saying that?

A.: Oh, no, not that I recall; that is, he gave me his assevera-tions—as I supposed, an impartial person—

Q.: You did not think of the injury inflicted upon you in charg-ing you with immoral conduct, did you?

A.: I don't recollect that I specially brought that into connection with the injury done by me to Mr. Tilton, through Mr. Bowen.

Q.: Then I will ask you . . . when you came to that conclusion that Mrs. Tilton had told a falsehood about it, and that Mr. Tilton was acting in good faith in making the charge against you, why didn't you hasten to vindicate yourself to him by telling him it was untrue?

A.: I thought I was doing it, sir. . . . This whole interview was a vindication and an explanation and was to be carried by him [Moulton] to a man that was excited, and whose interview with me would not be likely to be pacificatory in all respects.

Q.: Now, in that conversation with Mr. Moulton on that day, was the term "improper relations," or "improper advances," or "improper solicitations," used?

A.: I cannot recall that the words, those phrases—were used upon that occasion.

Q.: Well, you regarded that as the most serious charge against you, did you not? . . . Improper solicitations?

A.: Certainly that was the most serious part.

Q.: And yet you did nothing to single it out and vindicate yourself against it by sending any message to Mr. Tilton?

A.: I did not send *any* message to Mr. Tilton. I understood that Mr. Moulton was my message.

Whatever the effect of such testimony on the jury, it did nothing to shake the faith of most other Beechers in Henry Ward's innocence. From her Florida retreat, Harriet employed the busiest pen in commenting on the trial. She wrote to Mary that "this testimony of Tilton's is an outrage on human decency . . . the more the better *nobody* can believe that— They might believe something less but anything like *that* is a nightmare creation of insanity." A little later, in a letter to a friend, she said that "Henry's long cross examination is over and what evil have they found in him? . . . What can anybody allege but over trust in a false friend and a generous unselfish effort to shield what the true gentleman always thinks sacred, the weakness of a woman?" The trial was reported in England, and Harriet responded to a letter of sympathy from George Eliot by claiming that "never have I known a nature of such . . . almost childlike innocence. . . . In all this long history there has been no circumstance of his relation to any woman that has not been worthy of himself—pure, delicate, and proper." Charles wrote Henry Ward that "I think you will have a verdict—and I'm only afraid that the jubilant people will pull you to pieces among them." Writing to Henry Ward from Chicago, William struck a sad note: "During all the revelations made during the examinations & cross examinations you have endured I have been surprised to see how confiding & loving you have been to Bowen & Moulton & Tilton & I must confess I have been jealous—why have you never done so with me? You never put yr arm about me or open'd yr heart to me & yet no one could more admire & love every noble trait in you & every fine, beautiful & holy sentiment uttered by you. I have read & tears filled my eyes & my heart has bounded & my soul gone out to you and in all your afflictions I have been afflicted."

In his summation to the jury, Evarts took somewhat the same view as Harriet. He stressed "the incredibility of so flagrant and heinous imputation" against a man of Beecher's reputation. "You do not need to spend much time in finding out that the scarlet guilt of adultery, and the coarse, selfish purposes of seduction do not match the generous heart and loving kindness, and the nobility of Henry Ward Beecher. It is a miracle if he was guilty and you, gentlemen, on the part of the plaintiff . . . must produce sufficient evidence to convince the jury that a miracle has happened in our midst," he argued. Beach claimed that "great and good as Mr. Beecher may have been, he is yet, in the eye of God and in the eye of men, a fallible sinner. . . . Are we to have a new version of the Scriptures? Are we to have new teachings in regard to the fall of man? Are we to be told that there is no sin among the apparently pure and great?" In a rather unusual effort to underline his point of common human depravity, Beach told the jury that testimony about his client as "a harsh and unloving husband . . . an adorer of Victoria Woodhull . . . and immoral libertine . . . if true" should make no difference in their deliberations, since Henry Ward had nevertheless been guilty of defiling Tilton's home. It would later become questionable as to what Beach really had in mind in reminding the jury of his client's alleged character flaws when he let it be known that he had become convinced of Beecher's innocence during the course of the trial, and he told friends that "I felt then, and feel now, that we were a pack of hounds trying in vain to drag down a noble lion."

The jury was not as easily persuaded. For eight sweltering days, the twelve men, mostly local merchants, argued with each other while reporters spying on them from tree limbs and rooftops tried to keep the story alive by providing details like this: "The jury was extremely quiet last night. Its members laid themselves yawningly over the tables and gaped. Half-nakedness is its condition by choice." On July 2, 1875, the jury finally reported to the court that after fifty-two ballots they were still divided nine to three in the defendant's favor. This result was good enough to cause an immediate celebration at Plymouth Church, but uncertain enough that the church called a council of noted ministers early in 1876 to review all of the proceedings. Among the Congregational ministers in attendance was Hartford's Joseph Twitchell. He and his friend Mark Twain also had attended some of the sessions of the trial, but Twitchell had kept an open mind until he found himself in "a noble body of men bent on doing righteously without fear or favor" who as "they listened to him [Beecher] and watched him were conscious of ceasing to doubt his integrity." Twitchell agreed with the council's verdict that Beecher was innocent of the crime with which he was charged but guilty of folly in "falling so easy a prey to his enemies." Plymouth Church also launched a drive that would raise $100,000 of the $118,000 in costs incurred by its pastor.

The women's suffrage advocates who had been responsible for so much of the talk that brought about the trial were conspicuous by their absence during the event. Isabella Hooker stayed in Europe until it was all over. The Woodhull was summoned by the defense and made a very brief appearance simply to identify material exchanged between her and Tilton. Possibly through her sixth sense as a spiritualist she had foreseen how the trial would turn out and was in the process of joining the winning side, as her subsequent activities would reveal. Not everyone agreed that Beecher had won. One commentator in the press called him "a dunghill covered with flowers"; another said that "mankind fell in Adam, and has been falling ever since, but never touched bottom till it got to Henry Ward Beecher." But by the end of that year of deliverance, Henry Ward Beecher would be back on the lecture circuit, drawing larger crowds than ever.

10

"I will not lie there."

49 Forest Street, Hartford, Conn. Oct. 11, 1887

DEAR BROTHER [Edward Beecher]—I was delighted to receive your kind letter. *You* were my earliest religious teacher; your letters to me while I was a school-girl in Hartford gave me a high Christian aim and standard which I hope I have never lost. Not only did they do me good, but also my intimate friends, Georgiana May and Catharine Cogswell, to whom I read them. The simplicity, warmth and childlike earnestness of those school days I love to recall. I am the *only one living* of that circle of early friends. *Not one* of my early schoolmates is living,—and now Henry, younger by a year or two than I, has gone—my husband also. I often think, *Why* am I spared? Is there yet anything for me to do? I am thinking with my son Charles's help of writing a review of my life, under the title, "Pebbles from the Shores of a Past Life."

Charlie told me that he has got all written up to my twelfth or thirteenth year, when I came to be under sister Catharine's care in Hartford. I am writing daily my remembrances from that time. You were then, I think, teacher of the Grammar School in Hartford.

So, my dear brother, let us keep a good heart, no evil can befall us. Sin alone is evil, and from that Christ will keep us. Our journey is *so* short!

I feel about all things now as I do about the things that happen in a hotel, after my trunk is packed to go home. I may be vexed and annoyed . . . but what of it! I am going home soon.

Your affectionate sister, HATTIE

It is probable that Harriet Beecher Stowe's oldest brother got something of a chuckle out of his sister's letter. Wasn't she packing her trunk a little too soon? At eighty-four, Edward was still serving as pastor to a small flock at Parkville Congregational Church on Brooklyn's Eighteenth Avenue. Harriet had nearly a decade or more of living to do before catching up to him, and she seemed to be fit for her age and was certainly more comfortable in that place of hers at Nook Farm than he had ever been in all his life. It was good that she was still trying to write something, but he wondered what she might have left to say after putting out more books and articles than he had been able to keep up with. He did not know what, if anything, to make of the coincidence that brother Charles was talking about writing a biography of him, Edward, while his namesake, Harriet's Charles, apparently was working with his mother on her autobiography. As if that weren't enough in the way of Beechers writing about Beechers, Henry Ward's son William and son-in-law Sam Scoville were collaborating with Eunice to rush Henry Ward's biography into print. Edward suspected that their motive was to wipe out of the public mind any lingering doubts about their subject's character as a result of his troubles in the 1870s, though Henry Ward had done a good job of that himself these past ten years.

Edward had to admire the courage that his brother had displayed by going out on the lecture tour right after his trial. The first audiences that packed the halls to see what a celebrity sinner looked like greeted his entry with catcalls and taunts and his exits with applause. Sensibly, Henry Ward refrained from preaching personal morality and lectured instead on the state of a society in bewildering flux. The white Anglo-Saxon Protestant composition of the northern and midwestern cities on Beecher's circuit was being altered by the northward drift of African Americans and the rising tide of emigration from central and southern Europe. The rapid postwar expansion and industrialization of the American economy that was being spurred on by the Republicans' high tariff policy was faltering and leaving more than a million workers unemployed and in danger of starvation. In a development unknown during centuries of a rural economy, the rich were rapidly growing richer and the poor, poorer. Businessmen were building mansions on Fifth Avenue and at Newport; industrial workers were beginning to stage bloody strikes that usually were futile but nevertheless frightening to the middle class; farmers, squeezed between high tariffs and hard money, were forming associations and parties in the hope of easing their debts with bimetalism or paper. Henry Ward Beecher shot a bright ray of optimism through the gathering economic gloom. In one of his most popular lectures, "The

Reign of the Common People," he extolled the good sense and industry of the average American that could be counted on to set things right. He could be equally hard on the rich and corrupt, as when he called the flamboyant Jim Fisk, who was involved with Jay Gould in an attempt to corner the gold market, "abominable in his lusts and flagrant in his violation of public decency," and on the poor as when he claimed, "It is said that a dollar a day is not enough for a wife and five or six children. No, not if the man smokes or drinks beer. . . . But is not a dollar a day enough to buy bread with? Water costs nothing and a man who cannot live on bread and water is not fit to live."

As in theology, Henry Ward did not let himself get stuck in any school of political or economic thought. Whether he acknowledged it or not, he believed in a statement by his peer and rival on the lecture tour, Ralph Waldo Emerson, that "a foolish consistency is the hobgoblin of little minds, adored by little statesmen and philosophers and divines." Beecher's message would change with changing times and events and personalities. In 1876 he put what he saw as the best interests of the country above party loyalty in a contested election to determine the successor to President Grant. To profit from the corruption in Washington— so flagrant that Grant felt obliged to apologize to Congress for "errors of judgment not of intent" in a last address—the Democrats nominated Samuel J. Tilden, newly elected governor of New York because of his record as a reformer who had led a successful attack on Manhattan's corrupt "Tweed Ring." The Republicans picked a very solid but dull citizen in the form of Rutherford B. Hayes, a Union general and three-time governor of Ohio, who has been described as "hampered by virtue." Although Tilden won the popular vote by a 264,000-vote margin, he got only 184 electoral votes, one short of the required majority. Still in doubt at midnight of election day were electoral votes from Florida, Louisiana, South Carolina, and one from Oregon. White sentiment in those southern states was Democratic, but control there was Republican, still supported by federal troops. The states submitted two conflicting tallies of electoral votes, and Congress was left to decide the outcome. A fifteen-man electoral commission, weighed eight to seven in favor of the Republicans, was chosen to do the job. Feelings were running so high that some observers feared a resumption of the Civil War. Henry Ward Beecher's was one moderate voice suggesting that Hayes concede in view of losing the popular vote, and Hayes himself was said to have been resigned to defeat. But, being in control of the commission, the Grand Old Party would not consider such a sacrifice, although its leaders did agree to make a deal with the Democratic leadership in the disputed states to keep a lid on the conflict. In return for the gift of the White House, Hayes was persuaded to promise withdrawal of federal support for the existing carpetbagger governments and the appointment of a Southerner to his cabinet. It meant virtual disenfranchisement of the freedmen and a blow to their supporters in the North, most of whom were disillusioned Republicans such as the Beechers. To them and to Democrats generally, Hayes was known as "Rutherfraud" or "His Fraudulency" or "Boss Thief." Perhaps to overcome this stigma, Hayes made civil service reform an objective of his presidency, but his only notable act in that direction was the firing of a prominent Republican politician, Chester A. Arthur, from his lucrative post as customs collector for New York because he refused to investigate corruption in his organization as directed. With that act, Hayes managed to split his own party and contribute to a Democratic election sweep that gave them control of both houses of Congress for the first time in twenty years.

Just as it was a bad year for Republicans, 1878 proved to be a trying time for Beechers. In April, while Henry Ward was off lecturing, the *New York Times* published a letter from Lib Tilton, by then living in obscurity with a daughter, in which she stated "that the charge brought by my husband, of adultery between myself and the Reverend Henry Ward Beecher, was true and that the lie I had lived so well the last four years had become intolerable to me." Henry Ward brushed off this new change of mind on the part of his once good friend by saying that she was a clairvoyant prone to trances and to "kissing the feet of those to whom she most felt herself under obligation." The *Times* took the matter more seriously in an editorial comment on Lib's letter, since they had pronounced Beecher guilty despite the jury's failure to convict him. But the *Times* did admit that Lib's "card" was "worthless as legal evidence, however strongly it may confirm the moral presumption of Mr. Beecher's guilt. This weak and erring woman has so hopelessly forsworn herself as to forfeit all claim to attention or credence." The rest of the world must have agreed with that part of the editorial, since this confession caused no general stir. Henry Ward's astonishing ability to shrug the whole scandal off regardless of this disturbing echo is evident in a letter he wrote to Eunice in that same year. He spotted Frank Moulton on a train, and, although he did not speak to him, the experience evoked fond memories. "Could I be happier? Oh, yes, if another were only here—if only my T. T. [Theodore Tilton] could complete this Trinity! It was a comfort to see on Moulton's wrists a pair of noble jasper medallion sleeve buttons which I gave him.

It shows how tenderly he cherishes my memory. If only it were possible for us to be friends again."

At about the time that Lib Tilton surfaced for the last time, Tom Beecher was detecting worrisome behavior by the half sister who had become his permanent guest. Nobody in the greater Beecher family was surprised to learn that Catharine had at last alighted in Elmira, least of all Tom's wife, Julia. One of the things she had liked about Tom before she really knew him was what her friend Livy, Tom's first wife, wrote about him: "But when Miss Katy Beecher wants someone to run all over New York half a dozen times to get a crutch made for her—she knows *which brother to ask*." When Tom proposed taking Catharine into their home, Julia's response was "I think there are worse afflictions in the world than the care of an old Christian woman who has at least tried to do good all her life and needs someone's kind attentions till the Lord calls her home. I am not going to worry about *that*." There was, in fact, no cause for worry when Catharine first moved in, although she was as old as the century. She was a survivor. Catharine attributed her frequent nervous breakdowns and on-and-off paralysis of her limbs to being the only child of Roxana to inherit a weak constitution. She tried everything to keep going—a wide variety of medicines, psychological tricks such as staring at a silver piece for fifteen minutes at a time, baths of every known kind, and as many as thirteen rest cures in one twelve-year stretch. Aside from Tom's hospitality, the proximity to Gleason's water cure was an important motivation for Catharine's move to Elmira. Without any editorial or administrative project in view and "feeling stronger than for years," she soon complained of being bored and restless in a letter to Harriet, who replied, "I am relieved and glad to think of you at home at last with brother Tom. Too many years have passed over your head for you to be wandering like a trunk without a label. The government of the world will not be going on a whit worse that *you* are not doing it." Instead of trying to save the world, Catharine should consider using her "vein of humor" and natural good nature to cheer up the patients at the water cure, in Harriet's view. Harriet was striking a note that she felt sure would resonate with the sibling whom she knew better than any other but Henry Ward. She had shielded Catharine on many occasions; studied under her; worked with her; and, as she once tartly informed her father and Henry Ward, read her books, not only about housekeeping but also about theology. Like Harriet herself and Henry Ward and to a lesser extent most of the others, Catharine had substituted a gospel of love for the Calvinism that their father had thrust on them. Catharine had arrived at her beliefs more through her intellect than her emotions, and in one of her last books on the subject—*Common Sense Applied to Religion; or, The Bible and the People*—she attempted to analyze the workings of love:

> [W]e find that, both in sorrow and in joy, the mind seeks for the sympathy of others, while this grateful and soothing boon is delightful to bestow. So, also, the consciousness of being the cause of good to another sends joy to the heart, while the recipient is filled with the pleasing glow of gratitude in receiving the benefit. The consciousness of virtue in acting for the general good, instead of for contracted, selfish purposes, is another source of happiness.
>
> This same beneficial economy is manifested in a close analysis of all that is included in the affections of *love* and *gratitude*. It has been shown that, in the commencement of existence, the young mind first learns the sources of good and evil to self, and its sole motives are desire for its own enjoyment. Soon, however, it begins to experience the happiness resulting from the relations of minds to each other, and then is developed the superior power of *love* and its importance as a regulating principle.
>
> In the analysis of this affection, it is seen to consist, first, in the pleasurable emotions which arise in view of those traits of character in another mind pointed out in previous pages [basically, thoughts and feelings common to being human beings]. When these qualities are discovered, the first result is emotions of pleasure in contemplation. Immediately there follows *a desire of good* to the cause of this pleasure. Next follows the desire of reciprocated affection—that is, a desire is awakened *to become the cause of the same pleasure* to another; for the desire of *being loved* is the desire to be the cause of pleasurable emotions in another mind, in view of our own good qualities. When we acquire this desired appreciation, then follows an increased *desire of good* to the one who bestows it.
>
> Thus the affection of love is a combination of the action and reaction of pleasurable emotions, all tending to awaken the desire of good to another. This passion may become so intensified that it will become more delightful to secure enjoyments to another than to procure them for self.
>
> Gratitude is the emotion of pleasure toward the author of *voluntary* good to self, attended by a desire of good to the benefactor. This principle can be added to augment the power of love.

Whether from remembering her own recipe for happiness or from taking Harriet's advice, Catharine did throw herself into visiting patients at Gleason's and lecturing students at the female college in Elmira until the behavior that worried Tom came upon her. "Like a mirror fractured . . . Catharine 'went to pieces,'" Tom reported to Mary Perkins. "Incessantly, yet incoherently active, now with her hands fixing her well-worn conveniences of dress, shoes and writing apparatus, now writing a page or two of education . . . correspondence with bishops, statesmen, and capitalists, running ten times a day to play snatches of tunes from her antique repertoire, always ending with a quavering hymn refrain, 'It's better farther on.' Then back to her room, ready for metaphysics until would come the explanation, 'My head is tired, Tom.'" On a May night in 1878, Catharine Beecher went "farther on" when she suffered a stroke in her sleep. Edward came up from Brooklyn to conduct a memorial service in Tom's church, and wisely used the occasion to recall warm family relationships and his sister's extraordinary accomplishments in her chosen field of education instead of indulging in theological speculations.

Harriet did not come up from Mandarin for the funeral. She had finished yet another novel—*Poganuc People*—earlier that year. Nearing seventy herself, she felt in need of physical rest and the kind of spiritual refreshment she could get only when away from what she called "the world that hates Christ." Her mood at that time was reflected in her novel, which was set in "olden" times and about a family very like the Beechers in a town very like Litchfield. As she described it in a letter to Dr. and Mrs. Oliver Wendell Holmes, "It is an extremely quiet story for these sensational days when heaven and earth seem to be racked for thrills, but as I get old I do love to think of those quiet, simple times when there was not a poor person in the parish and the changing glories of the year were the only spectacle." It was the changeless glory of the year in Florida that Harriet found so enchanting, as she wrote to a friend, "We have days when the sun shines warm, and the lizards dart from all the shingles of the roof, and the birds sing in so many notes and tones the yard reverberates, and I sit and dream and am happy, and never want to go back North, nor do anything with the toiling, snarling world again." Actually, Harriet was quite active in most of her Florida days. She loved to take a picnic basket and go off with the twins to sail the river in a neighbor's boat, or fuss around with decorating the chapel that she built for black worshipers, or see to the management of her property and the pleasure of her guests. By contrast, Calvin stayed rooted to a chair on the veranda with a basket of books by his side, moving only to get in or out of the shifting spots of sun. He was such a fixture that, as Harriet once wrote, "His red skull-cap served mariners as a sort of daytime lighthouse." Because of her writings about Florida in magazine articles and a book called *Palmetto Leaves,* the Stowe establishment became a tourist attraction that steamer captains never failed to point out to passengers as they passed it, and not infrequently tourists on land would wander into the property uninvited and much to the annoyance of the reclusive, studious Calvin.

While they were in Florida, the famous biblical scholar often preached to small congregations of blacks and, when asked, to whites in some of the district's larger churches. In that year of 1878 a writer named Amanda M. Brooks happened to attend a Sunday morning service in Jacksonville where Calvin preached, and her account of the event was carried in the local press:

> Mrs. Harriet Beecher Stowe is here today from her home in Mandarin, for the purpose of attending church. Dr. Stowe, her husband, accompanies her, as he preaches. When they both entered the Southern Methodist Church a slight rustle was heard in the congregation, and a few persons left the house. Mr. and Mrs. Uncle Tom were more than a Sabbath dose for some of the Jacksonville community. Harriet B. had no resemblance to the perpetrator of discord or scandal, or one who has swayed the divining rod of Abolitionism with sufficient potency to immortalize herself with many coming generations, or probed the private life of a man, who, during the period of his checkered existence, never carved out virtue for his shrine. Three snowy curls on each side of her face gave her a matronly look, and her stout-built frame, well-covered with flesh, a substantial appearance.
>
> The service was opened by a very long prayer from Mr. Stowe, after which he preached a purely orthodox sermon on the subject of godliness. Mrs. Harriet had confidence in the ability of her husband, she knew the discourse would be right without her vigilant eye, and she went to sleep. Like other sleepers, she nodded naturally, her digits concealed beneath kid covers, and thrusting at no one. She looked the picture of content, and was no doubt dreaming of far-off, beautiful country where those who create dissensions and stir up strife never enter.

Calvin's presence in a Methodist pulpit along with the Stowes' participation in building and worshiping in Episcopalian chapels were evidence of their ecumenical view of the Christian mission in the world. Either despite or because of the fact that many of Lyman Beecher's fiercest battles were waged against other sects and denominations out of honest conviction, all of his children strayed from the narrow path he walked. If there was a common ground on which they took their stands, it was that no doctrine should stand in the way of agape, a Greek word commonly used for the kind of universal love for all other human beings that Jesus preached. Henry Ward's wide view was not limited to professing Christians as neighbors deserving of love. When Jews began flooding into the New World to escape pogroms in Russia, Henry Ward urged his fellow Americans to make them welcome. But he didn't just talk the talk, he walked the walk in the sense that Joseph Seligman, a banker and leader of New York's German Jewish community, and his family were among his best friends during his yearly retreats to Twin Mountain House. When in the summer of 1877 the Seligmans were refused accommodation by the Grand Union Hotel in Saratoga Springs at the instigation of A. T. Stewart, a wealthy Manhattan department store owner, and Henry Hilton, a judge tarred with the brush of "Boss" Tweed, Henry Ward was so incensed that he preached one of his most famous and controversial sermons, "Gentile and Jew." In his impassioned style, he credited the Jews with giving the world "a treasure of benefits such as no other people had ever conferred upon mankind"—among them respect for women; love of children and belief in education; and the establishment of a commonwealth based on an ethical religion, which became the foundation of Christianity. After all, the Christ who was worshiped by the Christians who turned Jews away was a Jew. And Yankees, as Beecher, a born and bred Yankee himself, reminded his people, were in no position to complain about the admirable industry and smart business tactics of Jews.

Pastor Tom was one of the most articulate Beechers on the subject of ecumenism. Asked by a young man about the best way to get to heaven, he said, "My boy, you can go to New York from Elmira by the Erie, the Lehigh Valley, the Lackawanna or the Northern Central. You can walk, ride horseback, or you can go by boat. One way may be somewhat more roundabout than the other but you will get there all right if you follow the sign posts. You can reach heaven by the Catholic church, or by the Synagogue, Universalist or Baptist, and you can even reach it through the Park Church [his own church in Elmira]—but, whatever you do, do it unto the Lord." Tom Beecher did not, however, believe in doing away with the variety of creeds and churches available to truth seekers in the ongoing social and political experiment called America. One of his few publications was a book, *Our Seven Churches,* in which he extolled the virtues of each of Elmira's places of worship. "I have walked in them as in gardens of the Lord; their beauties have filled my eye, and the air is fragrant roundabout." He argued that every church could learn from every other church, that variety was needed because "every man has his own horizon" and that "there are many churches but one religion."

Having been expelled from the union of churches in Elmira, Tom went his own way when he finally decided to build a church to accommodate the crowds he was attracting to the opera house and park. The edifice he built and the uses to which it was put were at first considered ungodly by his fellow pastors. There was a stage for theatricals, a kitchen capable of serving two hundred diners, the first public library in the city, a "Romp Room" for dancing, and billiard and pool tables. With no intention of pioneering, Tom was creating one of the first of the "institutional churches" that would spread across the country. Henry Ward was impressed. "Tom, when I go, I shall leave behind me no such great monument to my life's work," he told his brother when he saw the new building. The success of Tom's venture brought him favorable publicity and offers from big-city churches willing to pay him as much as ten thousand dollars a year to take over their pulpits. But Tom, who cherished the freedom that his congregation and the citizens of Elmira generally granted him to indulge his idiosyncrasies, heeded Henry Ward's sage advice: "Don't leave the Park Church—they can appreciate you and endure you!"

Tom was both a guardian and a companion to his brother James, who served churches first in Owego and then Poughkeepsie during the early 1870s. Like Tom and Julia, James and Frankie adopted orphaned girls—Kathie and twins named Margie and Mary. The brothers enjoyed hunting and fishing and camping in the Catskill Mountains wilderness and, by luck or design, had married energetic women who also enjoyed these pursuits. In 1876 James gave up his pastorate, bought a mile-square tract in Ulster County far from any town but blessed with a pond that he christened Beecher Lake, and took up residence with his family, first in a tent and then in a cottage built by his own hands. The Tom Beechers were frequent and willing guests who pitched in as James gradually cleared a twenty-acre patch to raise vegetables to go along with the fish and game on which they subsisted. Once they were aware of his presence, lumbermen scattered around the area asked James to preach in their schoolhouses, and, as she had done with the troops in Florida, Frankie established a school for the children whose few months' attendance in those poorly served schools left them nearly illiterate. It was the kind of busy and active life that James craved, and he did so well at it that he got national publicity as the "hermit preacher."

One reason for James's radical change in lifestyle was his hope that it might cure, or help him get through, the bouts of melancholy he shared with all of his brothers and sisters. In his view, he and his blood siblings were afflicted with the "blues" more deeply and more often than the others. As he wrote to his wife when she was away from camp, "I am sure that there runs a streak of insanity in our mother's three children—or rather monomania, assuming diverse forms. I recognize it in Tom and myself. The only advantage I have is in being thoroughly conscious of the fact. Tom is partially so. Belle is absolutely unconscious and is therefore the craziest of the three." Harriet had used the term "monomania" in relation to Isabella's defection from the rest of the family in the matter of Henry Ward's guilt. Its dictionary definition—"mental derangement restricted to one idea or group of ideas"—made the word even more suitable when Isabella returned from Europe in 1876 with a new obsession: spiritualism. As an associate of the Woodhull before she went abroad, Isabella had toyed with this increasingly popular belief that it was possible to get in touch with the spirits of the departed, but it was only when a vivid vision of her mother, Harriet Porter Beecher, began appearing to her and giving her advice as she lay in bed in her Paris hotel that she was completely converted. In a diary she kept for the balance of that year of her epiphany, she recorded a message from the spirit world that surely would have caused nearly everybody else in the family to agree with James about her mental state had she made it known. She had been informed that she would become president of the United States and, by effort and example, spread the concept of matriarchal government around the world as a prelude to the coming of Christ's kingdom. What she did share of other visions with the people around her was enough to make her either fascinating or frightening to them, and she was as much of a puzzling figure to reckon with in the respectable atmosphere of Nook Farm as she had been during her brother's trial.

Isabella's agitation for women's rights and the relationship with the Woodhull that had led to her break with Henry Ward and banishment from Nook Farm social circles had alienated her conservative sons-in-law to the point where she seldom had contact with her daughters. Her involvement with spiritualism made matters worse. Voices from the other world in 1876 were telling her that her eight-year-old granddaughter, Kathy Burton, whose home was within sight of the Hookers', would not live out the year. This incensed the girl's father, Eugene, and he would not let Isabella come anywhere near his house or his daughter. Living with her and communicating daily, Isabella's own son, Ned, studying to be a physician, and her husband, John, were tolerant and open-minded, though not convinced, about her powers. Even so, they felt obliged to stay up and keep watch all night and persuade policemen to patrol the Burton home when Isabella was warned that a burglar would break into the house and wound Eugene. Nothing happened, and this, like the warning of Kathy's death, created an embarrassment for which Eugene Burton was not grateful.

If her new obsession cost Isabella dearly by offending her nearest relatives, it also served as a bridge to some of the other Beechers. Catharine was staying temporarily with the Stowes, and her intellectual curiosity about matters such as faith healing, clairvoyance, and spiritualism prompted her to visit the Hookers and discuss them with Isabella. Catharine may have wanted to tell her sister of a meeting she had had years before with Kate Fox, one of the earliest and most famous mediums in the spiritualist movement. Fox reported seeing Lyman kneeling before Catharine and presenting her a rose as a sign of her purity. Catharine's response to this, as she told it, was "Such nonsense! When my father never in his life praised me, although he used to say that I was the best boy he had." Catharine invited Isabella over to play croquet on the lawn between the Stowes' and Mark Twain's house. When Harriet learned that the Hookers were having a hard time financially, possibly because of Isabella's long stay in Europe, she sent a gift of fifty dollars by Catharine, and it turned out to be an effective peace offering. Isabella was able to mend some other fences as well through the good offices of Susan Warner, wife of Charles Dudley Warner. Susan, a nearly professional pianist, was both amused and intrigued by Isabella's efforts to reach Beethoven for comment on Susan's performance of his music. Although that effort failed, too, Susan was appreciative enough to stage a luncheon in December 1876 for some twenty of Isabella's old friends, including Livy Clemens and her mother-in-law, Mrs. Langdon, at which Isabella found herself warmly received back into Hartford society.

From Isabella's point of view, the timing of the lunch could not have been better. It empowered her to take up again the role she had once played so well as a popular Nook Farm hostess and invite the Clemenses [the Mark Twains] and Warners, among others, to a New Year's Eve celebration. She wanted them to be present on that date when, as the spirits were predicting, the announcement of her election to rule the world would come from on high. Since the message might not get through to some of her old friends who were not psychically prepared for it, Isabella also invited, over her husband's objection, a number of the mediums from around the Hartford area with whom she had been meeting. The spirits out there were no respecters of social status, and the people they visited were not the kind of people with whom John Hooker associated personally, despite his liberal views on issues such as slavery and women's rights. In this instance, his worst fears were well founded. With the decorous Nook Farm set already munching on nuts and raisins and trading gossip in the parlor, the spiritualists, ungainly in manner and improperly dressed, began appearing at the door. Now realizing that John had been right, Isabella joined him in shunting these unsuitable guests up the stairs to a room she had set aside for her own communications with the spirits by way of devices such as a particular pen that would cause her hand to write out messages in different scripts. Isabella was in for another disappointment. Midnight came and went with no revelations either upstairs or down, and departing guests from both levels mingled in embarrassment at the door.

Both testy after the last guest had gone, Isabella and John got into an unusual argument in the early hours of 1877. He reached for the now familiar word "monomania" to define what he suggested was his wife's unstable mental condition—a concentration on spiritualism to the point where she was unaware of, or unconcerned about, all other aspects of life. She countered with the claim that she was still reading widely in the newspapers about public and cultural affairs and playing whist for social amusement and then added, according to her notes about the evening, "He had confessed to me lately, that he not only was a hypochondriac of *melancholy without a cause* from his grandfather which would make him positively insane in the his old age & a burden to his friends. Now I simply because I am investigating phenomena that claim the attention of the whole scientific world . . . now *you dare to call me insane*—I think this is the pot calling the kettle black." Ned stepped in to pacify his parents by assuring his father that his mother was not in any way crazy, and in time both Ned and John would come to share a good deal of Isabella's continuing interest and faith in spiritualism.

Another indication that Isabella might suffer from monomania was the way she eased off on her participation in the campaign for women's suffrage for a number of years after her return from Europe. In any event, a more pressing issue of those times had to do with the changing economy, which was resulting in widespread labor unrest and poverty. Blessed with memories of a society "when there was not a poor person in the parish," as Harriet put it, and imbued with the business ethic of one of America's richest communities that attributed poverty to laziness, even the so-called liberals of Nook Farm did not feel called on to do more about this growing problem than make contributions to local charities.

Anything like an action picture on scene was rare in the infancy of photography, but some efforts were made to leave pictorial records of meaningful events.

This picture was taken shortly before the death of Lyman Beecher, the family patriarch, when Harriet was visiting him in 1863 in Brooklyn, where he was living to be close to Henry Ward and the Plymouth Church. It may have been then that Harriet told her father that he was a handsome old man, to which he replied, "Tell me something new."

One of the great events of the year 1891 in Hartford, Connecticut, was the fiftieth wedding anniversary of two of its most famous citizens— Isabella Beecher Hooker and her husband, John. This photo was taken in the gardens of their suburban Nook Farm home before or after a daylong reception for hundreds of guests in the city.

Calvin Stowe can be seen indulging in his one and only outdoor activity—
sitting on a porch with book in hand—at the Nook Farm home where the
Stowe family spent the last decades of their lives. The house is still standing
and has become a major tourist attraction.

For twenty years, life in the Nook Farm community was enlivened for
the many Beechers living there by the presence of Samuel Clemens—
Mark Twain—and his family. Here they gather on the Ombra, or great
porch, of their home next door to the Stowe house where Harriet would
visit them, uninvited and unannounced, almost daily during mindless
wanderings in her dotage. This house, too, is a tourist attraction today.

It was Isabella's blood brother Tom, the Beecher least likely to get involved in social action, who was fired up by the plight of the poor. The only organized force in sight that seemed to care about the poor was the Greenback Party, which advocated using paper money to ease the crunch brought on by the drop of money in circulation from thirty-one dollars to nineteen dollars per capita in the decade since the end of the war. In the congressional elections of 1878, the Greenbacks collected a million votes and won fourteen House seats, and the Reverend Thomas Beecher decided to run for the House on that party's ticket in 1880. His doing so was regarded as a quixotic act by his acquaintances, including Mark Twain's friend the Reverend Joseph Twitchell. Tom felt moved to explain himself in a letter that Twitchell found important enough to preserve in his journal but not convincing enough to change the belief he shared with his Hartford flock that unbridled capitalism with decent people in the saddle would outrun poverty. Tom wrote,

> I wish you had any social convictions as to the welfare of the masses. I enclose the greenback platform—which with trifling exceptions I cannot gainsay. Read it and think, that's all. Dear Joe Twitchell whom I loved from the word go—as the healthiest and heartiest minister that lets me call him friend—this very mail brings me two letters, one from a widow—the other from a man of fifty in Idaho—whose struggles I have known for 20 years. Whatever you and I have felt in days by gone as the scared fugitives from slavery came shivering to us by night showing cracked pit scars, & in rags, until we could endure *slavery* no *longer*—the same I feel daily and hourly as the unending procession of my neighbors files by me—anxious, heartbroken, or worse, with eyes of hate & envy, as they know themselves the bleeding grist of our great financial mill—that, in defiance of Scripture & testimony of ages insists that to lend money—exact interest . . . & grow rich while brother men & partners are *cleaned out*—is honest Christian enterprise.
>
>   No—Joe—praise me for my patience. These twenty five years I have been of intenser convictions than Garrison [one of the earliest and most radical antislavery men] ever was. . . . You know I am not a party man . . . nor a . . . communist. I am only Jeremiah *redivivus*.
>
>   There, I love you & so I write as I never wrote other.

The election of 1880 did not send Tom Beecher to Washington. Greenback candidates made such a poor showing that most historians do not mention their participation at all. By contrast, brother Henry Ward landed again on the winning side by picking his way carefully through a minefield of factions that was threatening to blow the Republican Party apart when their delegates met in Chicago to nominate a replacement for Hayes, who declined to run again. Henry Ward at first went along with a group called the "stalwarts," who wanted to rerun Grant. Minister or not, Beecher's initial support of Grant had been so strong that he once told an audience, "I had rather have Grant a drunkard than Horatio Seymour sober!" Still seeing the general as "solid, unpretentious, straightforward," Henry Ward followed the lead of conservatives such as New York senator Roscoe Conkling as they battled a more liberal faction known as the "half-breeds," supporting Senator James Gillespie Blaine of Maine. The convention was deadlocked through thirty-five ballots until the Blaine faction threw their votes to a dark horse, Congressman James Abram Garfield of Ohio, a pious man with a good record as a major general in the Civil War. The stalwarts then agreed to support Garfield in return for the nomination of one of their number, the recently fired New York collector of customs, Chester A. Arthur, for vice president. Whatever he thought of the candidates, Henry Ward Beecher called for party loyalty during the campaign and was credited with providing the catchy, if rather irreverent, slogan "For God and Garfield." The Democrats nominated a popular war hero still in service, Major General Winfield Scott Hancock, in an effort to neutralize the advantage Republicans gained by appealing to patriotic sentiment through what was called "waving the bloody shirt" to remind voters of the winning side in the war. Garfield squeaked through with only a nine-thousand lead in the popular vote, but the Republicans recaptured the House that Tom Beecher would never enter.

The rancor of the nomination process and close election carried over into the next year, when on July 2, 1881, a clearly deranged man named Charles Guiteau shot Garfield in Washington's Union Station as he was boarding a train to attend a reunion at his alma mater, Williams College. Guiteau shouted, "I am a stalwart and Arthur will be president!" Garfield had to live through two hot summer months in agony before Guiteau's wish came true with his death on September 19 and Arthur's inauguration on September 20.

Despite these dramatic events, most of the developments that would have historic significance in their effect on American society were taking place outside the political arena in the late 1870s and early 1880s. Applications for life-altering devices, particularly from a laboratory in Menlo Park, New Jersey, where a man named Thomas Edison worked almost around the clock, were piling up in the patent office. There was one for a phonograph and another for an "incandescent lamp," the latter being put to practical use only two years after it was granted in the form of electric lights in sixty New York City buildings powered by a steam generator in a station on Pearl Street. George Eastman in Rochester, New York, patented a film roll that would make it possible for him to put a camera in every home that could afford one. Another inventive Rochester man, George Selden, developed a two-cycle gasoline engine to power a "horseless carriage," but it turned out to be a bitter irony that, although he was a patent attorney by profession, the patent he applied for was not granted until others beat him out. Enterprising businessmen came up with new ways to serve—some would say milk—the public. In Utica, New York, Frank Woolworth and W. H. Moore opened the first "five-cent store"; lawyers for John D. Rockefeller's Standard Oil thought up a device called the trust, which would bring forty companies and 90 percent of the nation's refining capacity under the control of only nine people. With businesses combining, workingmen who had suffered severely in scattered strikes took a step toward a competing form of organization when the Federation of Organized Trades and Labor, a little later to become the American Federation of Labor, was founded in Pittsburgh, with Samuel Gompers as president.

For the most part, Henry Ward hailed both the new things and the new thoughts he was seeing and experiencing. An exception was the widening gulf between rich and poor, which drove brother Tom to his uncharacteristic act of running for office. By 1882, in articles and sermons, Henry Ward was sounding an alarm that must have been startling to his middle-class readers and parishioners. Not only did he defend the right of labor to organize despite the violence and property destruction that their inevitable strikes would cause, but he added that "one thing is certain—our sympathies should be with the multitude, with the poor and weak against the rich and strong. The duty of the rich was to be on the side of the less fortunate—the mass of men—and to hold their wealth as a trust from God for the benefit of the poor. . . . Today the rich are about to learn, if they have not yet learned it, that they cannot separate themselves from the welfare of the whole great laboring multitude. . . . The man that stands today upon a pedestal simply because he is rich, will in another fifty years stand in the pillory if he does not make his riches serve mankind. . . . If the top of society bends perpetually over the bottom, with tenderness, if the rich and strong are the best friends of the poor and needy, that is a civilized and Christian community." Henry Ward was not spouting only liberal social views, he also was quoting Scripture, as he read it: "When he [Jesus] opened his ministry, the text that he gave—I have already read it in your hearing—is contained in Luke, where he says: 'The spirit of the Lord is upon me, because he hath anointed me to preach the Gospel to the poor.' That was His ministry and that was His mission: 'He hath sent me to heal the broken-hearted; to preach deliverance to captives, recovering of sight to the blind, to set at liberty those that are bruised, and to preach the acceptable years of the Lord.'"

Except as they may have played a part in the thinking behind Andrew Carnegie's impressive benefactions and his own *Gospel of Wealth*, published a few years later, Beecher's pleas to the rich were not notably effective in that "gilded age." As if giving Beecher a thumb to the nose, the commodore's son William K. Vanderbilt threw the fanciest dress ball the nation had ever known for twelve hundred guests at a cost of $250,000 in March 1883. But Henry Ward's welcoming attitude toward new thinking and the changes it required prompted him to take another kind of stand that would have profound effects through future generations. Back in the 1860s, when brother Edward expressed concern about finding a book by evolutionist Herbert Spencer on Henry Ward's crowded shelves, Henry Ward did not reveal how much what Edward regarded as an atheistic tract was shaping his thinking except to drop hints here and there in his sermons that, as against the opinion of almost the entire Christian establishment, he believed in Darwin's theory of evolution. By the time Herbert Spencer was given a dinner in Delmonico's to celebrate the end of a speaking tour of America in 1882, Henry Ward was willing to come out of the closet, as it were, and consent to be one of the speakers. He was generous in his praise of the guest of honor, who "will be found to have given more truth in one lifetime than any man who has lived in the schools of philosophy in this world," and lighthearted in describing his personal reaction to evolution: "I would just as lief have descended from a monkey as from anything else—if I had descended far enough."

Henry Ward was, however, very serious in the study and thought that he put into a series of sermons that would eventually be published in the book *Evolution and Religion*. After a decade of turmoil, he was enjoying a period when peace of mind allowed him to tackle a deep subject such as evolution as well as an assignment to write a life of Jesus. The Woodhull and Tennessee Claflin moved to England, where they reportedly and incredibly were marrying into wealthy families, and Theodore Tilton opted for a bohemian life as a freelance writer in Paris. From across the waters came only the faintest echoes of the scandal that Henry Ward had shrugged off. In 1881, in a British publication called the *Cuckoo*, the Woodhull tried to nail down the conversion to respectability and religious guidance that she had begun in the States. She blamed the whole affair on Stephen Pearl Andrews, an advanced social thinker who had been part of the ménage on Thirty-eighth Street and who had, in fact, been the creator and ghostwriter of much of the material in the Claflins' paper. She now claimed that Andrews had signed her name to the "Beecher Article" without her leave and that she had taken the blame for it to protect her then husband, Colonel Blood, who was the paper's nominal editor and who was being threatened with violence. One of the *Cuckoo*'s few readers was prompted to write to the publication that "barefaced mendacity has never been exceeded," and friends of Andrews and Blood reportedly laughed at Victoria's attempt to rewrite history. The Beechers apparently ignored it.

In trying to convince his own people and eventual readers of his book that evolution and the discoveries of science generally should deepen rather than cast doubt on religious faith, Henry Ward had to challenge the concept of the Bible as the infallible and only word of God. In effect, he had long been doing so by using illustrations from the observable workings of nature, such as the beauty of flowers, as much as Scripture to demonstrate the workings of God. But any kind of rational thought made it impossible to accept both the claims of evolution and a literal interpretation of the Bible. Henry Ward began his own discussion of the matter by pointing out that he was not alone among religious leaders in promoting this point of view. Among others he cited Professor Dana of Yale College, a Congregationalist; Professor Gray of Harvard University, a communicant of the Christian Church; the Episcopal bishop of London, Dr. Williams; and "Professor McCosh of Princeton College, a Presbyterian of the Presbyterians, and a Scotch Presbyterian at that." It is unlikely that Henry Ward could have added his most theologically minded brothers to this list in view of an exchange of letters between him and Charles while he was working on his sermons.

Newport, Fla.
Jan. 14, 1884.

Dear Brother,

I forgot whether you were to furnish the bear-skin and I the commentary on John or vice versa. I could supply the comm., on the Revelation, if that was in order, and it is said that bears are plenty not far from here. As we are wearing on, had we not better settle this? I am afraid if you set off on another lecturing tour, it may extend to 33,000 miles—or in fact never end. Any little matter like that alluded to above should be arranged at once.

What terrible fellows these reporters are! Somebody gave me an Atlantic paper with a report of your lecture there. He made you say some dreadful things. I don't know how to prevent it, unless you carry your own reporter along with you.

I think it a pity that we should go so long without writing to each other. Do you remember those great sheets we exchanged in College—And those big barn door letters circulars (tho' square) that were marked all over in red ink 25c. 50c. It would be better to go back to those than to tolerate such total non intercourse. I inferred from some remarks made when I last saw you, that you had some slight differences in opinion in matters theological from me and Edward. But that need not prevent our correspondence. We think man a fallen being, you think him a risen being,—but that need not prevent our writing letters to each other. Or is it a difference that must create a wide divergence, wider than might at first appear? It seems to me that a belief in the fall of man, may be tolerated in this era of liberty and liberality.

Your affectionate brother,
Charles

In an unsigned letter, Henry Ward responded:

Brooklyn, N.Y.
Jan. 19, 1884.

My dear Charles—

You were to furnish the bear skin, I the volume and my part of the contract will be fulfilled before yours. I am now on Romans and have made the Analysis of the book preliminary in next Homeletical Monthly (Funk & Wagnall, N.Y.)

I am amazed or ought to be, that you go back to Adam for an adequate supply of sin to furnish the needs of the world. About here, we can have it fresh, first class, too, manufactured on the spot, and all warranted, without adulteration. Who would eat *canned* fruit who could get fresh? The fact is, Adam's Sin, is like stale yeast, not fit to use, poor at best and now only fit to be trodden under foot of men.

In all sobriety—just now among thinking unchurchly men, and among many ministers the Choice is between Evolution and Infidelity. I prefer the former. The whole force of organized religion has been directed to *Fear and Conscience*. In a low and barbarous condition this works well. It is time that as much *power* upon the soul should be developed from the higher religious sentiments, hope, trust, faith, Love, as from its basilar powers. I believe the time will come, speedily, when revivals will be developed from the religion of love as from that of *Fear*. At any rate that is my endeavor.

The theory of evolution delighted Henry Ward Beecher because it provided a logical basis for his emotional optimism about God's creation in general and did away with what he considered the illogical and emotionally unacceptable Calvinist belief in original sin, or, as Charles put it, man as a fallen being. Edward and Charles also had been troubled by the doctrine of original sin because of what it implied about the nature of God—how could he be viewed as a loving Father if he condemned all of his creatures to hell because of Adam's supposed fall? They made God blameless and worthy of worship through their concept of a preexistence in which the creatures who would be reborn as human beings on this earth had made the choice to follow Satan and were thus damned unless they underwent a prescribed process of conversion. Henry Ward's concern about the doctrine of original sin was not what it implied about the nature of God, whom he worshiped unconditionally, but about the nature of man. He simply could not swallow the concept that human beings were born sinners, and he spelled out the effect of evolution on his thinking about this concept in one of his sermons:

> The old theory of sin, then,—which will be exterminated, I think, by the new light thrown upon the origin of man, and the conditions by which the race has been developed—is repulsive, unreasonable, immoral, and demoralizing. I hate it. I hate it because I love the truth, because I love God, and because I love my fellowmen. The idea that God created the race, and that two of them without experience were put under the temptation of the archfiend (or whatever the "creature" was), and that they fell into disobedience to what they did not understand anything about, and that God not only thrust them out of the Garden of Eden, as no parent would ever treat a child in his own household, but that he then transmitted the corruption that was the result of disobedience through countless ages, and spread it out and out and out, and kept on through the system of nature, mingling damnation on the right and on the left, before and behind—I hate it, because I love God, I abhor it, because I love justice and truth. People say to me, "It is generally understood that you are not a

Calvinist." John Calvin can take care of himself. But I am a teacher of righteousness. I am a lover of mankind. It is my business to make the truth, the path which men's thoughts travel, just as plain as I can, and take out all the obstructions that tend to unbelief. Among the mischievous things of this kind is this whole theory of sin and its origin, that lie at the base of the great evangelical systems of Christianity. I say, it is hideous, it is turning creation into a shambles and God into a slaughterer, and the human race into a condition worse a thousand-fold than that of beasts. The lion is never blamed for being a lion, nor the bear for being a bear, or for being no more than a lion or a bear; nor the horse, nor the swallow, nor the eagle, for not increasing the stature of their being. But man is made to start and not to stop; to go on, and on, and up, and onward, steadily emerging from the controlling power of the physical and animal conditions in which he was born and which enthrall him during his struggle upward, but ever touching higher elements of possibility, and ending in the glorious liberty of the sons of God.

This furnishes a ground of appeal which no man can very well resist. If I say, "You have inherited from Adam a corrupt nature," you may justly rise up and say, "I have not; I inherited from my father and mother as pure a nature as ever descended to a child. There has no drop of Adam's bad blood come through to me." But if I say to you, "God had made man a progressive creature, beginning at the very bottom, on the line of the material, first the animal, then the social, then the intellectual, the aesthetic, the spiritual, and every one of you should live so as to travel on and up; but you have not done it, you are living in the lower portions of your nature; you are not acting becomingly to yourself or your Creator"—if I say this, there is not a man here who can deny it. The doctrine of sin, as reflected in the philosophy of Evolution, will carry more power, and have more effect upon the conscience and the aspirations of men, and upon the desires for higher and better life than any other. It will explain to them the road by which they are to travel, and the directions they are to take, away from appetites and passions, and will enable them to live more and more perfectly in the higher ranges of emotion and more sensibility.

So long as it was taught that for the sin of one man the whole race was blighted, so long as it was believed that, the race left in ignorance, untended, oppressed, was yet emptying itself every thirty years into hell, and that this terrific work was going on from generation to generation—while this was the doctrine no man could justify God on any principle of justice, of truth or of humanity. You might call it a mystery; you might say that it was something which should be revealed hereafter; but the hereafter will not do for men who are already in the bonds of despair on account of what they think and feel now. And when you put in place of that hideous dream of an explanation which the mediaeval theology borrowed from the Roman, and the Roman from the old horrible Tuscan, whose deities had not one spark of anything but cruelty in them—when you put in the place of that hideous dream the conception of an orderly and regular progression, beginning as it were in the atom elements, set on fire of God, beaten on the anvil of creation into solid worlds, going on from change to change, perfecting even its material and visible forms, bringing up the lower forms of creation, advancing them step by step, at last bringing them into the human ranks, and thence in all their combinations, onward and upward, until the consummation, how beneficent, how glorious the vision! And in view of that, how do our hearts swell with grateful joy as we anticipate the wondrous chorus of the Apocalypse: "And every creature which is in the heavens and on the earth, and under the earth, and such as are in the sea, and all that are in them heard I saying. Blessing and honor, and glory, and power, be unto him that sitteth upon the throne, and unto the Lamb forever and ever."

Henry Ward viewed the church much as he viewed the Bible—a useful tool to employ along with others in opening the way to spiritual growth, but not possessed of any exclusive or mystical powers. He was as ecumenically minded as his siblings. One of the selections in his book *Autobiographical Reminiscences* could have been written by Tom:

When I was in England I attended the Episcopal Church more than any other, and since I came back persons knowing that fact have patted me on the shoulder and said, "You must be living contrary to your convictions: otherwise you would be an Episcopalian." They cannot begin to understand the largeness of the place that I stand in. I own the Episcopal Church, it is mine. I own the Presbyterian Church. There is not a good thing it in that I do not own. I own the Methodist Church, and I will go to that church when I have a mind to. I own the Baptist Church. I own the Lutheran Church. I own the Unitarian and Universalist Churches, if they have good ministers in them. I own the Swedenborgian Church. The earth is the Lord's and the fullness thereof. I am the Lord's and the Lord is mine. I am his son and heir. Anything that Christ loves I will love, anything that he uses I will use, and those whom he sits down among I will sit down among. I am not false to my ground here, because I have large sympathy with Christians everywhere. I do not regard their church systems as better than mine, though they have much that I respect and esteem. I say that they are all imperfect and all partial, but they all stand for Christ, and do him grand service.

In other statements, he included the Catholic churches and synagogues as "imperfect" places of enlightenment.

The man who knew and understood Henry Ward better than anybody else outside the family was Lyman Abbott, a member of Plymouth Church who succeeded Beecher in the pulpit there. In a biography, Abbott pictured Henry Ward in those years when, basking in the sunshine of greater popularity than ever after coming out of the shadow of scandal, he devoted most of his energies to defining and redefining his gospel of love:

In person he was slightly under six feet; powerfully built; not corpulent but stocky. His general appearance suggested great physical strength. Mr. Fowler [a college classmate of Beecher's], the phrenologist said of him that he was a "splendid animal," and no one looking on his magnificent physique could doubt the fact. . . . He had a good digestion and an excellent nervous system. . . . Vigor of health was characteristic of him throughout his life. No doubt nature had endowed him with a fine physique, but he cooperated with nature and took excellent care of his body. He used neither tobacco nor alcohol, until the latter years of his life when he made occasional rare use of the lighter forms of the latter. He did not use tea or coffee in excess, and in his diet was never self-indulgent. . . . He was an early riser, and usually finished his work in the study in time to allow some out-of-door exercise or excursion before a two-o'clock dinner hour. The afternoon was given to rest, part of it to sleep, part of it to social calling or out-of-door employment. After a light supper he entered on the work of the evening, which was almost invariably given up to some public engagement. He was always a sound sleeper, and had the gift, somewhat rare I think, of throwing off cares and anxieties, whether they belonged to him or others, when he believed that further carrying them would do no good to him or them. . . .

Mr. Beecher was one of the first ministers in the Christian Church if not the very first in this country, to advocate the doctrine of evolution as a doctrine which, so far from being inimical to the cause of Christ, was certain to prove its friend and supporter. . . . The doctrine of evolution . . . seems to deny the doctrines of revelation, redemption, and regeneration. It was regarded by substantially the whole Christian Church as subversive of the entire system of evangelical faith. . . . But if he [Henry Ward] cared very little what the great public thought of him, he cared a great deal about how those who knew him felt toward him. The expression uttered by him on his seventieth birthday represents his habitual mood. "I love men so much that I like above all other things in the world to be loved. And yet I can do without it when it is necessary. I love love, but I love truth more, and God more yet." For great as was his love for his fellow men and his desire for their love, the dominating motives of his life were his love for God—or his love for Christ,—and in his experience the two phrases were synonymous,—and his desire for God's love. No one who knew him intimately could doubt the simplicity and sincerity of his piety. Christ was a very real and very present Person to him. His disbelief in theology never involved in doubt his experience of vital fellowship with a living God.

The national election of 1884 would provide a showcase opportunity for Pastor Beecher to demonstrate in practice much of what he had been preaching. The Republican Party divisions that had opened up in 1880 grew wider at the convention in Chicago, when the elegant James G. Blaine, known as the "Plumed Knight," was finally rewarded for his long service in Congress and as secretary of state under Garfield and Arthur with nomination for president on the fourth ballot. Because of Blaine's record of trading the power of his offices for favors from business and his conservative policies, a group of liberal Republicans, calling themselves Mugwumps, broke off to hold their own convention and pledged their support to the Democratic nominee, Grover Cleveland, a reformer governor of New York. Although he was not a Mugwump, Henry Ward Beecher cast his lot with Cleveland because he deplored Blaine's attitude about labor unions and his reputation as a grafter. It was such a close contest that campaigning descended rapidly into character assassination. An incriminating letter Blaine had written to a friend named Fisher with the damning postscript "burn this letter" turned up and inspired a Democratic chant: "Burn this letter, burn this letter; Kind regards to Mrs. Fisher." Then, in midsummer, a rumor circulated that Cleveland had fathered an illegitimate child by a married woman. Much to his supporters' distress, Cleveland acknowledged the truth of this story and presented Republicans with their own chant: "Ma! Ma! Where's my pa? Gone to the White House Ha! Ha! Ha!" Toward the end of the campaign it became evident that the issue would turn on the vote in New York, where Blaine was believed to have an edge largely because of his popularity with the Irish and some remaining effect of the "bloody shirt." Although not established as an indisputable fact, there is good evidence that the views of two Protestant preachers may have determined the outcome. One was a Blaine supporter, Samuel Dickinson Burchard; the other was Henry Ward Beecher.

Burchard denounced the Democrats as "the party of rum, Romanism, and rebellion," and Blaine, experienced politician though he was, failed to denounce Burchard, with the result that both Catholics and presumably the saloon set were alienated. Instead of indulging in negative campaigning, Beecher spoke in defense of his candidate's character, much to the surprise and dismay of his friends and especially his wife, who feared that Henry Ward's support of an admitted adulterer would revive his own scandal. Speaking to a large crowd gathered at the Brooklyn Rink, Beecher first informed them that he was deserting the Republicans for their failure to act on issues such as reforming the civil service and acknowledging the rights of labor. Then he turned to the charges against Cleveland. Flourishing a paper in his hand, he began:

> My honored wife, unknown to me, cut from the newspapers certain passages with respect to the life of Grover Cleveland in Albany and sent them with a letter asking what truth there was in them? She received from Governor Cleveland a letter which I have had between two and three weeks which he meant to be private and marked private, but such a complexion has the canvass taken, that I telegraphed him and asked if I could use my

discretion in regard to that letter and he said "yes," and I will read Governor Cleveland's letter:

"Executive Mansion
Albany, Oct. 7, '84

"My dear Mrs. Beecher:

"Your letter as you may well suppose has affected me deeply. What shall I say to one who writes so like my Mother? . . .

"The contemptible creatures who coin and pass these things appear to think that the affair which I have not denied makes me defenseless against any and all slanders.

"As to my outward life in Buffalo the manifestation of confidence and attachment which was tendered to me there by the citizens must be proof that I have not lived a disgraceful life in that city. And as to my life in Albany all statements that tend to show that it has been other than laborious and perfectly correct are utterly and in every shade untrue.

"I do not wonder that your good husband is perplexed. I honestly think I desire his good opinion more than any aid he is disposed to give me.

"I don't want him to think any better of me than I deserve nor to be deceived. Cannot I manage to see him and tell him what I cannot write? . . .

"Having written this much it occurs to me that such a long letter is unnecessary and unexpected. It is the most I have written on the subject referred to and I beg you to forgive me if your kind and touching letter has led me into any impropriety.

Yours very sincerely,
Grover Cleveland."

Beecher had to wait for applause to die down before he was able to continue:

When in the gloomy night of my own suffering, I sounded every depth of sorrow, I vowed that if God would bring the day star of hope, I would never suffer brother, friend or neighbor to go unfriended should a like serpent seek to crush him. That oath I will regard now. Because I know the bitterness of venomous lies, I will stand against infamous lies that seek to sting to death an upright man and magistrate. Men counsel me to prudence lest I stir again my own griefs. No, I will not be prudent. If I refuse to interpose a shield of well-placed confidence between Grover Cleveland and the swarm of liars that nuzzle in the mud or sling arrows from ambush, may my tongue cleave to the roof of my mouth and my right hand forget its cunning.

Cleveland picked up just enough popular and electoral votes to become the first Democratic president in twenty-five years. Just a year later, in October 1885, when he delivered at Boston's Tremont Temple a eulogy on Ulysses S. Grant, who had died of cancer at age sixty-three in July, Beecher demonstrated again the compassion for the trials of others that may have been a blessing bestowed upon him by his own trials. Grant's funeral was a great event. While thousands lined the streets, five hundred celebrities led by President Cleveland and a military procession that included generals and troops from both sides of the Civil War followed the hearse from New York's City Hall, where the body had lain in state, to the tomb. Beecher's audience would have known of this and understood him as he said in part:

Another name is added to the roll of those whom the world will not willingly let die. A few years since storm-clouds filled his heaven, and obliquy, slander, and bitter lies rained down upon him.

The clouds are all blown away; under a serene sky he laid down his life, and the Nation wept. The path to his tomb is worn by the feet of innumerable pilgrims. The mildewed lips of Slander are silent, and even Criticism hesitates lest some incautious word should mar the history of the modest, gentle, magnanimous Warrior.

The whole nation watched his passage through humiliating misfortunes with unfeigned sympathy, the whole world sighed when his life ended. At his burial the unsworded hands of those whom he had fought lifted his bier and bore him to his tomb with love and reverence.

Grant made no claim to saintship. He was a man of like passions, and with as marked limitations as other men. Nothing could be more distasteful to his honest, modest soul while living, and nothing more unbecoming to his memory, than lying exaggerations and fulsome flatteries.

Men without faults are apt to be men without force. A round diamond has no brilliancy. Lights and shadows, hills and valleys, give beauty to the landscape. The faults of great and generous natures are often overripe goodness, or the shadows which their virtue cast.

In that fall of 1885, when Henry Ward Beecher was extolling the life and works of a veteran whose death seemed to symbolize for the whole nation an end to its most terrible conflict, another veteran nearer and dearer to the speaker was writing despairing letters from Winchendon, one of the mental institutions in which he kept finding himself. James Chaplin Beecher had been a general, too, and could have squeezed back into his old uniform to escort the body of his once commander in chief to its last resting place but for a baffling disorder of the mind that he could not comprehend or control. Back in 1881, James had come out of the woods to respond to a call from big brother Henry Ward to run a bethel that Plymouth Church was establishing in Brooklyn. Although life as the "hermit preacher" had been idyllic for James, it weighed on his conscience that he was not really doing a Beecher brother's share of the Lord's work, and the three young girls they were rearing needed decent schools and the stimulus of other children. It did not take much more than a year of dealing with the poor and wretched who sheltered in the bethel and with civilization generally before James began to have disabling bouts of disorienting depression, for which he sought help in various institutions, including that familiar refuge of Beechers, the Gleason water cure in Elmira. By 1885 he was more often away somewhere than at home, as his letters to Frankie from Winchendon reveal. The hand-writing differs so much from letter to letter that they appear to come from different people, as indeed they did in terms of his mental state.

In an early note he scrawled:

> But dont desert me my precious one. Believe me—believe me I am doing the best I can. I do try to keep up when before people. I can keep up when I can forget for a moment my burden of sorrow & pain. And so people do me fearful—cruel injustice—& blame me when if they only knew they would pity—and respect & help me. There are those here now who are doing everything to make me wretched who, if they knew the truth and knew me would do everything in their power to help—instead of harm—I could have been cured of disease long ago if that were all. But Ill write again as I wrote you before—if you knew—if you would believe—you could help but you dont believe. But living or dying my dearest & whatever suffering—I am yr true & loving husband—and it is not mere selfishness which makes me beg so to have you help me.

A little later, in a more controlled script, he wrote:

[Y]*ou must help me to come home.* I would come without your coming but you know the weakness from which I suffer. I wont reiterate the pain and agony—and misconception which I endure daily. I cannot endure it any longer. It makes me sick in body & heart and mind. I love you too dearly to be left of you alone when I am dying for want of a friend and worst of all is that it is the tenderness of your love which is killing me by inches. So come my dearest wife before it is too late . . . be true to the promise you made me many times that you would never let me be left helpless again.

Later still he wrote in a hand that supports his contention that

I am clear headed now. Dr. and Mrs. R are both kind now. I am very grateful to them, but I cannot endure that of which I have told you so often. If it were only my disease it could be cured by proper treatment. My precious—my beloved I wont reiterate— because it does no good. Only this, dont let man or devil—or appearances make you doubt even for one moment the tenderness & faith of my love for you and the dear children. I am sure I ought to be at Elmira this moment & yet it may possibly be too late. I am afraid of complete loss of self control. I cannot stand these agonies of mind and constant misdirections of judgment and other annoyances with which you are familiar though you will not believe they exist. . . . I want to write to Tom, but my hands seem tied fast. You write to him—tell him that excepting my wife only I love him better than anything in heaven or on earth, that I long for him with longing unutterable. Somehow I feel as though if he would take me by the hand I could walk and even hope. Send him this letter, wont you dearest.

In a reply in January 1886, Frankie declared that "I am sure we love each other all the better for the sorrows we share, as well as the years of joy we have had. Never doubt my heart & my love which is yours and yours only forever—in sickness & in health I am your true & devoted wife. . . . Our only trouble is that you are ill & weak. Oh, how I wish you could get the heart of trust & rest that a little child has in his mother. I am trying to have it, for faith is good to rest on. Do not think for a moment that I ever forget you a moment. . . . I shall write to the Dr. & ask what he thinks of your case now."

James did manage to get to Dr. Gleason's retreat in Elmira, but meeting people there who remembered and admired his sermons during his brief time in Tom's pulpit caused him more pain than pleasure. "You say stop thinking and Tom scolds about being unhappy," he wrote to Frankie. "I marvel that it seems to you both a light thing that in a years time I have lost the home I worked six years to make—have not a shelter I can call my own or a dollar except from charity—or a home I can live in or an employment I can set myself to—and yet every day tormenting me with some reminder of a time when I had home & friends—and work—and power both of body and mind." He ended that letter with "P.S. Remember my dearest, one thing. It is my chief pain that I show my worst side to you. It is because it is only to you that I talk of the past. I will stop it. . . . No, dont think of any other 'sanitarium.' Home is the only one. I will overcome selfishness and fear, both, by help of God & my wife."

Except for the references to Tom, there is no indication in James's letters that he had much, if any, contact with his other brothers and sisters. They were all getting older, older than he, and dealing with crises in their own lives that must have taxed their strength and sympathies. Living out his unlucky life with one of his children in Chicago, William fell mostly out of touch with his faraway siblings. Mary, living quietly at Nook Farm as always, had never been close to James, a child of another generation in her terms, and her relations with Frankie, who had ended her engagement to Mary's son Fred to pursue James, were awkward. Charles was in the midst of traumatic life changes for a man in his seventies—a move in 1884 from Florida back to Georgetown and then on to assume yet another pastorate to the Scotch-Irish community of Wysox, Pennsylvania. Henry Ward was back in England in 1886, dusting off the friendships he had made twenty-three years before and bringing with him an evolution-inspired religious message rather than a political one. In his absence, Edward, in his eighties, would doubtless have taken on some of the chores at Plymouth Church while tending his own flock. Regardless of the fences that she had been able to mend in Hartford, Isabella remained estranged from family members who, like James, had retained their faith in Henry Ward throughout his trials.

Harriet's hands and heart were simply too full to let her become deeply involved with James. Her Calvin had come down with Bright's disease, an incurable kidney condition, and was too feeble by 1884 to make the trip to their beloved Florida. Harriet sold everything but the orange grove and used the money to buy a house in Hartford for son Charlie, who had assumed a pastorate there. She was concerned about the deteriorating health of her daughter Georgiana, who had become addicted to the morphine that a doctor prescribed as treatment for the Beecher "blues" and the insomnia it caused. Ill or not, preacher's wife or no, Georgie was said to lead a fast life of too much wine and too many late parties when she moved to Boston with her husband. Harriet could not do much about that, since she and her spinster twin daughters were needed to nurse and keep company with Calvin, whose mind remained sharp until sunset of August 6, 1886, when he slipped away, murmuring, "Peace with God! Peace with God!"

Meanwhile, another sanitarium had been found for James, one of whose last letters must have been achingly hard for Frankie to take:

My beloved wife—You know how I have almost lost the faculty of writing . . . & . . . how I shrink from it. I wrote you . . . telling you how I grieved that I have been tampering with tobacco again and begging honestly your loving pardon for using it so offensively. You know I meant to have gone home with you. I had been longing, more than words can tell, for your coming. Why I let you go without me I cannot tell—any more than why the impulse came upon me to come up here in the first place. I cannot account for these.

I seem to be moved by a spirit other than my own. I have suffered beyond expression in all these days. I ought to be with you and at work. This inaction is unendurable and I know hurtful—I *will* write tonight before I try to sleep. I am trying and will try to exercise will power which seems almost obliterated. I want to go this moment but dread to start lest I shd get to vacillating as I have done before. I am as clear minded now as I ever was but what should I do when the cloud comes down and I am all adrift.

If even I could get to Hartford I think I could go alone from there—but I want some *will* that will guide me when my own fails. . . . I want a friend whom I can trust & lean on to go with me—I am mindful of you & your work every waking hour—I cannot endure this vacillation & inaction. It seems a sin & a shame but what can I do. Last night I could not have written this letter even if my life had depended upon it. Tomorrow I may be just so. But one thing my beloved wife, my every thought is homeward & every day a pain & almost agony except when for an hour or two I seem to be myself.

I *will* get home—I *will* break through the strange paralysis which has come upon me. I believe that it can be cured when some one will understand & treat it properly—God bless & help & strengthen you—You have been so patient—so enduring—so loving. Thank you for it—who are my heart & soul. YR Husband

Released in the early fall of 1886 in the custody of his nephew, Henry Ward's son Henry, James went to Elmira to visit Tom and the staff at the Gleason establishment. A group of men who were going to a private rifle range on the premises invited him along. Not surprisingly, a man who had learned to handle firearms as an officer on clipper ships and in the army and as an experienced hunter and who appeared to be in good shape at age fifty-eight outshot them all. After the contest, James joined the other men in a convivial dinner. When they were enjoying postprandial cigars and conversation on the veranda, James excused himself and went into the house. Minutes later the men outside heard a shot, ran in to investigate, and discovered that James had fatally shot himself through the mouth. Nobody in the Beecher clan would have to ask where James got the idea. As a sensitive teenager, he would have been horribly fascinated by the details of his much older brother George's suicide.

One of the first of the family to react was George's widow, Susan, in a letter to Frankie dated October 3, 1886:

> Words cannot express the deep sympathy I feel for you, such a sudden fearful death is so overwhelming as I know by sad experience. Though of more than forty years endurance, it seems as painful and real as of yesterday. The shock to the whole nature, physical, mental and moral, can never be overcome so long as life endures.
>
> In your case, my dear Frankie, the circumstances were peculiarly aggravating. Without doubt it is a blessed relief to James. At once to find rest, peace and perfect freedom from all fear and agony (unsupportable), a joyful entrance into the Heavenly Home, welcomed by father, mother, brothers and sisters. The very thought must in some degree give you consolation, you who are so unselfish, having so devoted your life and all to your husband for many years. But, all the same, your life must be desolate and in doing for others . . . must find consolation. . . . I had not heard of James illness until this summer when Sister Mary Perkins told George [Susan's son] in a general way without giving particulars and consequently I was overwhelmed with the news of his sudden death. Sister Bell has kindly sent me the account as written by Fred Beecher to his mother, also Julia in her kind and loving way has told me of four years of suffering and labor from you & dear Brother Tom have done all that could be done to alleviate and if possible mitigate the intense agony that James must have endured. I enclose a draft of $50 as a kind

remembrance and a small expression of the interest I feel for you my dear Frankie.

It fell to Edward as the oldest Beecher nearby to give out the news to the papers of the youngest Beecher's death. Ever mindful of the orthodox view of suicide, he stressed mental illness as the cause of an act for which the Reverend James Chaplin Beecher could not be held responsible.

The Beechers scarcely had time to make peace with James's tragic death before they were confronted with another unexpected and daunting loss. In the early months of 1887, Henry Ward was back from a refreshing trip to England, and he exuded his usual vitality as he threw himself into the busy schedule of Plymouth Church and took up the long-postponed writing of the life of Christ. He told friends and family that he was blessed with a new vision of the subject so grand that "twenty men could not in a life-time write all that I now see; how can I put it into one book?" He did not try. He decided on a two-volume work and was already on the twenty-fifth chapter with only three more to go in late February when an English minister of his acquaintance dropped by and inquired as to when the work would be finished. Henry Ward estimated a time of two or three months. After the man left, Henry Ward, kneeling in his armchair and staring out the window to watch his friend go, mused aloud: "Finish the Life of Christ! Finish the Life of Christ! *Who can* finish the Life of Christ! It cannot be finished."

In keeping with his vivid picture of the man he would succeed in the Plymouth pulpit was Lyman Abbott's account of events during the next few days:

Sunday evening, February 27, 1887, was the last service Mr. Beecher ever attended in Plymouth Church. It was remembered afterwards that he lingered for a few moments at the close of the service listening to the choir as they practiced a new musical setting by . . . the organist of the church to Faber's "Hark, hark, my soul, angelic songs are swelling," and that as he started to go out he remarked, "That will do to die on." "Will it not do to live on, Mr. Beecher?" asked a friend at his side. "That is the way to die," he said quickly. As he passed out, he saw standing by the furnace register, to warm themselves, a little girl about ten years old and her brother, only five years old, who had for some weeks been in the habit of going alone to church on Sunday evenings. Putting a hand on the little boy's head, he stooped and kissed him, saying, "It is a cold night for such little tots to be out.". . .

Interestingly—perhaps significantly—the two most famous of the Beecher women chose in the last years of their lives to pose for photographs with an image of their most famous brother, Henry Ward Beecher, prominent in the background.

The relationship between Isabella Beecher Hooker and her half brother, Henry Ward, was a stormy one. Because she expressed doubts about his innocence when he was charged with adultery, she was shunned for years by other family members, and yet, as a devout spiritualist, she claimed that her brother's spirit inspired her after his death when she was giving speeches for women's rights. Here she sits beneath a bust of Henry Ward.

For Harriet Beecher Stowe, her slightly younger blood brother could do no wrong. The feeling was mutual, and they went through life almost literally hand in hand.

On Wednesday evening, March 2, after a full day of shopping with his wife, for some refurnishing of the parlors of the church and a short evening of recreation with the family, he retired earlier than usual, and when a little later Mrs. Beecher went upstairs she found him already apparently sleeping. Early the next morning she was awakened from her sleep by an unusual sound in her husband's room, ran to his side, and found him suffering from nausea. To her inquiry into the matter, he replied, "Nothing but a sick headache," and dropped almost instantly to sleep again. He slept through the following day. Not until four o'clock in the afternoon was the physician sent for. An effort was made to arouse Mr. Beecher from his sleep; the response was brief and broken; and the doctor's conclusion soon reached: Mr. Beecher was dying of apoplexy. The end came on Tuesday morning, the 8th of March, 1887.

If his death had been unanticipated at that time, the manner of it had long been predicted—and wished for—by Henry Ward himself, struck down in full flight by apoplexy. And there was no question in the minds of family members as to how he had wanted his death to be greeted. He had preached—nearly ranted—about it often enough, as in this passage:

The scholastic conceptions of dying and death are unworthy of reason, unworthy of conscience, and are blasphemous to God and to His government. They have no foundation in the New Testament, none certainly in the Old, and they ought to be purged out of our imaginations. Yet it lingers with us, and when death has come the household has not one note of triumph, not one star shines through the grief, not one door of flashing light is opened. We cover the pictures, we shut up the instruments of music, we close the windows and shut out the light, we have a black hearse with plumes plucked from the wings of midnight, and we send for our minister, who doles out lugubrious, mournful themes, and we sing awful hymns. And then because one's child has gained the coronation of glory, and is in the arms of Jesus, and rests from all labor and trial and temptation, we put on black—black over the head, black around the neck, black down to the feet, black inside! We carry the habiliments of woe and darkness and gloom, and think that we can see death everywhere. No other thing is as this. The one thing that men carry everywhere with them, and they are bound to share alike with brothers, strangers, friends, is that one thing that is borrowed from the despotism and cruelty of heathenism. Not one joy, not one thanksgiving, not one gleam of faith and hope, not one promise of Jesus Christ, not one single second of immortality and glory, is permitted to cheer the soul. All is night, black night, hopeless night. Sinful, the whole of it, unchristian, ungrateful! . . . When I fall, and am buried in Greenwood, let no man dare to stand over the turf and say, "Here lies Henry Ward Beecher," for God knows that I will not lie there. Look up; if you love me, and if you feel that I have helped you on your way home, stand with your feet on my turf and look up; for I will not hear anybody that does not speak with his mouth toward heaven.

The door of the Beecher home was not draped with black but adorned with a wreath of pink and white roses under a white bow. Lying in state and silent by the pulpit from which he had so often spoken, his body was nearly buried in a colorful field of the flowers he had loved in life. There were several services—a private one at home on Thursday, a public one in Plymouth Church on Saturday, with simultaneous ones in other Brooklyn churches before the burial, and a Sunday morning memorial, again at Plymouth Church, at which representatives of every creed, including Jews and Roman Catholics, took part. At Henry Ward's own request, the Reverend Dr. Charles H. Hall, pastor of Holy Trinity Church, presided at the first two services. He was chosen because of an unforgettable act of friendship. In the dark days when Beecher's innocence was in doubt in so many minds and his presence unwanted in so many sanctuaries, Dr. Hall spotted him in the audience during a service at Holy Trinity, walked down the aisle, took him by the hand, and led him up to sit beside him.

The only shadow to fall across what Harriet would call "Henry's exaltation" was Isabella Hooker's arrival on the scene. Among the visions that had come to her in her séances was one of Henry Ward asking her forgiveness and telling her that she had been right all along. In the few days that he lay dying, Isabella rushed to Brooklyn to see whether she could realize her vision but was turned away at the door by Eunice. Reporters were holding a celebrity death watch on the sidewalk outside the Beecher home, and Isabella walked among them, spilling out her bitterness. Veterans of the "Plymouth Company" that Beecher had helped to raise and arm during the war provided a kind of honor guard at the home and at the church, and they were instructed to keep an eye on Mrs. Hooker to see that she made no trouble when she attached herself to the end of a line of an estimated fifty thousand mourners filing by the bier. Although she got a last look at her brother's silent face, Isabella was not permitted to attend the Saturday services. Her blood brother Tom was at the services but, true to his reputation for eccentricity, would not go along to the burial. It is quite probable that Tom agreed with Henry Ward's assertion that "I will not lie there."

Up in the Nook Farm area of Hartford, Isabella's behavior reopened old wounds. Some, like the Reverend Mr. Joseph Twitchell and his wife, who had examined the evidence during Henry Ward's trial and found Isabella's charges wanting, would have nothing to do with her socially. In a sermon on March 13, he expressed his attitude about the scandal by saying that "on the day he became the subject of such a joy and such a sorrow as has been seldom witnessed in our communities—the day when the glad exultant cry went up from all the ranks and haunts of iniquity that he had fallen—and that into a depth of baseness and falseness that was unfathomable, while on the other side, among the hundred of thousands who had loved and honored him and whose years he had comforted and strengthened, there was equal distress of consternation and grief—I found it practicable in the face of all plausibilities that told against him to keep my faith in him—as I did—and I have an abiding confidence that as time passes and distance more and more reveals the proportions of his greatness and the nature and magnitude and lasting beneficent consequence of the work he wrought (he is too near now to be measured in his full stature and little men can pick at him) whatever mists cloud his name will dissolve, his integrity will be accepted in the judgment of men, and he will be recognized and felt to have been in his whole life a true-hearted and mighty servant of God and of Christ, all because he was a mighty believer in God and Christ."

Not a churchgoer by desire or habit despite his friendship with Twitchell, Mark Twain could not help reading the sermon as published in the paper the next day and wrote to Twitchell: "It is a noble sermon, & I am glad I did not hear it. The mere reading it moved me more than I like to be moved—or, rather, *would* like to be moved in public. It is great & fine, and worthy of its majestic subject. You struck twelve. What a pity—that so insignificant a matter as the chastity or unchastity of an Elizabeth Tilton could clip the locks of this Samson & make him as other men, in the estimation of a nation of Lilliputians creeping and climbing about his shoe soles."

Later in that year of 1887, there would be an uncelebrated death in Boston when the once spritely Georgiana Stowe Allen yielded to the ravages of her illness and addiction at age forty-four. It is no wonder that her mother, Harriet Beecher Stowe, was moved to sit down and inform her brother Edward that "my trunk is packed to go home."

11

"In the flickering light of the dying embers"

WHEN ISABELLA BEECHER HOOKER, turned silver-haired and regally hand-some in her seventies, stood before a large gathering at the 1896 World's Congress of Religions to read quotations that she had chosen from all of the major faiths and blended into a universal creed, the last of Lyman Beecher's children to shine in the public eye was calling into question not only her inherited Calvinism but also the claims of orthodox Chris-tianity itself. In doing so, she was not in any sense giving up on the self-assigned task of saving the world that she shared with all of her siblings. Although once called mad by her half brother Henry Ward and the cra-ziest of them all by blood brother James, Isabella clearly thought of her-self as the most spiritual of the Beechers in the light of her letters and diaries. Instead of forgetting about the spiritualism that she had grafted onto the trunk of Christianity when her anticipated elevation to ruler of the world failed to come about on that embarrassing New Year's Eve of 1876, Isabella used spiritualism to overcome the deaths and disappoint-ments of the next decade and to sustain her drive to realize the reform that had so far resisted all Beecher efforts—to bring about women's suffrage.

At a time when deaths all around seemed to be draining the heart of Harriet Beecher Stowe, the most famous and successful of the Beecher sisters, one death, in 1886, energized the much younger Isabella. Her old-est child from whom she had been estranged in part by her spiritualist visions, Mary Hooker Burton, died of consumption. Isabella, who always was a hypochondriac and fastidious about physical contact with her chil-dren, was filled with remorse that she could not bring herself to hug her

335

dying daughter. After Mary's death, the Hookers set aside a place in the house as a kind of altar where Isabella and John, by then a convert to spiritualism, would converse with their departed daughter. Apparently relieved and forgiven by what she heard, Isabella launched herself once more into political activity and took pains to stay closer to her surviving daughter, Alice Hooker Day, as revealed in letters that she wrote to Alice.

February 5, 1889:

I wrote you a hasty line from Washtn my dear daughter and now am in the dear old room once more, facing the dear picture [of Mary] while I write. I find when I am away I think of that as my precious daughter and it takes the place of the sweet but pale and sometimes sorrowful face that always has come to me, lying on her little bed . . . patiently waiting to be translated. And it is a great comfort, I saw so little of Mary when she was well, and always that heavy cloud of separation from Kate [Mary's daughter], that I cannot recall any sweet expression of face except perhaps at the little lunches I gave in the dining room here after we began housekeeping once more. I remember how she enjoyed my broiled chicken from the poultry yard—and can see her face light up with some witty remark that was just on the way. I am so glad now I had those little gatherings—though I little dreamed that they would be the last. Sometime now I seem to catch the same peculiar turn of head and quiet smile as she talks with friends on the other side as I feel sure she does, in a genial happy way . . . mother love is such a tremendous thing. I doubt if there is anything like it in the heavens above or the earth beneath or the waters under the earth—and I do hope that some day it may find its own and be satisfied—if not there never will be any heaven for me. . . .

I tell you Alice the day is not far off when we can begin to work for our country and leave behind us all this terrible conflict for our right to work. And it will be none too soon—Olympia Brown [a national suffragette leader] has been studying the census and finds that so large a proportion of *foreign* population are men, (the women are coming in small numbers comparatively) and so large of native pop. are now women, (the war having killed so many men) the result is that in many States, the foreigner has two votes to the native American's one. It was startling to the Judiciary Comm. of the House when she made the same assertion and showed the figures. They asked her to pursue her investigation and send the paper to the Comm. And she finds the matter confirmed at every step . . . the native *women* enfranchised will put foreign and native *men* on equal footing as nothing else can. There are other most cheering indications but I have no time to enlarge. . . .

I send you some hair that you can put in a locket for your bracelet or neck and there is nothing like the life there is in hair you know—and I have saved a great deal of that and used it to grace her [Mary's] beautiful head. When the sun shines through the curls in her picture it makes a veritable halo such as no painter has yet given to his saint—you will be surprised and comforted when you see it.

May 17, 1889:

Dear Daughter—Much as I love you and enjoy your letters I can hardly bring myself to writing you on this last day for mailing, because I am so absorbed in our work. I will enclose your father's Circular to the members of the [Connecticut] Legislature—so you will understand about the two bills yet to be voted on and I will tell you a little about the vote this week on striking out the word *male* from the Constitution 44 in favor, 90 against—but already the ayes are coming to us and saying "we are of the 44"— and they bring us the reprobates to be converted. The speeches of the opposition were so weak and silly that even Maj. Kinney said to a friend, "if I had to vote according to the *arguments* made today there is but one way I could vote." The [Hartford] Courant has been bitter and vigilant all the way—and is now complacent and rejoicing. But it looks as if some of the noes are ashamed of their advocates and many are willing the women should vote on school matters so we may carry the School Bill and possibly the Temperance Bill—tho' the great fight now a days is from the liquor dealers. In our hearing before the Committee on Constitutional Amendmts—which had charge of this Bill on striking out male six were strongly in favor and only two against—and of these two one was a young man who did not attend either of our hearings, and the other an *Irish saloon keeper*—but even he was so much impressed that he listened to me with his mouth wide open and in the public debate last Tuesday said that Mrs. Hooker was fit to be President of the U.S. but that she was an exception. . . .

I have been to Litchfield, Winsted and South Manchester . . . and formed Clubs at each place for the study of political science and . . . I mean to have such a Club in every town in this State in the course of the year—then in parlor meetings women will be reading and talking about the same things and getting ready to manage town affairs as they should be managed. My first and chief proposition is that if the towns and villages are well cared for in sanitary matters, in schools, in jails and poor houses, in temperance regulations and in police then the State is safe—and the States being well regulated the republic is safe and can never be brought low, as other republics have been. But masculine wisdom and patriotism cannot be depended on to protect and educate even a village community as experience has shown—so we must compel women to bear their share of burden and responsibility. At Litchfield lately, a young teacher on her way from school through some woods, was seized by a young man of respectable family and violated twice in same afternoon—being nearly choked to death—so much for our protectors!

Nook Farm all well—Clemens deeply interested in W. Stuff. Thinks it more important than anything else for the good of the country and race he tells Lilly—but whether he will give me the $100 I need remains to be seen. We have given $150 already—and all my time and strength and much of your father's.

February 18, 1890:

My dear daughter, I came from Washtn on Monday and was so exhausted by mental strain day and night that I slept in the cars much of the time and so took cold—but Ned [her doctor son] has helped me out of the sore throat and gradually I shall get back to life again. . . . I was better in Washington—but the personal consultations, Committee work, and Convention of four days, all coming after the Susan Anthony banquet which lasted till two o'clock, were enough to disable the strongest, so I am rather triumphant than otherwise and feel sure that with the help so constantly and manifestly given me from the spirit world I shall live to do much more work and see its results.

I spoke half an hour Monday evening, without an idea in my head to begin with—I mean I was too tired from the banquet and from Sunday's consultations which lasted long past midnight to think out any plan—so gave myself up to the inspiration of the moment. The result was most gratifying—very many said "it was most refreshing—not a set speech, but so many points, never to be forgotten and such with humor! etc"—To tell the truth, as nearly as I could recall the scene it seems as if brother Henry [with whose spirit she claimed to be in contact] had it all his own way—one gesture I remember especially and the house was convulsed with laughter and moved to tears alternately. He has entreated me many times to give myself up to his control—but I have not been quite ready to trust him to speak for a woman's soul—possibly he saw his opportunity and used it so well I shall never be afraid of him again.

But my daughter—I am more than ever impressed with the superior mental and moral power of womankind. In all those four days there was not a weak word uttered from young or old and every phase of patriotism and statesmanship was clearly manifest. No body of men that ever came together for righteous purposes I verily believe showed as much common sense and uttered it in such elegant language—yet scarce a woman there has had a liberal education and most of us have gathered our wisdom and knowledge while caring for our children in the family or teaching other peoples children in the schools. Oh I am proud of my sex— I am so glad men have had to have mothers as well as fathers. Though you wouldn't suspect it from history or current literature.

By passing along messages from departed family members—Catharine, for instance, as well as Henry Ward was a frequent visitor to the Hooker home—Isabella tried to convert her living siblings, with little success. Charles, the most mystical in his own thinking and once the closest to Isabella, was so intrigued by the phenomenon of spiritualism that he wrote a book about it—*Spiritual Manifestations.* He believed in the existence of spirits and tried to relate them to Christianity as he understood it, but he warned Isabella that they could be *"of the devil."* Tom shared that feeling, and he told his congregation that, after studying spiritualism for twenty years, "the whole habit of my mind has changed in this regard. Instead of being surprised to hear that there are spiritual manifestations abounding throughout the land, I am daily more and more surprised and grateful that as yet I have been able to keep them out of my own house and out of my own body. . . . There is very little doubt in my mind that the clamor and confusion and strife of opinion of these days are to be attributed largely to spiritual influences."

Tom remained concerned about the more tangible realities of life that he saw so clearly. A typical sermon was one he titled "Beware of the Bargains of Life," and he made his point with an illustration from his own experience rather than the Bible. Walking down Elmira's East Hill on a summer afternoon he passed a boy selling lemonade at three cents a glass, fished the coins out of his pocket, and got what went down as a refreshing drink in exchange. Farther along he spotted a competing lemonade stand and felt obliged to be evenhanded with his largesse. Holding out another three cents, he asked for a glass and was told, "It's five cents, here, mister." Tom asked, "How do you expect to compete with your rival up the hill who is selling his for three cents?" The unexpected reply was the substance of the sermon: "Oh, but a puppy fell into his!" Tom was never a man to preach do-as-I-say instead of do-as-I-do. Since early in the century, temperance had been a continuing cause for the Beechers, as attested to by Isabella's letters. But temperance did not mean abstinence for most of them. This was especially true of Pastor Tom, who not only lifted a glass in public but also discussed the finer points of making beer, wine (one of his hobbies), and "ardent spirits" in a column he wrote for the local newspaper. He got a kick out of once informing a friend that "there's a temperance revival here. And there's ale in my cellar." But in 1886 and at age sixty-one, he surprised his congregation with a sermon titled "Prohibition," in which he said that long years of firsthand experience with alcohol had convinced him that the number of people who could use it in moderation and beneficially were so few compared to the many for whom it was injurious that the time had come to replace futile attempts at regulation with absolute prohibition. Although he was convinced that his own use of alcohol was doing him good, he had given it up himself and was "ready to stand forward with my fellow-citizens of agreeing mind and temper, and demand that this public enemy shall be declared contraband in time of peace, and beyond the pale of protection."

Tom's sad experiences with his sister-in-law Annie and nephew Fred Stowe would certainly have influenced his thinking about the uses of alcohol, and their ghosts gave Harriet a sympathetic interest in Isabella's spiritualism. Although she never became a convert and participant in séances like the Hookers, Harriet had been understanding and accepting when Calvin talked of the strange creatures from another world who had visited him in childhood and stayed with him in memory through the rest of his life. She had experienced a number of inexplicable dreams and visions herself, not excepting God's gift to her of Uncle Tom. When Annie was in deepest trouble, she reached out to Harriet for help in a dream, but Harriet had been either unwilling or unable to respond. In the 1880s it remained as unfinished business in Harriet's mind along with the disappearance of her son Fred, which could account for a note she wrote to Isabella: "I wish dear sister you would do me one other favor. Copy and send to me the supposed communication from my poor Fred—also poor Annie. Mr. Stowe wants to see them and I want to see them again. I committed Fred to my Savior, who knows all—who lives to save and goeth after that which is lost until *he find it*."

It may be significant that Harriet did not seek messages from Calvin after he died in 1886, judging by available reports. She showed the same confidence in his happiness in the heavenly kingdom as she had in his preaching when she slept through his sermon in Florida. But almost from the time of Calvin's death, Harriet's mind began to give way, alternating between looking forward to her own death and slipping backward into a second childhood. With the help of son Charles she did manage to finish her autobiography—a bland collection of memoranda—that was neither a critical nor a commercial success when it was published in 1889. Thereafter she only sporadically recalled that she had ever been any kind of a writer, let alone one of the most notable of her times, and seemingly lost interest in, or awareness of, public affairs, about which she had once been so passionate. Except in the most inclement weather, she would wander around the safe environs of Nook Farm, plucking flowers, playing with children wherever she found them, acting as sidewalk superintendent at a site of new construction, dropping in on neighbors unannounced.

As her closest neighbors, the Mark Twains bore the brunt of visitations by the new Harriet. For the most part they welcomed her. Recording in her diary an incident when Harriet spied her sitting on their Ombra, as the Twains called their large porch, and brought a gift of flowers, Livy wrote that "Mrs. Stowe is so gentle and lovely." Even though it was a somewhat pathetic witness to her state of mind, Mark appreciated Harriet's reaction to his *The Prince and the Pauper*. Stopping him on the street one day, she told him, "I am reading your Prince and Pauper for the fourth time, and I *know* it is the best book for young folks ever written"; only weeks later she spotted Twain on the Ombra and came up to tell him that she had just finished her sixth reading. Mark was not quite as appreciative of some of Harriet's antics, such as raiding his greenhouse for blooms, ignoring the scissors hung by the door for that purpose and plucking them off with her fingers, or sneaking up behind a person to "fetch a war whoop that would jump that person out of his clothes." On those occasions, he blamed Harriet's twins, whom he labeled "Soft Soap" and "Hell-fire" in his notes, for failing to keep an eye on their mother. In a pathetic instance of Harriet's derangement, she saw what should have been a familiar neighbor on Forest Street walking by, ran out, and flung herself on him, crying, "Fred! Fred!"

Not content with the popularity and brisk sales of his works, Mark Twain tried to get in on the wealth of the gilded age by investing in various business propositions, all of which proved disastrous and prompted him by 1891 to close up his expensive Nook Farm residence and take the family to Europe, where he hoped the dollars he did have would go further. What with Harriet's decline, Mark's departure was the beginning of the end of the community's reputation as a remarkable cultural colony. But if the empty house beside hers would be a sad reminder of better times for Harriet, it would suggest an open place at the top of Nook Farm's social hierarchy for Isabella and John Hooker. The year of the Twains' departure was the year of the Hookers' fiftieth wedding anniversary, and their celebration of that date prompted the kind of full description in Hartford newspapers that constituted an acknowledgment of the high standing they had reclaimed. The *Courant* of August 6 reported:

> The Hooker golden wedding reception, which took place yesterday afternoon and evening at the City Mission rooms on Pearl Street, was unique and one of the most noteworthy social gatherings which ever occurred in Hartford. Seldom has a more distinguished company of people been brought together in this city, and in addition to this the whole occasion was marked by a cordiality, spontaneous good-fellowship, and unconventionality which made it enjoyable and significant. . . . Down stairs, Wright Hall was used for a supper room, two long tables being spread with sandwiches, cake, fruit, ice cream, and coffee, and the entrance hall was prettily fitted up, as was the business office. Ascending the steps, the large reception hall was given up to the inflowing guests. At the farther end of this spacious room, Mr. and Mrs. Hooker sat on a dais over which evergreens were tastefully draped, while the dates 1841–1891 were prettily worked below the greenery in rustic lettering. Mrs. Hooker wore a dress of silver-gray silk, with point lace overlaid with gold, the gown having been made for her silver wedding, and her queenly and beautiful appearance was subject of common remark throughout the reception. Beside Mr. Hooker sat the venerable Dr. Edward Beecher, and his wife occupied a similar position with regard to

Mrs. Hooker. The walls were gracefully hung with golden-rod, nasturtiums and black-eyed susans and other blooms.

Shortly after 3 o'clock the invited guests began to arrive, and by 4 a large number of people were distributed among the various rooms and halls. The number steadily increased up to 6 o'clock when there was a thinning out, the nearer family friends, however, and the relatives remaining. At about half-past 5 Mrs. Virginia T. Smith, in behalf of the Equal Rights Club of Hartford, made a speech, presenting a bride's loaf covered with fifty shining gold dollars. This cake was afterwards cut up into small pieces and placed in envelopes, which were for the asking for all who wished this souvenir of the occasion. Mrs. Hooker rose and responded . . . and she was followed by Mr. Hooker, who made a characteristically witty speech. . . . A cordial invitation was extended by the Hookers to all who could to remain through the supper hour and listen to some quartette singing. . . . After supper . . . the numbers began to swell and from 8 to 9 the rooms were crowded with a brilliant assemblage composed of Hartford's leading citizens, and of many from abroad known throughout the land. Shortly before 9 o'clock General Hawley addressed the company, saying that the reception would close by the united singing of hymns printed on cards which were handed to one and all, and by remarks and a prayer by Dr. Edward Beecher.

Among the guests named by the *Courant* the only other Beechers were the Reverend Thomas K. Beecher, the Reverend Charles E. Stowe, and "the Misses Stowe." With her celebrity status, Harriet would have made that list had she been able to come. William had died in Chicago two years before, unattended by siblings. Both Mary and Charles and, of course, Henry Ward's Eunice were still shying away from socializing with Isabella, who had never joined them in proclaiming Henry Ward's innocence. In view of his own strong faith in Henry Ward, Edward's prominent part in the Hooker celebration might have baffled anyone not aware of the fact that he and his wife, Isabella, who had been a Porter and related to Isabella Hooker's mother, had lately been joining the Hookers in their séances. It was something of a leap for Edward, who had once pronounced spiritualism evil, but, as with Charles, his belief in preexistence made it hard to deny the existence of spirits who just might be good as well as bad. Edward was a crusty old survivor. As noted in the news accounts of the Hooker party, he had fallen under a train in 1889 on the way home from a meeting at the church he was pastoring and lost a leg. Thanks to the body he had built in those years of performing gymnastics and shifting sand with father Lyman, Edward had the strength and stamina to get around on an artificial leg with the help of a cane. As he had accepted the deaths of nine of his eleven children, Edward accepted his own injury as a test of faith and compared notes on this with Charles, who was losing his hearing, an even crueler fate for a sometime musician than the loss of a leg. But Edward's Isabella was not as indestructible as he, and when she was diagnosed with incurable cancer, Edward used his new spiritualist connection to hire "an educated clairvoyant who has brought wonderful results in desperate cases"—Voice Adams, a young woman whom the Edward Beechers first employed and finally adopted to care for them, since she could also soothe Isabella's pain with her nursing and lift Edward's spirits with nightly hymn singing and mandolin playing. Charles, whose near worship of Edward inspired him to work on an unpublished biography of his brother, and his wife, Sarah, were disturbed by this turn to spiritualism and advised Edward's son that they had "grieved ourselves ill over the strange change in your parents, but 'tis a temporary hallucination. When the soul lets down the bars of the spirit world without placing the Holy Spirit to keep watch and ward—lying spirits in the body or out can forge the name of loved ones—for instance Uncle Henry (who sends wonderful letters which your dear mother accepts as genuine)."

Aside from family members at the Hooker party, the reporters spotted nationally famous suffragettes, including the esteemed Susan B. Anthony, and fellow members of the Board of Lady Managers of the World's Columbian Exposition, to which Isabella had been appointed as Connecticut representative. The exposition, another name for a world's fair, was scheduled to be held in Chicago in 1892 to mark the four-hundredth anniversary of Columbus's discovery of America, but it would not open officially until the spring of 1893 when Grover Cleveland, beginning a second term as the only Democrat to occupy the White House since before the Civil War, cut the ribbon. Isabella's participation in years of planning the exposition's programs and erecting 150 buildings to house them brought her back onto the national stage, where she was credited with star quality. The *Chicago Herald* praised her "drollery, her picturesqueness, her very faults," which made of the woman's board "an Isabella society." Although Isabella seethed inwardly and confided to herself that "my soul is indignant and I keep wondering how a gentleman can look me in the face and declare that he was born to rule and I to obey—he a sovereign, I a subject, from the cradle to the grave," she had the wit to present a public image of grace and humor. She endeared herself to the Chicago reporter with a typical comment: "I want the Fair gates opened early on Sunday and let everybody in, but I want somebody else to get up to open them."

In her arguments for women's right to vote, Isabella was consistent and coolly logical. She kept ringing variations on the same theme, which she sounded most compellingly in an address titled "the Constitutional Right of the Women of the United States" and delivered to the International Council of Women. In essence she argued that there was no need for new legislation to establish that right, since it was already inherent in the Constitution. In most instances that document does not use the words "man" or "woman" but the word "people," as in the preamble, which begins: "We, the people of the United States, in order to form a more perfect Union. . . ." Therefore Isabella claimed that "women are included in this word 'people' of the preamble, and were intended to be included as much as men, and that their nonuse of the ballot in the past, because they chose to exercise their people's powers in other ways, has not cut them off from their right to use the ballot at any time they may see fit, and you will perceive by a careful examination of the whole constitution which follows the preamble, and which became the law of the land so early as 1789, that women were embraced in its provisions precisely as men were, and that the word 'people' so frequently used, always included them."

Isabella went through the Constitution article by article to nail down her point. Even where the word "man" or "men" is used in legal language, it is used by custom and generally understood to mean all human beings. To argue otherwise was absurd in Isabella's view. "As well may theologians interpret 'Whatsoever ye would that men should do unto you, do ye even so to them,' to mean literally men and therefore demand a new Scripture specially to include women in these and like injunctions: 'He that believeth shall be saved, and he that believeth not shall be condemned,' 'No man can serve two masters,' 'A good man out of the good treasure of his heart bringeth forth good things,' etc. No, friends, the truth is, precedent and prejudice, custom and blind conservatism, are the only barriers against women in government to-day. Constitutions are all right when properly interpreted and shorn of their man-made inconsistencies, and the laws are right save the voting laws. Every other law recognizes woman by the use of the masculine pronoun, compels her to pay taxes, to be fined, imprisoned and hung as he, his and him, and it is simply absurd and wicked to tax and hang a woman by one statute and deny her right to vote by another, when the phraseology is precisely the same in both."

Isabella could sometimes employ emotion more effectively than logic to move her audiences, as Henry Ward so often did, which may account for her thought that his spirit was speaking through her. Her remarks on those occasions often went unrecorded, as in one of her appearances at the annual meeting of the National Suffrage Association. When she began to read from the manuscript of a carefully crafted speech, her voice was nearly inaudible, and cries of complaint were heard. Susan Anthony, presiding, asked the gathering to be quiet and just enjoy the silvery presence of their handsome speaker, who made "a picture to delight an artist." Isabella would have none of that. She told the audience that she was delivering a written speech only because Miss Anthony had insisted on it and then took off on an extempore address that brought the gathering to their feet, applauding. Deeply affected herself, Susan Anthony hugged Isabella and turned to the crowd: "To think that such a woman belonging by birth and marriage to the most distinguished families in our country's history, should be held subject and have set over her all classes of men, with the prospect of there being added to her rulers the Cubans and the Sandwich Island Kanakas. Shame on a government that permits such an outrage!"

Unfortunately for the sake of her cause, Isabella was usually preaching to the converted, as in this case, but she did take every opportunity she was given to deliver her message to the doubters among the other sex, such as the Irish saloonkeeper in Connecticut. With respect to public affairs, Isabella was exhibiting a form of her monomania throughout the last decades of her life by concentrating so exclusively on suffrage while the nation was undergoing so many rapid changes in nearly every aspect of its development. As foreseen by brothers Henry Ward and Tom, the inescapable social problems of the world's most advanced experiment in unbridled capitalism intensified. When the bloody Homestead strike of 1892 led the news, Isabella revealed a sentiment she shared with her siblings in a recorded comment: "Only think of Carnegie with 30-odd millions grudging his faithful workmen the trifle that would help them to lay a mite by for a rainy day, and preparing hot steam and rifles to protect his works." But other than the way in which it further unbalanced the power of disenfranchised women, the nation's pursuit of its manifest destiny across the continent and abroad through war seemed to bypass Nook Farm. Nor is there any recorded reaction of any of Lyman Beecher's remaining children to the wonders that the experiment in capitalism was producing, such as turning night into day through the spread of electrification and liberating individuals from the slow pace of foot and horse by harnessing the power of oil. Few who knew the family well would disagree with the statement of another famous divine of the time, Theodore Parker, who called Lyman Beecher "the father of more brains than any man in America." But as their turbulent century drew to a close, the merciful God in whom they believed began loosening the grip of those brains on earthly matters.

Although his strength and energy kept him on his feet literally, Edward's mental acuity began to dull gradually but certainly after his commanding appearance at the Hooker anniversary celebration. He was no longer up to serving a church or writing another book, and would wander around in frustration that he could not find anything useful to do. He began losing track of time and, as his wife reported, "He thinks every day is Sunday. He wonders why we do not go to church." He was ninety-one years old when his physical strength gave out in 1895, and his death, like all Beecher deaths, was looked on as an ascent to the heaven he preached. Tom came from Elmira to give the eulogy at the funeral service. With an admiring Charles presumably still available to do the honors, Tom's presence in the pulpit must have been a surprise to Beecher watchers. It was Tom, after all, who had almost been driven from the faith by the theories that Edward had hoped would enshrine him as a theological Copernicus. Perhaps the biography that Charles, who agreed with Edward's theology, had written was thought to be tribute enough, or perhaps Charles was too emotionally involved with Edward to perform the service. In any event, Tom steered clear of theology, as he always did, and stressed the holy life that his brother had led, but he could not resist pointing out the likelihood that Edward's departure from the scene would not hold back mankind's ongoing search for spiritual truth, since "an avalanche does not stop for a tiny grave stone."

If they had bothered to tell her about it at all, Harriet would not have been able to comprehend the passing of her "earliest religious teacher." By then Harriet was living so completely in another world—and very happily, by all appearances—that the family had engaged a sturdy Irish woman to keep watch over her during every waking moment so that she would not be lost or injured during her rambles. One of Harriet's great pleasures was to escape this watchdog, and she was cunning enough to do it frequently. In 1893 she had experienced her last extended periods of lucidity. In the letters she wrote, she displayed a flash of her old way with words as well as an unsuspected degree of self-awareness. One of these went to eighty-four-year-old Oliver Wendell Holmes:

> My mental condition might be called nomadic. . . . I wander at will from one subject to another. In pleasant summer weather I am out of doors most of my time, rambling about the neighborhood, calling upon my friends. . . . Now and then I dip into a

book much as a humming-bird, poised in air on whirring wing, darts into the heart of a flower, now here, now there, and away. Pictures delight me and afford me infinite diversion. . . . Of *music* I am also very fond. I could not have too much of it, and I never *do* have as much of it as I should like. I make no mental effort of any sort, my brain is tired out. It was a woman's brain and not a man's, and finally from sheer fatigue and exhaustion in the march and strife of life it gave out before the end was reached. And now I rest me, like a moored boat, rising and falling on the water with loosened cordage and flapping sail.

The other letter went to her friend Mrs. Howard in Brooklyn, the same friend to whom she first revealed her feeling that God was the real author of *Uncle Tom's Cabin:*

"My sun has set. The time of work for me is over. I have written all my words and thought all my thoughts, and now I rest me in the flickering light of the dying embers, in a rest so profound that the voice of an old friend arouses me but momentarily and I drop back again into repose."

Harriet's tired body was finally released to follow her mind on July 1, 1896, as the Irish guardian she could no longer escape sat by her bedside. Although most of the people who knew her and her work had long gone before her, her funeral was still an event, best described in a letter to Mark Twain by A. B. Pond, the New York lecture agent who had represented and befriended Henry Ward, Harriet, and Twain himself for many years:

I have just returned from Hartford with Mrs. [Henry Ward] Beecher. We attended Mrs. Stowe's funeral yesterday. Mr. Twitchell conducted the service. It was a pathetic incident, and I might almost say, event. There were present most of the distinguished people of Hartford, and all of your old neighbors. Within a few minutes walk lay Mrs. [Mary Beecher] Perkins. In her ninety-second-year—a physical invalid with an intellect as brilliant and sparkling as ever. She is quite deaf. I called on her and she seemed quite delighted to see me. She had not seen Mrs. Stowe for eight years, although she had been stopping in Hartford for two years. She said she preferred to remember her sister as she saw her eight years ago. Mr. and Mrs. Warner and Susie [Clemens] were present. Charley Stowe [Harriet's son] was there with his family. I received a gracious reception from everybody.

I called at Mr. Warner's and Mrs. Warner went with me to your house where we found Susie in possession of the old place. She, and her faithful Katie, spend their days at the house. She seemed very glad to see me. She told me that she had heard from you about two weeks ago, that you had decided to spend the winter in England (near London), and that she and Jean [Mark's third daughter] expected to sail in September. She seems quite happy where she is. She says it seems very much like home to her, and she wished you would come back. The place is beautiful, but there is a terrible atmosphere of lonesomeness there. . . .

I started to write you about Mrs. Stowe, but it seems to me my thoughts are of the living more than on the dead. Susie told me that she (Mrs. Stowe) was in the habit of coming over nearly every day to your place for a chat, and was pleasant and childish. Hattie Stowe told me that her mother had played with the children and seemed more like a child for the last four years than a woman. Her memory seemed to have failed, and she seldom referred to the past. She was in good physical health until she was stricken last Friday. There are none of her old friends left to write of her. The familiar poet friends and men of letters, she has outlived; even Mrs. Gov. Claflin of Boston, died on the 13th of May last. Mrs. Beecher, in her eighty-fifth year, accompanied me. She is quite feeble. Mrs. Hooker was at the funeral, but she and Mrs. Beecher did not meet,—a very pathetic condition of affairs.

Pond failed to mention that eighty-one-year-old Charles Beecher was on hand, but a much younger Tom was not able to make it. Mary Perkins's reluctance to see a Harriet who might not recognize or remember her was an indication that she was husbanding what strength she had left to achieve a distinction that was so far eluding all of her illustrious siblings—living to be a hundred. If she had imparted this ambition to Pond, he would have found it pathetic as well in view of a sentiment she often shared with people around her: "When I was a young woman I was known as the daughter of Lyman Beecher. In my middle age, I was introduced as the sister of Harriet Beecher Stowe and Henry Ward Beecher. Now in my old age I am identified as the mother-in-law of Edward Everett Hale [author of *The Man Without a Country*]." Pond also failed to note an aspect of the service that would have had the most meaning for Harriet in her right mind—a chorus of black singers who were in Hartford on tour from a southern school came to sing spirituals. A similar sign that she was remembered and appreciated by the people who owed their freedom in part to her work appeared at the graveside in Andover, where she was laid to rest between Calvin and son Henry—a wreath from Boston with a card reading "From the children of Uncle Tom."

Mary did not reach her goal, although she made a good run for it by staying alive until 1900, when she died at age ninety-five, to become and remain the longest-lived of her father's children. It was not a good year for Beechers. Eighty-five-year-old Charles, finally retired and living with a daughter in Georgetown, also died. His last published book—*Patmos; or, the Unveiling*, a fanciful work based on the Book of Revelations—had appeared in the year of Harriet's dying. His use of words and images suggests that deafness inspired him to try to create a different kind of music, as in his description of the heaven he hoped to enter: "Cloudland above cloudland, thick sown with incandescent angel-forms, like fireflies in a tropic night! No frost in that electric city, even to the surface of the atmospheric sea. . . . The delicate network walls of filmy gold, the diamond panes, shut out frost and shut in millions of spirit song-birds. . . . The posts and bars and sash of that aviary intangible but infrangible; geometric lines without thickness, mathematical points of force without magnitude; planes of electric magnetic action, the continental cube ethereal, yet stronger than steel or adamant, sparkling, flashing, blazing, phosphorescent . . . and in the center the cherub-borne throne, with thunder-voice, saying, 'Holy, holy, holy!' and throned elders responding, 'Thou has redeemed us by thy blood, and we are reigning on earth!'"

Yet another Beecher—seventy-six-year-old Tom—died on that threshold of a new century. Some intimation of mortality had come to him in 1894, when he arranged to have a ministerial couple—the Reverend Mr. Samuel E. Eastman and the Reverend Mrs. Annis Ford Eastman—come to Park Church as joint assistant ministers. Although Tom stayed on as pastor emeritus, the Eastmans took over responsibility for keeping the church going. Young Mrs. Eastman was so fascinated by the dynamics of the Beecher household that she put her observations into a little book. She concluded that Tom was right when, speaking of Julia, he joked that he was "as well as a man could be who had been hitched to a steam engine for so many years." But in another mood he paid her a serious tribute by calling her "my strong, courageous, energetic Julia—to whom belongs the credit of nine-tenths of the achievement of our long life in Elmira" in a letter to a friend. But Mrs. Eastman wrote:

> Some have felt that Mrs. Beecher's natural endowment of enthusiasm hindered rather than furthered her usefulness; that it carried her sometimes beyond the limits of good taste and a nice sense of the fitness of things. But those who knew her real life,

her task, realized that she had need of every increment of vital energy and spiritual fervor she possessed. Often, when seeing her press on with some matter of domestic improvement or of church work in the face of Mr. Beecher's despair and disapproval, I have thought of a strong swimmer in a heavy sea, needing all the strength and courage he could command to keep his head above water. She had her own little ways of beguiling the spirit of gloom which used to descend so causelessly upon the head of the house. She thus tells her mother of a little catechism she used to put him through:

"Q.: What have the people done for Tom?
"A.: Given him a house and lot—or given him $50 (whatever the last kindness may have been).
"Q.: What ought Tom to be?
"A.: Grateful.
"Q.: What ought Tom never to be?
"A.: Blue.

"It almost always brings him 'round."

It is sad to know during the priceless service of those forty years by which she enabled a great prophet and teacher to declare his message and live his noble life, she had no sense of success in that which was always uppermost in her desire. How often . . . she has said, "When I get to heaven I will find Tom and take him to Livy and say, 'Here he is, Livy, I have done my best, but I could not make him happy, now take him.'"

In keeping with his character, there was no such golden vision as Charles saw in Tom's eyes. He simply told his congregation in one of his last sermons that they soon would not see him in the flesh because he would be going into "the other room" but that his spirit would be with them always. Uncharacteristically, the supposedly levelheaded, practical Julia took him literally. She kept his favorite chair empty at home in case his spirit came to call, said that she could "almost but not quite see him" in church where she was sure he would come to be with his flock, and joined the Society for Psychological Research to sharpen her awareness of spiritualism. She was honest enough to admit that his spirit never did turn up, and one wonders whether she would find it necessary to take him to Livy if she did join him in heaven.

But for her increasingly intense involvement with spiritualism, Isabella, the only remaining member of her birth family, might have felt quite alone when her faithful husband died in 1901. He simply joined the rest of the spirits with whom she had visitations every morning before stepping into her earthly role as charming Nook Farm hostess and determined political activist. She had no fear of her own inevitable death because of the messages she was receiving and recording from beyond. She had come to believe that she was the twin sister of Jesus Christ, the "Counselor, the Holy Spirit, whom the Father will send in my name," as reported in John 14:26, and that she would reign as his coequal in the government of the world. But she was in no hurry to rejoin her husband, John, and enter into her exalted state while the task of securing women's rights remained unfinished. She was still burning bright on that score in 1905 when she wrote that "the degradation of my political classification with minors, criminals, and idiots is harder to bear than ever before and rouses within me a storm of indignation that shakes my very soul of souls." So she kept up an active correspondence in an effort to light the same kind of fire under others.

However rocky their relationship became when they had differing views of Henry Ward's involvement with Mrs. Tilton, Isabella kept in touch with Mark Twain, who was an ally in the suffrage cause. Mark never returned to the Nook Farm house where his family had enjoyed such happy times because the memories it held would have made more painful the events befalling the Clemenses after they left it. When word filtered back to their old acquaintances that Livy and then two of their daughters died, Isabella was moved. As a neighbor, Mark had been put off by the Hookers' interest in spiritualism, yet Isabella, never one to give up, evidently hoped to share with him her source of comfort after the deaths of loved ones by sending him a copy of husband John's book *Some Reminiscences of a Long Life*. Because of John's deserved reputation as a well-bred, sane, and witty lawyer, Mark might believe his testimony as to the spirits he had encountered while alive and his conclusion that "there is one very comforting fact we learn from Spiritualism. It is that the suffering in the spirit-world is reformatory, and not everlasting, that erring and perverse souls, when they have suffered for a time, perhaps for years, and have come to see and feel ashamed of their evil-doing, repent, and are uplifted, good spirits helping them to find the way to light. And from frequent expressions of these spirits . . . they get great help from coming to us for sympathy and encouragement. The one task given them all is to come back here, and try to influence others to do better than they have done."

When there was no response from Mark, Isabella remained undaunted. In the summer of 1905 she took a medium from Hartford named Mrs. Lazarro to her cottage at Norfolk in the cool hills of northern Connecticut. Together the women had satisfying communication with the spirit of John Hooker. Hearing that Clara Clemens, Mark's only living daughter, was in a sanitarium nearby, Isabella made contact with Mark and invited him over for a meeting with the medium. He clearly did respond this time in a way that, either by joking or establishing some conditions for the occasion, aroused Isabella's ire. A woman who expected to become at least coruler of the universe was not at all in awe of a man who was by then America's, if not the world's, most famous author and humorist, and she sent him this tart note:

Dear Friend Clemens,

I find I must recall my invitation to you to meet my friend Mrs. Lussarro [Lazarro] in my cottage for friendly converse on the great questions of life & immortality. My thought was that being a psychic yourself & understanding in part the laws of spirit intercourse you were ready to enter the whole realm under the guidance of competent teachers such as Mr. Hooker and myself. So I sent you his book of Reminiscences & waited to hear from you. . . . I find that you are still in the attitude of most so called *"investigators."* You know it all—but you demand through these public mediums an elucidation of the wisdom & justice of the omniscient Creator of the Universe. You have certain tests in your mind & till these are satisfied you decline to listen to evidence.

Well dear friend it will be a long and wearisome journey that way, so I thought of inviting you to meet the little woman who stands by the little wicket gate to immortality & quietly opens it to every traveler that has the countersign—it is closed to all others. But we were admitted, my beloved & I, long years ago as I told you—& have almost walked the heavenly streets *together* for years and years—till he entered in, & *still we are together*. So I meant to invite you to talk with *us* in a friendly way through our good friend who holds the key to the wicket gate.

But I see you are not ready for such humble entrance, so I must withdraw my invitation for this afternoon but am most cordially & affectionately your old friend

Isabella Beecher Hooker

In that year of impressive activity for a woman of her age, an article by Isabella Beecher Hooker appeared in a 1905 issue of *Connecticut Magazine*. The first half of the title—"The Last of the Beechers: Memories of My Eighty-third Birthday"—might have proved a bit startling, if not offensive, to some sons and grandsons of her brothers and even women who harbored the blood regardless of their names. One of the latter most certainly was Charlotte Perkins Gilman. By then forty-five years old, a writer of note and nationally recognized promoter of such causes as peace, women's rights, and socialism, Gilman freely attributed her drive and courage to trumpet controversial views to her illustrious great-aunts. Ironically, this most famous "Beecher" of her generation was directly descended from Mary Perkins, the least famous of Lyman Beecher's children. Her father Fred, Mary's son, was once described as a "freelance intellectual"—a dropout from college and law school courses, an itinerate editor and writer, a sometime teacher. Fred married Charlotte's mother on the rebound from a blighted romance with Frankie Johnson, who then married Fred's uncle, James Beecher. Early on, Fred Perkins deserted his wife and daughter, and they were then taken in for long periods of time by one or the other of the Beecher women living in Hartford, including Isabella. As a growing girl, Charlotte was fascinated and inspired rather than shocked by the scandals surrounding great-uncle Henry Ward or spooked by Isabella's flirtation with the spirits. An aggressively unconventional woman herself, Charlotte was delighted in 1894 when her finally widowed father married, as she wrote, "the love of his youth, his widowed aunt. By this combination my father became my great-uncle, my great-aunt became my mother, and I became my own first cousin— once removed." A Californian by adoption, Charlotte came East in 1899 and stayed at a New York boardinghouse in a "comfy" family atmosphere with Frankie and her three adopted daughters while she made visits to her father at the Delaware Water Gap Sanitarium, where he was slowly dying of a familiar Beecher complaint: "a softening of the brain."

Even with Charlotte Perkins Gilman on the scene, it must be acknowledged that after Isabella Beecher Hooker drifted off to her spirit world at the reasonably ripe age of eighty-five, America was no longer a country "inhabited by saints, sinners, and Beechers," as the family's old friend Dr. Leonard Bacon of Yale once described the nation to emphasize their influence. But the echo of their pioneering footsteps still can be heard whenever an African American takes a seat at a cabinet meeting in the White House, whenever a woman enters a voting booth and pulls the curtain behind her, whenever a union wins for its members better working conditions, whenever a mind is able to accept a new scientific discovery in place of an old "truth," wherever the doors of a house of worship stand open to all who would enter. Although the Beechers may not have saved the world as they set out to do, it also must be acknowledged that the lives they led made a difference.

Bibliography

In researching this book, the author was blessed by the fact that the Beecher family lived by, and for, the word and in a time before the development of electronic communication. They had to stay in touch by writing letters to each other. As remarkable as the quality and volume of letters they wrote is the amount of these letters that the recipients saved. It is a sign that, although they were not always happy with each other's activities and opinions, they respected each other and evidently were aware that the reputations of some of them, at least, would outlast their lives. These letters can be found in a number of well-managed collections and, of course, have been quoted in virtually all the books written about the Beechers. In this case the author has made use of them to tell their story as much as possible in the characters' own words and let the reader know how they viewed their lives and their world in their own time frame. Parentheses are used in quotations as they appear in the original; brackets indicate an addition by the author.

Books

Abbott, Lyman. *Henry Ward Beecher*. Boston: Houghton Mifflin, 1903.

Adams, John R. *Harriet Beecher Stowe*. New York: D. Appleton-Century, 1963.

Andrews, Kenneth R. *Mark Twain's Hartford Circle*. Cambridge, Mass.: Harvard University Press, 1950.

Beecher, Catharine E. *Common Sense Applied to Religion*. New York: Harper & Brothers, 1857.

———. *Miss Beecher's Housekeeper and Healthkeeper*. New York: Harper & Brothers, 1873.

Beecher, Charles. *Redeemer and Redeemed*. Boston: Lee & Shepard, 1864.

Beecher, Edward. *Conflict of the Ages, or The Great Debate*. Boston: Phillips, Samson, 1853.

Beecher, Eunice W. *From Dawn to Daylight, or The Simple Story of a Western Home by a Minister's Wife*. New York: Derby & Jackson, 1859.

Beecher, Henry Ward. *Autobiographical Reminiscences*. Edited by T. J. Ellinwood. New York: Frederick A. Stokes, 1898.

————. *Evolution and Religion*. New York: Ford, Howard, & Hulbert, 1886.

————. *Patriotic Addresses in America and England, 1850–1885*. Edited by John R. Howard. New York: Ford, Howard, & Hulbert, 1888.

Beecher, William C., and Rev. Samuel Scoville, assisted by Mrs. Henry Ward Beecher. *A Biography of Rev. Henry Ward Beecher*. New York: Charles L. Webster, 1888.

Boydston, Jeanne; Mary Kelly; and Anne Margolis. *The Limits of Sisterhood*. Chapel Hill: University of North Carolina Press, 1988.

Caskey, Marie. *Chariot of Fire*. New Haven, Conn.: Yale University Press, 1978.

Clark, Clifford E., Jr. *Henry Ward Beecher: Spokesman for a Middle-Class America*. Urbana: University of Illinois Press, 1978.

Cross, Barbara M., ed. *The Autobiography of Lyman Beecher*. Vol. 1 of *Religion and the Beecher Family*. Cambridge, Mass.: Harvard University Press, Belknap Press, 1961.

De Toqueville, Alexis. *Journey to America*. Translated by George Lawrence. Edited by J. P. Mayer. New Haven, Conn.: Yale University Press, 1960.

Dickens, Charles. *American Notes and Pictures from Italy*. New York: Charles Scribner's Sons, 1902.

Eastman, Annis Ford. *A Flower of Puritanism: Julia Beecher, 1826–1905*. Elmira, N.Y.: Snyder Bros., 1910.

Eastman, Max. *Heroes I Have Known*. New York: Simon & Schuster, 1954.

Fields, Annie, ed. *Life and Letters of Harriet Beecher Stowe*. Boston: Houghton Mifflin, 1898.

Finch, Earl A., and Diana Royce, eds. *Portraits of a 19th Century Family*. Hartford, Conn.: Stowe-Day Foundation, 1976.

Fox, Richard Wightman. *Trials of Intimacy*. Chicago: University of Chicago Press, 1999.

Furnace, J. C. *Goodbye to Uncle Tom*. New York: William Sloane Associates, 1956.

Graff, Mary B. *Mandarin on the St. John*. Gainesville: University of Florida Press, 1953.

Grant, Ellsworth S. *The Miracle of Connecticut*. Edited by Oliver Jensen. Hartford: The Connecticut Historical Society and Fenwick Productions, 1992.

Harlow, Alvin F. *The Serene Cincinnatians*. New York: E. P. Dutton, 1950.

Hedrick, Joan D. *Harriet Beecher Stowe: A Life*. New York: Oxford University Press, 1994.

Hertz, Emanuel. *Abraham Lincoln: A New Portrait*. New York: Horace Liveright, 1931.

Hibben, Paxton. *Henry Ward Beecher: An American Portrait*. New York: George H. Doran, 1927.

Hill, Mary A. *Charlotte Perkins Gilman: The Making of a Radical Feminist*. Philadelphia: Temple University Press, 1970.

Hooker, John. *Some Reminiscences of a Long Life: With a Few Articles on Moral and Social of Present Interest*. Hartford: Belknap & Warfield, 1899.

Johnson, Paul. *A History of the American People*. New York: HarperCollins, 1997.

Johnstone, Johanna. *Mrs. Satan: The Incredible Saga of Victoria C. Woodhull*. New York: G. P. Putnam's Sons, 1967.

Lancaster, Clay. *Old Brooklyn Heights*. Rutland, Vt.: Charles E. Tuttle, 1961.

Linton, Calvin D., ed. *The Bicentennial Almanac*. Nashville, Tenn.: Thomas Nelson, 1975.

Martineau, Harriet. *Autobiography*. 2 vols., London: Smith, Elder, 1877.

————. *Society in America*. Garden City, N.Y.: Doubleday, Anchor Books, 1962.

McLoughlin, William G. *The Meaning of Henry Ward Beecher*. New York: Alfred A. Knopf, 1970.

Merideth, Robert. *The Politics of the Universe: Edward Beecher, Abolition, and Orthodoxy*. Nashville Tenn.: Vanderbilt University Press, 1968.

Morison, Samuel Eliot, and Henry Steele Commager. *The Oxford History of the American People*. New York: Oxford University Press, 1937.

Reynolds, David S. *Walt Whitman's America*. New York: Alfred A. Knopf, 1995.

Rugoff, Milton. *The Beechers: An American Family in the Nineteenth Century*. New York: Harper & Row, 1981.

Sachs [Arling], Emanie. *The Terrible Siren: Victoria Woodhull*. New York: Arno Press, 1972.

Sandburg, Carl. *Abraham Lincoln*, 1-vol. ed. New York: Harcourt, Brace, 1934.

Schlesinger, Arthur M., Jr., ed. *The Almanac of American History*. Greenwich, Conn.: Brompton Books, 1993.

Shaplen, Robert. *Free Love and Heavenly Sinners: The Great Henry Ward Beecher Scandal*. New York: Alfred A. Knopf, 1954.

Simmons, James C. *Star-Spangled Eden*. New York: Carroll & Graf, 2000.

Sklar, Kathryn Kish. *Catharine Beecher: A Study in Domesticity*. New Haven, Conn.: Yale University Press, 1973.

Stowe, Charles Edward. *Life of Harriet Beecher Stowe*. Boston: Houghton Mifflin, 1889.

Stowe, Harriet Beecher. *Lady Byron Vindicated: A History of the Byron Controversy*. London: Sampson, Low, Son, & Marston, 1870.

————. *Oldtown Folks and Sam Lawson's Oldtown Friends Stories*. Boston: Houghton Mifflin, 1896.

————. *Uncle Tom's Cabin, or Life among the Lowly; The Minister's Wooing; Old Town Folks*. New York: The Library of America, 1982.

Stowe, Lyman Beecher. *Saints, Sinners, and Beechers*. Indianapolis: Bobbs-Merrill, 1934.

Trollope, Frances. *Domestic Manners of the Americans*. Edited by Donald Smiley. New York: Vintage Books, 1960.

Waller, Altina L. *Reverend Beecher and Mrs. Tilton: Sex and Class in Victorian America*. Amherst: University of Massachusetts Press, 1982.

Wetter, Rush. *The Mind of America, 1820–1860*. New York: Columbia University Press, 1975.

Wilson, Forrest. *Crusader in Crinoline: The Life of Harriet Beecher Stowe*. Philadelphia: J. B. Lippincott, 1941.

Winik, Jay. *April 1865: The Month That Saved America*. New York: HarperCollins, 2001.

Other Sources

Beecher Collection, Harvard University, Radcliffe Institute for Advanced Study, Schlesinger Liberary, Cambridge, Mass.

Beecher Family Collection, Yale University Library, New Haven, Conn.

Beecher, James C. "Report on Land Reform in the South Carolina Islands." Retrieved from http://occawlonline.pearsoned.com/bookbind/pubbooks/divine5e/chapter16/medialib/primarysources3_16_3.html

Hooker, Isabella Beecher. "The Constitutional Rights of Women of the United States: An Address before the International Council of Women." Retrieved from http://gos.sbc.edu/h/hooker.html

Letters Collection, Harriet Beecher Stowe Center, Hartford, Conn.

Lincoln, Abraham. "Cooper Union Address." Retrieved from http://showcase.netins.net/web/creative/lincoln/speeches/cooper.htm

Singleton, William Henry. "Reflections of My Slaving Days." *Independent Weekly* (March 22, 2000), www.refdesk.com

Theodore Tilton v. Henry Ward Beecher. Vol. III. New York: McDivett, Campbell, 1875.

Worcester Aegis and Transcript. "First Carolina Colored Infantry/Thirty-fifth United States Colored Troops." Retrieved from www.refdesk.com

Index

Note: Page numbers in *italics* refer to illustrations.